Taking Back Control?

Taking Back Control?

States and State Systems after Globalism

Wolfgang Streeck

Translated by Ben Fowkes and Joshua Rahtz

VERSO

London • New York

The translation of this work was funded by Geisteswissenschaften International – Translation Funding for Work in the Humanities and Social Sciences from Germany, a joint initiative of the Fritz Thyssen Foundation, the German Federal Foreign Office, the collecting society VG WORT and the Börsenverein des Deutschen Buchhandels (German Publishers & Booksellers Association).

This English-language edition first published by Verso 2024
Translation © Ben Fowkes and Joshua Rahtz 2024
First published as *Zwischen Globalismus und Demokratie:
Politische Ökonomie im ausgehenden Neoliberalismus*
© Suhrkamp 2021

1 3 5 7 9 10 8 6 4 2

Verso
UK: 6 Meard Street, London W1F 0EG
US: 388 Atlantic Avenue, Brooklyn, NY 11217
versobooks.com

Verso is the imprint of New Left Books

ISBN-13: 978-1-83976-729-6
ISBN-13: 978-1-83976-731-9 (UK EBK)
ISBN-13: 978-1-83976-732-6 (US EBK)

British Library Cataloguing in Publication Data
A catalogue record for this book is available from the British Library

Library of Congress Cataloging-in-Publication Data
A catalog record for this book is available from the Library of Congress

Typeset in Minion by Biblichor Ltd, Scotland
Printed and bound by CPI Group (UK) Ltd, Croydon CR0 4YY

Contents

Introduction

Political Economy beyond Globalism: States, War, and Capitalist Democracy

In this book I explore the conditions of a possible, although not very probable, revival of democracy as a counterforce to both capitalism and authoritarian rule, in a historical moment when neoliberal globalisation is breaking up to give way to a new, as-yet-unknown political-economic formation. In doing so, I avail myself of literature on the rise and fall of neoliberalism; the transformation of the global state system, first in the transition to and then in the decay of a unipolar global order under US hegemony; the demise of representative social democracy; the economic crises of capitalism in the era of globalisation and hyperglobalisation; the governing capacities of different architectures of states and state systems; and, not least, the role of 'national security' and military capacity in the political economy of late neoliberalism and neoliberal imperialism. Special attention is paid to Europe, Western and Eastern, as a region in the global world organised, in part, in the European Union, an international organisation linked in multiple ways with the multiple institutions of global governance under Western-American auspices.

In terms of my theoretical and intellectual ambitions, I aim to merge a political theory of the state with a political-economic theory of capitalism and capitalist development, on terms that are not functionalist, not economically deterministic, and grounded in historical time and space.

'Not functionalist' means that the concern is not with 'the state' as such, as in much of Marxist 'state theory', but with the living variety of states and the international systems they form. 'Not economically deterministic' implies a concession to states and state systems of a – political – logic of their own that exercises a causal influence of its own on the course of political-economic events – an attribution, in other words, of independent agency. 'Grounded in historical time and space', then, means that the book is not about capitalism and statehood in general but about a particular historical form taken by the two in a concrete historical relationship between them. That particular form, the subject of this book, is the political economy of neoliberalism and the global state system of the New World Order, in the three decades after the collapse of Soviet Communism in the early 1990s, with a special focus on the state system of Europe, in particular Western Europe as organised (during the period of interest) in the European Union.

As behoves any discussion of capitalism and its relationship in the neoliberal period with the global state system and its regional subdivisions, a central theme must be that of so-called globalisation. In the book, this, too, is historicised. Globalisation has been around for a long time, in historically changing forms. It may be said to have been conceived in 1492 when the two branches of humankind, having left Africa about 50,000 years earlier, first moving north, then one moving west and the other east, reunited on an island in the Caribbean named Guanahaní, renamed San Salvador by its 'discoverer', Christopher Columbus. The reunion gave rise to the first global empire, 'the Empire on which the sun never sets', under the Spanish-Habsburgian Holy Roman emperor, Charles V, who ruled from 1519 to 1556. From then on, what took place between the major powers in international politics inevitably had global consequences, intended or not, with the territorial reach of international politics continuously increasing, especially in the form of colonialism and the modern slave trade. Then, the defeat of Russia in the 1904–05 Russo-Japanese War heralded a new era in which Asian countries would increasingly play an active role; as a by-product, the war also, in 1905, triggered the first Russian revolution. In the nineteenth century, it had been England which became the centre of a European global empire, while in the twentieth century, two world wars were fought over who would inherit from the United Kingdom an increasingly densely connected world. In the Second

World War, from 1939 to 1945, the United States became the dominant global power, having fought and won two major wars at the same time, one in the East and the other in the West, rivalled only by Russia in the form of the Soviet Union, in what was seen as a struggle between global capitalism and global communism. Forty-five years later, another era in the history of globalisation began when the Soviet Union collapsed and the United States became the only global superpower standing, while capitalism became the only surviving form of modern political economy. It is the globalisation of the period after 1990, celebrated by the older, neoliberal ideology of globalism and referred to as 'hyper-globalisation' by its critics, that this book addresses, with a special emphasis on the manifold tendencies towards deglobalisation in appearance since the world financial crisis of 2008, the COVID-19 pandemic, and the war in Ukraine.

Inevitably, another central subject of this book is the nation-state, in particular the nation-state in a global world and its state system. In fact, one of my objectives is to rehabilitate the nation-state as a site of political debate and political action, precisely in an era of globalisation, and, indeed, hyperglobalisation. Nation-states, I argue, their sometimes grim history in the nineteenth and twentieth centuries notwithstanding, are the only social site – the only institutionalised polity – that is potentially available for democratisation in opposition to capitalist distributional justice. Essentially, as I will point out, this is because nation-states tend to be small in comparison to superstates and empires undertaking to govern entire continents or the world as a whole. Their relatively small size enables them to serve as a substructure of subdivided, or distributed, governance responsive to and reflecting, if allowed national sovereignty by the state system of which they are part, the diversity of interests, experiences and practices associated with different societies – not least their diverse settlements with the demands made on social life by a capitalist organisation of the economy. Nation-states may be imagined as sitting on top of a landscape of neighbouring societies that, while different, blend into each other at their margins. By demarcating and organising national societies, nation-states enable them to form, express, and pursue a collective will. Management of the complex relationship between states and societies requires artful architectures of statehood, within and between national states – which in fact are often multinational with respect to their citizenries – which may be designed to give voice to collective diversity while, at the same time, integrating it in regimes of peaceful coexistence, both nationally and internationally.

Democracy, too, I discuss with indices of time and space attached to it, in particular in the historical form into which it evolved during the three decades of globalist-neoliberal capitalism after the apparent 'end of history'. During that time, I argue, democratic institutions and practices in the states of mature capitalist societies underwent profound transformations, all linked to the new condition of democratic nation-states embedded in global markets instead of national markets embedded in nation-states. Neoliberalism I conceive in this context as associated with a retreat of democratic politics and democratic states from their post–Second World War mission of protecting their societies from the pressures of capitalist markets, in particular markets for capital, and from capitalism's 'creative destruction'. Indeed, under neo-liberalism, national governments actively invited pressures from global markets in pursuit of 'reforms' aimed at restarting capital accumulation by increasing the 'competitiveness' of national societies and national firms. In the process, political parties, programmatically pre-empted by a new economic reality, withdrew from their constituencies into the safety of state institutions; party membership and electoral turnout declined, trade unions and collective bargaining withered away, and social inequality increased.

As democratic politics dissociated itself from the political economy by preventing itself from discretionary intervention in market opportunities and outcomes, leaving economy and society to their own devices, the plebeian dimension of democracy, acquired with the extension of universal suffrage in the nineteenth century and the welfare state in the twentieth, dried up. Democracy was redefined, by democratic theory–cum–ideology, from a regime for egalitarian correction of market outcomes into a practice of public deliberation among citizens guided by 'post-material' middle-class social values, adopted or transmitted on the assumption that the post-industrial societies of today, capitalist or not, can and should be normatively integrated. I believe that the idea of a classless democracy, going back to 'democratic theory' as developed in the slave-owning societies of Athens and Virginia, where the working class was excluded from political voice – the idea of democracy as a debating society among consenting citizens – opens the door for a materially emaciated 'identity politics'. This, in turn, goes easily together with the idea of a self-regulating economy shielded from egalitarian politics, in a polity ridden with conflicts over collective identities in both domestic and international social relations. A central question I raise is under what conditions, national and international, and with what sort of state and state system, a kind of democracy can be instituted, or restored, that can again become a countervailing power rather than a subordinate side-show of modern capitalism – that can, in other words, re-domesticate an economy released into the global open by neoliberalism at the peril of society and of itself, and, in the process, rebuild it as an economy of, by, and for the people.

Considerable space is devoted in this book to the institutional structure of states and state systems, and its consequences for the substance of the politics that may possibly be produced within it. I argue that directions of capitalist development, modes of globalisation and deglobalisation, the role of nationalism and the nation-state, and the opportunities for democracy and dictatorship are closely connected to structures, and easily organised around theories of modern statehood. From the perspective of this book, a main dimension here is the centralisation and decentralisation of statehood. Centralisation comes with integration by unification in large political entities, whereas decentralisation recognises diversity and difference, and breaks up statehood into multiple smaller-sized, independently sovereign units (or, in large states as distinguished from state systems, allows for highly autonomous 'federal' – or, better, confederal – subunits). I argue that large and centralised states, or centralised state systems, given the diversity of the societies underlying them, are governable only by bureaucracy, technocracy, or marketocracy – meaning self-regulating free markets – or, more likely, by combinations of the three. They are not, however, governable as democracies by means of democratic participation. In fact, as a rule they have to be kept together by military force or economic incentives. This is why large centralised states that insist on unifying their inevitably heterogeneous society, or collection of societies, tend to become dictatorships, while state systems, in order to be governed centrally and uniformly, must become empires divided between a centre and a periphery, along a gradient of power between member states. I will argue that the European Union may, in this sense, be considered an empire, and indeed one, as I will also argue, that is doomed to fail.

Both empires and centralised large states are difficult and costly to hold together, although, of course, the circumstances make a difference – for example, their position in the global system, territorially and otherwise. Especially where territorial subunits – regions in large states and small states in empires – claim autonomy or sovereignty, embarking on a quest for decentralisation or secession, the benefits accruing to national (as distinguished from regional) social elites or to the hegemonic state tend to decline in comparison to the – then rising – costs of compensation or repression. In the present period of capitalist development, global centralisation, in the sense of the provision of a borderless playing field on a world scale, is inseparably connected with neoliberal capitalism, whereas deglobalisation and a return of the economy from capitalist to democratic control would have to be associated with political decentralisation in smaller units of self-government, which may be parts of locally rooted systems of sovereign nation-states. Here, institutional form and political-economic substance are deeply linked. Endemic technical and political dysfunctions make globalised empires and extended large states unstable, a condition which, in turn, undermines neoliberal capitalism by denying the latter its optimal state form. Globalism therefore remains a neoliberal ideology, a utopia for a capitalism pressed to expand globally while leaving behind national idiosyncrasies. Globalist capitalism, however, is unviable in the longer term and, once its deficiencies have accumulated long enough to become unmanageable, must be replaced by something else.

In this book, I argue, with much caution, that the failure of neoliberal globalism and the decay of neoliberal globalisation may open a historical window for political experimentation with deglobalised systems of production and reproduction, not just within but also, perhaps, beyond capitalism. Ultimately, my objective is to provide a realistic assessment of the possibilities, limited as they may be, of a democratic-socialist response to the capitalism of the early twenty-first century, in the course of the ongoing transformation of the global state system. An important factor to be considered in this is the war in Ukraine and the confrontation, perhaps the approaching war, in East Asia between the United States and China. Here, as well, special attention must be paid to the structure of states and state systems as the only possible institutional framework for a new democratic politics potentially allowing for a constructive and effective answer to capitalist crisis, including the crisis of the global environment. Here, again, I focus on Europe, inside and outside the European Union, in its relationship with the United States and the North Atlantic Treaty Organization (NATO), and within Europe on Germany, a pivotal country for any future European state architecture.

I treat as an open question the impact of international warfare on the character and the direction of the deglobalisation process currently underway. While wars are a central feature of statehood, and were very much so during the thirty years of 'forever war' under the New World Order, the unpredictability of their event, as the military theorist Carl von Clausewitz (1780–1831) prominently noted, makes them a powerful stochastic source in history as well as for the development of capitalism: a generator of random events if there ever was one, if not for the longue durée then certainly for the short run, which may well run as long as a generation. It is not least for this reason that I abstain from any attempt to make predictions, although I do consider probabilities. Grand evolutionary tendencies and the logic of historical evolution, if there is one, matter; indeed, they seem to matter a lot. So, however, do the contingencies of current events that temporarily overlay them, forcing them to take sometimes tortuous detours and making their destination, again to the extent that there is one, invisible as they proceed, to be discovered and reconstructed only with hindsight by future observers.

I also resist the temptation to offer political recipes, strategic blueprints, or 'road maps', partly for the same reason and partly because this would attribute a power to scholarly argument that, compared to the power of the powerful or of current events, can be nothing more than a narcissistic illusion. If there is any advice I feel confident enough to offer, having written this book, it is the general insight that it will not do damage to the interests of citizens and peoples – of ordinary people – if they, as they increasingly do, resist further centralisation, unification, and integration, and, to the contrary, insist on a return of power and responsibility, and, indeed, sovereignty, to political formations more down to earth, closer to the ground, after the failure of global governance and similar neoliberal chimeras. There are, I have come to conclude, no functional reasons at all today to move political authority and state sovereignty further upwards, while there are good functional as well as democratic reasons to move them, to the contrary, downwards and return them to lower levels of social and political organisation. There is no reason, this implies, for a further disempowerment of nation-states, and much reason for relying on them, the only political institutions capable of being democratised, to re-establish popular-democratic control over the political economy. It is, I argue, only in a world of non-imperial, and in this sense small, sovereign states bound together by extensive networks of voluntary cooperation – what further on I shall call 'Keynes-Polanyi states' – that there may be a chance for new progressive, less crisis-prone, perhaps even post-capitalist modes of production and forms of social life, as well as for stable international peace, globally or regionally.

This book was written at the Max Planck Institute for the Study of Societies in Cologne, which grants its emeritus directors – of which I am one of three – the privilege to pursue their scholarly work as they please, as long as they feel they can make a contribution. While thanking the current directors, Lucio Baccaro and Jens Beckert, for their support, I would also like to absolve them, and the institute as a whole, from any suspicion that the occasionally somewhat uncompromising conclusions I have reached reflect any kind of 'institute line'. We have never had such a line in the past, nor shall we in the future. At the same time, it is true that I could not have written this book without keeping current of the research going on here, particularly on 'Europe', and the opportunity to participate in discussions of the subject with colleagues such as Renate Mayntz, Fritz Scharpf, and Martin Höpner. I also benefited immensely from the excellent technical support provided by the institute, above all its incomparable library and the equally incomparable people working there. And special thanks are due to a succession of 'research assistants' – a term that is entirely inadequate to do justice to their abilities and commitment – on whose input I continue to draw. In relation to the present book, Salvatore Mancuso, Rex Panneman, Martin Möller, and Benjamin Hendricks deserve special mention. Finally, my thanks go to Eva Gilmer, my editor at Suhrkamp for the original German edition, who performs her work as a martial art and has cured me of more than a few eccentricities – all for my good. For anything that may still have gone wrong, despite her help, I am solely responsible.

PART I

The Demise of Centralism

1

Global Politics and Regional Planning

How must horizontal and vertical, cooperative, and authoritative relations in a state system combine to satisfy the civilisational need for a democratic regulation of capitalist market economies? In 1945, a year after the appearance of *The Great Transformation*, the political economist Karl Polanyi published a short, concisely argued article in a journal called the *London Quarterly of World Affairs*, under the title 'Universal Capitalism or Regional Planning?'.[1] In it, he investigates the relationship between what he calls 'the organisation of international life' and the politics and structures of the most important states of his time.[2] Polanyi

---

1 Karl Polanyi, *The Great Transformation: The Political and Economic Origins of Our Time*, Boston: Beacon Press, 1957 [1944]; Karl Polanyi, 'Universal Capitalism or Regional Planning?', *London Quarterly of World Affairs* 10, no. 3 (1945), 86–91, available at karlpolanyisociety.com.

2 Polanyi's perspective was taken up more than thirty years later by Peter Gourevitch on the basis of the rich literature that had grown up on the subject since then, in a seminal journal article that is often cited: Peter Gourevitch, 'The Second Image Reversed: The International Sources of Domestic Politics', *International Organization* 32, no. 4 (1978), 881–912. Here is how Gourevitch summarises the conclusion of his comprehensive examination of the relation between the structure of domestic politics and of the international system: 'The international system is not only a consequence of domestic politics and structures but a cause of them. Economic relations and military pressures constrain an entire range of domestic behaviours, from policy decisions to political forms. International relations and domestic politics are therefore so interrelated that they should be analysed simultaneously, as wholes' (911). I regard Polanyi's analysis of the way 'regional planning' is conditioned by the structure of the international state system as an early predecessor of the type of theory sketched out by Gourevitch.

believed that the immense changes then in progress offered a glimpse of 'far-flung and meaningful policies which may, albeit incidentally, fulfil the deeply-rooted aspirations of the common man'. Referring to the US, Russia, and the UK, the three global powers left standing after the war, Polanyi thought that what was 'at issue between the powers is not so much their place in a given pattern of power, as the pattern itself'. In this respect, 'the tremendous event of our age' was 'the simultaneous downfall of liberal capitalism, world-revolutionary socialism and racial domination – the three competing forms of universalist societies'.[3] According to Polanyi, this had made possible 'a new era in international politics', one of peaceful coexistence of diverse regimes in the regions of the world, based on differing ways of settling class conflict:

> World-revolutionary socialism was overcome . . . in the sufferings and glories of the Five Year Plans, the tribulations of the trials and the triumph of Stalingrad; liberal capitalism ended with the collapse of the gold standard, which left millions of unemployed and unparalleled deprivation in its wake; Hitler's principle of domination is being crushed on a battlefield co-extensive with the planet he attempted to conquer; and out of the great mutation various forms of inherently limited existence emerge – new forms of socialism, of capitalism, of planned and semi-planned economies – each of them, by their very nature, regional.

Polanyi's most important example of the beneficial international consequences of what he regarded as the end of universalism was the collapse of the gold standard in the inter-war years, which he argued marked 'the end of the nineteenth century system of world economy'. This was because the overcoming of universalism had led to 'the immediate emergence of economic units of limited extent', each of which was compelled to 'look after its own "foreign economy"', which had previously "looked after itself"':[4]

---

3   Polanyi leaves open what he means by 'racial domination'; I assume that the expression stands for both German National Socialism and British colonialism.

4   Polanyi's concept of 'foreign economy', which he several times puts in quotation marks, is presumably a somewhat clumsy translation of the German *Außenwirtschaft*. In a footnote, Polanyi defines 'foreign economy' as 'the movement of goods, loans and payments across the borders of a country'.

New organs had to be developed, new institutions had to be set up to cope with the new situation. The peoples of the world were now living under these new conditions . . . Their 'foreign economy' is the governments' concern; their currency is managed; their foreign trade and foreign loans are controlled. Their domestic institutions may differ widely, but the institutions with the help of which they deal with their 'foreign economy' are practically identical. The new permanent pattern of world affairs is one of regional systems co-existing side by side.

Discussing the subdivided international order that he saw taking shape, Polanyi looked first at the United States. That country, he wrote, was a 'notable exception' to the rule, and therefore a potential source of systemic instability. The US had 'remained the home of liberal capitalism' and was 'powerful enough to pursue the utopian line of policy' of attempting 'to restore the pre-1914 world order, together with its gold standard' – utopian because it was, he believed, 'inherently impossible' to restore that order. Nevertheless, for whatever reason, Americans still believed 'in a way of life no longer supported by the common people in the rest of the world, but which nevertheless implies a universality which commits those who believe in it to re-conquer the globe on its behalf'.

The case of the Soviet Union was different. There, 'the victory of Stalinism over Trotskyism meant a change in her foreign policy from a rigid universalism, relying on the hope of a world revolution, to a regionalism bordering on isolationism'. The 'startling novelty of Stalin's policy' consisted in his readiness, according to Polanyi, to limit his ambitions to establishing a cordon sanitaire around Russia, made up of countries which did not have to be socialist or communist so long as their class and political structures were altered in such a way as to rule out any inclination to support deadly attacks on Soviet Russia. All that was needed was 'to destroy the political influence of the feudal class' by a revolution 'far safer than the traditional, unlimited socialist ones which, at least in Eastern Europe, would either provoke a fascist counter-revolution, or else could maintain themselves only with the help of Russian bayonets, which Russia has no intention of providing'. 'Nothing', Polanyi continued, 'could be less appealing to the conventional revolutionary' than the Stalinist turn from revolutionary universalism to a new regionalist particularism.

The British Commonwealth and the USSR having become 'part of a new system of regional powers', it was only the US which still insisted 'on a universalist conception of world affairs', one that tallied 'with her antiquated liberal economy'. According to Polanyi, regionalism as a formula for peace between neighbouring countries takes account, in accordance with the communitarian particularism of human life, of the lessons learned during the war from observing 'how overwhelmingly the people rally behind policies designed to protect the community from external danger'. The Soviet Union of 1945 promised its regional neighbours 'a secure national existence' on condition that 'they rid themselves of incurably reactionary classes' through 'expropriations and ... confiscations'. After this, they would reorganise their governments according to their own wishes – not in order to introduce a universal communist model of a good society but simply to live with their neighbours in peace. 'Socialisation of a new kind', writes Polanyi in relation to Eastern Europe and the regions in the neighbourhood of the victorious Soviet Union, 'is emphatically not an article for export. It is a foundation of national existence.'[5]

Continuing his investigation into the possibility of a peaceful post-war order for the East European region in particular, Polanyi arrives at the core of his argument for a regionally subdivided world system characterised by diverse modes of decentralised government. Eastern Europe, he argues, traditionally suffered from 'at least three endemic political diseases – intolerant nationalism, petty sovereignty and economic non-co-operation'. As elsewhere, the rise of nationalism took place especially in 'territories brought under the control of a credit system by autochthonous middle classes'. Ethnic conflicts – in Polanyi's words, 'unresolved racial issues' – were magnified by unrestricted economic competition between countries, whose governments were compelled by the gold standard in external economic relations to leave it to the market to bring their balances of trade and payments into equilibrium. In the inter-war years, this had been overcome whenever, under Soviet Russian leadership, 'market methods were discarded for

---

5   I cannot judge whether Polanyi's conclusions were correct when he was writing. On the surface, there is much to be said for them; things turned out differently, but not necessarily following the intentions of the Soviet leadership at that time. As my argument is concerned with systems, not history, it does not matter for it whether Polanyi's intuition was historically correct or not.

planned trading'. From then on, 'intractable chauvinisms lost their viciousness, national sovereignty became less maniacal, and economic co-operation was regarded again as being of mutual help instead of being feared as a threat to the prosperity of the state' – the reason being that 'as soon as the credit system is based no longer on "confidence" but on administration, finance, which rules by panic, is deposed, and sanity can prevail'.

The conclusions Polanyi drew from this were far reaching. 'If the Atlantic Charter', he writes, 'really committed us to restore free markets where they have disappeared, we might thereby be opening the door to the reintroduction of a crazy nationalism into regions from which it has disappeared.'[6] In that case, liberal capitalism would be 'a matter of foreign policy' based on 'buying and selling, lending and borrowing, and the exchange of foreign currencies between individuals, as if they were members of one and the same country', with the expectation that the market would balance the foreign currencies 'automatically – that is, without the intervention of their governments'.

That system had failed in the 1930s, and the gold standard had to be abandoned. Now, 'regional planning' – the cooperative administration by neighbouring nation-states of selected sectors of their economies – had made possible 'new methods of "foreign economy" . . . more effective for the purpose of international co-operation', because they could solve previously intractable problems such as 'the distribution of new materials, the stabilizing of prices, and even the ensuring of full employment in all countries'. Only the United States continued to hope for a 'universal system of marketing' and would need time to understand that its conception of international political economy was doomed to fail. Meanwhile, elsewhere in the world, work could get underway on 'an alternative to the reactionary utopia of Wall Street', with 'the deliberate development of the new instruments and organs of foreign trading, lending, and paying, which constitute the essence of regional planning'.

---

6   The Atlantic Charter was worked out by Franklin D. Roosevelt and Winston Churchill in August 1941 on the battleship HMS *Prince of Wales* in the vicinity of Newfoundland. It defined the political and economic goals of the Allies for the period after the war, months before the United States officially entered it. One of its eight points referred to the general dismantling of obstacles to trade, in anticipation of the later drive towards globalisation by the General Agreement on Tariffs and Trade (GATT) and, above all, by the World Trade Organization (WTO).

Polanyi ended his discussion with an analysis of the situation of the UK – the country where he was living at the time and where the Labour Party, under Clement Attlee, was in the process of building the first comprehensive welfare state in history, while nationalising a large part of the country's industrial capacity. Britain was dependent on imports both in order to maintain 'a civilised standard of living' and to ensure 'the survival of the Commonwealth' through 'free co-operation with overseas dominions', which were, or soon would be, colonies no longer. A 'planned foreign economy' would allow the country 'to reap the huge economic and political advantages of the new regional organisation of the world'. After the changes it had undergone since the 1930s, Britain was 'no longer a free-trading country' – which had made the country more of a democracy than it had ever been: 'more healthily united with every year that has passed since she left the atmosphere of liberal capitalism, free competition, the gold standard and all the other names under which a market-society is hallowed'. Thus, 'the real issue today', Polanyi wrote, 'is that reactionaries still hope that it is not yet too late for Britain's own system of foreign economy to be changed back so that it may fall into line with that of America'. The UK would thereby not only lose the advantages of equal cooperation with the USSR and the US; the country would also be deprived of 'those organs of external trade which she needs for her survival'. It would also, for a long time, lose 'freedom of action, a rising standard of life, and the advantages of a constructive peace'. Economic universalism on the American model would require a return to the gold standard in substance, if not formally, because 'the balancing of "foreign economy"' would have to be entrusted to the 'automatic movement of trade', which is 'the undirected trade of private individuals and firms'. The revived battle at the time over the gold standard was 'in reality a battle for and against regional planning'. The fact that the old ruling classes of British society were on the side of a 'universalist conspiracy' to 'make the world safe for the gold standard' showed that they dreaded 'the new egalitarian impulse' that could 'fuse Disraeli's two nations into one . . . Contrary to national interest, they might attempt to restore universal capitalism, instead of striking out boldly on the paths of regional planning.'

The Neoliberal Interlude

What became of the world Karl Polanyi thought was possible at that fateful historical juncture, the end of the Great Destruction? While some of his predictions were falsified by the course of events, others came astoundingly close to fulfilment. However, even where Polanyi was largely, or completely, wrong, his speculations seem remarkably fruitful for the description and analysis of post-1945 developments. What particularly distinguishes Polanyi's approach is the way he connects the political institutions of states, especially their democratic institutions, with their system of foreign trade, relating this, in turn, to the architecture of the surrounding global state system. By placing regional nationhood within the context of the latter, Polanyi succeeds in illuminating the relation between the embedding of capitalism in national democracy and the embedding, or lack thereof, of national states in international markets and international state systems. In order to do this, he provides a conceptual tool which makes his analysis relevant far beyond its historical time frame. In subsequent chapters, I shall attempt to apply Polanyi's analytical framework to the present-day European state system, in order (with his help) to outline a perspective for the continent's future.

First, it is necessary to understand that the regionalisation of socialism within the cordon sanitaire around the Soviet Union's 'communism in one country' proved to be less resistant to the universalist expansionism of the US than had been hoped. Just as Polanyi had expected, the United States did everything it could, in the course of confronting the other superpower, to export its system to the rest of the world. As the hegemonic power of an expansion-dependent capitalism, the US could not but act in this way, and it was remarkably successful. The Marshall Plan's offers of assistance to Eastern European countries, conditional on the introduction of a market economy, in line with the provisions of the Atlantic Charter, threatened to change the regional neighbours of the Soviet Union into hostile states, allied to the expansionist US. The Soviet Union, in turn, replied by lending military support to a revolutionary transition to a Soviet political and economic system in those countries. As a result, Eastern and Central Europe were incorporated into a closely integrated Soviet Russian empire and ensnared into a cold war with a Western alliance of democratic-capitalist states, organised domestically on the model of the American New Deal. This other empire, the Western one, continued to hold together even when in the 1980s its hegemon, the United States of America, pushed for a worldwide return to the fundamental principles of economic liberalism, becoming increasingly disinclined to allow its client states to pursue different national economic and social policies under the protection and within the limits of Bretton Woods Keynesianism. Its new objective was to convert the world into a field of expansion for the American version of capitalism, having hit its limits at home. This coincided with the Soviet Union's final loss of political legitimacy, not only in the eyes of the nations under its domination but also those of its own citizens, as a result both of harsh repression and the attractions of a consumer capitalism that the states of the Eastern bloc were unable to match, not least under the conditions of an intensified arms race. By 1990, then, communism was ready to collapse into global capitalism, which, as a result, felt free to abandon even the appearance of redistributive democracy at home and of liberal and pluralist institutions abroad.

What looked like a victory, however, indeed like an unconditional surrender, only lasted a short while. Very soon, the only surviving superpower – the (ad interim) undisputed hegemon of a world which was, by now, becoming thoroughly and completely capitalist – began to suffer from overextension, like other imperial powers in earlier times. Lost wars, beginning already with Vietnam and not, presumably, ending with Afghanistan, and failed projects of nation-building as in Iraq, or of regime change as in Syria, Iran, and Libya, were accompanied by continuing neglect of domestic problems such as a decaying infrastructure, failing social services, and increasing social divisions. This was associated with a form of economic growth which only favoured a tiny oligarchy made up of the private beneficiaries of the financialised global empire. Increasingly isolationist tendencies among the country's electorate, and vociferous demands for protection against a world market in which the United States could no longer guarantee its citizens (unlike its oligarchs) a share of the profits, smoothed the path to the presidency of the demagogue Donald Trump, who presented himself as an isolationist and protectionist – 'America First'.[7] The upshot was a

---

7   During his presidency, Trump proceeded to retrace, in reverse, the United States' historical road from protectionism to globalism. For a sophisticated examination of the

stalemate between, on the one hand, the capitalist imperialism of the East Coast cosmopolitan elites, in alliance with a national military and security apparatus at its post-9/11 global peak, and, on the other hand, a new populist mainstream interested neither in international adventures nor in handing over the country's 'external economy' to the play of the free market.

Western Europe, too, has undergone an evolution that can be described in Polanyian terms, even though it has not followed the path he envisioned, or hoped for, in 1945. At first, in the 1950s, Western European countries, to a great extent at the instigation of the United States, embarked on a process remarkably similar to what Polanyi had meant by 'regional planning'. The European Coal and Steel Community (ECSC) was set up, along with other similar organisations, to jointly administer certain sectors of the economies of neighbouring European countries while considering the differing economic needs and interests of each, thereby ensuring peaceful relations between the European members of the US-led anti-communist alliance. Placing the key industries of the industrial capitalism of the time under joint control was to prevent defeated Germany from using them as it had done in the 1930s to rearm itself. It also gave other European states secure access to the coal produced in Germany while helping to administer industries with strong trade unions and a tradition of labour conflict in an internally peaceful and externally coordinated manner. Later on, a further sector, nuclear energy, then regarded as the future basis of any modern industrial economy, was entrusted in the same way to a joint international authority, the European Atomic Energy Community (Euratom), which, like the others, corresponded in principle to the model of regional planning Polanyi had had in mind in 1945.

Soon, however, sectoral regional planning morphed into something different. The area of jurisdiction of the international organisations set up for this purpose progressively extended, and the number of participating countries increased from the original six to twelve in

development of American commercial policy towards 'legalised multilateralism' and 'globalisation as an institutional project', see Nitsan Chorev, *Remaking US Trade Policy: From Protectionism to Globalization*, Ithaca, NY: Cornell University Press, 2007. Chorev's book appeared a year before the world financial crisis and contains remarkably accurate predictions of the further course of events under the impact of the emerging resistance against the kind of globalisation instituted through the World Trade Organization.

1989, and no less than twenty-seven at present. What had started as an instrument of a cross-nationally coordinated sectoral industrial policy appeared in the 1970s, for a short time, to be the prelude to the construction of a single European state. Technocratic administration by sector was imagined to be a stepping stone towards a generalisation of political authority, with a view to replacing the variety of European national states with the unity of one European supranational state, or indeed a supranational welfare state, as the original confederal system of horizontal cooperation appeared to be turning into a vertical-hierarchical federalism.[8]

Then, however, instead of joining together to form a sovereign multinational state, member states, eager to preserve their sovereignty – and, in any case, unable to gain the consent of their citizens with their self-dissolution into a compound superstate – limited themselves to merging their national economies, by means of international treaties, into a single supranational market economy. What came to be called the single market, later, for most member states, completed by a single currency, was immunised against democratic-redistributive political

---

8   Wolfgang Streeck, 'Reflections on Political Scale', *Jurisprudence* 10, no. 1 (2019), 1–14. There are important variations in the way the concept of federalism is used. In the Anglo-Saxon countries, where states (and organisations in general) tend to be looked at bottom up, as compound structures made up of older, smaller units, 'federalism' has almost the same meaning as centralism, implying the surrender of originally separate jurisdictions to a common central authority. Thus, the public pronouncements in favour of a strong central state, composed under the pseudonym Publius by Alexander Hamilton, James Madison, and John Jay during the struggle over the US Constitution, were referred to summarily as the *Federalist Papers*. In Germany, in contrast, where states and organisations are, rather, conceived top down, federalism signifies a delegation of specific areas of jurisdiction by a central state to member states, or by the headquarters of an organisation to its subdivisions – the emphasis being on decentralisation rather than, in the Anglo-American version, on centralisation. In both versions, however, federalism is distinguished by its vertical, hierarchical component from horizontal cooperation. Therefore, when I refer to horizontal cooperation, in the sense of a free, guild-like association of political units with equal sovereignty, I do not speak of a 'federation' but of a 'confederation' – in other words a formation that is structured, or has come into existence, confederally or federatively, not federally. See also Dirk Jörke, *Die Größe der Demokratie: Über die räumliche Dimension von Herrschaft und Partizipation*, Berlin: Suhrkamp, 2019, 66ff, where he rightly stresses the essential difference between a federation and a confederation, and between a federal state (*Bundesstaat*) and a federation of states (*Staatenbund*). He uses the distinction to good effect in his final chapter, where he calls for the transformation of the European Union into a 'confederation of European States' (245ff).

intervention, not by a democratically correctable political will of its citizens but through a regional international authority instituted irreversibly by member states and their governments, with the aim to keep each other within the neoliberal integration camp. In this way, the return of the United States to unrestricted market liberalism after the final demolition of the New Deal was accompanied, following the collapse of Soviet communism and the disintegration of its empire in Eastern Europe, by a shift from a free common market in a politically still-subdivided and therefore only negatively integrated Western Europe, to an inter-state *liberal empire* consisting of twenty-eight states (after Brexit, twenty-seven) encompassed by a constitutionalised supranational market economy, bound together by a hard German-style common currency.[9]

Polanyi would not have been surprised to note that the transition of the EU, in the final decades of the twentieth century, away from 'regional planning' to a renewed capitalist universalism, internationally institutionalised in a neoliberal, region-wide super-market – for Polanyi, a relapse from the historical progress achieved since the end of the war – was accompanied by a return of the national and international conflicts of the era of the gold standard. Within the EU's Economic and Monetary Union, in particular, relations between the member states are worse today than they have ever been since 1945. Germany, the hegemon under the hard currency it had shared more or less voluntarily with its Western European allies, has become the target of nationalist hostility, particularly in the Mediterranean countries but, increasingly, also in Eastern Europe. One symptom of how Germany's economic strength and dominance have disturbed the peace of Europe is the demand raised repeatedly by countries like Greece and Italy, but also Poland, for Germany to pay compensation for the devastation inflicted on them during the Second World War, more than seventy years after its end. In Greece and Italy, as if accidentally, the amount asked for is roughly equal to the size of their current national debt.

When, as in the Economic and Monetary Union, countries and their 'foreign economies' find themselves in all-out economic competition

---

9   Fritz W. Scharpf, 'Negative and Positive Integration in the Political Economy of European Welfare States', in Gary Marks et al., eds, *Governance in the European Union*, London: Sage, 1996, 15–39.

with each other involving their national institutions and their traditional ways of life – a competition they cannot curb within the straitjacket of the 'four freedoms' of the single market and under the common currency – national conflicts over distribution are turning into international ones – this, too, a theme found in Polanyi.[10] Thus the political issue ceases to be about classes or markets and instead concerns societies as integrated collective actors locked in conflict with each other, each perceiving the other holistically – consolidated as if an individual actor – as greedy, lacking in solidarity, and even hostile. This can give rise to nationalist countermovements, which rediscover the institutional resources of national democracy in an effort to compel their governments to abandon their studied passivity and return to protecting the welfare and the way of life of their societies from the creative-destructive forces of capitalist globalisation, shielding them from the dominance of other states and societies as mediated through international organisations.

A Critical Moment

By the time of the COVID-19 pandemic at the latest, the two unification projects of the post-Communist end-of-history era – George Herbert Walker Bush's one-world 'New World Order' and the Maastricht Treaty's European superstate – had both got stuck. Globally, the end of unity, and with it the *end of* the end of history, manifested itself in the 2016 election of Donald Trump to the American presidency. The triumph of Trumpism was widely perceived as a turning point towards a revival of American isolationism in some new form, under the slogan of 'America First', heralding a return to a new kind of global bipolarism. While still highly competitive and expansionist, it differed from the previous American project of a unified world by recognising the durable presence of a powerful other, no longer the Soviet Union but, in its place, China. This was, or seemed to be, accompanied by a sort of détente vis-à-vis Russia, so as to focus what had remained of American power on the confrontation with what would soon be its sole global competitor.

---

10   I have analysed the process in *Buying Time: The Delayed Crisis of Democratic Capitalism*, 2nd ed., London: Verso, 2017, 54–62.

By the mid-2010s, like global union, European union, in the form of the EU, had hit a wall. At that point, Brexit was just a matter of time, waiting to be consummated, shrinking the European Union by one of its three (heretofore) most powerful members. Italian decline under the straitjacket of monetary union had been going on for years, and fewer and fewer people could make themselves believe that the attempts by the European Commission, the European Central Bank, and the European Council to end the rot could possibly be enough. At the same time, Poland, Hungary, and other Eastern member states were learning how to go their own, non-liberal ways, culturally and politically, and to success-fully resist the kind of liberal re-education prescribed for them by the powers that be in Brussels and Berlin. Moreover, the material and politi-cal costs for the German hegemon of keeping 'Europa' together, not to speak of keeping it united, were growing, and a moment was on the horizon when the German electorate, and perhaps the German judiciary, would no longer condone the ever-new under-the-table manoeuvres *extra* or *contra legem* by which the centre of the Union subsidised and thereby pacified, if not the periphery, then its political elites.

Add to this the Greens' attempts to expand the jurisdiction of the European Parliament and use it to establish Europe-wide moral and cultural leadership for themselves, which not only failed to unify Euro-pean societies but came at the price of more conflict between and within member states, and with the European Commission. Furthermore, national governments had, during the three decades since the Maastricht Treaty, perfected the practice of designating uncomfortable problems as 'European', and therefore in need of a 'European solution'. An example is immigration, where Germany managed to sustain an unsustainable regime of de facto open German borders by holding countries like Greece and Italy responsible for enforcing the Union's external borders while at the same time funding an armada of rescue vessels to collect migrants from unseaworthy boats provided by refugee traffickers.

How far the rot had gone by the time of the COVID-19 pandemic became more visible than ever when the European Council set up the 'Next Generation EU' (NGEU) fund for the 'recovery' of member coun-tries.[11] To circumvent the prohibition on the Union taking on debt, the

---

11   Preceding this had been the complete failure of the EU in its attempts to define and govern a unified collective European response to the pandemic. The disaster is

inflowing money from the capital markets had to be distributed to all twenty-seven member states without exception, even though the declared purpose was to respond with an act of European solidarity to the 'pictures from Bergamo'. When the Italian government proved unable to decide how to spend its share of the 750-billion-euro handout in a way that would have fit 'European' prescriptions, Brussels and Berlin sent the former European Central Bank chief Mario Draghi as an EU viceroy to Rome. There, he was appointed prime minister by the Italian president and celebrated all over Europe as the long-awaited 'Super Mario' who would finally rid the Continent of its Italian calamity. Hardly one and a half years later, unable to come up with a credible programme to restore to his country what economists call 'competitiveness', he resigned. This, however, did not keep Brussels from contemplating another round of 'Next Generation' borrowing, in another effort to keep Italy in, and thereby stabilise, the German-style monetary regime ultimately to be imposed on all of Europe, western and southern, eastern and northern.

With global unity broken and European unity disintegrating and drifting out of reach, the late 2010s seemed to resemble, in an interesting way, the constellation that Polanyi described in 1945: two global superpowers potentially balancing each other, one of them – China – neither willing nor able to be the master of the world, the other – the United States – potentially expansionist but perhaps healed from it after its experience with the New World Order. Between the two, a multitude of medium-sized European states seemed potentially free, after the collapse of EU superstatism and the erosion of its hierarchical dimension, to choose a specifically European mode of living and working together – one that would respect the lessons both of the inter-war years, especially the outbreak of internal and external war under the gold standard, and of the neoliberal decades, with their *forever war* and their unending economic crises as a consequence of overextended political and economic integration.

Then came the war in Ukraine. If ever there had been a moment when an era of decentralisation could have begun, after the failed centralisation at both global and European levels, a moment which in Europe

---

described in no uncertain terms by Luuk van Middelaar (*Pandemonium: Saving Europe*, Newcastle upon Tyne: Agenda Publishing, 2021), who rightly emphasises the superior capacity of nation-states politically and technically to deal with matters of life and death.

even offered a chance, if small, of a simultaneous restoration of national sovereignty and national democracy – with new ways of handling countries' 'foreign economy' such that, together with permanent war, the permanent capitalist crisis might finally be overcome – then all of this was again up in the air. What, for a critical moment, might have offered a new perspective in Europe for 'regional planning' to rise from the ashes of neoliberal European integration, now conjured up the possibility of a Western Europe united under American hegemony against a Russia transformed into a Eurasian dependency of China. With Russia's Western border turned into the Eastern border of a NATO-ised Western and Central Europe, the Eurasian continent would be divided between an American-led European, or 'Western', and a Chinese-led Asian, or 'Eastern', section. Both would be subject to imperial control by a great power – one of which would be exterritorial, hostile to both political sovereignty and economic self-sufficiency of its subordinate states.

2

The Demise of the New World Order

When Communism collapsed in 1990, an old American dream seemed to come true: one world growing out of many, *e pluribus unum*, as it says on the Great Seal of the United States, its dollar bill, and its presidential plane, Air Force One. In the early 1990s, there were not a few who understood this to mean the end of statehood as one knew it – certainly the end of nation-states, with governance, now global, transferred to a new kind of world government, most likely the United Nations in one form or other. In fact, during the salad days of the New World Order, as proclaimed by none other than George H. W. Bush, then president of the United States, the United Nations were, for the first time, truly united as the two critical veto players on the Security Council, Russia (the former Soviet Union) and China, were now willing to follow the lead of the United States. A first test for the kind of global rule that might have been emerging at the time was the 1990 Gulf War, fought by an international coalition assembled and commanded by the United States under an official mandate from the UN. In fact, it was against this backdrop that Bush Sr. – who, under the presidency of Richard Nixon, had served as US ambassador to the United Nations – abstained, after Iraq had been defeated, from proceeding all the way to Baghdad to remove Saddam Hussein from power – such action being outside the UN mandate.

Notably, this kind of international legalism was not well received in the US. It took Bush's son, George W., advised by disappointed members of his father's administration, to finish what he and others thought was the job that should have been finished by his father in 1990. When Bush Jr. started the second Gulf War in 2003, without a UN mandate and at the head of a 'coalition of the willing', there was still a lingering memory in the US of the deep frustration among American veterans of the 1990 war, who did not understand why the local victory parades upon their homecoming, held all over the country, had to celebrate an international rather than a national victory. President Bill Clinton (1993–2001), having denied Bush Sr. a second term, had to put up with an armed militia movement in the forests of northern Michigan and neighbouring states, which was preparing to fight supposed plans by the American federal government to surrender its sovereignty to the UN, which would then send foreign troops to the US to disarm its citizens. One outgrowth of this was the bombing, by Gulf War veterans, of the Murrah Federal Building in Oklahoma City in 1995, which killed 168 people. The main perpetrator was sentenced to death under federal law and executed during the presidency of George Bush Jr. in 2001.

The role of the nation-state under the New World Order also loomed large with respect to political economy. The American dream of one world, a United World grown out of the United Nations under the guidance of the United States, which envisaged the disappearance of national state borders dividing national economies and polities, was not just an American but also a neoliberal dream. From a neoliberal perspective, as it had emerged in the inter-war years, nation-states – having arisen, in particular, after the end of the First World War in 1918 – were hotbeds of political interference in free markets, in pursuit of irrational ideas like social justice or economic equality. Since they stood in the way of a reconstruction of the old liberalism of the empires of the long nineteenth century, they had to be, if not removed, economically neutralised in one way or other. In the inter-war period, neoliberalism became a movement that called for the resurrection of the old liberalism, for any number of reasons: the need for international peace, the ungovernability of the complexity of modern societies by national politics, the refusal by political majorities of a just reward for entrepreneurial acumen and risk-taking, the protection of honest markets from corrupt politics, and so on.

After 1945, of course, when a programme like this seemed more unrealistic than ever, with the New Deal still in place and the capitalist economy, national and international, reorganised along Keynesian lines, the postwar settlement provided for the integration of sovereign nation-states into a global regime of managed international trade with mutually adjustable national currencies. For the three decades after the Bretton Woods agreement of 1944, as the capitalist world was confronted with a political alternative – a different, non-capitalist organisation of industrial society in the form of Communism – the neoliberals turned into an exotic political-economic sect hibernating in Freiburg and Chicago. When Communism collapsed, however, the capitalist nation par excellence, the US – where capitalism had turned into Americanism in the decade after 1918 and had remained Americanism during and after the Great Depression – was the only global power left. Thus, the neoliberal utopia of a state-free global economy could rise from its ashes to experience a second spring, with two of its principal architects, Friedrich Hayek and Ludwig von Mises, still around to see it.

Although not quite. While the end of history was the end of Communism, it was far from the end of the nation-state. There is no capitalism without a state, except in its neoliberal utopian self-image. Just like the New Deal, or, indeed, any other historical version of capitalism, the depoliticised free market of neoliberal capitalism is a state construction. What makes it different is not that the state had disappeared but that it had become a different state, under the impact of a different domestic and international politics. It takes a strong state to eliminate the state from the economy, just as eliminating redistributive politics from a capitalist economy and society in the name of free markets means nothing other than the institution of another redistributive politics, a politics of redistribution by capitalist default, from the bottom to the top.

In the post-Communist New World Order, the need for a state to institute a stateless free market was fulfilled, as a second-best realisation of the paradoxical utopia of state-organised statelessness, by the United States, finally powerful enough to imagine itself, and make others imagine it, as a world government in waiting – indeed, as a de facto world state. While this was less ambitious than the anarchism of the pure neoliberal faith, it was immensely more practical, and indeed indispensable if that faith should ever fulfil its destiny and rule the real world. The political economy of the New World Order, the era of post–New Deal neoliberalism, of an integrated global market economy, rested on the global hegemony of an imperial nation-state that had made the spread of free market capitalism by political means, including military muscle, its raison d'être, its *Staatsraison* – a nation-state so powerful after 1990 that it could fancy itself as, for all practical purposes, if not the only remaining state, certainly the only real one. In its world, that of the Project for the New American Century, all other states were expected to behave like non-states, as though they were non-existent, so as to not stand in the way of a reordering of the global political economy as an integrated entity, one economy under the United States, indivisible, with the same free market for all.[1] The decades after 1990, the era of Bush I, Clinton, Bush II, and Obama, were a time when the US, as a matter of course, perceived for itself a historic mission to unite the world in its own image, so as to make it safe for capitalism and, inseparably, democracy. In this, the latter became defined operationally in terms of a state's willingness to cooperate with the US and the UN, transformed into the chosen instrument of the former for global governance, which would eliminate national borders and national sovereignty by making the states of the world 'interoperable' with their imperial, indeed 'indispensable' super-nation and indistinguishable from – 'isonomous' with – each other.

Globalisation and Hyperglobalisation

The objective of the neoliberal revolution was to overcome the stagnation of capitalism during the 1970s, caused among other things by the rising expectations of an increasingly self-confident working class empowered by state policies of full employment. Falling profits in the heartlands of capitalism were accompanied by rising inflation and growing demands on social security systems, lessening capital's readiness to settle down and be invested. The result was unemployment, which could be blamed on a 'Keynesianism' reduced, in the spirit of

---

1   The Project for the New American Century was a neoconservative think tank set up by Dick Cheney, Robert Kagan, and William Kristol in 1997, after Clinton's re-election as president of the United States. It was closely associated with the American Enterprise Institute. Its goal was 'to promote American global leadership', on the assumption that 'American leadership is good both for America and for the world'. It sought to build support for 'a Reaganite policy of military strength and moral clarity'. 'Project for the New American Century', wikipedia.org.

Paul Samuelson, to a set of instruments of technocratic macro-economic management. The situation was worsened by increasing energy prices and the rise of Japan and Germany to become world economic rivals to the US. Both developments undermined two important implicit prerequisites of the Bretton Woods system: the access of the leading capitalist nations to cheap energy, guaranteed by military strength instead of free trade (and indirectly paid for, in part, by defence spending), and the tremendous economic pre-dominance of the post-war United States, which, for a long time, enabled it to tolerate the trade deficits needed to spoon-feed its former wartime opponents-turned-allies. Moreover, the post–Bretton Woods de facto world currency, the US dollar, had increasingly escaped the control of its native land. In part, it had moved to an unregulated international money market, in the process transforming itself into the so-called eurodollar. Together, these developments destroyed the reputation of the Bretton Woods system and, finally, led to the US decision to terminate it.

The transition to a neoliberal economic policy in the 1980s was intended to revive capitalism by disciplining a labour force which had, by that time, come to feel by and large protected by national systems of social security. The neoliberal transformation of social, wage, and labour market policies was to be achieved above all by a shift to a new external economy of a liberal rather than a Keynesian type. The departure from post-war democratic capitalism began in the late 1970s, driven by increasing internationalisation not just of trade but also of production. The concept by which it came to be referred to was 'globalisation', presented as the linear continuation of a long, natural, and irresistible coalescence of humankind into a peaceful and pacified world society, held together by a shared universalist value system. Later, during the 1990s, after the fall of Communism, globalisation, as it had by then developed, took on a new form for which one of its earliest and most acute observers suggested a new concept, that of 'hyperglobalisation'.[2] What was involved here was nothing less than a worldwide change from national specialisation in accordance with Ricardo's law of comparative advantage, where nations organised in

---

2 Dani Rodrik, *The Globalization Paradox: Why Global Markets, States, and Democracy Can't Coexist*, Oxford: Oxford University Press, 2011.

states trade with each other (wine and cloth, Portugal and England), to the elimination of nations as self-governing political units, with their own economic policies and wealth-creation practices, in favour of global 'value chains' in a borderless global economic area.[3] In it, states no longer play a role, apart from a legal duty and economic need to establish and enforce, domestically and internationally, uniform regulations to protect the rights of internationally operating enterprises and investors from arbitrary state intervention in pursuit of values such 'social justice'. Under hyperglobalisation, states become facilitators of a denationalised world market with a uniform set of rules, established by global governance rather than government, so as to free profit-dependent movers of capital from fear of attacks on their property by national states, encouraging them to take risks and thereby make national economies maximally efficient.

The move from Ricardian globalisation to neoliberal hyperglobalisation was, not least, an answer to the long-term decline in the industrial competitiveness of the United States under the first globalisation regime. By the end of the 1980s, the US – or, more precisely, American business – was no longer in a position to meet the challenge from more efficient and qualitatively superior products made in Japan and Germany, even in its domestic markets. But protective duties were as incompatible with the US claim to worldwide leadership as they were with the appetite of the American working class for cheap consumer goods. As a cosmopolitan alternative, the liberal part of the spectrum of public opinion focused on the restoration of national competitiveness through social reforms, as a precondition for the 'high road' approach to industrial policy thought to be present in Germany and Japan. In concrete terms, the goal was

---

3 Ricardo's argument for the advantages of international trade is an extension of Adam Smith's. According to Smith, countries which cannot produce a commodity as cheaply as other countries can obtain it from them instead of continuing to produce it themselves. Ricardo's theory, however, concerns decisions about national specialisation, and it compares the price of production of commodities not between countries but within them: countries should specialise in products for which they enjoy 'comparative advantage' to the extent that they require less effort to produce in comparison with other products of the same country; in other words, they give rise to lower opportunity costs. For all participating countries, then, more wealth is created when they specialise in the commodities they can produce most cheaply, export those commodities, and import the others.

reindustrialisation through raising the skill level of the labour force and instituting a kind of social partnership.[4]

By 1994 at the latest, with the overwhelming victory of the Republicans under Newt Gingrich at the midterm elections during Clinton's first term in office, it had become evident that this was politically unrealistic. As a result, a different strategy gained favour. It amounted to using the United States' international power to open up the world, particularly the countries at the periphery of the capitalist system, to its giant domestic companies. The aim was to enable them to shift production abroad into international supply chains, develop transnational business structures, make worldwide financial investments, and spread the American consumption model. This was supported by a gigantic financial sector, increasingly deregulated for the purpose; by the US dollar as the de facto world currency; by the omnipresence of the American armed forces; and by the dominant position of the country's leading universities in the global knowledge industry, staffed with the world's best and brightest and ready to be put to commercial use once international law had been comfortably extended to cover intellectual property. Add to this the exertion of American economic control through international organisations such as the World Bank and the International Monetary Fund, originally Keynesian institutions set up to safeguard the Bretton Woods system but now repurposed as instruments of a nationalistic denationalisation of the world economy in the form of an American mono-nationalisation, with America's giant financialised enterprises as commanding heights.

If it had come to pass, the conversion of the world into a single gigantic free trade zone for everything would have realised the most adventurous dreams of the neoliberal globalists. As neoliberalism's 'cunning of reason' – or, rather, as the triumph of neoliberal strategy – the removal of the subdivision of global capitalism into state-organised societies would have given rise to a level of aggregate political-economic complexity sufficient to make a mockery of all government endeavours to control it. It would have produced a supersystem so clearly ungovernable politically that there would have been 'no alternative' to leaving the task of ordering it to

---

4   Michael L. Dertouzos, Richard K. Lester, and Robert M. Solow, *Made in America: Regaining the Productive Edge*, Cambridge, MA: MIT Press, 1989; Lester C. Thurow, *Head to Head: The Coming Economic Battle among Japan, Europe, and America*, New York: Warner Books, 1992.

market forces. The result could only be unpredictable and unplannable, and in any case could be neither 'rational' nor 'socially just', two concepts deeply detested by hardcore neoliberals of the Hayekian persuasion. Growth and economic progress within the world as a global free trade zone would have been secured, as a side effect of the gains made by the most risk-inclined participants in the free market, by implacable pressures to adapt, as exerted by market forces on businesses, their subcontractors, and their workers. Above all, the proletarian tendency to be content with life at a subsistence level, so adverse to the advance of capitalist civilisation, would have been suppressed by an institutionalised compulsion to respond with vigilant watchfulness to the danger to a traditionalist way of life emerging from the unpredictable catastrophes that could, at any moment, be inflicted by a denationalised world market.[5] Faced with the heightened complexity of a world economy released from political government, the non-capitalists, still needed to help the capitalists accumulate capitalist capital, would then have nothing to rely on apart from their human capital, optimised to a state of unlimited flexibility.

Hyperglobalisation may be described as an abdication or expulsion (or both) of the nation-states from their position as masters of their domestic and external economies, in favour of a 'free play' of global 'market forces'. But, as noted earlier, that is not the whole picture. For one thing, worldwide market forces are less anonymous than their abstract characterisation might suggest; they are embodied and put into effect by strategic actions of firms whose size grows in accordance with the reach of their global markets.[6] The subordinate position of the allegedly free markets of hyperglobalism is shown by the fact that since 1992, almost 50 percent of the imports and 30 percent of the exports of the American economy took place within firms (figs. 1 and 2), a proportion that is even more striking in the case of services alone (fig. 3). To that extent, neoliberal globalisation involves not the replacement of state hierarchies by the market but that of public hierarchies by private ones. This, however, does not preclude a powerful state presence in the hyperglobalised world of neoliberalism, for example when they impose

---

5   See below, chapter 5.
6   See Colin Crouch, *The Strange Non-death of Neoliberalism*, Cambridge, UK: Polity Press, 2011, where he contests neoliberalism's claim to be a market economy by pointing to the dominant position of the largest international businesses in the decisive national and international markets.

economic sanctions on other states, demand that 'the markets' take account of the requirements of 'national security', deny the firms and governments of other countries access to superior technology, or use military means 'to secure their trade routes' – typically behind a veil of liberal rhetoric about human rights and the freeing of markets from state control. Not all states are equally able to participate in this, which on closer examination turns the globalist *absence of the state* into a *global presence of large states*. In practice, this comes down, or came down during the golden age of neoliberal hyperglobalisation between the end of the Soviet Union and the rise of China, to a *single state system,* run by the American superstate integrating the world, in the name of the unrestricted freedom of the market, into its empire, in the process extending the playing field of its national enterprises to the world as a whole.

Figure 1. Intrafirm foreign trade, United States, 1992–2018, as a percentage of total foreign trade

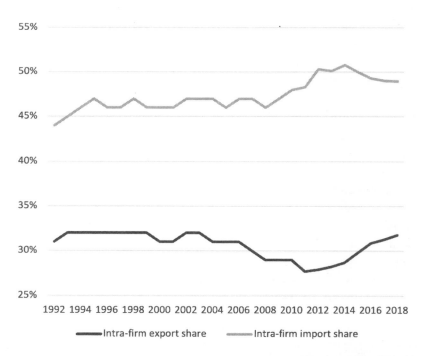

Source: Kim Ruhl, 'An Overview of US Intrafirm-Trade Data Sources', NYU Working Paper No. 2451/31994, November 2013, ssrn.com. Supplemented for the period 2013–18 by author's own calculations from the same data source (US Census Bureau).

Figure 2. Intrafirm trade and trade conducted by transnational firms in 2010, as a percentage of world trade

	2010
Intrafirm trade	33.2%
Trade conducted by transnational firms *	78.9%
Total world trade	100%

*Including intrafirm trade

Source: Patrick Kaczmarczyk, 'Growth Models and the Footprint of Transnational Capital', MaxPo Discussion Paper 20/2, Max Planck Sciences Po Center on Coping with Instability in Market Societies, Paris, 2020, 9.

Figure 3. Intrafirm foreign trade in services, United States, 1986–2017, as a percentage of total US foreign trade in services

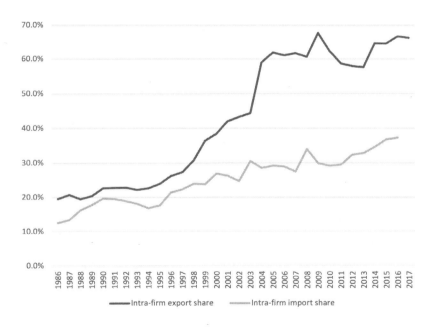

Source: US Bureau of Economic Analysis and author's own calculations. From 2004 onwards the figures include the services of the subsidiaries of US banks, which for their part may either be banks or not. Intrafirm exports of services are services abroad which are performed by majority-owned subsidiaries of American multinational firms. Intrafirm imports of services are services to US clients performed by the US branches of majority-owned foreign multinational firms.

A New European Order: The European Union

One outgrowth of neoliberal globalism after 1990, and indeed of the New World Order, was the European Union of the Treaty of Maastricht (1992; in force since November 1993). In central respects, the post-Maastricht EU amounted to a perfect realisation of the prescriptions of post-Communist neoliberal economic globalism, indeed hyperglobalism: a common market embedding states rather than states embedding markets; centralised, depoliticised – 'bureaucratic' – rule-making and rule enforcement; quasi-constitutionalised freedom of movement in the Union's internal market for goods, services, labour, and capital, with an explicit prohibition on capital controls, not just inside the Union but also in relation to its outside world; and one currency for – ultimately – all, centrally administered by a politically independent central bank according to politically non-negotiable legal rules and expert judgements.[7]

In the post-Maastricht EU treaties, 'the economy' figures as a socially detached, non-political engine for the production of prosperity for all, a subject of govern*ance* rather than govern*ment*, instead of a battleground between conflicting economic and social interests in the vexing relationship between capitalist profitability and social prosperity. By this it qualifies as a perfect creature of the age of unification and centralisation under the New World Order after the end of Communism. For a while, not all neoliberal globalists shared this view, just as it was not shared by trade unionists and social democrats of various provenance. For example, the British Conservatives, led by Margaret Thatcher, saw the EU as a potential Fortress Europe under socialist command, a politicised island in an emerging global sea of depoliticised neoliberal universalism they were hoping to expand with the help of their American friends. Others in the neoliberal camp, to the contrary, saw Western Europe as a practice ground for neoliberal globalism, considering European 'integration' as a field experiment that would demonstrate to the world beyond Europe the extent to which neoliberalism had become

---

7   Article 63 of the Treaty on the Functioning of the European Union (TFEU) prohibits all restrictions on the movement of capital not just between EU countries but also between EU countries and non-EU countries, unless they are necessary to pursue legitimate public interests (the latter to be determined by the Commission and the European Court of Justice).

politically conceivable after 1990, and how much good it would do to capitalism and capitalist society. (They could also point to the European Treaties' prohibition on political interference with capital movements across the EU's outside borders, which links European finance inseparably into global finance.) That the moderate European left – including, importantly, the British labour movement – forecast the arrival of precisely the kind of EU that frightened the Thatcherites may have made it easier for the neoliberal proponents of the EU as a forerunner to global integration to get what they wanted, as it helped keep alive social democratic hopes for a 'social Europe', if not now then in a not-too-distant future.

Soon, however, Thatcher's fears proved as unjustified as the left's hopes. The death of Communism, not only in the Soviet Union but also in countries like Italy and France, coincided with, and both called and allowed for, the EU's turn towards supply-side economic policies. In the 1990s the so-called 'European social dimension', promised to European trade unions and social democratic parties by the then president of the European Commission, Jacques Delors, gradually petered out before it had fully materialised, never to be seen again.[8] Also, Thatcher's successors in the United Kingdom learned from experience, to their satisfaction, that even hardcore neoliberal policies – such as the introduction of so-called zero-hour contracts in employment law and the malevolent neglect of declining regions in structural policy, resulting in ever-increasing social inequality – were possible without EU institutions even taking notice.

In any case, as the decade wore on, the EU was increasingly occupied with a task quite different from that of protecting its member states' social order against 'creative destruction' by capitalist progress. What was to seize a growing share of its attention in subsequent decades was transforming the former Communist countries of Eastern and Central Europe, including some former member states of the Soviet Union, into willing and able participants in the New World Order of a 'West' on the way to becoming the world. To serve as something of a foster home for the new ex-Communist member states in the East, teaching them the ways of the West so they could successfully join it, from the European single market to NATO, the EU needed to switch to a new sort of social

---

8   Wolfgang Streeck, 'Progressive Regression: Metamorphoses of European Social Policy', *New Left Review* 118 (July/August 2019), 117–39.

policy – one no longer domestic, in pursuit of 'social justice', but international, aimed at regional coalition and global empire-building. In subsequent years, an ever-growing share of EU resources went into all sorts of 'structural funds'. From there, they were distributed to the new member states to bolster the electoral prospects of national governments willing to play by the rules of the hyperglobalised New World Order, economically as well as politically. In this respect as well, the EU became a pillar of globalisation, rather than, as some had feared and others had hoped, a continent-sized exclave in a world-sized market.

Forever Unfinished

The New World Order did not last long – if, indeed, it ever existed. The roughly three decades during which it was supposed to be under construction, from the end of Communism to the economic war on Russia and China, were simultaneously a period of self-destruction – a time of endemic crises resulting from both fundamental flaws in its neoliberal blueprint and growing resistance to its expansion as it was put, partly and gradually, in operation. There was not a single day during the New World Order's lifetime when its would-be one-and-only state, the United States, was not at war, in a protracted effort to wipe out growing resistance around the globe, after the end of history, against inclusion in the global empire. Stabilisation and expansion of the world of hyperglobalisation required unprecedented violence, perhaps most visible in the US 'War on Terror', although far from limited to it. After the turn of the century at the latest, and, in particular, after 9/11, 'political Islam', or 'Islamism', replaced Communism as Global Enemy Number One. This drove an increase in American military spending unparalleled in the history of warfare, at its highest point amounting to one and a half times the maximum of US 'defence' expenditure during the Cold War era.

The War on Terror had been preceded, among other things, by the development in the US of the so-called duty-to-protect doctrine, which, in practice, amounted to an unlimited license for the US, and no one else except for its confederates, to intervene in the internal affairs of any country deemed not to respect human rights as determined by the US government. The first time the new international law was applied was the bombing of Belgrade after the break-up of Yugoslavia. This resulted in the creation of 'Western' satellite states and statelets at the expense of the traditional Russian ally, Serbia, in a first effort to extend the New World Order to the territories of the former Communist bloc. Next was the extension of the mission of NATO to so-called out-of-area operations, which secured the US the assistance of its European allies basically anywhere in the world, whenever it felt it needed it. Such need arose already in 2001, when the US invaded Afghanistan, starting a twenty-year effort to re-educate the country in line with 'Western' concepts of good government and family life, so as to turn it into an outpost of the New World Order in the heart of Asia. As we now know, this was to no avail.[9] Two years later, the US and a 'coalition of the willing' invaded Iraq, this time without legal pretext, to allow the younger Bush to 'complete' the 'mission' of the elder Bush. At this point, at the latest, any country, even the most peaceful one, that harboured ideas about avoiding inclusion in the new American global regime would have felt a need to reach for whatever gun it might conceivably have or acquire – and not just figuratively speaking.

On the side, to make it clear that a new era had begun, the United States cancelled, one by one, the arms-control agreements it had inherited from the Cold War. Moreover, when the Arab Spring bloomed, the US, together with a collection of European allies, intervened in different ways in Libya, Syria, and Egypt, to ensure that local democratisation was compatible with the new global order under construction. In all these places, however, what the US left behind when it departed was not order but chaos, civil war, social anomie, starvation, and waves of refugees leaving their native lands. Concurrently, NATO was expanded, under American pressure, to former Warsaw Pact states, and from there to former member states of the Soviet Union, in particular the three Baltic republics. The advance came to a halt, for the time being, when Russia attacked Ukraine in early 2022, in an apparent attempt to prevent the country being admitted to NATO and the European Union.

Economically, the three decades of the New World Order were a time of severe financial crises, from the Asian crisis in 1998 to the global

---

9   During the twenty years of the war, the US spent $2.31 trillion on it, an average of $300 million per day. More than 240,000 people were killed, among them 48,000 civilians and 67,000 Afghan government troops. Of the American invasion force, 2,445 soldiers died, about 120 per year. By the end of the war, 5.5 million of Afghanistan's population of 40 million were refugees.

crisis a decade later, in between a Russian crisis and the breakdown of several large financial firms. One example was the Long-Term Capital Management (LTCM) hedge fund, which needed to be saved by a major rescue operation as early as 1998. Financial instability reflected a lack of regulation of financial markets at the global level, where national deregulation and the end of national capital controls had resulted in the formation of a global financial system in the absence of a political-administrative system at the same level. Inevitably, global finance was infected with the pathologies of the oversized American financial industry, which after its deregulation from the 1980s on had become the foremost profit-making machine of the de-industrialising national economy of the US. Financialisation was allowed to proceed by the US central bank on the premise that, according to its chairman Alan Greenspan, while it was impossible to anticipate and prevent the occasional financial crisis, governments had learned to clean up afterwards so that no lasting damage would occur. Here, too, states were still needed – importantly, for crisis management, but also to open up the world for Western and especially American capital, often acting through global institutions like the World Bank and International Monetary Fund.

Instability became the hallmark of the New World Order economy in yet other respects. Throughout the neoliberal era, on the United States' watch over peace, democracy, and prosperity in the world, economic inequality increased sharply in both old and new capitalist countries. Contemporaneous claims that the gap between those two had been closing, making inequality decline at least at the international level, turned out to reflect, more than anything else, the rise of China, which internally became one of the most unequal economies and societies. Worldwide, the number of billionaires shot up over the thirty years, among them not just Arab sheikhs but also a variety of oligarchs from different countries, in particular Russia and other successor states of the Soviet Union. After the end of Communism, they had managed privately to appropriate large shares of the productive resources of their countries, which they transferred to Western banks and invested in Western stock markets, firms, sports clubs, and big-city real estate, particularly in the United Kingdom. They were surpassed only by the nouveaux riches of Silicon Valley, whose fortunes were derived from the commercialisation of new information technologies developed and funded not least under the auspices of American national security policy.

At the same time, throughout the countries of advanced capitalism, real wages stagnated – or, in any case, lagged behind productivity – and everywhere, the share of precarious employment in national labour markets went up. Also, there is scarcely a country left in the capitalist First World without rapidly growing numbers of food banks sustaining, for free, a growing clientele of the indigent – unemployed and low-paid workers, pensioners, immigrants, and single mothers – something virtually unknown up to the 1980s. As the New American Century approached, neoliberal economic policy, which was what was left to nation-states in the one-state empire of an ostensibly stateless global economy, was undercutting stabilising social institutions such as trade unions and worker representation at the workplace. The result was a broad decay of the social fabric. Efforts by Third Way social democracy to stem the tide at best delayed the deterioration of working and living conditions for large segments of the population in presumably rich democracies. All the new social policy could and would do was to urge workers at risk to take more responsibility for themselves, as the state now had to provide for international economic competitiveness rather than social equality. In particular, workers had both to work harder and to acquire the skills necessary for the more intellectually demanding jobs waiting to be filled by them in a new era of flexible, more competitive, and increasingly digital capitalism.

By the financial crisis of 2008, it became clear that the golden age of neoliberalism in a unipolar world, born out of the domestic and international needs and politics of the United States of America, was coming to an end. Several developments had progressed enough to be widely visible. Most importantly in the present context, states had not gone away, or turned into invisible hands enforcing the freedom of markets out of some global governance backstage; in fact, they increasingly refused to be turned into outposts of the American New World Order in their respective societies. Nation-state sovereignty and discretionary policy-making power remained highly valued and in strong demand, regardless of globalist rhetoric trying to persuade societies to give it up for cosmopolitan prosperity. Thus, an institution like the World Trade Organization (WTO) got stuck midway towards becoming a unified, consolidated, rule-bound, bureaucratic economic government detached from all states save one. A similar fate befell a wide range of other globalist trade agreements, either before or after being put in place. The European Union, originally conceived as a continent-wide model of non-discretionary, 'rule-bound', technocratically depoliticised economic management to be extended to a global scale, was held together only by a variety of compensation payments from states favoured by the common, one-size-fits-all regime to states that were not. Indeed, by the time the war in Ukraine began, the UK had already left the EU, wanting to be able to govern itself by its own rules rather than the rules of others. And the damage done by the common currency to a country like Italy could be papered over only by ever more brazen fiscal emergency manoeuvres bypassing and thereby undermining the Union's de facto constitution, the European Treaties.

Most importantly, with hindsight, two large states included in the New World Order at its origin, Russia and China – one a former empire, the other potentially a future one – had, each in its own way, so benefitted economically from the advance of hyperglobalisation that they could increasingly feel encouraged no longer to deny or forget national interests on which previously, as peripheral and subordinate participants in the unipolar globalist architecture of post-1990 international relations, they had been unable to act. In a truly dialectical turn, the revival of the two countries' aspirations for national sovereignty came about as an unintended, and indeed self-destructive, consequence of the neoliberal globalisation of the world economy. It had been their participation in the American-ruled global market that had enabled them to build up enough economic power to be able to challenge the constraints imposed by US rule on their national self-determination. It may be useful at this point, and in view of the events that ultimately ended the New World Order in the early months of 2022, to briefly look at these two cases that were central to the ultimate demise of neoliberal globalism and will be equally central to the future of the global political economy and, indeed, to war and peace on a global scale.

When, in 1992, the Russian Federation under Boris Yeltsin rose from the ashes of the Soviet Union, the country was firmly in American hands, where it remained until the end of the decade. Not only was Yeltsin's re-election in 1996 engineered with American money and public relations expertise; more importantly, Russian economic policy, at its centre the management of the 'transformation' of the national economy from communism to capitalism in its globalist version, was tightly controlled by American government agencies, foundations, and NGOs of all sorts, among them think tanks and universities, including various enterprising consulting firms operating out of Harvard University.[10] Densely networked into Russian government authorities – or what there was left in their place – they in particular designed and oversaw the gigantic privatisation programme that was to bring Western-style prosperity to Russia – supposedly in only a year or two. What happened, of course, was the opposite. During the 1990s, Russia was stripped of its assets by an emerging class of superrich oligarchs, often grown out of the now-obsolete power structure of the Soviet Union. Endowed with excellent connections to the West, especially to Western financial institutions, they were received with open arms by American corporations and, not least, the London real estate market. Meanwhile, organised crime of all sorts, national and international, blending into legal business, made Moscow one of the most dangerous places in the world, with gangland killings in its streets an almost daily occurrence. Until the end of the century, with Russia firmly in American hands, the per capita gross domestic product had declined by no less than 39 percent. During the decade, inequality exploded: consumer price inflation exceeded 900 percent in 1992, then declined to 224 percent in 1994 before returning, after a few years of stability, to above 100 percent in the late 1990s, at the end of the Yeltsin era. At the same time, life expectancy among males fell from sixty-five years in 1988 to fifty-nine twelve years later. Nevertheless, in spite of all this, Russia remained a loyal ally of the United States, fully included in the latter's global effort to transform the bipolar world of the Cold War into an American-dominated, unipolar world of hyperglobalisation – a second-class state, having to content itself with being on the periphery of the only first-class state left, the US, and a reliable ally when it came to UN Security Council votes.

Boris Yeltsin, ever more unable to exercise any kind of public authority, resigned suddenly on 31 December 1999, a little more than three years into his second term, to turn the country over to Vladimir Putin. By then, Russia was a basket case economically and a non-entity internationally. Its domestic political economy had become an anarchic Wild East hunting ground for capitalist profiteers, including an army of adventurers and speculators (with a complement of organised crime) mostly, but far from exclusively, from the US. At the same time, Russia's

---

10   Janine Wedel, *Collision and Collusion: The Strange Case of Western Aid to Eastern Europe*, New York: St. Martin's, 2001.

fall from its status as one of two global superpowers was evidenced by the admission of its former Eastern European satellite states, one after another, to the EU and NATO, followed, to top it all off, by three former Soviet republics in the Baltics. As the Western military and economic alliance tightened its ring around Russia, Russian political elites, to the extent that there still were such, had to realise that the American side had forever ended the Cold War practice of mutual respect for each other's national security interests. With Ukraine next in line to accede to the Western alliance, Putin saw it as his mission to restore something like statehood internally and great power status externally – internally by building a power bloc, a sort of crony capitalism, with some of the oligarchs against the others, and externally by seeking some kind of integration into the Western European peace and prosperity zone, without giving up his goal of regaining national sovereignty for Russia. This would include protection from American pressure by a cordon sanitaire of the kind on which great powers have always insisted, as exemplified by the United States' so-called Monroe Doctrine of 1823.

It was on this background that Putin, in 2010, called for a European, in fact Eurasian, free trade zone 'from Lisbon to Vladivostok'. While this went nowhere due to, among other things, American opposition, the Putin regime's search for, if you will, 'strategic sovereignty' was favoured by a booming international energy market, allowing Russia to quickly become one of the world's largest oil and gas exporters. On the one hand, this imparted on the country the typical pathologies of an extractive political economy, reinforcing endemic corruption, oligarchic politics, gross economic inequality, neglect of investment in human resources, and the like. On the other hand, it provided Russia with resources that it could use for rebuilding its capacity to project power internationally, for example by modernising its nuclear arsenal to keep up with ongoing American efforts. Russian arms spending had remained far behind the United States, especially during the American 'War on Terror' (fig. 4) when, in its peak year, the US spent about twenty times as much on its military as did Russia. (Russian defence spending also lagged behind that of China, which increased steadily from the early 2000s.) Still, from the US vantage, the recovery of the Russian military budget under Putin added an unwelcome potential for national independence to what, since the 1990s, had been one world kept together by the one indispensable nation, the United States of America.

Figure 4. Military expenditure by country, in constant (2020) US $billions, 1990–2021

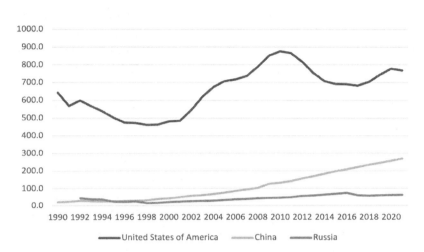

Source: SIPRI Military Expenditure Database.

The place where a possible Russian desertion from the global regime of the New World Order was to be nipped in the bud was Ukraine, which happened to be a place where, beginning in the middle of the 2010s, the newly won American energy autarchy could effectively be brought to bear. Putin invaded Ukraine in what, for him, must have been a last-ditch effort to halt the American advance into the territory of the former Soviet Union, at a time when Russia was still decades away from matching the military capacity of the West. The exact reasons for the invasion must be left to future historians to discover. In any case, rather than repelling the United States, Putin dealt it an opportunity to enlist the support of Western Europe for its defence of the unipolar world order.

The Chinese story differs in many ways from the Russian one. What they have in common is that, at the beginning of the 1990s, both were members in good standing of America's 'one world'. Corresponding to the end of Communism in Russia was the beginning of capitalism in China – capitalism after Communism in Russia, inside Communism in China. The Tiananmen Square massacre of democracy movement demonstrators in 1989, ordered by Deng Xiaoping, was not long held against him. As a faithful neo-capitalist, or so he had made himself appear, the butcher Deng was as welcome in Washington as the putschist Boris Yeltsin. Bush Sr. and Clinton, the latter even more than the former, considered China an indispensable partner in their effort to rescue American capitalism from itself by transforming it in a neoliberal direction. Not only had China become a reliable ally on the UN Security Council, just as Russia, but, because of the tight discipline the Chinese Communist Party was able to impose on the Chinese working class – unlike Russia, which at the time was sinking into disorder – China offered itself as an extended workbench for the American economy on its way out of material production into financialisation, and unable to develop an industrial strategy of profit-making that would have dispensed with the need to further depress real wages at home. As social inequality continued to rise in the US, while 'welfare as we know it' was, under Clinton, abolished, Chinese exporters were allowed unlimited access to the American market. In fact, soon their country was invited to join the World Trade Organization, on preferential terms as a 'developing' economy. In subsequent years, American firms like Apple drew unimaginable profits from relocating production to equally unimaginable sweatshops in China. At the same time, American consumers benefited from an unending supply of consumer goods affordable for the lower classes with their stagnant wages and increasingly precarious employment conditions, making them forget for a while their collective social decline.

One outgrowth of American de-industrialisation as a result of production moving to China was the rise of the giant department store Walmart. Hailing from Arkansas, the state where Bill Clinton had been governor until he was elected president in 1992, Walmart became the prototypical distributor of cheap Chinese goods to an increasingly impoverished American working (or no longer working) class. Owned by the Walton family, Walmart rose during the 1990s to be the world's largest retail firm, with a turnover of no less than $611 billion in 2023. (Hillary Clinton had been a member of the Walmart board from early on, when her husband was making a career in Arkansas state politics.) The restructuring of the US economy that had begun with the high-interest anti-inflation policy of the US central bank under Reagan was accompanied by a huge and growing trade deficit, in particular with China. At first, this did not bother the US government as long as the Chinese central bank held its surplus dollars as reserve or invested it in

US public debt. This kept the dollar strong while signalling to the world Chinese confidence that the US currency would continue to be in high international demand regardless, or even because, of its being issued in infinite supply by the US government.

This, however, did not remain so. As China continued to grow at phenomenal rates, there were increasing concerns in the US that it might, at some point, use its dollar hoard and its position as America's biggest creditor to make demands on American foreign and even domestic policy. More disturbing, as the Chinese capitalist economy began to seek outlets for its products other than the US, the Chinese state used parts of its trade surplus for infrastructural investment in Western Europe, Africa, and South America, and generally to buy political influence there. This, of course, was in violation of the New World Order's First Commandment, which prohibits countries other than the US seeking independent political status. Moreover, imperialistic trade-craft knows that where trade and, in particular, credit go, the military tends to follow. Also, with growing economic muscle China might, like Russia, rediscover older desires for national sovereignty, especially from the West, and for being treated as equal rather than being humiliated as a second-class power in global affairs. Observing the US and its national and international politics, Chinese political elites might also develop a fear of preventive American action, if only in the form of obstructing Chinese foreign investment – for example, its Belt and Road trade routes. Moreover, as the American economy continued its decline, its trade balance deteriorating and its public debt rising, China might be tempted to try setting up an international payment and credit system of its own, with the renminbi taking the place of the dollar. It seems plausible that the steady increase over the last two decades in Chinese military spending, financed out of the country's rapid economic growth (see fig. 4, p. 37), was not least in response to potential American hostility, accepting that it might, in turn, be seen by the American side as a threat, calling forth a strategic response of one sort or another.

In the final phase of the New World Order, the United States had come to see China as a dangerous strategic rival rather than a compliant junior partner, a deadly threat to American global supremacy that urgently needed to be contained and, if possible, eliminated. Much faster than expected under Bush I and Clinton, China had changed from an offshore support base for American financialisation and de-industrialisation, part of a US-led international community, where it was given time to slowly develop into a Western-style democracy, into an authoritarian evil empire that had to be subdued by economic (if not military) means in the interest of global order. Already under Trump, the US had designated China as its next international enemy number one, among other things playing up Taiwan as another site for America's 'duty to protect' in its worldwide battle for democracy and against authoritarianism. Across the otherwise unbridgeable divide in US politics, both Republican and Democrat political strategists felt what may be called a Thucydidean temptation: to attack the rising rival rather earlier than later, as long as one can still be reasonably sure that he will be defeated. By the time of the Ukraine war, there seemed to be agreement in the US that a trial of strength with China – a battle for hegemony in the Pacific, on the western coast of the North American continent – was overdue. It was a battle the US would do well to fight before China, already a high-tech superpower, could become invincible not just economically but also militarily. (The remaining disagreement concerned whether winning the war with China was easier with or without NATO, in parallel with the war in Ukraine or after ending it.) Putting China in its place now would do away with the danger of a relapse into global bipolarism; it could even open up a historic opportunity, not just for a restoration of American-controlled unipolarism but also for a new international monetary regime including debt forgiveness (as after the Second World War), centred around a dollar rejuvenated in a worldwide battle for a New World Order Mark II.

3

Stuck: Between Globalism and Democracy

By the time of the 2008 financial crisis, globalisation, in its new iteration as hyperglobalisation, had come to a standstill. The centralisation
of the global political economy by way of a simultaneous deregulation
of national political economies – the extension of the American
model of political economy to the world – had ground to a halt well
before the COVID-19 pandemic and the war in Ukraine. An increasingly intensive struggle began over an alternative where there was
allegedly none, in an exhaustive search for a refoundation of politics in
rejection of a globalism for which politics is limited to an unlocking of
market forces. Suddenly, the neoliberal establishment had to put up
with a growing aversion to the submersion of national economies in a
unified world economy and the attendant replacement of national state
sovereignty with supranational global governance. The result was an
impasse in which it seemed impossible to move in either direction,
whether upwards towards complete globalisation or downwards
towards renewed nationalism.[1] Distantly, the situation recalled
Vladimir Lenin's definition of a 'revolutionary situation': 'when the
"lower classes" do not want to live in the old way and the "upper classes"
cannot carry on in the old way'.

---

1   I use the concept of nationalism as a neutral characterisation of a mode of
political action based on the nation-state and in pursuit of the collective interests it
stands for, which may (but need not) be associated with international aggressiveness or
the disparagement of other nations on racist or other grounds.

The political impasse that marked the crisis of the neoliberal era had developed over a longer period. It had been preceded by phenomena such as a continuous decline of political parties with a will to shape the future and with programmes to do so, both classical social democratic and communist parties, as well as parties of conservative provenance; a dramatic fall in the membership of parties and trade unions; a long-term decline in electoral participation; and an increase in the proportion of voters who literally make up their minds in the voting booth. At the same time, there was a decline of trust in the established media, perceived as too close to the state, and in the number of people reached by them, while doubts have proliferated as to the representativeness and effectiveness of democratic institutions. Hence the formation of parties and social movements of a new type, which question the ruling political order to which they ostentatiously refuse to belong, insisting on acting outside the system 'in the name of the people'; in not a few countries, this has led to a new increase in electoral participation.[2] A common theme, which ran from Trump to Sanders, from the Yellow Vests to La France Insoumise, and from Syriza to the Alternative for Germany (AfD) through the Lega Nord and the Five Star Movement, was the nation-state's loss of control, whether desired or suffered by its governors, over the social situation of broad strata of the population – that is, over regional cohesion, income trends, employment opportunities and social security, state borders, the preservation of traditional ways of life, protection from internal or external violence, and the future in general. All this adds up to a crisis of political legitimacy, with intense struggles over nothing less than the constitutive foundations of the political order: the nature and demarcation of political communities and their mutual relations; the relationships between politics and market forces, and between collective and individual interests and values; and the legitimate claims of a society on its members and vice versa.[3]

I would maintain that the clueless stagnation of normal politics in the democratic nation-states under present-day capitalism resulted from

---

2 For more on this, and on so-called 'populism', see below, chapter 6.

3 This crisis, unlike the one diagnosed, or at least anticipated, at the beginning of the 1970s by the critical theorists of the Frankfurt school (Jürgen Habermas, *Legitimationsprobleme im Spätkapitalismus*, Frankfurt am Main: Suhrkamp, 1973), developed in parallel with and in the context of a crisis of the capitalist economy.

the failure of the globalist and neoliberal model of society, dramatically made plain in Western societies by the 2008 crisis and the popular demand, in reaction to this crisis, for the restoration of political control by 'the people' over social and economic development. Neoliberal internationalism had run aground; so long as it remained unclear what a successor regime would look like, and how it could be brought into existence, it seemed fitting to describe the situation as an interregnum.[4] According to Gramsci, an interregnum is a condition in which an old order is dying but a new one cannot yet be born – a transitional situation without a foreseeable end and with an open exit.[5] As long as it persists, says Gramsci, we must expect the appearance of 'a great variety of morbid symptoms' – unexpected, structurally underdetermined, critical events that lead to a loss of normality and social order.

What Next? A Tug of War

The post-neoliberal interregnum could be described as a temporary stalemate in a tug of war between the elites of the neoliberal coalition, who sought to break out upwards, towards a uniformly governed world economy in a globally unified polity, and forces which hoped to break out of the stalemate downwards, the new 'populists' – separatists, nationalists, and so on – seeking greater control over their present and future lives.[6] There were two central themes here: the *economic functionality* and the *moral value* of the two alternative levels of political

---

4   Wolfgang Streeck, *How Will Capitalism End? Essays on a Failing System*, London: Verso, 2016, 36–7. The expression has become a commonplace among contemporary diagnoses. The war in Ukraine is seen by many as an opportunity to end the interregnum by remilitarising the Western democracies outside the United States and subjecting them to US leadership. I return to this infra.

5   Antonio Gramsci, *Selections from the Prison Notebooks*, ed. and trans. Quintin Hoare and Geoffrey Nowell-Smith, London: Lawrence & Wishart, 1971, 276.

6   I use this expression and its derivations as a quasi-quotation, which is why I often put inverted commas around it. In most cases, 'populism' serves as a defamatory term for political opponents of practically every kind, from Donald Trump to Bernie Sanders, with a few exceptions in which it is used analytically, as in Ernesto Laclau and Chantal Mouffe, *Hegemony and Socialist Strategy: Towards a Radical Democratic Politics*, London: Verso, 1985; Ernesto Laclau, *On Populist Reason*, London: Verso, 2005; Chantal Mouffe, *On the Political*, Abingdon: Routledge, 2005; and Chantal Mouffe, *For a Left Populism*, London: Verso, 2018.

action and institutionalised government, global and national, engaged in a contest over technical competence and political responsibility. Both themes are closely bound up with the question of the possibility and desirability of democracy as an organisational principle of modern societies and the degree to which modern politics can be democratised – a connection that makes them highly loaded emotionally. The globalists, who are striving to move upwards towards a world society, regard democratic decision-making as a fundamentally unsuitable way of finding adequate answers to the 'complexity' of worldwide social and economic systems and therefore want to replace them either with technocratic agencies like the International Monetary Fund – in Europe, the European Commission and the European Central Bank – or with a 'free play of market forces', or both, in a coordinated side by side. The 'populists', on the other hand, who are looking for a downward exit, place their faith in a decentralised state and governmental system and a halt to or reversal of globalisation, with the aim of restoring democratic self-government and popular self-determination. This is an ambition which the globalists pronounce to be, if not immoral from the outset, then at least unrealistic, in view of an alleged impossibility of comprehending from below worldwide interdependences and external effects.

The battle lines between globalism and democracy, globalists and nationalists, centralisers and decentralisers, supporters of market technocracy on the one hand and democracy on the other, are by no means always obvious, and a certain amount of effort is required to disentangle them. Two circumstances, in particular, have repeatedly caused confusion. *Firstly*, it is not the continued existence of the nation-state as such which is at stake in the conflict between neoliberal globalists and protectionist nationalists, whatever the two sides may assert. Although neoliberal ideology presents this differently, neoliberalism does not aim to 'transcend' the nation-state, because it needs it to implement and protect the freedom of the world market. This requires an energetic and sustained policy of 'liberalisation', adapted to the prevailing local conditions. Neoliberal globalism is, to that extent, self-contradictory. The neoliberal policies carried out by supranational organisations and institutions, including the European Union, differ in practice from the way they are presented: they are not in fact aimed at absorbing individual nation-states. Supranational institutions serve to impose on these jointly created obligations of liberalisation – 'reforms' – which as national policies independently arrived at could be sold only with difficulty, if at all, to a national electorate. Seen from this angle, the supranational political circuit functions as a convenient repository for national political responsibilities which cannot, or should not, be exercised any longer. What is involved here is a paradoxical situation in which a political-economic theory which has at its centre the freedom of the market from state interference cannot in reality dispense with state coercion – that is, a scenario in which the 'free economy' is obliged to rely on precisely the 'strong state' its ideological defenders claim they want to abolish.[7]

Left Globalism

At least as confusing, *secondly,* is the fact that the globalists, in handling the legitimation problems which unavoidably arise from their anti-democratism – their need to abandon egalitarian, market-correcting, protectionist national democracy standing in the way of the world market – have been and are able to count on the assistance of former factions of the left which have, in practice, shifted to the liberal centre.[8] That was and still is possible because neoliberalism, with its demand, if only ideologically, to overcome the nation-state, can align itself with a universalist sense of justice, as has taken shape and solidified among a new middle class in parallel with economic globalisation and the disappearance of the organised working class as a historical subject.[9] On

---

7   Andrew Gamble, *The Free Economy and the Strong State*, Basingstoke: Macmillan, 1988. That the nation-state is, in practice, indispensable to its globalist enemies entails a possibility for its reconquest with the goal of its (re)democratisation, and, with it, its rededication to other purposes than the implementation and protection of a 'free' market economy. Such rededication is the objective of, for example, those advocating a 'left Brexit', or 'Lexit', many of whom are organised in the group 'The Full Brexit' ('for Popular Sovereignty, Democracy, and Economic Renewal', thefullbrexit.com).

8   The parallel migration by the New Green Centre towards a new-old bellicism, which could be observed in the course of the war in Ukraine, might bring about a correction of neoliberal globalism in an economic sense in the shape of militarily founded restrictions of free trade, which would have to be accompanied by new forms of state intervention. Economic sanctions for military purposes would be another nail in the coffin of neoliberalism and its internationalist ideology of liberation. This will be further discussed below.

9   For a recent trenchant critique of left cosmopolitanism, see Martha Nussbaum, *The Cosmopolitan Tradition: A Noble but Flawed Ideal*, Cambridge, MA: Belknap Press, 2019.

the political level, this development had its origin in the perplexity of the Third Way left of the 1990s over what it might offer to its voters after its turn towards globalism – no longer, in any case, protection from market forces and international competition. Propagation of liberal and libertarian 'post-materialist' values appeared a way out – one that seemed to align with a historical trend and was bound up with the attractive image of an approaching world society with unlimited mobility.[10] In this way, 'globalisation', originally the path to a free worldwide market, could be reframed as a universalist extension of the nationally limited solidarity model associated with the old working class, now supposedly rendered obsolete by economic and social change. In the course of the transition from the Third Way as an emergency measure for the revitalisation of capitalism, to cosmopolitanism and cosmoliberalism, seen as a liberation from particularisms of all kinds, a notion of solidarity was smuggled into the public consciousness, by which the refusal of the working class of the old industrial countries to expose their income and prospects of employment to a worldwide competition with low-wage countries could be presented as a betrayal of the socialist tradition of international solidarity.

Elites whose legitimacy is under threat may portray conflicts with their opponents as moral and cultural in nature, by drawing on their political and cultural capital and exploiting their control over the institutionalised channels of public discourse.[11] Alongside economic theory, advocates of the neoliberal system can deploy traditionally left notions of democracy and solidarity in pursuit of a discursive strategy in which

---

10   Ronald Inglehart, *The Silent Revolution: Changing Values and Political Styles among Western Publics*, Princeton, NJ: Princeton University Press, 1977.

11   The concept of discourse is treacherous. Sometimes it is only a grander synonym for 'discussion'. But, most of the time, it also comprises the notion of boundaries of what can be said within it, or the premises which must be accepted by all who want to take part in a particular 'discourse' – thereby splitting the deliberating subject along the lines of obligatory fundamental assumptions. Those who come up against these typically implicit boundaries and premises must construct their own alternative discourse, if they can. A search for 'discourse' and 'debate' using Google Ngram brings up the result that between 1920 and 1980, 'discourse' was practically unused, whereas 'debate' appeared with increasing frequency. After 1980, the use of 'discourse' expanded rapidly, catching up with 'debate', while 'debate' declined steeply from roughly the turn of the century. By 2015, 'discourse' was used more frequently than 'debate'. If I use the concept of 'discourse' at all, I prefer to keep my distance by putting it in inverted commas, so as to draw attention to its restrictive, even repressive connotation.

they associate internationalism with globalism and the nation-state, and national policies with internal authoritarianism and external aggression. In this way, hegemony is sought according to the idea that democracy can only bring about morally justifiable results if it applies globally. To achieve this, democracy has to be redefined in at least two respects: as a universalist canon of values instead of a system of institutions which gives the losers in the loaded lottery of the capitalist market a chance to change the results in their favour, in however limited a fashion; and, in the classical liberal sense, as respect for freedom and individual property, instead of the sense characteristic of communitarian republicanism, in which democracy offers the starting point for legitimate political intervention in those freedoms for the realisation of equal welfare. Democracy is thereby redefined as no longer a *plebeian institution* but a *moral attitude*, with the remarkably enthusiastic assistance of parts of academic 'democratic theory' and in harmony with the worldview of a neo-libertarian and neo-elitist middle class which regards itself as cosmopolitan.[12] The intended result is the normative disarmament of the territorially defined nation-state as a locus of obligatory rather than simply voluntary solidarity, and its de-legitimation in favour of a universalism ascribed to a global economy and a global society – which cannot, in practice, be anything other than the universalism of the global market. Democracy, once redefined *as a universalist system of values*, can be present only where it is simultaneously absent *as an institution*; whereas in places where it *does* exist as an institution, it is made to appear inherently narrow-minded and self-serving.

Culture versus Unculture

In sociological terms, the conflict between democracy as a system of values and democracy as a political institution reflects a new kind of class division, as it were, on the left flank of the capitalist democracies as they were opened up to the world market. In historical terms, this

---

12   One can then be – or not be – a 'democrat' as an individual, or a group of individuals, and in Germany official bodies like the Office for the Protection of the Constitution (*Verfassungsschutz*) can and do decide, with the help of appropriate experts, whether the functionaries and supporters of a particular party are 'democrats' or not.

division is a product of the collapse of the post-war coalition between the progressive middle class and industrial workers – or, more generally, 'ordinary people' – a coalition in which bourgeois intellectuals were content to help workers' parties and trade unions express the collective interest of the working class, thereby helping them devise a common strategy. This relationship was never without its tensions, and it became increasingly precarious in the 1970s with the creeping takeover of the social democratic parties by a growing academically trained service class. After 1989, with the end of the age of social democracy and the, for the time being, victory of neoliberalism, it disintegrated completely.

There is a growing literature on the withdrawal of the new middle class from its alliance with the old, and new, working class and its ideological consequences, and I do not aspire to add anything original to it.[13] If we apply the class concept in an appropriately flexible way, defining class in the Weberian sense by an individual's market situation, the new class division can be understood as a result of divergent interests vis-à-vis globalisation: a definition of the new middle class as a group who are believed to, or actually do, profit from globalisation, who have an

---

13   An often-used term for the milieu referred to here is *bourgeois bohémiens*, or Bobos. The expression was invented by David Brooks, a conservative columnist for the *New York Times*, who in 2000 published a book entitled *Bobos in Paradise*. The reference was intended to be favourable: Brooks described himself as a Bobo. The term later made its entry into France, where it was applied critically against the new-left 'cosmopolitan' middle class (Christophe Guilluy, *Le Crépuscule de la France d'en haut*, Paris: Flammarion, 2016). Since then, a vast amount of literature has appeared on the subject, extended to cover the left-liberal intellectual elite in the widest sense and their view of themselves. See, for the German-language area: Ulrike Ackermann, *Das Schweigen der Mitte*, Darmstadt: wbg Theiss, 2020; Dirk Jörke, *Die Größe der Demokratie: Über die räumliche Dimension von Herrschaft und Partizipation*, Berlin: Suhrkamp, 2019, 222–44; Philip Manow, *Die Politische Ökonomie des Populismus*, Berlin: Suhrkamp, 2018; Philip Manow, *(Ent-)Demokratisierung der Demokratie*, Berlin: Suhrkamp, 2020; Robert Misik, *Die falschen Freunde der einfachen Leute*, Berlin: Suhrkamp, 2019. For the US: Michael Lind, 'The New Class War', *American Affairs* 1, no. 2 (2017), 19–44; Michael Lind, *The New Class War: Saving Democracy from the Managerial Elite*, New York: Penguin Random House, 2020; Thomas Frank, *The People, No: A Brief History of Anti-Populism*, New York: Metropolitan Books, 2020; Michael J. Sandel, *The Tyranny of Merit: What's Become of the Common Good?*, New York: Allen Lane, 2020. For the United Kingdom: David Goodhart, *The Road to Somewhere: The Populist Revolt and the Future of Politics*, London: C. Hurst & Co., 2017; and Paul Collier, *The Future of Capitalism: Facing the New Anxieties*, London: Allen Lane, 2018; in each case among many others.

interest in open international markets for their human capital, and who do not want to be held responsible for satisfying the parochial demands of the losers of globalisation for material or cultural compensation. Their world is the planet, not the nation, at least in their self-image, and they see their opportunity in a progressive opening of national societies, both for themselves and, through migration from outside, for people ready to perform basic, menial services for low pay. As always, the discovery of collective material interests goes hand in hand with the construction of appropriate cultural justifications, including positive images of self and negative ones of others. In this case, what is involved is a moral elevation of universalist social orientations and a corresponding depreciation of localist-particularistic ones, emigrating from the nation-state's *context of obligations* towards a morally superior, but at the same time largely obligation-free, *context of commitment*. With Weber, again, we might speak of an estate-type (*ständisch*) milieu, which endows itself with a particular concept of honour, one that is linked by elective affinity to its economic interests.

The conflict between the old working class and its former allies, now feeling themselves to be cosmopolitans, is exacerbated by a particular asymmetry. In so-called post-industrial society's economic division of labour and social class structure, it is typically the representatives of the new middle class who end up in possession, or, in any case, in control, of the means of cultural production and communication. This enables them to present and express their particular perspective as a general one – which is, of course, exactly what is meant by the production of ideology. As a result, in the ideal image of globalist politics *the representation of the underclass in a democracy conceived as a system of institutions* is replaced by *the education of the underclass in democracy as a system of values*. This reversal in the direction of political communication is additionally favoured by the fact that a large part of the new class works in the field of education, where they believe their task to be to dissuade the less learned by friendly encouragement or bad examination marks from holding erroneous opinions. The resulting culture wars, in which a newly standardised way of writing and speaking sometimes becomes a requirement for full moral citizenship, are conducted with a passion and emotion which is all the greater because the two hostile camps were previously allies, or at least thought they were.

Democracy as a De-proletarianised Value System

Discussions in late neoliberalism about the true essence of democracy are in large part confrontations between two social strata, status groups, or indeed classes (the latter certainly in cultural production), who emphasise different aspects of the concept and whose interests require that what was once summarily described simply as democracy, thanks to a conveniently syncretistic renunciation of sharp distinctions, should now appear divided by the course of events into two subcategories (fig. 5). Both versions, which I call 'social' and 'liberal', can be explained both *systematically* and *historically* in terms of their respective affinity with different interests: systematically as ideal types, which can be conceived as standing for the opposite ends of a continuum; and historically as the starting point, and (tendentially) the conclusion, respectively, of a process of political-economic transformation from social into liberal democracy, hence from democratic into neoliberal capitalism. Democracy, *as a system of social institutions under capitalism*, offered *plebeian* interests disadvantaged by the capitalist market and capitalist society an opportunity to assert themselves by mobilising *political majorities.* Its mode of action was *the struggle*, a *trial of strength* between more or less well-organised camps within society, *represented* by parties and associations, settled by a *compromise* which could be extended, repaired, or cancelled and replaced, while there continued to exist and be recognised a *pluralism* of interests grouped essentially around the relation between capital and labour, but also between traditionalism and modernism, the latter often intertwined with the former.

In the self-image of democracy as a *value system of a society of citizens*, in contrast, a market economy turned over to technocratic management or left to its own devices replaces capitalism as a relation of political and social domination. Democracy, in this sense needs, an elite capable of an authoritative interpretation of its authoritative values; it is not plebeian but *elitist* or meritocratic;[14] its 'values' are determined by legal experts instead of by the decisions of contending citizens;[15] they are

---

14   On this, see, recently, Sandel, *The Tyranny of Merit.*

15   On the function of the 'human rights discourse' in the neoliberal revolution, see Samuel Moyn, 'A Powerless Companion: Human Rights in the Age of Neoliberalism',

constitutionalised, that is to say withdrawn from the purview of the majority, to protect them from voters who might misuse democracy to produce faulty decisions; interests are *converted into laws* and thereby made subject to judicial oversight; politics is no longer a struggle but a *discourse*, no longer plebeian but *elitist*; and *interpretation of the law* by experts replaces the political trial of strength. Instead of being represented by democracy, people are *educated* into being 'democrats', by citizens who know what 'democracy' is; and at the end of 'discourse' beckons, if everything runs smoothly, a freely constituted (*herrschaftsfrei*) *consensus*, which relegates to the past, as a product of civilisational backwardness, the compromise based on relative power. Thus, the bad pluralism of capitalist democracy gives way to the virtuous *monism* of a middle-class post-capitalist society united under universalist values, and the division between social classes is ideally and ideologically transcended by the notion of a normatively integrated society, where faithfulness to the law replaces partisanship, and an all-embracing universalism eradicates both national and social particularism.[16]

Figure 5. Social and Liberal Conceptions of Democracy

Social	Liberal
System of institutions	System of values
. . . in capitalism	. . . in civil society
Plebeian	Elitist
Majoritarian	Constitutionalised
Interest	Law
Struggle	Discourse
Test of strength	Law interpretation
Representation	Education
Compromise	Consensus
Pluralism	Monism

Law and Contemporary Problems 77, no. 4 (2014), 146–69; Samuel Moyn, *Not Enough: Human Rights in an Unequal World*, Cambridge, MA: Harvard University Press, 2018.

16   As impressively analysed by Mouffe, *On the Political*.

Discussions about the essence and limits of democracy, as have arisen in the political stalemate of the twilight of neoliberalism, reflect a conflict liable to wreak lasting damage on one of democratic capitalism's central peace formulas – namely, that the same competence to decide fundamental questions of political life, including questions of social justice, is ascribed to every citizen, whether rich or poor, a member of an academy or a high school dropout. This formula is institutionally anchored in a system of universal suffrage, in which everyone possesses one, and only one, vote, with the possibility in principle for even the great unwashed to turn their notion of common sense into society's, or at least to make it socially influential. The involution of social into liberal democracy, as promoted by the new middle class, attacks this premise, which profoundly challenges the structure of class society in two ways: firstly, by implying that citizen majorities do not have the capacity to deal with 'complex problems' in the proper manner, for which reason the power of decision should be removed from them and handed over to an expertocracy certified by an educational aristocracy; and, secondly, by constitutionalising 'democratic' moral values to protect them from a potential majority of citizens whose moral sense is judged by experts to be insufficiently developed.[17] In this way, the argument over the nature and scope of democracy is turned into a cultural struggle (a *Kulturkampf*) of 'democrats' against 'populists', in which the former aim at the intellectual and moral exclusion of the latter. The sense of insult arising from the various attempts to disenfranchise citizens on grounds of functional and moral incompetence could be one reason why right-wing 'populist' counter-movements attract not only a declining working class but also a petty bourgeoisie which, while reasonably well situated economically, experiences the critique of democracy by the new middle class as denying its claim to equal civic competence and dignity.[18]

---

17   For the UK, where this syndrome was particularly pronounced during the struggle over Brexit, see Paul Embery's book on the theme: *Despised: Why the Modern Left Loathes the Working Class*, Cambridge, UK: Polity, 2021.

18   I suggest that it is only on the background of its historical break with social democracy and its falling out with the uneducated that the support of the new middle class for the Western war effort in Ukraine may be understood. That support came unexpected to almost all, especially in Germany, where post-1945 pacifism seems to have disappeared from one day to the next. (Other, more nationally specific factors were clearly also at work there.) What was most surprising, at first glance, was that the

Complicating a resolution of the impasse between globalism and democracy in favour of the latter is the fact that historically pro-democratic forces have changed sides, by turning against distributed sovereignty and joining a coalition supporting supranational bureaucracy, technocracy, and marketocracy, who are perceived as patrons of individual liberty and opportunity. Large segments of the former left, having given up on the socialist ideal of a *classless society*, turned to and continue to be rooting for the liberal, indeed neoliberal, 'anti-totalitarian' ideal of a *stateless society*, a society without borders and, as a consequence, without a capacity for authoritative regulation – including, importantly, a capacity to tax its members and generally impose binding obligations on them.

Calls to 'take back control,' as made by resident losers of hyperglobalisation, thus no longer find the support of factions of the pro-democracy coalition of the past that have in the neoliberal era discovered the secret charm for people like them of globally centralised

---

globalist former left was so easily converted to the Western cause, although the war was claimed to be fought by the United States and NATO in defence of the right of the Ukrainian people to a sovereign nation-state, one free to choose its military alliances without having to take into consideration the security interests of its neighbours – and one that insisted on its sovereign right to apply harsh methods of nation-building to its Russian-speaking minorities in particular, including outlawing their language and incarcerating their religious leaders. Embarrassing as this could have been for cosmopolitan human rights advocates, it was overlaid by a firm identification in the Green worldview of its domestic enemies – the despisers of anti-nationalist and pro-libertarian, liberal democracy – with the international enemy, Russia, both of which equally called 'fascist' in Green progressive rhetoric. Fighting 'Putin' in the Manichean battle between democracy and autocracy – between the good empire and the various evil ones, as imagined by Clintonian Democrats and Republican neocons in the 1990s – simply extended the fight at home against AfD (in the United States: against Trump) to the world at large, making it internationalist and anti-nationalist as well as domestic – all the more so since the right in most countries, and the AfD in particular, did (and does) not feel a strong desire to fight a war, even one purportedly for national sovereignty, side by side with the 'internationalist (in the sense of imperialist) West', sacrificing their own national sovereignty and security for that of Ukraine. As international front lines become identified in the new middle-class worldview with domestic ones, supranational centralisation, this time of 'the West' rather than the world, as in NATO and a militarised EU, even if, on the surface, for the cause of defending national sovereignty – for restoring the 'rules-based international order' of the unipolar world of the post-Communist era – turns war into an indispensable requirement of an anti-fascist anti-nationalism that relegates not just pacifism but also 'diplomacy' and 'détente' to the rubbish heap of history.

regimes of governance – or better, of non-government – even though these cannot by their nature be democratic in any redistributive sense. What is more, not only are such regimes beyond the reach of any intermediary organisation citizens might be able to form to communicate their collective interests to those that make decisions on their behalf; they are also too far removed from the realities of social life to implement effectively the decisions they pretend to make, making them mostly symbolic and turning them into empty promises, especially where they are supposed to mitigate the adverse effects of capitalism on societies and social structures. The crisis of centralised neoliberalism as the New World Order drew to an end was, therefore, due to a lack not just of democratic legitimacy but also of technical efficacy, as evidenced, for example, by the recurring crises of economic management. However, while towards the end of the neoliberal era the dysfunctionality of the neoliberal regime became increasingly obvious, calling forth various forms of 'populist' revolt from below, the trahison des clercs prevented the formation of a pro-democracy coalition willing and able to do away with neoliberalism and restore social (as distinguished from liberal) democracy.

Those who have abandoned decentralised democracy in favour of globally centralised capitalism may today watch with surprise as the global market and its unipolar stateless state system are being broken up, not by victorious pro-democracy forces but by profit-minded capitalist firms seeking to 'de-risk' ungoverned supply chains, and then, even more forcefully, by military planners in pursuit of 'national security'. Economic costs, as inevitably ensue from sacrificing centralised economies of scale for decentralised autonomy, include public subsidies to international firms for 're-shoring' and 'friend-shoring', not of course for a restoration of democratic self-government. In fact, today decentralisation, in the sense of a fragmentation of the New World Order global economy, as expedited not just in response to the Ukraine war but also in preparation for a coming Sino-American war in the Pacific, is pursued by social agents who never cared about the anti-democratic effects of centralisation and, indeed, insist that they be preserved even as globalism is not. In their vision of the future, those who demand democratic self-government in the only places where it can exist, in sub-global social communities, figure as enemies of democracy. Rather than embedded in a revival of democracy and distributed sovereignty, decentralisation at the end of neoliberalism is driven by economic interests and national security concerns. What this may mean for the future of globalist neoliberalism, on the one hand, and national democracy, on the other, is the central political-economic question of our time.

4

Breaking the Deadlock: Democracy and the Politics of Scale

This book is, put briefly, an attempt to rehabilitate the nation-state as the main arena of democratic politics under capitalism. Its aim is to contest its moral demonisation and the disparagement of its technical capacity to govern, in order to open the way to a sober evaluation of the possibility of a *downward exit* from the post-neoliberal stalemate.[1] The argument connects the themes of capitalist crisis, political democracy, the structure of states and state systems, and the sovereignty and governing capacities of states with the choice between centralisation and integration of political regimes, on the one hand, and their decentralisation and differentiation, on the other. In what follows, I will give an overview on the book's remaining chapters.

---

1   Here I am in harmony with an extensive range of recent literature. In addition to Mouffe, there are many other examples: John B. Judis, *The Nationalist Revival: Trade, Immigration, and the Revolt against Globalization*, New York: Columbia Global Reports, 2018; William Mitchell and Thomas Fazi, 'Make the Left Great Again', *American Affairs* 1, no. 3 (2017), 75–91; Erik S. Reinert, *Globalization, Economic Development and Inequality*, Cheltenham: Edward Elgar, 2004; Dani Rodrik, *Has Globalization Gone Too Far?*, Washington, DC: Institute for International Economics, 1997; Dani Rodrik, *Straight Talk on Trade: Ideas for a Sane World Economy*, Princeton, NJ: Princeton University Press, 2017; and Dani Rodrik, 'The Great Globalization Lie', *Prospect* 226, January 2018.

Economic Crisis and State Systems

The next two chapters attempt a summary account of what I consider to be the two structural roots of the political impasse that has materialised in the post-neoliberal configuration, productive of a 'dual crisis': of capitalism (chapter 5) and of democracy (chapter 6). *First*, the workings of international high capitalism, set free and financialised by neoliberalism, have increasingly become a mystery to the societies subject to it. It is not simply that they do not know how, and indeed whether, to govern it; they are also faced with the questions who should bear the growing costs of saving it from itself and when they will finally exceed capitalism's – declining – utility to even the majority of its beneficiaries. My discussion on this follows up on earlier observations on the crisis of 2008–10, taking into consideration as far as possible the more or less exogenous new crises after 2019, unleashed first by the COVID-19 pandemic and then by the war in Ukraine.[2]

Second, the societies of developed capitalism are suffering from the way the internationalisation of the state system has become bogged down in a contest between the neoliberal internationalism of its elites and the newly emerging nationalism, or localism, of growing sections of their populations (chapter 6). The main theme here is the relation between national democracy and the international rule of the market or, as the case may be, of technocracy, with its implications for the possibility or impossibility of protective democratic market regulation and the egalitarian correction of market outcomes. I describe the situation in the final phase of neoliberalism as a result of the dissolution of the standard model of capitalist democracy, the kind that developed after the end of the Second World War. Today, the role of democracy as a counterforce inside a nationally organised capitalism appears to be just as severely eroded as the latter itself. The ensuing struggle over how to reorder the relationship between nationalism and internationalism, localism and centralism, particularism and universalism is driven by a deep-seated conflict over what would be an acceptable new settlement between capitalism and society – a conflict that takes place in a multiplicity of

---

2   See, in particular, Wolfgang Streeck, *Buying Time: The Delayed Crisis of Democratic Capitalism*, 2nd ed., London: Verso, 2017, xxxiv–xli.

forms differing from one country to the next, within and over the respective local remnants of the standard model of the democratic nation-state. Today, that conflict has assumed a new and unexpected form, as it has become involved in the global struggle over the unipolarism of the post-1990 New World Order.

This leads into part III and chapters 7 and 8, where I develop what is probably the key concept of the present analysis: that of *state system*. Guiding notions are those of *differentiation* and *integration*, drawing on the work of two classic authors from different centuries, Edward Gibbon and Karl Polanyi. According to both of them, states do not exist in isolation or as such but always together with other states; they are members of state *systems* constituted by the relations between their members – based on law or power, or, normally, on both – and by their number and internal structures, their number depending on how their territories are demarcated. From Gibbon's observations on the end of the Western Roman Empire and its consequences for Europe, I have taken the idea of a politics of *political scale*. With respect to statehood, in Polanyi, one finds the notion that the social embeddedness of markets in democratic politics depends on how far the states which embed the markets are themselves embedded in an international state structure which respects their sovereignty and is, in this sense, pluralist rather than universalist. Gibbon, for his part, asks what is more advantageous for a region of the world: to be ruled by a single large state or by a multitude of smaller states; he comes down in favour of a world divided into small states, with many centres rather than just one. Polanyi, in turn, considers it a civilisational necessity for capitalist market economies to be socially embedded and democratically regulated in distributed rather than unified sovereignty, as proven by history, particularly the collapse of the gold standard in the 1930s and the outcome of the Second World War.

Inspired by the insights of Gibbon and Polanyi, I argue that the architecture of state systems is related to the presence on their territories of historically grown *heterogeneous ways of social and economic life*, arising from what I conceive as the *constitutive pluralism* of human socialisation and the associated, territorially distinct communal and political interests associated with this heterogeneity. A given extent of social diversity located on a given territory can, other things being equal, either be politically divided into a multiplicity of independent small states or, in an extreme case, be included in a single large state. In the former case, conflicts and interdependencies between localised community and class interests must be managed through an inter-state system of 'foreign policy', the design of which may be more or less appropriate to this task. In the latter case, relations between communities must be handled as domestic politics, the more so the larger the state that encompasses them, and the more communities it comprises. To remain viable as a unitary polity for a multiplicity of societies, large states require a strong central power so as to subject the conflicts between the societies they have internalised to centralised hierarchical control and adjudication and suppress secessionist tendencies. If centralised power does not do the job, a federal state structure can be adopted in which the different communities embraced by the state are granted rights to substate or even quasi-state self-government. In extreme cases, a large state comprising many communities differs very little, if at all, from a state system consisting of a large number of small states. In both cases, the quality of what we may call an *architecture of statehood* will be assessed, in the view of both the sovereign small states of a distributed state order and the more or less autonomous substate units of a more or less federalised large state, on the basis of how far it allows the characteristics and interests of the communities covered by it to assert themselves, in particular in relation to the logic of accumulation in the capitalist economic and social formation and its nationally diverse incarnations.

The central theme of chapter 7, then, is the *politics of scale* of the modern state system under capitalist globalisation. I consider the growth of that system after 1945 and then examine the metamorphoses the nation-state has undergone in the societies of democratic capitalism in connection with the globalisation process. To illustrate the complex political and institutional requirements for the embedding of the particularism of social life in an encompassing state architecture – the historical and institutional dynamics of nation-state formation – I use the cases in the nineteenth and twentieth centuries of Scotland and Catalonia in comparison with Germany, adding remarks on Brexit in a Polanyian perspective.

Following this, in chapter 8, I apply the concept of a state system to the European Union and the conflict between 'pro-European' attempts to build it into a centralised superstate, and 'nationalist' demands for decentralisation and national sovereignty. In drawing this connection, a historical examination of the development of the Western European state system as organised in the EU proves helpful, not only from the point of view of the increasing heterogeneity which has resulted from its expansion from six to twenty-eight (now twenty-seven) member states, but also as regards its implications for the relationship between markets and states as well as for the possibility of political democracy in general. The chapter, then, discusses the special case of the EU as an example for both the politics and the limits of neoliberal centralisation and integration. After the end of the social democratic age, which, at the level of the EU, lasted longer than in some of its member states, the EU became a showcase of a neoliberal political economy, as long intended by the pragmatic 'Europe now, the world later' wing of the neoliberal movement, as distinguished from the globalist *tutto-e-subito* wing led famously by Margaret Thatcher. In the 'single market' era of the 1990s, neoliberal economic integration seemed to be well on its way, accompanied by neofunctionalist hopes that if you merge societies into a common market, after a while, their hearts and minds will follow. The Monetary Union, however, instituted at the end of the decade as the logical next step in the elimination of the nation-state from the governance of the European political economy, soon turned out to be sustainable only with the help of ever-new informal fixes of its utopian one-size-fits-all design, which carried with it growing economic disparities and political tensions between member states. At the end of the 2010s, having vastly overplayed its centralist-integrationist hand and torn between the increasingly hierarchical character of its internal relations and the insistence of its member states on their national sovereignty, in particular their capacity for political-economic action on behalf of their citizens, the European Union was on track, nolens volens, towards a 'Europe à la carte', a 'Europe of variable geometry', and even a 'Europe of fatherlands', through an unending series of backroom political compromises and informal modifications of its cast-in-stone quasi-constitutional supranational regime. Then came the Ukraine war, which raised the question whether the centralist-integrationist project of European state-building might be salvaged by rededicating it, under NATO leadership, to military instead of economic purposes, in what seemed to be on its way to becoming a divided world of warring states.

Before I continue, a brief comment on terminology. German advocates of a united, centralist Europe, including Jürgen Habermas, have accused doubters, including the author of this book, who draw attention to the political-economic opportunities offered by a subdivision of political and economic sovereignty, of *Kleinstaaterei* (small-statism).[3] The concept has its origin in the disputes of the early nineteenth century over a future German state. It was applied polemically by German nationalists to the inherited state structure of the Holy Roman Empire, also called Old Empire (*Altes Reich*) – a constitutional order last laid down in 1648 by the Peace of Westphalia, which envisaged a multiplicity of mostly small sovereign principalities and free imperial cities. The dominant argument of the advocates of a refoundation of the *Reich* in the shape it took in January 1871 after the victorious war against France was the supposed need for Germany, as a 'nation of culture' (a *Kulturnation*), to turn into a 'nation of power' (a *Machtstaat*), in order to survive in its struggle for existence against other, more 'modern' nations.[4] Now it resurfaces in Habermas, with the difference that he refers to 'way of life' (*Lebensweise*) instead of 'culture', and, indeed, as an argument for a European army as a vehicle for the formation of a centralised supranational European Union.[5] My answer to the charge of *Kleinstaaterei* was to propose the concept *Großstaaterei* (mega-statism) for the quest to establish a European *Reich*.[6] One reason was to introduce into the discussion the admittedly speculative idea that Europe might perhaps have

---

3   Jürgen Habermas, *The Lure of Technocracy*, Cambridge, UK: Polity, 2015; Jürgen Habermas, 'Demokratie oder Kapitalismus? Vom Elend der nationalstaatlichen Fragmentierung in einer kapitalistisch integrierten Weltgesellschaft', *Blätter für deutsche und internationale Politik* 58, no. 5 (2013), 59–70.

4   See, for example, Max Weber, *Gesammelte Politische Schriften*, Tübingen: J. C. B. Mohr (Paul Siebeck), 1988 [1921], 142–5.

5   The episode deserves attention as a forerunner to the European participation in the Ukrainian proxy war against Russia. See Hans Eichel et al., 'Für ein solidarisches Europa – Machen wir Ernst mit dem Willen unseres Grundgesetzes, jetzt!', *Handelsblatt*, 21 October 2018, handelsblatt.com. The call was issued by Habermas along with a group of, then retired, CDU and SPD politicians. I will return to the call, in particular to its 'way of life' concept, in view of its amazing career in denoting a shared cultural particularism of the peoples inhabiting (Western?) Europe, but also in justifying the militarisation of Europe. Note that the department of the vice-president of the von der Leyen European Commission in charge of, among other things, refugee policy, Margaritis Schinas, is called the 'Office for Promoting our European Way of Life'. Originally, it was 'for the Protection' instead of 'for Promoting'; the change had to be made because of Green objections.

6   Wolfgang Streeck, 'Vom DM-Nationalismus zum Euro-Patriotismus? Eine Replik auf Jürgen Habermas', *Blätter für deutsche und internationale Politik* 58, no. 9 (2013), 75–92.

been spared a series of catastrophes if the *Altes Reich*, rather than being transformed into a new (and eventually a 'Thousand Year') *Reich*, had turned into a kind of large-scale Switzerland: too decentralised to be able to project power abroad, capable of defence but not of attack, constitutionally decentralised and democratic to reflect its internal diversity, and, possibly for that reason, immune to irredentist and separatist tendencies, and highly motivated to defend itself against hostile takeover from the outside.

Megalomania?

I now return to my introductory overview of the contents of the book. Part IV, 'Beyond Globalist Centralisation', investigates the two alternative escapes from the deadlock between centralisation and decentralisation, focusing on the limits of mega-statism (*Großstaaterei*) and the possibilities – the potential for effective democratic and democratically effective self-government – of small-statism (*Kleinstaaterei*). First, in chapter 9, I discuss the problems of globally unified, centralised statehood supporting a global capitalist economy organised as a unified single market – in other words, of institutionalising political-economic globalisation in a neoliberal format. My thesis is that globalist-capitalist *Großstaaterei* of whatever kind cannot be governed democratically. In fact, to the extent that it is tried, it is intended precisely not to be democratic, its purpose being to protect the capitalist economy from the (potentially democratic) nation-state. Undemocratic by design, a centrally unified global capitalism would need to be sustained by a depoliticised technocratic social order as what I call a *marketocracy*; desirable, and indeed indispensable, as it may seem for global capitalism, a regime like this is no more than a figment of overheated capitalist imagination, as it will never be supported by any real (as opposed to fictional) society. This holds for global governance by a unitary single *state*, but as the experience of the New World Order has shown, it holds for a unipolar state system as well. As the size of the unit to be governed increases, so does, ceteris paribus, its internal heterogeneity, and with it the extent of internalised conflict. The larger a unitary state, the more force required to hold its society – or, better, its collection of societies – together under a centrally unified regime, unless conflict can be bought out by bribes rewarding loyalty and compliance; both repression and bribery are, however, costly.

An alternative would be internal decentralisation in the form of an institutionalised recognition of heterogeneity and the conflicting interests arising from it – in other words, some sort of decentralised governance, which comes with a risk of encouraging tendencies towards secession. Similarly, in an expanding imperial state system, perhaps a predecessor of a global state in a globalist worldview, like in the New World Order of the 1990s, advancing expansion begets growing heterogeneity, and, as the two increase, so too does the resistance of peripheral states against centrally imposed unity, increasing the cost of suppression or conciliation. Both large states and empires, global or continental, to the extent that they encompass substantially different societies, including societies with deeply rooted 'varieties of capitalism' – that is, with different settlements of the foundational conflict between capitalism and society – can be ruled without suppressing local ways of life and justice only if their central powers forgo the ambition to rule their societies *uniformly*.[7] The more, however, they commit themselves to something like political-economic federalism, the more functionally similar they become to multi-state *Kleinstaaterei*, and thereby risk laying themselves open to demands for democracy.

As my discussion proceeds, I shall repeatedly return to the constitutive particularism and pluralism of social integration, which I consider to be so fundamental that it cannot be neglected even in the distant perspective of a future global convergence, whether democratic or neoliberal. What interests me about it is its significance for the governance and the governability of societies, and for the structure of modern state systems and the political-economic role of national sovereignty in them, hence also for the sustained enforceability of political-economic orders. From the point of view of centralised government, as needed for the implementation of a one-size-fits-all regime, the contingent diversity of human socialisation, with its territorially consolidated institutional groundwork, appears problematic in its functional and social complexity, and, indeed, rightly so: if such complexity exceeds a certain level, it

---

7   Wolfgang Streeck, 'E Pluribus Unum? Varieties and Commonalities of Capitalism', in Mark Granovetter and Richard Swedberg, eds, *The Sociology of Economic Life*, 3rd ed., Boulder, CO: Westview, 2011, 419–55.

can make it impossible for governments and states, technically or demo-cratically, to bear the burden of social as well as system integration.

To illustrate the functional obstacles in the way of an upward exit from the neoliberal stalemate, it seems appropriate to recall two twentieth-century debates about what we might call the *governability of complexity*. One took place in inter-war Europe over the possibility of socialist planning, the other in the US during the 1960s over the limits of political 'solutions' for 'social problems' associated with capitalist progress. At the end of the debate on the planned economy, the market economy faction, led by Friedrich Hayek and Ludwig von Mises, had won the argument as they were able to offer the price system of 'free' markets as a coordinating mechanism. The advocates of a planned economy could only place their hopes in a new kind of bureaucracy, to be created some time in the future, which would direct the production and distribution of use values without self-regulating markets and more efficiently than the latter. In 1939, shortly before the outbreak of the Second World War, the cunning Hayek developed the idea of a federally organised world state as a prerequisite for eternal peace between the nations – a large-state project if there ever was one. But there was a price to pay: the state had to renounce any political intervention into the complex play of market forces, because, owing to the heterogeneity of the local interests in a federation that necessarily had to be far flung in order to be genuinely peace promoting, this would overstrain the capacity of any central government to build political unity and act strategically.[8] I have shown, in *Buying Time*, how the political-economic logic of Hayek's plan for world peace, which in reality was a neoliberal logic of market expansion accompanied by state contraction, has unfolded in the development of the European Union and its gradual enlargement.[9]

The plan-versus-market controversy saw a brief revival in the Soviet Union in the 1960s, when new computer technology appeared to open the prospect that the masses of information required for the central administration of a complex economy could, after all, be processed so as

---

8   Friedrich A. Hayek, 'The Economic Conditions of Interstate Federalism', in Friedrich A. Hayek, ed., *Individualism and Economic Order*, Chicago: University of Chicago Press, 1980 [1948], 255–72.

9   See Streeck, *Buying Time*, 97–110.

to render a realistic model of the world.[10] Interestingly enough, similar expectations emerged at the same time in the United States, where, after the collapse of Lyndon B. Johnson's 'Great Society', the new discipline of 'policy research' discovered the concept of 'complexity' as an ontological description of a condition of modern societies which democratic systems of government, as inherited from the past, were incapable of managing.[11] Here, too, it was expected, in the atomic age's exuberant faith in technology, that the instruments of electronic information processing which had just come into existence (or were expected to be available shortly) could offer a remedy, either by creating models of social processes that were as complex as the processes themselves, or by continuously collecting current data and processing the result in real time. In relation both to the governability problem of the United States after the boom of the Golden Years and the planning problem of Soviet Communism after Stalin, a technocratic utopia thus became the last, very soon disappointed hope for managing a complex centralised system from above. That it remains utopian to this day has hardly diminished its attraction – and certainly not for parts of the cosmopolitan left who had gone over to globalist liberalism – because however unrealistic the prospect of solving problems of governance with the help of intelligent machines, it appears to open the possibility that there could still be other instruments of coordination for Hayek's global federation than a Hayekian free market.[12]

The theme of chapter 9, then, is the limited viability and the internal contradictions of *Großstaaterei* – mega-statism – as an upward escape from the post-neoliberal political stalemate. The empirical core of the chapter is the 'globalisation' of the economy in the second half of

---

10   Francis Spufford, *Red Plenty: Inside the Fifties' Soviet Dream*, London: Faber & Faber, 2010.

11   See Ariane Leendertz, *Der erschöpfte Staat: Eine andere Geschichte des Neoliberalismus*, Hamburg: Hamburger Edition, 2022.

12   It is one of the ironies of modern capitalism's historical development that today, roughly half a century after the collapse of the socialist dream of cybernetic control (Stephen Kotkin, *Armaggedon Averted: The Soviet Collapse 1970–2000*, updated ed., Oxford: Oxford University Press, 2008), the neoliberal market, denationalised on the pretext of freeing the state from the burden of excessive complexity, has given birth to social and economic control systems, in the shape of the privately owned 'social media', whose information-processing capacity exceeds everything that either side, communism or state-administered capitalism, could ever have imagined.

the twentieth century, its quasi-government referred to euphemistically as global governance, intended to eliminate the nation-state and take the place of national democracy while getting stuck on the road to hyperglobalisation after the end of the systemic conflict between capitalism and communism. What was optimistically proclaimed to be a post-statist cosmopolitan world government replacing the nation-state was and remained in reality an imperially structured state system around a US centre, supposed to function as an institutional scaffolding for a unified, *one-capitalism-fits-all* world while describing itself as a 'liberal', 'multilateral', 'rules-based' international order.[13] Like every empire, this too had a tendency to overexpansion, with a corresponding decline in effectiveness and legitimacy, also within its central state. Moreover, it suffered from the inherent centralism of the neoliberal programme with its hostility to nation-states and its unrealistic goal of a unified worldwide political economy. Hence, instead of a progressive construction of a new world order, if not non-statist then at least single-statist, what happened was an increasing fragmentation of a regime conceived for nothing other than the global expansion of neoliberal capitalism, and certainly not for regulating it in line with social needs and in order to contain the damage it causes.

------

13   I avoid following the practice of much of the literature referring routinely to a 'liberal international order' (often abbreviated to LIO). My reason is the ambiguity of the word 'liberal'. In American usage, 'liberalism' can mean something in the nature of social democracy; thus, when John Ruggie referred to the post-war order as 'embedded liberalism', he meant an international regime which tolerated the different versions of a social democratic class compromise between capital and labour, as embedded in different nation-states whose political economy varied according to the prevailing configuration of political forces within each country – in other words, the world of Keynes and Bretton Woods: John Gerard Ruggie, 'International Regimes, Transactions and Change: Embedded Liberalism in the Postwar Economic Order', *International Organization* 36, no. 2 (1982), 379–415; John Gerard Ruggie, 'Globalization and the Embedded Liberalism Compromise: The End of an Era?', in Wolfgang Streeck, ed., *Internationale Wirtschaft, nationale Demokratie: Herausforderungen für die Demokratietheorie*, Frankfurt am Main: Campus, 1998, 79–97. Today, however, a 'liberal' international order could be, and indeed is, understood to mean an order in the neoliberal sense, which no longer has anything to do with the social democratic meaning of 'liberalism'. In this usage, the dramatic difference between the world of Keynes and Ruggie and that of hyperglobalisation in the late-twentieth and early twenty-first-century world is conceptually hidden.

Decomposing Complexity

Finally, chapter 10 investigates the possibility of a downward exit from the post-neoliberal stalemate and looks at the possibility that a system of small states – in other words, a domestic and international order which is decentralised and tolerates particularism – may be able to achieve structural democratisation and political governability, and maximise economic welfare. Having argued that there can be no further upward move, no further increase in political scale, either in Europe or the world as a whole, I now undertake to show that there is still free space below, in terms of not just subversive anti-neoliberal but also constructive post-neoliberal policy. The fundamental idea is to increase the capacity of complex systems, in this case the globalised world, for political self-government by *decomposing* them. This is uncomfortable for universalists who favour large states, which is why it never features in discussions in the neoliberal camp and is morally denigrated by cosmopolitan globalisation enthusiasts as an ideological cover for dubious motives. Taking up a theme of the countermovement from below, which has brought globalisation and, with it, the advance of neoliberalism to a standstill, I suggest that decentralisation makes it possible to do without not only the technological utopia of a computer system at the centre of a post-national world order, but also without the self-regulating world market, the dream of the globalists and the all-too-realistic nightmare of those who cannot, or do not wish to, depend exclusively on markets. Only through decentralisation, I argue, can encompassing social systems maintain a sustainable existence. Indeed, even norms with a claim to universal validity can take effect only under particular conditions and must in their application be allowed to be interpreted differently, if only because no universal law-maker can grasp the present complexity of the real world, let alone anticipate its complexity in the future.

As pointed out, in the capitalist political economy of today, the choice between large and small statehood, between integration and differentiation of state systems, is a choice between globalism and democracy, or, rather, the possibility of democracy. A combination of the two, globalism and democracy, is not on offer, nor is democracy without and outside of nation-states.[14] Chapter 9 recalls Herbert Simon's general model of controlling complexity through the decomposition of unmanageable large units into manageable small ones. It also refers to Keynes's reflections on national sovereignty and self-sufficiency in a world economy with international trade, based on his experience of the collapse of the gold standard after the First World War. The closeness of Keynes to Polanyi, or Polanyi to Keynes, on this decisive issue is so remarkable that I feel encouraged to speak of a *Keynes-Polanyi model* of statehood – involving economic protectionism, or nationalism, as a precondition of social stability and international peace, as well as of cooperation between states in what Polanyi calls 'regional planning'.

Small-statism, or restored distributed sovereignty, as a way out of neoliberal stagnation requires a supportive international order. A downward resolution of the post-neoliberal stalemate demands a retreat from a regime of international hyperglobalisation which, at its core, could not be anything other than an empire based on power rather than rules. With the US as declining global hegemon, and China rising, such a retreat appeared possible even in the European region, certainly before the Russian invasion of Ukraine. Today, a prerequisite would be preventing the European Union from using the militarisation of its external relations, under its own or under American command, as a means of halting, or reversing, the loosening of its internal centralisation set in motion by the crisis of neoliberalism. Beyond Europe, the continuing crisis of Western capitalism had, long before the Ukraine crisis, given rise to surprisingly far-reaching considerations about deglobalisation, regionalisation, and even 'responsible' or 'progressive' protectionism. I will argue that there is much to be said for the idea that the growth crisis of financialised global capitalism, together with the

---

14   See also Dirk Jörke, *Die Größe der Demokratie: Über die räumliche Dimension von Herrschaft und Partizipation*, Berlin: Suhrkamp, 2019, where he raises democratic theory to a new level by showing that any upscaling of effective political jurisdiction beyond a certain magnitude is inevitably accompanied by a downscaling of democracy. What I add to this is the insight, gained from a theoretical concept of complexity and from observing neoliberalism in action, that it is not just democracy but the very ability to govern that declines as the size of a state – more precisely, of an integrated uniform regime – increases. Hence a world without effective nation-states – or a world ruled by a world state – would be dystopian in two senses: not only would it be undemocratic but it would also be ungovernable – the latter being partly, although not exclusively, on account of the former.

globalisation crisis associated with the pandemic and now with the war, not only makes possible but positively demands a new turn towards the local and communal, or even communitarian, foundations of economic activity.[15] To the extent that financialised capitalism's crisis of growth and legitimacy also derives from the volatility of capital that has become too mobile to be reliable, decentralisation towards sovereign democracy could also encourage a search for less mobile forms of property and capital, perhaps of a cooperative or communal kind; the paradoxical result might be something like an expanding socialist supplement to, or substructure of, capitalism. Needless to say, this would be impossible within the internal market regime of the European Union in its present centralised and unitary form.

---

15   Julie Froud et al., *Foundational Economy: The Infrastructure of Everyday Life*, Manchester: Manchester University Press, 2018.

PART II
After Three Decades

5

A Dual Crisis I: Capitalism

Why has global neoliberalism, and the New World Order in which it was enshrined, ended in disaster? In the following, I will offer three main reasons. First, not only did the New World Order fail to repair the crisis of capitalism that began with the breakdown of the post-war Keynesian settlement; it extended it into a *crisis sequence* in which it took increasingly destructive forms as political solutions successively turned into problems themselves. With the failure of ever-new attempts at crisis management, popular confidence in future growth compensating for present decline, essential for capitalist stability, began to wither away across broad sections of capitalist society.

Next, the politics of the New World Order undermined the historical compromise between capitalism and democracy by setting in motion a deep *transformation of democratic institutions and practices* – one that cut off institutional channels for local demands for political intervention in the general logic of capitalist development. This excluded growing sections of the population of capitalist democracies from the democratic class struggle, by removing the capitalist economy from the reach of democratic politics. As a result, the reformist democratic opposition of the social democratic era was sidelined, and liberal democracy was reduced to dealing with diffuse political discontent, disorganised and therefore difficult to address, and with conflicts over identity rather than interests. This, in turn, created ample political opportunities for neo-authoritarian social movements that tend to grow more powerful the more they are excluded from influencing policy or entering government.

Third, the globalist architecture of the New World Order was designed to subdue independent local expression and the autonomous pursuit of distinct collective interests rooted in the constitutive particularism of the human experience, as embodied in the modern era in national societies and represented by sovereign national states. But the attempt to merge the world into an all-encompassing, unified political economy governed by universal norms and values rather than by local politics stirred up powerful popular resistance that proved invincible, in spite of the application in various parts of the globe of inordinate military force. Efforts to eliminate *national sovereignty* for the sake of *international unity* also failed in the EU, where the national institutions of post-war social democracy resisted the onslaught of the triple power of bureaucracy, technocracy, and marketocracy. With supranational rule, global or continental, perceived as foreign rule, attempts to maintain the unity of the post-1990 international order proved futile. This manifested itself not least in the Russian war against Ukraine – a war, in fact, over the terms of the US-dominated, allegedly 'rules-based' New World Order as well as those of its approaching sequel, the war in the Pacific between the United States and China.

Economic and political crises fall within the responsibility of different scientific disciplines and are therefore, as a rule, treated separately; here, too, this practice will be followed initially, for simplified presentation. But the connection between the two is of great interest, and it goes further than simple causal relations as when either the economy stagnates because there is disorder in a state, or there is disorder in a state because the economy no longer 'delivers'. What is important for a theory of political economy which approaches its subject historically rather than in terms of efficiency theory is to view changes in the relation between crises in the state and crises in the economy in the context of changes in capitalism in general and in democratic capitalism in particular. What kind of policy does present-day capitalism 'demand' of present-day states so that the accumulation of capital may continue?[1] What does state policy require of today's capitalist economy so that it can create legitimacy both for the state and for capitalism? And what

---

1   Bruno Amable, *Structural Crisis and Institutional Change in Modern Capitalism: French Capitalism in Transition*, Oxford: Oxford University Press, 2017.

requirements must be fulfilled by the institutions of democratic capitalism as they have historically grown? How must they change, or allow themselves to be changed, for neoliberal progress to continue – or, where possible, to be replaced by another kind of progress, in another direction? Both problems, economic and political, are entangled in the crisis of the European Union, which will be addressed briefly at the end of this part of the book.

Stagnation

As far as the condition of the capitalist economy at the end of the New World Order is concerned, a prominent concept in the public discourse has, for some time, been that of stagnation. It was introduced – or, better, revived – at a conference of central bankers in 2013 by Larry Summers, a man who did several stints as chief engineer in the engine room of globalised capitalism.[2] In his address, Summers asked whether Western capitalism had not been living through an epoch of 'secular stagnation', or 'a continuing situation of slow growth', for some time, including the period between 1995 and 2001, when he was a prominent member of the Clinton administration.[3] Since then, there has been as much contention over a precise definition of the concept as over the origin of the disease and its therapy. Summers himself diagnosed a 'savings glut', coinciding with low growth, minimal increases in productivity, and, strangely enough, interest rates tending towards zero or even turning negative. Others have added to the list increasing inequality, a declining wage share, a tendency of the new gigantic global enterprises towards net saving, uncertainty over the future (*Angstsparen*), public and private indebtedness at a level unparalleled in peacetime, and a rapid growth in the money supply divorced from any connection with the real economy. I cannot attempt to adjudicate between the numerous more or less standard economic theories of stagnation available. I admit, however, that I have a certain preference

---

2 On Summers, see 'Lawrence Summers', wikipedia.org.

3 I have discussed this in more detail in the preface to Wolfgang Streeck, *Buying Time: The Delayed Crisis of Democratic Capitalism*, 2nd ed., London: Verso, 2017.

for a Keynesian explanation, in which a central role is played by the increasingly unequal distribution of income and wealth resulting from the advance of neoliberalism and the financialisation of capitalism. To put it simply: without trade unions, no mass purchasing power; without mass purchasing power, no investment.[4]

For a brief phenomenology of the continuing economic crisis in the countries of mature capitalism, it is well to begin with the long-term decline of their growth rates in the neoliberal era. For twenty members of the Organisation for Economic Co-operation and Development (OECD), the rapid slowdown in economic growth, as measured in five-year moving averages, began in 1997, in the first decade of the New World Order. It came to an end only in 2010, after thirteen years in which it had declined continuously from about 3.5 percent to slightly under zero (fig. 6). Subsequently, in the wake of the 2008 financial crisis and assisted by the emergency measures taken by governments to prevent a global depression, it rose to a little over 2 percent, until it fell again after 2016. Note that the peak of 2015 was not much above the cyclical troughs of 1981 and 1992, and growth after both 1981 and 1992 always peaked below the level of the 1960s, when it was dependably above 5 percent. Following 2016, 2 percent growth, the point of inflection of the new cycle, was no longer the lower limit but the upper one, which continued the long-term downward trend since the end of the mixed economy. This, it would seem, leaves little hope for a new wave of growth causing, for example, social inequality or public debt to be reduced, even without taking into account the effect of the COVID-19 pandemic and the war in Ukraine.

---

4   Remarkably enough, in the meantime, Summers has moved towards the present author's position. Before that, he had broken with Goldman Sachs, as he explained in a Twitter post: 'Today, Goldman's CEO received a 20 percent raise to $27 million. Apart from the juxtaposition with the worst American health disaster in a century, there is the fact that the stock is down more than 35 percent during the last year.' A little later, on 26 June 2020, an article by Summers appeared in the *Washington Post*, written jointly with a Harvard University doctoral student, with the title 'US Workers Need More Power' (washington.post.com). Its last paragraph reads: 'Overall, we believe that increasing worker power must be a central and urgent priority for policymakers concerned with inequality, low pay and poor work conditions. If we do not shift the distribution of power to workers, any other policy changes are likely to be short-term and insufficient.'

Figure 6. Growth rates, 1970–2019, five-year moving averages

———5-Year Moving Average

The following countries are included: Australia, Austria, Belgium, Canada, Denmark, Finland, France, Germany, Greece, Ireland, Italy, Japan, the Netherlands, Norway, Portugal, Spain, Sweden, Switzerland, United Kingdom, United States. The calculation of the moving average ends with the year 2021 (data point 2019), and it therefore takes into account the initial impact of the COVID-19 crisis but not that of the war in Ukraine.

Source: OECD Economic Outlook No. 111. Database and the author's calculations.

Average figures hide considerable differences between countries (fig. 7). Of eleven countries we have chosen as examples, Germany, France, the United States, and Ireland had, already by 2011, returned after the 2008 crash to their pre-crisis performance. Indeed, Sweden had arrived there a year earlier. Japan and the United Kingdom followed in 2013, Spain in 2017, and Portugal in 2018. In 2021, Italy and Greece were still below their performance at the beginning of the decade, Italy very slightly (94.3 percent) and Greece dramatically (75.8). The frontrunners in the race to overcome the crisis were Ireland (206.0 percent), Sweden (126.1), the US (124.2), the UK (114.1), and Germany (112.4); in 2021, despite COVID, Germany and the UK, in particular, displayed a perceptible rise in employment since 2008, alongside a fall in the rate of unemployment.

Figure 7. Growth, employment, and unemployment in eleven countries, 2008–2021

		2008	2009	2010	2011	2012	2013	2014	2015	2016	2017	2018	2019	2020	2021
Germany	GDP	100.0	94.4	98.2	102.1	102.7	103.3	105.6	106.9	109.2	112.4	113.7	114.9	109.2	112.4
	Employment	70.1	69.4	70.3	71.8	72.1	72.5	72.8	73.0	73.7	74.3	74.9	75.7	76.2	75.8
	Unemployment	7.4	7.6	7.0	5.9	5.4	5.2	5.0	4.6	4.2	3.8	3.4	3.2	3.9	3.6
France	GDP	100.0	97.2	99.0	101.2	101.5	102.2	103.2	104.3	105.3	107.9	109.9	112.0	103.1	110.1
	Employment	65.3	64.4	64.4	64.3	64.4	64.4	64.5	64.7	65.0	65.6	66.2	66.4	66.1	67.3
	Unemployment	7.5	9.2	9.3	9.3	9.8	10.4	10.3	10.4	10.1	9.5	9.1	8.5	8.1	7.9
Italy	GDP	100.0	94.7	96.3	97.1	94.2	92.4	92.5	93.1	94.4	96.0	96.8	97.3	88.4	94.3
	Employment	58.7	56.9	56.3	56.4	56.1	55.0	55.3	56.0	57.1	57.9	58.5	59.1	57.5	58.3
	Unemployment	6.8	7.8	8.5	8.6	10.9	12.3	12.7	12.0	11.7	11.3	10.6	9.9	9.3	9.5
Japan	GDP	100.0	94.3	98.2	98.2	99.5	101.5	101.8	103.4	104.2	106.0	106.6	106.3	101.5	103.2
	Employment	70.9	70.2	70.3	70.8	70.6	71.8	72.8	73.4	74.5	75.5	77.2	78.1	77.7	77.9
	Unemployment	4.0	5.0	5.0	4.6	4.3	4.0	3.6	3.4	3.1	2.8	2.4	2.4	2.8	2.8
Sweden	GDP	100.0	95.8	101.2	104.5	104.2	105.4	108.3	112.9	115.0	118.2	120.6	123.0	120.2	126.1
	Employment	74.3	71.7	71.6	73.1	73.3	74.0	74.4	75.0	75.7	76.3	76.9	76.6	74.9	75.4
	Unemployment	6.4	8.5	8.8	7.9	8.1	8.2	8.1	7.6	7.1	6.9	6.5	7.0	8.5	8.8
United Kingdom	GDP	100.0	95.8	97.8	99.2	100.7	102.6	105.6	108.4	110.9	113.2	115.1	117.0	106.2	114.1
	Employment	72.6	70.9	70.5	70.3	71.0	71.6	72.9	73.7	74.4	75.0	75.6	76.2	75.4	75.2
	Unemployment	5.7	7.6	7.9	8.1	8.0	7.6	6.2	5.4	4.9	4.4	4.1	3.8	4.5	4.5
United States	GDP	100.0	97.4	100.0	101.6	103.9	105.8	108.2	111.2	113.0	115.6	118.9	121.7	117.5	124.2
	Employment	70.9	67.6	66.7	66.6	67.1	67.4	68.1	68.7	69.4	70.1	70.7	71.4	67.1	69.4
	Unemployment	5.8	9.3	9.6	8.9	8.1	7.4	6.2	5.3	4.9	4.4	3.9	3.7	8.1	5.4
Greece	GDP	100.0	95.7	90.5	81.3	75.5	73.6	74.0	73.8	73.5	74.3	75.5	76.9	69.9	75.8
	Employment	61.4	60.7	58.9	54.9	50.4	48.5	49.2	50.7	51.8	53.2	54.5	56.1	53.7	57.3
	Unemployment	7.8	9.6	12.7	17.9	24.4	27.5	26.5	24.9	23.5	21.5	19.3	17.3	16.3	14.7
Spain	GDP	100.0	96.2	96.4	95.6	92.8	91.4	92.7	96.3	99.2	102.1	104.5	106.7	95.1	100.0
	Employment	64.5	60.0	58.9	58.0	55.8	54.8	56.0	57.8	59.6	61.1	62.4	63.3	61.0	62.7
	Unemployment	11.3	17.9	19.9	21.4	24.8	26.1	24.4	22.1	19.6	17.2	15.3	14.1	15.5	14.8
Portugal	GDP	100.0	96.9	98.6	96.9	93.0	92.1	92.8	94.5	96.4	99.8	102.6	105.4	96.5	101.2
	Employment	68.0	63.0	62.3	61.9	59.3	58.8	61.2	62.8	64.2	67.0	69.0	69.9	68.5	70.2
	Unemployment	8.4	10.2	11.6	13.4	16.5	17.1	14.5	12.9	11.5	9.2	7.2	6.6	7.0	6.6
Ireland	GDP	100.0	94.9	96.1	97.0	96.8	98.4	106.7	133.8	137.0	149.5	163.2	171.6	181.7	206.0
	Employment	69.7	63.6	61.0	60.0	59.9	61.8	63.1	64.7	66.4	67.6	68.5	69.5	66.6	69.9
	Unemployment	6.8	12.6	14.6	15.4	15.4	13.7	11.8	9.9	8.4	6.7	5.8	5.0	5.8	6.2

Source: OECD Economic Outlook No. 111 Database, OECD Short-Term Labour Market Statistics (current publications).

It appears that the US and the UK, the two countries with a strict neo-liberal approach to labour market and social policy, overcame the economic crisis relatively successfully, but, in return for this, both had to contend with deep political crises.[5] (Japan was still more successful, with a clear rise in employment and an extremely low level of unemployment.)

As to Germany, the figures reflect its privileged position at the time as an industrial exporter within the EMU (the European Economic and Monetary Union), under which it can avail itself of a currency that is permanently undervalued. Here, the contrast with France is striking, where growth was slower, employment was almost 10 percent below Germany's, and unemployment in 2019 was over two and a half times as high as in Germany. Note, though, that none of this changed the general downward trend in the growth rates of rich capitalist countries. How the shocks of the pandemic and the Ukraine war will eventually affect countries' relative economic performance, given the different magnitudes of those shocks by country and wide differences in national conditions, cannot be foreseen. There is, however, no reason to believe that national performance will differ in the same way as it did after the financial crisis, let alone that aggregate performance will reverse the trend towards ever-lower growth.

How can secular stagnation be explained, if indeed there is – or was – one? In the early 1980s, the central banks of the big capitalist countries pushed interest rates upwards, in order to end the inflation which had become endemic in the previous decade. The operation, led by the Federal Reserve Bank of the United States, came to be called the 'Volcker shock', after Paul Volcker, appointed by Jimmy Carter to head the bank in the summer of 1979. Volcker's anti-inflation measures contributed heavily to the de-industrialisation of the US economy. By 1982, the rate of inflation had fallen from 11 to 4 percent, while the rate of interest rose temporarily to as high as 18 percent. Volcker's policy 'broke the back', to

---

5   As one may suspect, this was a consequence of the very neoliberal reforms that allowed for an early recovery. Flanked by national monetary sovereignty, neoliberal policies may have made it easier to overcome the economic crisis, although at the expense of large sections of the population. In Italy, in contrast, the political crisis – which was, like in the UK and the US, accompanied by a collapse of the political centre – was the result not of neoliberal reform but of successful resistance to it, intensifying the economic crisis because, in the absence of monetary sovereignty, there was no alternative to so-called structural reforms.

use the customary violent metaphor, not just of worldwide inflation but also of American trade unions. Until the two crises after 2019, most 'experts' considered the main threat to economic stability to be no longer inflation but deflation – an overall fall in prices on account of a lack of demand, which, with high indebtedness, can have the dramatic consequence that loan repayments become more expensive in real terms (debt deflation), rather than becoming cheaper as they do when there is a fall in the value of money.

As a consequence, central banks found themselves struggling not against *too much* but rather against *too little* inflation. The European Central Bank, for instance, began to aim for a rate of inflation of '2 or slightly under 2 percent', a target that it failed to achieve until 2021 when, all of a sudden, inflation threatened to return to a 1970s level. The method of choice to stimulate inflation and, hopefully as a result, economic growth was a reduction in the rate of interest commercial banks had to pay to the central bank for loans they needed for the issue of credit; low or negative interest rates were to induce them to be more generous to would-be creditors. Thus, in Europe as governed by the EMU, the central bank's rate of interest long remained at zero. More-over, banks which kept money on deposit at the central bank, for speculation or safekeeping, had to pay interest on their accounts, just as they increasingly charged their customers a kind of storage fee for money deposited with them. The effect, however, was neither the end of the savings glut diagnosed by Summers and others, nor the increase in inflation that was meant to drive off the spectre of deflation. Although interest rates were lower than ever, and although whoever parked money in the bank risked having to pay for it, there was no prospect of an end to stagnation and low growth. Indeed, there is no indication that the surge in inflation in 2021 and, in particular, in 2022, at levels far beyond 2 percent, would have changed or will change this; in fact, the opposite seems to be the case, like in the infamous era of so-called stagflation in the 1970s.

Why, until 2022, was there neither new growth nor inflation, despite zero or even negative interest rates? The mystery is compounded if one bears in mind that the world's central banks had long ceased to limit their attempts to resuscitate capital accumulation by lowering interest rates. After 2008, when fiscal policy was immobilised by the financial crisis, the central banks had turned to so-called quantitative easing

(QE), aimed at expanding the money supply. For this, they began to purchase huge amounts of debt securities from the private sector, providing sellers with fresh money in hopes that they would reinvest it. This was attractive to the sellers, as it freed them from the risk of creditor default – a risk that need not worry a central bank which can balance any losses by using its sovereign powers to create new money. As a result, the balance sheets of the world's central banks tripled in absolute terms during the ten years after 2007 (fig. 8), and, as a proportion of GDP, the holdings of the four biggest central banks of the OECD world rose from 5 percent in 2008 to 40 percent in 2019, the last year before the COVID crisis (figs. 9 and 10). This obviously contributed to the fact that the quantity of money in circulation in OECD countries – which, in the case of 'narrow money', had up to the mid-1980s declined and had, for 'broad money', remained largely constant at around 50 percent of GDP up to the end of the 1970s – increased until 2016 from below 20 to 45 percent of GDP for narrow money and more than doubled for broad money from 50 percent to slightly under 110 percent (fig. 11). Even this did not raise inflation, nor did it increase the propensity to invest enough to cause growth by transferring the savings overhang back into the real economy.[6]

---

6   The easy money policy of the central banks did not fail to attract criticism by liberal and neoliberal economists. In October 2019, a group of German, French, Austrian, and Dutch former central bank officials published a memorandum directed against the 'accommodative' monetary policy of the ECB. They argued, among other things, that there was in fact no danger of deflation; that attempts to raise inflation to 2 percent might unleash an uncontrollable inflationary dynamic; that, by purchasing state papers, the ECB was in breach of its statute which barred it from using its money to finance states, a practice which would exempt governments from having to engage in financial consolidation; that the very low interest rate was redistributing resources in favour of owners of assets, which might lead to dangerous social tensions and, in addition, cause asset market bubbles; that weak banks and firms would be artificially kept in existence, leading to a 'zombification' of the economy; and that, as time went on, it would become ever more difficult to exit from the easy-money policy. See 'Das Memorandum der EZB-Kritiker im Original', *Frankfurter Allgemeine*, 4 October 2019, faz.net. What this shows to a non-economist is that highly regarded economists can arrive at diametrically opposed diagnoses on a life-and-death economic issue. Among other things, this may be interpreted as indicating a severe crisis, not only in economic theory and policy but also in the economy itself, with central bank leaders so desperate about continuing economic stagnation as to be willing to accept the plethora of risks spelled out by their predecessors in the 2019 memorandum.

Figure 8. Assets of central banks, 2007–2017

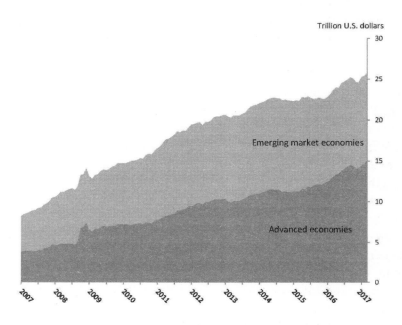

Advanced economies: Australia, Canada, Denmark, Eurozone, Japan, Norway, Sweden, Switzerland, United Kingdom, United States. *Emerging market economies*: Argentina, Brazil, Chile, China, Columbia, Czech Republic, Hong Kong, Hungary, India, Indonesia, Korea, Malaysia, Mexico, Peru, Philippines, Poland, Russia, Saudi Arabia, Singapore, South Africa, Taiwan, Thailand, Turkey.

Source: Bank for International Settlements, 87th Annual Report (2016/17), statistical data

Not that no one had taken up the offer of cheap credit. In contrast to what one might have assumed, public debt in OECD countries, notwithstanding their proclaimed policies of 'austerity', rose sharply in the six years following the financial crisis of 2008, from an average 68 percent of GDP in 2007 to 105 percent in 2013 (fig. 12). Subsequently, in parallel with central banks extending their balance sheets under QE, there was a slight decline, which, however, was soon completely wiped out by the enormous burden of debt resulting from the pandemic.[7] In large part, the increase in state indebtedness since 2008 amounted to a

---

7   And one can, with certainty, expect a big further increase in public debt as a result of the war in Ukraine.

Figure 9. Assets of four large central banks, in percent of GDP, 1960–2021

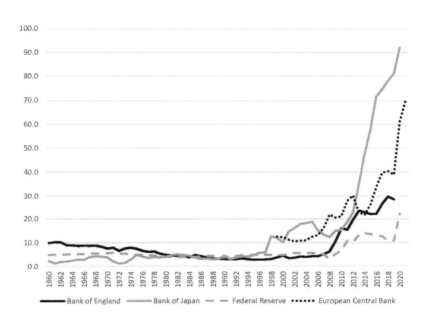

Sources: Bank of England (1960–2019): The Bank of England's Balance Sheet, 1696–2019, consolidated balance sheet as a percentage of nominal GDP, bankofengland.co.uk. Bank of Japan (1960–2020): World Bank, Central Bank Assets to GDP for Japan, retrieved from FRED, Federal Reserve Bank of St. Louis, fred.stlouisfed.org. European Central Bank (1999–2021): Annual consolidated balance sheets of the Eurosystem, Eurostat: GDP at market prices, author's calculations. Federal Reserve (1960–2020): World Bank, Central Bank Assets to GDP for United States, retrieved from FRED, Federal Reserve Bank of St. Louis, fred.stlouisfed.org.

shift in the overall debt burden from private to public borrowers – something creditors probably favoured, owing to the instability in the private capital market which had become apparent during the crisis. A similar restructuring of debt, although in the opposite direction, had taken place during the 1990s, when the United States had placed the consolidation of state finances on the international agenda. Very likely, this reflected a growing concern on the part of the financial industry concern over the ability and indeed willingness of the increasingly indebted states to honour their obligations to their creditors – states which had gone deeper and deeper into debt during the various capitalist crises that followed the end of post-war stability; after all, the average debt burden of OECD countries had roughly doubled in the two decades

Figure 10. Assets of three (up to 1998) and four (from 1999) large central banks, in percentage of GDP, unweighted average, 1960–2019

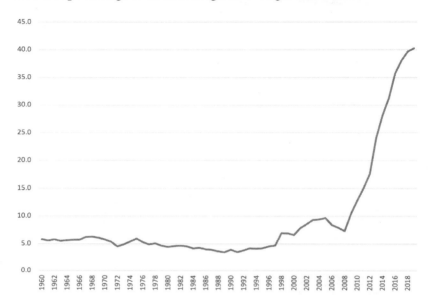

Sources: Bank of England, Bank of Japan, European Central Bank, Federal Reserve Bank.

after 1974, from 40 percent of GDP to almost 80. To compensate for the decline in household income and the fall in public and private demand caused by fiscal consolidation, private borrowing was made easier through deregulation of national and global capital markets; the partial replacement of public by private debt that resulted was, at the time, described as a privatisation of Keynesianism. After 2008, when the interest of the financial industry in economic stabilisation and the restoration of its borrowers' solvency began to outweigh the industry's fear of expropriation through sovereign bankruptcies, it was the states' turn to go back into debt, with the consequence that all the achievements of consolidation since the 1990s were more than lost (fig. 12).[8]

---

8   More on this in Wolfgang Streeck, 'The Rise of the European Consolidation State', in Hideko Magara, ed., *Policy Change under New Democratic Capitalism*, London: Routledge (2017), 27–46; Wolfgang Streeck, 'A New Regime: The Consolidation State', in Desmond King and Patrick Le Galès, eds, *Reconfiguring European States in Crisis*, Oxford: Oxford University Press (2017), 139–57; Streeck, *Buying Time*.

Figure 11. The OECD world: Aggregate quantities of money, narrowly and broadly defined, in percent of GDP, 1950–2016

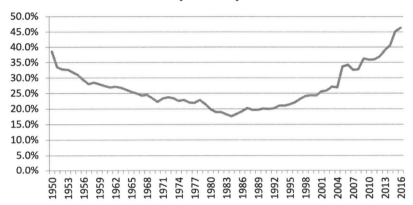

OECD World: Narrow Money Supply (%GDP)

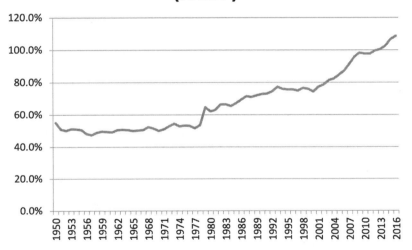

OECD World: Broad Money Supply (%GDP)

The following countries are included: Australia, Belgium, Canada, Denmark, Finland, France, Germany, Italy, Japan, Netherlands, Norway, Portugal, Spain, Sweden, Switzerland, United Kingdom, United States.

Source: Ò. Jordà, M. Schularick, and Alan M. Taylor, 'Macrofinancial History and the New Business Cycle Facts', in *NBER Macroeconomics Annual 2016*, vol. 31, ed. Martin Eichenbaum and Jonathan A. Parker, Chicago: University of Chicago Press, 2017.

Figure 12. Public debt in twenty OECD countries, 1995–2021, in percent of GDP

Unweighted average, including the following countries: Australia, Austria, Belgium, Canada, Denmark, Finland, France, Germany, Greece, Ireland, Italy, Japan, Netherlands, Norway, Portugal, Spain, Sweden, Switzerland, United Kingdom, United States.

Source: OECD Economic Outlook No. 105 Database, author's calculations.

The rise in public debt since 2008 did not, however, entail a lasting reduction in private debt. While in the rich economies the ratio of public debt to GDP increased between 2007 and 2014 by 35 percent, the corresponding ratio for private debt fell by no more than 2 percent.[9] According to Bloomberg News, total household debt in the US fell slightly following the 2008 collapse of collateral security, but from 2013 it started to rise again. By 2017, it was greater than the entire GDP of the People's Republic of China expressed in US dollars.[10] As to global

---

9   Richard Dobbs et al., *The Debt and (Not Much) Deleveraging: Executive Summary*, McKinsey Global Institute, 2015, mckinsey.com. According to McKinsey, after 2008, private household indebtedness in the countries most affected by the crisis fell back roughly to its level in 2000. But in most of the other rich countries, it continued to rise.

10   'Household debt outstanding – everything from mortgages to credit cards to car loans – reached $12.7 trillion in the first quarter of 2013, surpassing the previous peak

Figure 13. Global indebtedness and debt structure, 2000–2014

Global debt has increased by $57 trillion since 2007, outpacing world GDP growth

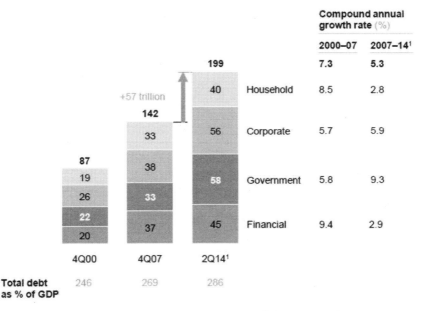

Global stock of debt outstanding by type[1]
$ trillion, constant 2013 exchange rates

		Compound annual growth rate (%)	
		2000–07	2007–14[1]
	199	7.3	5.3
Household	40	8.5	2.8
Corporate	56	5.7	5.9
Government	58	5.8	9.3
Financial	45	9.4	2.9

4Q00   4Q07   2Q14[1]

Total debt as % of GDP   246   269   286

[1]   2Q14 data for advanced economies and China; 4Q13 data for other developing economies. NOTE: Numbers may not sum due to rounding.

Source: Richard Dobbs et al., *The Debt and Not Much Deleveraging: Executive Summary*, McKinsey Global Institute, 2015, mckinsey.com (Haver Analytics; national sources; *World Economic Outlook*, IMF; BIS; McKinsey Global Institute analysis).

indebtedness, the McKinsey Global Institute estimates that it rose faster after 2007 than worldwide GDP, increasing from 269 to 286 percent of the latter, almost as quickly as in the seven years before (fig. 13). Although government debt registered the fastest growth, private sector debt also increased significantly (business debt more so than household debt), rising, in US dollars, from $71 trillion to $96 trillion.

in 2008 before the housing market collapse took its toll, Federal Reserve Bank of New York data show. To put the borrowing in perspective, it's more than the size of China's economy or almost four times that of Germany's.' 'In Debt We Trust for U.S. Consumers with $12.7 Trillion Burden', *Bloomberg News*, 10 August 2017, bloomberg.com.

What the accumulated indebtedness of governments, businesses, and households had to do with the fact that, despite zero or even negative interest rates, the available capital appeared unable or unwilling in the era of secular stagnation to find investment opportunities, ending in a 'savings glut', is something I cannot and need not explain. Nor do I have to know why, despite a worldwide flood of liquidity until 2021, the rich economies did not exhibit inflationary tendencies and, indeed, in the opinion of their central banks, operated at the border of deflation. A possible contributing factor may be that a large part of the world's assets today already consists of debt, the servicing and repayment of which is in its nature uncertain; it is difficult to maintain optimism for the future on the basis of a long-term rise in indebtedness. Creditors may, under such conditions, hold back from issuing credit for fear of losses, or they may refrain from passing low central bank interest rates on to their customers, while potential borrowers may already be so highly indebted that they have reasons to fear, in a coming crisis, being unable to service their debts.

Opinions are not unanimous on this – far from it. But, then, a social scientist trying to understand the changing relationship between capitalism and democracy need not necessarily be able to take sides in disputes among the experts over what is 'correct' in economic theory and practice, and what is not. For them, it seems sufficient to note that the deep differences of views among those who empathise with and operate capital bear witness to a fundamental uncertainty about the direction at present of capitalist development and of the resulting susceptibility of capitalist democracy and democratic government to crisis. It seems reasonable to assume that this uncertainty is not just unlikely to be resolved in any foreseeable future, but that it plays a major part in the long-term decline of the political legitimacy of the neoliberal economic system as well as of the scientific and economic elites who interpret and rule over it. I shall return to this in the next chapter..

Not that there have been no attempts to explain why not even zero interest rates and an open-ended expansion of the money supply were for so long unable to cause growth or inflation (or both). Some partly compete with each other; others are partly complementary, stretching from the technocratic – that 'the politicians' are working with bad theories, and that better theories would improve their performance – to the unorthodox. One unorthodox explanation is that the increase in inequality – the concentration of an ever-larger share of a society's wealth in the hands of the upper '1 percent', the simultaneous shrinkage of the middle class, and the declining income of those at the lower end of the income distribution – together with the downward pressure on wages exerted by global competition and by the individualisation of wage setting – have so severely impaired effective demand in the rich capitalist countries that it no longer pays to invest there to expand production, and with it employment. Compatible with this is the conjecture that the declining global hegemony of the United States has made it riskier to transfer excess capital to the periphery of the capitalist world system; towards the end of the neoliberal era, even the US could no longer guarantee a secure environment and a trustworthy legal basis for capitalist enterprise in such diverse countries as Russia and China, not to mention Egypt, Afghanistan, Iraq, or Pakistan.

Another theory, related to the increase in inequality and the incapacity or unwillingness of governments to combat it through either tax or wage policy, is that low interest rates, as long as they could be maintained, after all did have inflationary effects, not in markets for goods or labour but in asset markets.[11] While excluded from standard calculations of rates of inflation, general price increases in real estate and stock markets make possible lucrative capital gains and speculative profits, and, in any case, increase the available collateral for borrowers with access to low-interest credit. In this way, a large share of existing capital can circulate in a thoroughly globalised financial universe, without ever having to come into contact with real people and the real economy. And, even if low interest rates do nothing else, the central banks can, by keeping them low, help ease the burden on indebted states, allowing them to refinance their debt at a favourable rate, thereby reducing the fiscal burden of indebtedness.[12] Of course, this comes at the expense of small private savers whose capital income, if it does not entirely disappear, in any case remains below the going rate of inflation which

---

11   For example, according to data from the Flossbach von Storch Research Institute, in the fourth quarter of 2019, the assets of private households in Germany rose in value by 7.6 percent compared with the previous year.

12   The same is true of the purchase of government securities in the context of quantitative easing, which reduces their yield, thereby reducing both the cost of refinancing borne by the indebted state and the spread between the interest rates at which states of different 'levels of credit-worthiness' have to pay their creditors.

monetary policy was for several years hoping to raise. That hope was to be more than fulfilled in the aftermath of the COVID pandemic and during the Ukraine war.

The Neoliberal Crisis Sequence

Neoliberal globalisation, in its iteration as hyperglobalisation, promised to restore economic growth and thereby resolve the crisis of capitalism that had returned in the 1970s, after the end of post-war reconstruction and the exhaustion of the institutions created for it. Neoliberal reform aimed to build a worldwide unified economic order, a global economy liberated from discretionary interference by the parochial politics of democratic nation-states. To this end, it ushered in an era of unprecedent centralisation of economic governance in what was supposed to be one big state-free, depoliticised market (while, in fact, it was governed by one big state on the pretence that it was not a state but merely a set of rules). The result was a continuous decline in economic growth accompanied by a continuous increase in public debt, together with higher-than-ever profits for global enterprises in industry and finance, with stagnating real wages for growing sections of national workforces, accompanied by declining employment security in 'flexible' working arrangements proliferating at the lower end of the labour market. Among the results were sharply rising inequality in incomes and wealth and, generally, increasingly aggressive pressures on social life for untiring adaptation to changing needs of capital accumulation under conditions of competitive hyperglobalisation.

Throughout the three decades of the New World Order, the failure of globalist unification and centralisation to revitalise the capitalist economy, and the fundamental instability of neoliberal capitalism as a social formation, found expression in a sequence of political-economic crises (on the latter, see fig. 14). Government economic and social policies were confronted with ever-newer manifestations of the inability of globally integrated free markets to provide for the social and political conditions of uninterrupted capital accumulation. Economic policy, at national and international levels, was kept busy responding to the changing expressions of the incompatibility of the dynamic requirements of profit-making with the much less dynamic institutions governing social and political life – with the locally established different ways of life, *Lebensweisen,* of distinctive human societies. None of those responses was able to break the long-term downward trend of growth and the equally long-term upward trend of public debt; both continued regardless of how the crisis sequence unfolded and the form it took, and regardless of what was done to stop it.

Figure 14. The crisis sequence since the 1970s

Period	Problem addressed	Goals pursued	Solutions tried	Problems caused
Inflation state (1970s)	Labour militancy Social disorder	Social peace	Inflation Political exchange	Investment strike Stagflation
Debt state (1980s to mid-1990s)	Inflation	Stable money International-isation	Structural change De-unionisation Financial deregulation	Public debt Declining confidence in financial markets
Consolidation state (mid-1990s to 2008)	*Marktvolk* discontent	Financialisation Retrenchment of the state International competitiveness	Austerity Balanced budgets Privatisation Private debt Welfare state reform	Financial instability Savings glut
Central bank state (2008 to 2020)	Secular stagnation Failing banks Debt deflation	Monetary dominance Depoliticis-ation Technocratic governance	Low interest rates Quantitative easing Fiat-money	Asset-price inflation More inequality More public debt
Emergency state (2021 to ??)	Supply-side inflation Income losses *Staatsvolk* discontent	Political stability Citizen submission	High interest rates Quantitative tightening Cost-of-living subsidies Cost-of-producing subsidies	Public debt out of control

Capitalist crises have two faces: they are, at the same time, political crises of confidence and economic crises of profitability, posing political problems as they express themselves in social conflicts, and technical problems in their nature as economic disequilibria. Hidden behind the statistical aggregates of the macro-economy – investment, consumption, savings, employment, the money supply, and so on – are aggregates of action, more or less coordinated and, in this sense, collective, and driven by class interests as informed by different market positions. Especially when it comes to modern capitalism, economics is always politics, and politics is always economics. Thus, in the first decades after 1945, under the auspices of a state-administered New Deal capitalism of US provenance, economic growth – in other words, continued capital accumulation – was made compatible with social and political stability by the institutionalisation of strong trade unions, politically as a counterweight to capital and economically to coordinate supply and demand. Political consensus and the motivation of workers to work and cooperate with employers were secured through credible promises of a slowly but continuously rising standard of living, of a progressive reduction of economic and social inequality, of stable employment and an increasingly comprehensive welfare state. After fewer than two decades, however, it was precisely the successful stabilisation of the capitalist political economy that caused an all the more intense outbreak of distributional conflict at the end of the 1960s. By then, the propensity of capital to let itself be invested could (or would) no longer keep pace with the now firmly established expectations among ordinary industrial citizens of growing incomes and living standards for all. The result in 1968 and 1969 was a worldwide wave of unofficial strikes that challenged the social partnership mode of the pacification of distributive conflict between capital and labour under the auspices of capitalist democracy.

It was here that the sequence of crises – or, more precisely, of different manifestations of the inherent crisis-proneness of capitalism as a mode of production – began that has, to this day, not ended. At each stage, governments faced new economic problems caused by changed configurations of the conflicting interests of capital and labour that threatened to disrupt the smooth accumulation of capital, asking for political intervention to remove the newly emerged barriers to growth and clear the way for a resumption of profitable realisation of capital. Each time, however, the solution adopted for the problem of the day, or the decade, became a problem itself that demanded a new solution – one that could do no more than buy time before ushering in the next crisis. The drama began in the 1970s with the attempt to heal the rift between capital and labour – then widened by the appearance of a third party in distributive conflict, the energy producers in what was at the time called the Third

World – by concessions to organised labour in the form of high wage settlements and improved job security. Since the real economy, governed by the owners of capital, could (or would) no longer make such concessions, full employment and rising nominal wages, and, with them, social peace, had to be protected by an increase in the money supply in excess of the increase in productivity. However, keeping interest rates low to enable employers to finance concessions to trade unions by credit produced high rates of inflation, accepted for the sake of social peace – of continued willingness of labour to cooperate with capital – by what emerged as the *inflation state* of the 1970s. This was the first time after the post-war growth period that states took to introducing not-yet-existing future resources into the conflict between labour and capital, as a way of increasing the available mass for distribution. Then, as later, however, this worked only temporarily – in the 1970s, until capital, towards the end of the decade, began to refuse to be invested for fear of its devaluation by inflation. As a result, what had been a solution became a problem as unemployment rose alongside and in spite of inflation, leading to what came to be called 'stagflation'.

Neoliberalism was, above all, a political-economic project to end the inflation state and free capital from its imprisonment in the post-war settlement. The 1980s became the decade of an anti-inflationist economic policy offensive, aimed at making capital optimistic again by subduing labour. The campaign, led by the United States under Reagan and Britain under Thatcher, was pursued mainly by breaking trade union power through high interest rates and, as a consequence, high unemployment, together with increased international competition as a result of global expansion of markets, which resulted in accelerated de-industrialisation in the course of a deep restructuring of the old industrial economies. As part of this, the 1980s saw the rise of a *debt state*, with rapid growth of public debt replacing low interest and cheap credit as a way of bringing into the game not-yet-extant resources to, for the time being, keep the political and economic peace. It was at this point that a 'fiscal crisis of the state' began that, among other things, manifested in a secular rise of public debt. In part, then-increasing deficits in public finance reflected rising unemployment and impoverishment among the lower classes due to structural change, causing a rise in welfare state expenditures that could not immediately be cut. Another contributing factor was a decline in the taxability of capitalist societies, due to growing tax resistance among voters, more intense competitive pressure on industries and companies following globalisation, and expanded opportunities for oligarchs of all sorts to hide their money in the depths of a globalised financial system. In addition, there was the attempt by the United States to outcompete the Soviet Union militarily by investing in a new type of weapons technology – the 'Star Wars' project – and, as a spin-off, bring the domestic economy back onto a growth course; while the former succeeded, the latter did only in Silicon Valley and its environs.

Soon, however, it became apparent that the debt state, having replaced the inflation state, could not last long either. Beginning in the mid-1990s, in view of the growing mountains of debt in mature capitalist countries, it became necessary to reassure the states' creditors – mostly banks and pension funds – of the solvency and further creditworthiness of their debtors. Thus began the age of the *consolidation state*, inaugurated by the United States, first with the temporary help of the so-called peace dividend after 1990, which, of course, did not last long, and then, more seriously, with diverse methods of privatising public activities. In the course of welfare state reform and under the auspices of what would later become the so-called Third Way, deep cuts in social spending followed. Welfare state reform, which had still been politically too risky in the 1980s, was facilitated by declining trade union power and growing competitive pressures in the global markets of the 'New World Order' after 1990. To replace the resulting gap in demand and avoid social unrest, but also to help the financial sector grow to be the lead sector of a de-industrialising political economy, financial markets were deregulated, such that even low- and non-income earners could take on debt as a substitute for income from work and social benefits. In principle, this amounted to a relocation of debt from public to private, in analogy to the privatisation of public services. As a result of the austerity policies of the 1990s and early 2000s, public debt declined, or at least increased only slowly, while private household debt increased as if in a system of communicating pipes.

The consolidation state, in turn, came to an end in the financial crisis of 2008, when the global securitisation pyramids of an internationalised and thus under-regulated financial sector collapsed and financial firms – *too big to fail* – had to be rescued from themselves by the states that had released them into the wild. Once this was achieved, 'secular stagnation' entered the state as capital was taken out of circulation by its handlers to be relegated to a 'savings overhang'. As a result, growth declined further. To avoid having to address inequality and thereby scare away the owners and movers of capital, desperate attempts were made to lure listless capital out of its sulking corner through savings in public expenditure, that is, by offering the prospect of a small state with correspondingly low taxes – in other words, by a policy of austerity. But, as it turned out, this did not do the trick either; on the contrary, aggregate demand continued to fall, now also because of declining public spending. Thus, after a while, the danger of deflation loomed on the horizon – that is, of falling prices that would make it difficult or impossible for borrowers, states, and private individuals alike to service their debt denominated at the old, higher price level. As states found themselves forced to do something against debt deflation, a new phase in the capitalist crisis sequence – or capitalist debt trajectory – began, in which the consolidation state gave way to a *central bank* – or fiat-money – *state*, and neoliberal capitalism turned into *money-state capitalism*.

As pointed out above, the central bank state was a response to the failure of fiscal policy to restore growth by way of first increasing, then reducing, public spending and public debt. In a sense, it can be seen as the last stage of neoliberalism: an attempt to govern capitalism without fiscal policies controlled by democratic governments, relying exclusively on monetary policies wielded by the expertocracy of autonomous central banks. Low interest rates and liberally created fiat-money, resulting in a freely growing money supply, were deployed after 2008 to spare governments from going further into debt. But, just like fiscal policy earlier, monetary policy turned out to be unable to stem the tide of growing debt and declining growth. As the central bank state proved incapable of restoring stable growth, its masters, the wizards of central-bank money-making, began to hand responsibility for the health of capitalism back to governments and public spending. Their sales pitch was that if states would expand their budgets by taking up credit, central banks would ensure that this could happen at interest rates governments could afford. With a little good luck, then, states would be able to grow out of their debt provided their rate of new economic growth exceeded – as promised – the low rate of interest they would have to pay on their debt, especially if the borrowed money was used wisely, that is, accompanied by productivity-enhancing 'structural reforms'. (The assumption that interest rates would remain low was based on the idea that inflation had been so thoroughly rooted out that there would be no need to raise interest rates to fight it.)

After a few further remarks on the central bank state, I will turn to the issue of the changed view towards its end of public debt and the way public debt was sold to the left side of the political spectrum as a rehabilitation of Keynesianism. This will lead to a discussion of the next and (hitherto) final stage of the crisis sequence, the *emergency state* (see fig. 14), which overtook the central bank state when the capitalist political economy was hit by the two more or less exogenous crises of 2020 and 2022 – the COVID-19 pandemic and the war in Ukraine – which together put a sudden end to the end of inflation 'illusion'.

The Central Bank State as the Last Stage of Neoliberalism

Is money-state capitalism as sustained by a central bank state still capitalism, or is it already something else – something like post-capitalism? In the central bank state of the second decade of the twenty-first century, capital accumulation still went on, although predominantly in the form of seemingly endlessly rising asset prices. Asset-price inflation was driven by the cheap money provided by the central banks and distributed through the private banking system, for astonishing fees, to those with sufficient collateral to borrow money to buy shares, real estate, debt papers of all sorts. In doing so, in competition with each other, they drove up asset values, meaning prices, including the value of their own assets. Thus, accumulation continued, albeit no longer having to take the detour through material production but, as it were, self-referentially.

What was also growing in money-state capitalism, however, was economic and social inequality, now between the classes of those deemed worthy and unworthy of big-scale credit. For capitalism, this is not in itself a problem: the credit unworthy, as sociology, reassuringly, keeps finding, measure themselves against their neighbours rather than their oligarchs. And, unlike the factory owners of Manchester capitalism, the oligarchs of today are so far removed from ordinary people that they seem to them more like mythical figures, like Homeric war heroes in the battle for Golden Troy, or like Elon Musk and Co. struggling for precedence in the privatised ascension to outer space. Economically, if a central bank state can produce surplus value by pumping up asset markets, redistribution downwards to strengthen effective demand is no longer necessary for capitalism, as distinguished from capitalist society, to prosper. To ensure that an old systemic risk – inflation resulting from conflicts over distribution between capital and labour, the so-called wage-price spiral of the 1970s – does not return, a new, post-industrial, anti-union organisation of work is supposed to take care of it: precarious employment in the dispersed production sites of a new service sector, de-professionalisation of work, individualisation of wage-setting, new methods of selecting and monitoring workers, and the maintenance of work discipline, not least by generous access to loans to be paid off over a lifetime.

Still, nobody among those in the know really believed that the central bank state would and could last forever. If its predecessor, the now obsolete consolidation state, somehow entailed a promise of a stable distribution of power – to be clear, in favour of capital – and of a renewal of profitability and, perhaps, growth – a promise, in other words, of a neoliberal renaissance of capitalism – there was never a hope that the central bank state that had grown in the aftermath of 2008 would be more than a short, precarious stage of transition into a hopefully more stable but as yet unknowable future. Already before 2019, when a new wave of crises beset the capitalist world, central banks had (as noted above) realised, with growing despair, that there were limits to easy credit and fiat-money as means to restore growth. On the one hand, while quantitative easing as a way to keep capitalism going could not be continued forever, it could not easily be abandoned either, as that might bring on systemic disaster. As flooding the world with cheap money had failed to bring back prosperity, fears emerged, first probably behind the closed doors of capitalism's inner circles, of a return of inflation, posing to central banks the stark question of how they could curb looming increases in the cost of living by raising interest rates without thereby bursting the asset-market bubble. If they chose to stabilise asset prices by keeping interest rates low and endlessly blowing up the money supply to protect the prosperity of the rich, the streets and squares might fill with uncounted Yellow Vests protesting their declining standard of living and demanding protection not just for the prosperity of the rich. If, on the other hand, they opted for stabilising the cost of living by means of higher interest rates and tighter money, they might bankrupt banks and states no longer able to refinance their debt. The flight forward into expansion blocked, the accumulation of new capital at a standstill, the accumulated credit, private and public, rotting – in a world like this, there would very soon be little space for consumerist compensations of the masses for the 'creative destruction' inflicted on them in the course of capitalist progress. It was only by accident – in the shape of the two crises of 2020 and 2022 – that the managers of the capitalist central bank state were spared the dilemma between a capital ready to walk out and a citizenry ready to revolt, both paths that risked getting out of the frying pan into the fire.

Keynes from the Ashes?

Notwithstanding the self-confidently proclaimed scientific nature of the practice of macroeconomic theory and expertise, one should not underestimate its practitioners' deep-seated technocratic pragmatism, coupled with an emphatic 'optimism of the will' for which there are no intractable problems (or for which intractable problems are not problems at all). With continuing 'secular stagnation', a growing number of experts apparently began to suspect that monetary methods of revitalising capitalism had reached their limits, and that even the last resort of monetary policy, the deployment of 'helicopter money', if indeed it were ever to be resorted to, would still be unable to overcome the demand shortfall that was proving so detrimental to growth.[13] But if monetary policy cannot deliver the goods, all that remains is fiscal policy – a reversion to an expansionist policy of state expenditure, which means abandoning the neoliberal hope of achieving growth through austerity.[14] In the US and the UK, in particular, this was associated with a re-evaluation of

---

13   The idea of introducing 'helicopter money', a free distribution of cash, thrown down from the sky by the central banks, as a way of 'stimulating the economy', comes from Milton Friedman. One economic objection to it is that if there is a high level of indebtedness, those who pick up the free money might misunderstand the purpose of the exercise and use it to clear their debts rather than increase their consumption. That the distribution of money 'for free' might raise doubts about its legitimacy as a means of maintaining work discipline and for the assignment of status in a capitalist meritocracy is not an issue for macroeconomic technocrats, at least not publicly.

14   No one has described the neoliberal policy of austerity better than Marc Blyth, *Austerity: The History of a Dangerous Idea*, Oxford: Oxford University Press, 2013.

public debt, which, for a while, came to be viewed in an entirely positive light because of its expected positive impact on growth.[15]

The reconversion of macroeconomic practitioners to a fiscal policy of debt-financed expansion, which would later pave the way for the previously unheard-of borrowing spree that followed the emergence of the COVID-19 virus (see below on the *emergency state*), did not, in the Anglo-American world, require any ambitious theory explaining the failure of neoliberal austerity to restart capitalist capital accumulation; the fact that it *had* failed was justification enough. This was very different in traditionally debt-averse Germany, both for the government, which cleaved (and cleaves) stubbornly to the constitutional 'debt ceiling' from 2009 and its political promise of a balanced federal budget ('black zero'), and for the majority of German economists. Even here, though, there had long been, if not a rethink, at least some serious deliberation under way, initiated largely by Carl Christian von Weizsäcker, a liberal economist highly regarded in the mainstream of his discipline, who had, for years, been arguing for a debt-financed increase in German government expenditure.[16] In the following, I shall briefly summarise his most important suggestions and locate them in the political context of the exhaustion of neoliberalism and the development of what was often understood as, or declared itself to be, a new 'Keynesianism'.

As a supporter of global free trade and the EU single market, including the currency union, Weizsäcker was an early advocate of debt-financed expansion of German government spending. This would lead to an increase in imports, which would lessen the growing resentment of the country's European trading partners over Germany's trade surplus, which was endangering the euro. It would also take the wind out of the sails of protectionist pressures in the international markets

---

15 The presidential address by Olivier Blanchard to the annual meeting of the American Economic Association in January 2019 (Olivier J. Blanchard, 'Public Debt and Low Interest Rates', Peterson Institute for International Economics Working Paper No. 19-4, 2019) was an influential interim statement which opened the way to a return to fiscal policy. Blanchard was the chief economist of the International Monetary Fund from 2008 to 2015.

16 And it could do this. Sitting at the centre of the spider's web of the Monetary Union, Germany was able to reduce its public debt from 80 percent to under 60 percent of GDP without suffering any economic damage, and, on the whole, lived well, at least in the short run, with its national variant of austerity.

which were so vital to the German economy. When the discussion over 'secular stagnation' began, Weizsäcker started to move beyond considerations of political expediency. He began to look for an explanation for the coexistence of high excess savings with low interest rates, compatible with the requirements of a new fiscal policy, which would both be theoretically sustainable and practically useful. He found the answer in the 'natural rate of interest' theory of the Swedish economist Knut Wicksell (1851–1926), combined with an ambitious extension of the theory of capital advanced by the Austrian economist Eugen von Böhm-Bawerk (1851–1914).

Weizsäcker's thesis was worked out in detail in a book written jointly with Hagen Krämer and published under the title *Sparen und Investieren im 21. Jahrhundert: Die große Divergenz.*[17] The theory explains the savings glut as an outcome of two (and, in essence, no more than two) parallel historical developments, which, taken together, are claimed to have produced nothing less than a new epoch in the history of the capitalist economy. They are, firstly, a change in the nature of productive capital in the 'knowledge societies' of twenty-first-century capitalism – to increase the productivity of a mind demands less investment capital than to increase the productivity of a steel works – and, secondly, by a change in the demography of the industrialised countries – the result of greater life expectancy, which leads to longer periods of retirement, during which individuals must finance themselves from their savings. This, according to Weizsäcker and Krämer, leads to an increase in the supply of capital combined with a fall in the demand for it, as higher life expectancy requires more savings than needed for the formation of productive capital, especially in post-industrial societies. The result is a fall in the 'natural rate of interest' towards, or even below, zero.

People who make provisions for their old age are cautious investors; in fact, they do not even count as investors, because they eschew any risk of loss. Thus, their savings turn into the glut of money described by Summers – money which does not dare penetrate into the riskier peripheries of the capitalist world system and remains stuck in the labyrinths of the financial system at its centre, where it exerts downward pressure on the rate of interest. Only a borrower who could, as a matter of course, be

---

17   Carl Christian von Weizsäcker and Hagen M. Krämer, *Saving and Investment in the Twenty-First Century: The Great Divergence*, Cham: Springer, 2019.

accepted by everyone as permanently liquid could reactivate the capital laid aside to provide for old age and thereby withdrawn from the capitalist growth dynamic; according to Weizsäcker, the only entity that comes into consideration for this is the state. Only the state can activate risk-averse capital of this type, borrowing it in order to purchase more collective investment goods than its tax receipts will finance, and thus to provide a macroeconomic supplement to the inadequate private demand for individual investment goods. Of this the state is all the more capable in that the downward pressure exerted on the rate of interest by the savings glut makes it possible to borrow at a rate of zero percent, and sometimes even to levy storage charges, when a negative interest rate means that the sum to be repaid to the creditor falls below the nominal value of the original loan (and below any positive rate of inflation).

Weizsäcker's theory absolves the central banks of responsibility for secular stagnation, including the low yield for saved capital in risk-free investments which is a special concern for a German electorate. For him, the central banks are not the drivers of a new, permanently low 'natural rate of interest' but, rather, driven by it. A monetary policy, however, which is a victim of secular stagnation rather than its cause will not be able to bring it to an end. Here, the state must intervene with its fiscal policy. But it is exactly such state action that neoliberalism rejects as it limits the role of the state to the local implementation of an intervention-free global market.

Debt without Remorse?

On the other hand, Weizsäcker's combined diagnosis and therapy leave numerous questions open, even if we set aside the theoretical problems posed by his two-factor theory of the savings glut and of 'secular stagnation'. This is all the more relevant as Weizsäcker's is an argument for a return to fiscal policy and a departure from the central bank state, and not solely for the purpose of restoring growth. For example, it remains unclear whether the debt-financed expansionist fiscal policies he prescribes could be beneficial for *all* countries, or only for a country like Germany which, towards the end of the neoliberal era, managed to reduce its public debt. Also, for Keynes, government debt was to be paid back once the economic upsurge it was to stimulate had materialised. But can one expect, considering the almost linear increase in government debt in the rich democracies since the 1970s, that new debt will, from now on, really remain Keynesian in this sense? And what is the significance of an already-existing high level of national debt, built up over many years, and as a rule not reduced 'of itself' by an upsurge in growth? Can and should countries like Italy (138 percent of GDP in the second quarter of 2019) or Belgium (105 percent) take on fresh debt to the same degree as Germany (61 percent) or the Netherlands (51 percent), especially under the shared umbrella of a common currency? If the answer is no, how should different rights to take on fresh debt be determined and allocated in a currency union between sovereign states, and how should states be prevented from exceeding their quota? Or, should European debt be contracted centrally and supranationally by the EU, as the European Commission and the European Parliament have long envisaged, even though they presently lack any of the institutions required to work out the amount of public expenditure which can legitimately be allocated to each state?

Above all, however, Weizsäcker's argument in favour of a debt-financed increase in state expenditure presupposes that the interest to be paid by states will remain low forever – even that, for all practical purposes, it will move towards zero. The purpose of Weizsäcker's extension of the theory of capital is to make this assumption plausible. The idea is to convince not only his fellow economists but also, most importantly, governments that a state – perhaps not every state, but many of them, including, in any case, the German state – can take on new debt essentially for free, and, indeed, without incurring long-term costs; and, indeed, that it can refinance its old debt at a low, or even a zero, rate of interest. As noted earlier, similar assurances, though not so apodictic, are to be found in the work of French economist Olivier Blanchard, and they are, in any case, unlikely to be questioned by the European Central Bank, which then was (and now is) run by the former head of the International Monetary Fund, Christine Lagarde – whose chief economist at the time was none other than Blanchard, having long shared with her an institutional interest in passing the economic buck from monetary to fiscal policy.[18]

---

18   Blanchard, 'Public Debt and Low Interest Rates'. What is also involved here is an internal conflict between international organisations and nation-states such as Germany.

Weizsäcker's proposals for overcoming secular stagnation offer an opportunity for an exemplary clarification of some of the fundamental problems of capital-centred economics, such as its blind (or perhaps not so blind) partisanship, the political self-deceptions of its proponents, and the unaccounted-for institutional blockades which arise from the conflict between globalism and democracy. Looking at the enthusiasm of social democrats over the shift from monetary to fiscal policy – the retreat from the blind alley of neoliberal austerity and the embrace of a new debt-financed 'Keynesianism' – we find that it ignores the fact that raising public money by borrowing instead of democratically imposed taxation, particularly in an epoch of rapidly rising economic inequality, can be at best an emergency measure, and a possibly dangerous one too. What is fundamentally at stake here is the same savings overhang which the state could just as well confiscate, in the sense of taxing it out of existence.[19] If it is borrowed rather than confiscated, the inequality in income and wealth remains unchanged, the increase of which, along-side the corresponding reduction in mass purchasing power, is one of the causes of secular stagnation.[20] Capital which is borrowed by the state rather than expropriated by taxation can be passed on by its owners-turned-creditors to the next generation of their families, thereby contributing to a long-term rigidification of the distribution of wealth, especially when associated with a reduction in inheritance taxes. Even if, temporarily, no interest is received, with the result of no increase, or even a decline in the value of lent-out capital, the state remains a very safe haven for footless capital looking for a home to be its castle.

A liberal economist like Weizsäcker cannot really be expected to point out the distributional inverse of an indirect privatisation of government expenditure and activity through credit financing. This might be

---

This conflict came into public view by mid-2016 at the latest, with the appearance of an article by three members of the Research Department of the International Monetary Fund under the heading 'Neoliberalism: Oversold?', which was widely perceived as sensational: Jonathan D. Ostry, Prakash Loungani, and Davide Furceri, 'Neoliberalism: Oversold?', *Finance and Development* 53, no. 2 (2016).

19   See, on this, Streeck, *Buying Time*, 76–8.

20   This was caused in no small degree by the reduction in the top rates of income and business taxation during the supply-side policies since the 1990s. It is plausible to assume that without neoliberal tax reductions, there would not only be less of a savings glut, if at all, but also less need to finance public expenditure through borrowing rather than through taxes. See ibid., 62–9.

different for left-of-centre economists, but there, the internationalists appear to have made their peace with international tax avoidance, seeing it as an irreversible cosmopolitan side effect of opening national economies to the world market.[21] There is also tacit acceptance of the situation that indebted states become dependent on their creditors – on the 'people of the market' (*Marktvolk*; see fig. 14) of the international financial industry – and have to accept their supervision. If, for example, through 'socialist experiments', governments gamble away capital's 'confidence' in their 'creditworthiness', as measured by the assessments of the American rating agencies, or if they fail to achieve the obligatory annual net surplus in their regular budget, the cost of refinancing their debt can, at any time, be adjusted upwards as warning and punishment. From a liberal point of view, this is not a problem. After all, the subjection of states to the discipline of 'the markets' ensures that politics is kept within the framework of capitalist reason and that competitors for political power resist the temptation to indulge in the excessive public spending postulated in 'public choice' theory. Of course, a left which is still concerned with democracy, rather than with the moral desirability and political irreversibility of 'globalisation', would have to regard the possibility that the policy of a nation-state might come under the control of the international capital market as, at the least, a problem for the new debt 'Keynesianism' and discuss it in those terms.[22]

In any case, a central prerequisite for a high-debt 'Keynesianism' supported by a permanently low interest rate remains a long-term absence of

---

21   This is not true of Thomas Piketty, who, unlike others on the left, refrains from playing down the problem of state indebtedness and looks at it in the context of 'the distribution of wealth, particularly between the public and private spheres'. Thomas Piketty, *Capital in the Twenty-First Century*, Cambridge, MA: Harvard University Press, 2014, 540. According to him, public debt often boils down to an invisible way of transferring wealth from the poor to the rich, 'from people with modest savings to those with the means to lend to the government (who as a general rule ought to be paying taxes rather than lending)' (566). Debt reduction is, therefore, not anathema for Piketty, also because he is aware of the burden interest payments represent for democratically elected governments (544). He furthermore notes that inflation, the politically preferred instrument for the reduction of state debt, is a 'relatively crude and imprecise tool' (547). In general, Piketty warns against the negative distributional effects of debt reduction by monetary means, a method the ECB repeatedly attempts to use (550). I leave aside the question of whether, and to what extent, Piketty's proposals for a tax rise on high income and wealth are realistic.

22   Streeck, *Buying Time*, 79–90.

inflation, not necessarily in asset values but in the living costs of ordinary people. When, in the second half of 2021, the first signs appeared on the horizon that this condition might no longer be assured and that the long phase of monetary stability in the rich capitalist countries might have ended (see fig. 15), it could be heard from the relevant 'experts', including those at the head of the central banks, that the situation would, after no more than a few weeks, return to normal – to low inflation allowing for low interest rates allowing, in turn, for debt-financed government under a new regime of debt-financed quasi-Keynesianism. As justification, the very development was invoked that some of the same experts had used to explain secular stagnation: the breaking of trade union power since the end of the 1970s. Hence, when the pandemic struck, fresh debt could be (and was) taken on without hesitation; and, indeed, for a while, interest rates remained low. National governments took on debt on a vast scale to rescue endangered sectors and jobs with economic assistance programmes of all sorts, which was supposed to continue until national economies returned to their previous performance. The EU, which was for the first time allowed to enter the credit markets as a borrower – and was pleased with what it regarded as an increase in its sovereign powers – contributed its share with the €750 billion COVID recovery fund for reconstruction and modernisation, in the hope of thereby reducing some of the long-worsening tensions between its member states.

Figure 15. Annual inflation, consumer prices

	2019	2020	2021	2022	Q2-2023
France	1.1	0.5	1.6	5.2	5.2
Germany	1.4	0.1	3.1	6.9	6.5
Italy	0.6	−0.1	1.9	8.2	7.4
Japan	0.5	−0.0	−0.3	2.5	--
UK	1.7	1.0	2.5	7.9	7.7
US	1.8	1.2	4.7	8.0	4.0
EU	1.4	0.7	2.9	9.2	7.2
OECD	2.1	1.3	4.0	9.6	6.5

But then, in early 2022, there appeared first signs that inflation might have come back to stay for longer. Slowly, it was realised that the interruption of the long, often global, supply chains of the neoliberal age by the pandemic and by national measures taken against it, especially in China, would not soon be repaired. Only shortly later, the Ukraine war and the economic sanctions imposed on Russia – and increasingly also on China – created further shortages on the supply side, above all in fossil fuel markets, but also in food, which then caused price increases over the whole of industry. The accelerated changeover to wind and solar energy, driven in part by new shortages in import markets and previously subject to long delays in many places, entailed a further rise in the costs borne by both industry and consumers. The modification of the already ongoing trend towards *reshoring* into *friend-shoring* – namely, the acquisition of products and raw materials exclusively from friendly countries and the division of the global economy into geostrategic camps – also added to inflation, so that in mid-2022 inflation in OECD countries suddenly began to approach 10 percent, without any prospect of near-term improvement. This situation was increasingly perceived by governments as dangerous to 'social peace', requiring political intervention rather than patient trust in the free play of market forces.

As inflation continued, it undermined the business model of the central bank state by demonstrating that fiscal expansion supported by low interest rates and an ample supply of money was unable to return neoliberal capitalism to stability. What was only rarely mentioned, if at all, was the possibility that the new inflation might also have been a delayed result of the piling up of public debt and the liberal production of fiat-money during the neoliberal era. Still, the dilemmas posed to political-economic management by the prospect of enduring inflation were stark enough to herald the rise of a new political-economic configuration which I will provisionally call the *emergency state*, shortly to be addressed in more detail. The problem which, in effect, ended the central bank state was that while, in principle, inflation can be fought by raising interest rates, as after 1979, today this may cause the collapse of complex structures that have grown around asset markets which depend on credit driving a continuous increase of market values. Fighting inflation by raising interest rates may therefore interrupt financialised capitalism's privileged mode of accumulation and thereby set off a general economic crisis with uncertain outcome – and not just for asset holders. Higher interest rates might also compromise the ability of states to deal with their debt by restructuring it, more than offsetting the benefits of inflation for creditors, private and public. Small wonder, then, that governments initially tried to wait out inflation, sticking to meanwhile-established central-bank-state practices like quantitative easing and keeping interest rates reliably low. In fact, what was fought was not inflation but the political damage potentially caused by it, through temporary measures such as subsidies of all kinds, from cash handouts to tax relief, on petrol, heating costs, public transport, and so on – that is, by fiscal measures financed, inevitably, by more public borrowing.

An interesting case of a government trying to fight inflation by fighting the discontent over inflation was Germany. While trade unions had been eliminated as a cause of inflation after 1980, they returned to the scene when inflation returned, although this time not by causing but by responding to it. If in the past inflation could be seen as resulting from a *'wage-price* spiral' set in motion by redistributive wage demands by powerful trade unions, in the summer of 2022 what governments feared was a *'price-wage* spiral' resulting from unions fighting and striking for, and winning, nominal wage increases compensating their members for the increase in their costs of living. To prevent inflation causing wage militancy and industrial conflict – rather than the other way around – and thereby feeding on itself, the German government early on considered making moderate wage settlements below the rate of inflation palatable to trade union members by throwing one-off tax reductions into the bargain, or otherwise by using public coffers to pay part of the costs of inflation-compensating wage increases. That this would result in a further increase in public debt was accepted, as well as that it would make later increases in the rate of interest still more of a problem to public finances than they already had been; the same holds for the continuing accumulation of future obligations of the state towards private creditors.

Fighting inflation on borrowed money by way of public subsidies for private production and consumption tested the limits of the capacity of states to get credit in financial markets at acceptable rates. In any case, it was never more than a stopgap that remained dismally ineffective. In 2023, the central banks gave up on the central bank state's low interest rates and took the risk of abruptly ending the asset boom they themselves had caused, by ending quantitative easing and incrementally raising the rate of interest (fig. 16). Governments, in turn, let go of all restraint and begun to rely, as a matter of course, on debt-making as their principal response to the old problems of neoliberalism and the new problems of COVID and the fall of New World Order, with the militarised deglobalisation of the global political economy that followed. By then, the central bank state had finally ended and a new stage in the capitalist crisis sequence began.

Figure 16. Rates of interest as set by four major central banks, 2020–2023

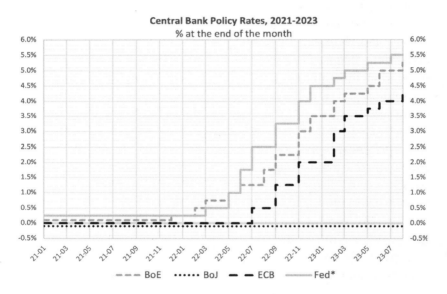

* Federal Funds Target Range – Upper Limit
Sources: Bank of England, Bank of Japan, European Central Bank, Federal Reserve Bank.

The Emergency State

Capitalist crises do not necessarily come from within, out of capitalism itself; they may also come from without, caused by external shocks. Today's capitalism finds itself attacked by three horsemen of the apocalypse: climate change, which is possibly approaching one or another tipping point; the global spread of a deadly disease; and the collapse, in the capitalist heartlands, of the post-1990 international order into war, indeed potentially nuclear war. Of course, while all three may, at first glance, seem exogenous to capitalism, they might as well be considered by-products of the normal course of capitalist development: of its relentless penetration into nature and its violent transformation of social life and social structures on a global scale. Be this as it may, the virus and the war did impart a final blow on the fiat-money central bank state, disposing of its hope to restore stable growth and stable finance to a neoliberal global economy – a hope that had already, for some time, become unrealistic. Prospects of capitalist governance by central banks and their miraculous powers of money-making becoming a new normal – a lasting, reliable, confidence-inspiring solution to the inherent contradictions of capitalism as a political-economic system – no longer seemed realistic. If the purpose of the central bank state was to stabilise the financial system after the 2008 crisis, now, under the emergency state that followed it (fig. 14), what takes precedence over everything else is *the stabilisation of society as a capitalist society*, by any means necessary.

The concept of the emergency state refers to a state overwhelmed by unpredictably emerging calamities, events that require immediate short-term address without attention to long-term consequences, even though they may cause lasting damage that may be impossible to repair later. COVID, for example, deeply disrupted established work and consumption patterns, threatening entire industries with extinction and forcing governments to financially compensate losers – individuals and firms – on a large scale. This was not just to secure compliance with public health measures such as lockdowns or work from home; it also was to preserve the possibility and the promise of a full return to a pre-COVID life once the virus was conquered. To counter popular discontent, packets of emergency measures were, and had to be, stitched together, disregarding all other concerns, including in particular fiscal ones. COVID also caused widespread interruptions of international value chains that had already, in the wake of 2008, become unstable, with global trade stagnating in key economic sectors due to the complexity and limited governability of finance and production on a world scale. Shortly thereafter, deglobalisation was reinforced by the war in Ukraine, which turned the 're-shoring' under way since the financial crisis into what came to be called 'friend-shoring': a reorganisation of the global economy into hostile political blocs, resulting in fragmentation of the neoliberal world economy along political and geostrategic lines and, at least for an uncertain transition period but possibly also for the duration, creating shortages of both outsourced components and consumption goods.

Today it is, above all, the preparations under way for a Third World War that are breaking up the supply chains of yesterday's neoliberal one-world capitalism, including in particular the provision of cheap energy for consumption and production in the capitalist heartlands. Among other things, this led to an increase in the cost of living that made itself especially felt among ordinary people, more so than in the inflation state of the 1970s, severely testing mass loyalty to consumer capitalism. The new type of inflation, originating on the supply side, joins with the hitherto-hidden inflationary tendencies produced by quantitative easing and the revival of the debt state inside the central bank state and is reinforced by opportunistic profit-making. Unlike the 1970s, today's wave of worldwide inflation is not caused by strong trade unions representing the interests of their members. To the contrary, as noted above, emaciated as trade unions are after three decades of neoliberalism, they may hope for a recovery by fighting for wage increases to match price increases, setting in motion a price-wage spiral – the obverse of the wage-price-spiral of the 1970s. Failing this, union members and non-members alike may take to the streets and cause all sorts of political havoc as they resist their unfolding impoverishment. As with the loss of earnings during the pandemic, emergency-state governments confronting supply-side inflationary pressures are reduced to 'populist' firefighting by way of compensating real income losses of families and subsidising accustomed mass standards of living by cash handouts from the state treasury – that is, by even more debt.

Fiscal giveaways in compensation of sudden losses in real income for ordinary people are improvised responses by political elites in panic over a breakdown of political consensus and the social order, with the prospect of political and social chaos. They are not precursors to a new version of a capitalist state: no new production system, no new model of capitalism like neoliberal capitalism was in relation to state-administered capitalism, or state-administered capitalism to pre-war liberal capitalism. There is only a desperate hope to protect private industry from bankruptcy and private households from sudden poverty by shifting the burden of the crisis onto the public budget. As a longer-term political regime, the emergency state is unsustainable: the way it uses public resources to buy political support is ultimately self-destructive. Underlying the politics of the emergency state is a hope, both desperate and indispensable, that a return to the world before the two 'exogenous' crises will be possible, making it unnecessary to build a new capitalist growth model or prepare for a lasting downward adjustment of economic expectations. A strategy of flooding the masses with fiat-money to make them sit still cannot continue forever: something else will have to take its place after the hastily invented solutions to the crises of today cause the next one, as they inevitably will. The emergency state can only be a transitional state, even more so than the other versions of a capitalist state that preceded it: not a social order, like neoliberalism aspired to be, but a condition of disorder, of what the Italian social theorist and Communist Party leader Antonio Gramsci called an 'interregnum'. The term is increasingly felt to be an apt description of our time: a situation, as Gramsci put it, 'in which the old is dying, but the new cannot yet be born'.

Clueless

By the time of the pandemic and the war in Ukraine, there was not even a vague consensus over how the disease of secular stagnation and public debt might be healed or who the physician might be: the nation-states, the central banks, or perhaps, rather, the G20, the G8, the US, or the EU? Should they act together or on their own? With or without China? At the end of the twelve years between the financial crisis and COVID, the disputes among the wise and powerful had produced nothing capable of lightening the mood of depression in the centres of capitalism – not in the US under Donald Trump, the UK of Brexit, the France of the 'Yellow Vests', Italy with its obliterated political centre, or Germany with the rise of the Alternative for Germany (AfD), particularly in the east, where its electoral results were on the way to overtaking the parties of the old political centre.

A brief look back over the various patent medicines for curing capitalist stagnation that have been tried but found wanting since the 'end of history' reveals the deep uncertainty that had befallen economic management under neoliberalism, long before the collapse of the 'rules-based international order'. In the 1990s, it was thought that a return to growth could be achieved by consolidating government finances, that is, by reducing state debt and switching to a restrictive fiscal policy. But, towards the end of the second decade of the new century, the opposite was hoped to do the trick: increased state expenditure financed by increased borrowing, even though after 2008 public debt above a fixed upper limit had been declared by economic authority to be an insurmountable obstacle to growth.[23] And, whereas the eradication of inflation after 1980 was celebrated throughout the neoliberal era as an epochal achievement of economic policy – in particular, of strictly separating monetary from fiscal policy, involving the emancipation of the central banks from government control and the imposition on them of a firm obligation to maintain monetary stability – after the mid-2010s, every possible method was tried to bring inflation back for the purpose of, astonishingly enough, restoring economic growth.

While in the heyday of neoliberalism, money had to be kept in short supply to keep it stable and trustworthy, now the central banks were urged to issue it in unlimited quantities ('and believe me, it will be enough' – Mario Draghi), and, instead of concerning themselves with monetary stability and nothing else, they were suddenly expected to take responsibility for growth, employment, and the environment. When inflation, suddenly an engine of rather than a barrier to growth, failed to return in spite of an unprecedented increase in the supply of money, central banks threw up their hands to return the buck to governments, insisting on the natural limits of monetary policy as a means to restore growth. To remain in business, growing sections of the economics profession converted to some sort of twice-bastardised Keynesianism, letting it be known that fears of inflation and of government debt ruining public finances were unjustified after all; that inflation had been wiped out by low interest rates and the destruction of trade unions; and that government debt would pay for itself as central banks would keep interest rates down while 'structural reforms', enhancing productivity, would provide for stable growth above the level of interest. Not much later, beginning in 2021 and getting into full gear in 2022, inflation

---

23   Carmen M. Reinhart and Kenneth S. Rogoff, 'Growth in a Time of Debt', *American Economic Review: Papers and Proceedings* 100, no. 2 (May 2010), 573–8.

returned with a vengeance, accompanied, however, not by renewed but by further declining growth.

Macroeconomic debates among experts escape the attention of ordinary people; nonetheless, one can be certain that a sense of the helplessness of capitalism's economic wizards, when faced with the mysterious end of one crisis and the equally mysterious beginning of the next, is penetrating downwards in some way, and that it has a demoralising effect. The age is, more than ever, dominated by uncertainty – and it is a time in which the most surprising theories and therapies sprout from the most astonishing soil. In August 2019, at the annual meeting of central bankers held at Jackson Hole, Wyoming, the governor of the Bank of England, Mark Carney, proposed the introduction of a global digital currency, which would replace the US dollar as the international accounting unit; the effect of this was supposed to be that the countries of the world would liquidate the dollar reserves they had built up as insurance against fluctuations in the global economy. Here there was yet one more explanation for the 'savings glut', and yet one more solution to it.[24]

Two months later, Carney's predecessor, Mervyn King, speaking at a conference of the International Monetary Fund, lamented that since 2008 (hence including his stint as governor from 2003 to 2013), nothing had been done to prevent a recurrence of the financial crisis: 'By sticking to the new orthodoxy of monetary policy and pretending that we have made the banking system safe, we are sleepwalking towards that crisis.'[25] The report in the *Guardian* goes on to say:

King said the world entered and departed from the global financial crisis with a distorted pattern of demand and output. To escape permanently from a low growth trap involved a reallocation of resources from one component of demand to another, from one sector to another, and from one firm to another. 'There has been excess investment in some parts of the economy – the export sector in China and Germany and commercial property in other advanced

---

24   Phillip Inman, 'Mark Carney: Dollar Is Too Dominant and Could Be Replaced by Digital Currency', *Guardian*, 23 August 2019, theguardian.com.

25   Larry Elliott, 'World Economy Is Sleepwalking into a New Financial Crisis, Warns Mervyn King', *Guardian*, 20 October 2019, theguardian.com.

economies, for example – and insufficient in others – infrastructure investment in many western countries. To bring about such a shift of resources – both capital and labour – will require a much broader set of policies than simply monetary stimulus.'

As a therapy, King proposed secret discussions between central bankers and politicians to make legislators aware of how vulnerable they were: 'Congress would be confronted with a choice between financial Armageddon and a suspension of some of the rules that were introduced after the last crisis to limit the ability of the Fed to lend.' The helplessness of the maestros of capital, to the extent that it percolated downwards in some form – and clearly it did – could not have any other result than to aggravate present-day capitalism's constitutive problems of industrial motivation and political legitimation, which we shall examine more closely further down.

The Great Uncertainty

As of 2023, a little more than a year into the war in Ukraine, the confusion surrounding how to manage a post-neoliberal capitalist economy is enormous, with the economic and political legacy of neoliberalism both persistent and dysfunctional. There are no signs, as yet, of an end of the secular tendency of declining growth in the capitalist centre. Moreover, neoliberalism has left behind massive piles of public debt and a bloated global money supply, as well as the huge balance sheets of the leading central banks that the banks believe need to be cut – probably to keep capitalism capitalist – without knowing how. Inflation is high and will be around for some time, and interest rates are high and likely to remain so, the dream of a steady decline of the 'natural rate of interest' remaining just that – a dream. At the same time, the fragmentation of the global economy is shortening supply lines and interrupting long-distance trade routes, not as a result of politically willed deglobalisation but for reasons of both technical ungovernability and national or imperial security, adding to inflationary pressures and shedding doubt on the future viability of existing industrial structures and the ways of life of those who have become dependent on them.

As always in capitalist crises, the problem is not that there would be no work to be done. It is not demand that is lacking but, rather, *effective demand.* This is at least the case with the arms industry, which faces a glorious future, although it entirely depends on government orders. When it comes to accumulating new means of destruction, there seems to be effectively no limit to modern states' ability to pay. There is also growth potential, and much more of it, in the huge efforts now finally overdue at mitigation of the effects of climate change, from urban renewal to dike building to reforestation. But this must be paid out of public budgets, and, as things stand, it can be financed only by debt, tax increases being politically impossible and technically unenforceable. New debt, however, would add to the old debt, the servicing of which is becoming more expensive due to the higher interest rates, testing the limits of public borrowing as set by the confidence, or lack thereof, of private capital. In any case, high interest, inflation, and interrupted supply lines add to the cost of infrastructural investment, increasing the amount of public money needed. Private-investor confidence is also required for the greening of energy generation, away from coal and imported oil and gas towards renewables and nuclear; here, too, public subsidies may be needed, and certainly reliable assurances of political resolve that cannot easily be given, not just because of fiscal constraints but also because of the unpredictability of political support.

Moreover, neoliberal austerity has left deep gaps in public services, such as elder care and health care, that demand urgently to be closed. That the inequality of incomes increased over three decades makes it imperative that such repair work be paid for not by user fees or social security contributions but by governments already suffering from an endemic fiscal crisis. In many countries, including Germany, there are now also significant skills shortages caused by decades of malevolent neglect of education. This has contributed to keeping productivity increases low, even with digitisation. Demographic change – a rising number of old people and pensioners coincident with a declining number of young people due to decades-long low fertility – not only adds to the fiscal burden but has begun to cause labour shortages of a magnitude that cannot nearly be compensated by immigration. There also seems to be, in several countries, a tendency among workers to minimise their participation in the labour market, perhaps in response to a decline in career prospects, or in order to better balance work with social and family life, as work outside of the household is becoming both more demanding and less rewarding. For all these reasons, hopes for a new wave of economic growth seem unlikely to come true.

It would seem that the restructuring of social and economic life in response to the climate crisis would entail major opportunities for economic growth and prosperity, much like reconstruction after the Second World War. For this, however, a large-scale redeployment of capital and labour would be needed, moving production factors out of old economic sectors into new ones, a scenario in which the fiscal capacities of the states and the monetary capacities of the central banks would appear to be already at their limits. Also, the long years of neoliberalism have shrunk the planning capacities of governments at all levels, for the benefit of the private sector, at the expense of citizens' loss of confidence in the technical competence of public bureaucracies. Rather than support for a collective effort, with an equitable distribution of the burden, one can more likely expect local outbreaks of discontent, similar to the COVID crisis but dragged out over a long period of social and economic transformation when the purpose of the exercise may recede from sight while the necessary public means will be hitting their limits. Will there be a post-neoliberal state system able to project not just the appearance but also the reality of technical competence combined with social justice, demonstrated by successfully reining in opportunistic attempts by capital to let the costs of ecological restructuring be paid by society alone? Is there a societal regime emerging that would end post-neoliberal uncertainty and provide the world with a less anarchic and more stable and reliable economic and political order, one in which sovereign democracies command a capacity to protect their citizens and the world from the invisible hands of blind market forces and the visible hands of imperial *Großstaaten* (large states)?

Capitalism and Nothing Else

Capitalism is about the infinite accumulation of privately owned capital for investment in its continuing infinite accumulation. All members of a society that has allowed its economy to be conducted in the capitalist way must allow themselves to be used for this purpose, although the result of their (in principle) open-ended efforts ends up in the hands of a small minority, in accordance with the nature of capitalism. The cooperation of those who cannot expect to have a share in the result of society's collective production efforts – those whose life enters as a cost in the calculations of the profit of others – needs to be won through effective techniques of motivation which must be constantly adapted to changing means and relations of production. These take the form of 'work incentives', which can range from promises of religious redemption through threats of physical punishment and prospects of economic misery to, more recently, housing loans, consumer credit, remuneration over and above market price (so-called 'efficiency wages'), a social policy designed to extend the labour supply, career ladders in 'internal labour markets', 'bonuses' related to 'performance', and, something very important since the rise of consumer capitalism, an unending stream of mercilessly 'improved' consumer goods.[26] The problem which is solved in this way was identified by Marx in his inquiries into economic history in *Capital*, volume 1, as (although he expresses it differently) a constant *temptation* among non-capitalists to backslide to a *subsistence economy*: to be satisfied with what they have and content themselves with a constant level of consumption defined by tradition as *good enough*. Traditionalism, in this sense, is considered also by Weber as a deadly enemy of capitalism whose flourishing depends on the members of a capitalist society being successfully socialised to squeeze out as much of their labour power as possible, instead of allowing it to rest once a given level of need satisfaction has been achieved – in short, to maximise output instead of minimising input.[27]

26 Max Weber, 'Die protestantische Ethik und der Geist des Kapitalismus', in Dirk Kaesler, ed., *Max Weber: Schriften 1894–1922*, Stuttgart: Kröner, 2002 [1904/5], 150–226; Karl Marx, *Capital: A Critique of Political Economy*, vol. 1, Moscow: Progress Publishers, 1887.

27 Seen this way, the problem of 'original accumulation' was not solved, as Marx probably assumed, by the formation of a modern working class during the nineteenth century; on the contrary, it has turned out to be permanent. See Wolfgang Streeck, 'Niemand wird freiwillig Arbeiter', in Mathias Greffrath, ed., *RE. Das Kapital: Politische Ökonomie im 21. Jahrhundert*, Munich: Verlag Antje Kunstmann, 2017, 111–28. Even Keynes assumed that once a certain level of need-satisfaction was attained, people would withdraw gradually from the capitalist labour market, to the extent that higher productivity made it possible for them to reach their accustomed standard of living with a correspondingly reduced expenditure of labour. He estimated that at some point in the twentieth century, this would lead to a fifteen-hour working week. John Maynard Keynes, 'Economic Possibilities for Our Grandchildren', in *Essays in Persuasion*, New York: W. W. Norton & Co., 1963 [1930].

Post-war capitalism, when it was institutionalised after the global economic and political crisis of the first half of the twentieth century, gained the cooperation of capitalist society's non-capitalist majority by a general promise of political-economic progress. Backed by political democracy and trade union representation, this promise included constantly rising wages, participation of the labour force at the workplace and within the enterprise, full and stable employment in different national forms, a social policy which mitigated and warded off market pressures, and a range of egalitarian policies to correct the primary, market-driven distribution between capital and labour of their jointly produced social product. All of this was underpinned by a political and social contract, known in the English-speaking countries as the *post-war settlement*, which safeguarded the continued accumulation of privately owned capital by politically mediated and guaranteed concessions to the non-capitalist majority of the members of capitalist society who, as such, had no direct interest in the unending growth of capitalist capital.

By the 1970s at latest, this solution to the capitalist motivation problem proved to be counterproductive, as indicated by the crisis of the 1960s which culminated in the mass strikes of 1968 and 1969. What had originally been intended to restore growth now threatened to obstruct it: high wages, expected by wage earners to get higher year by year; a 'rigid' employment regime in the labour market and at the workplace; and industrial citizenship rights which could, not least, be invoked to ration the labour supply by limiting the hours of work.[28] This led to the neoliberal revolution, directed against the democratic nation-state as the social locus of the post-war compromise and its promise of social progress, with the danger it entailed of the rise of a new subsistentialist traditionalism.[29] The search was now on for improved motivational techniques, aimed at making the progress of capitalist accumulation

---

28   T. H. Marshall, 'Citizenship and Social Class', in *Class, Citizenship and Social Development: Essays by T. H. Marshall*, Garden City, NY: Anchor Books, 1965 [1949], 71–134.

29   On the turn to neoliberalism in the late 1970s, see Streeck, *Buying Time*, 26–31; and many others, including Andrew Glyn, *Capitalism Unleashed: Finance Globalization and Welfare*, Oxford: Oxford University Press, 2006; David Harvey, *A Brief History of Neoliberalism*, Oxford: Oxford University Press, 2005; David M. Kotz, *The Rise and Fall of Neoliberal Capitalism*, Cambridge, MA: Harvard University Press, 2015; and Wendy Brown, 'Neo-liberalism and the End of Liberal Democracy', *Theory and Event* 7, no. 1 (2003).

more independent of politically mediated social and economic concessions. A central role in capital's fight against the apathy of its retainers, and the stagnation of capital accumulation caused by it, was played by increased competitive pressures on the workers of the 'affluent societies' of the West, domestically by 'deregulation' and across national borders by 'globalisation', forcing them to work harder and submit themselves more obediently to unpredictably fluctuating market conditions, by developing the new kind of 'governmentality' that has been so strikingly portrayed by Michel Foucault.[30]

The neoliberal revolution replaced the promise of social progress as a work incentive with a formula that had become current by the end of the twentieth century: *fear and greed*. As Colin Crouch put it, neoliberalism set about turning what had been secure citizens of a democratic welfare state with guaranteed social rights into insecure workers who were simultaneously confident consumers: driven, on the one hand, by existential worries and enticed, on the other, by constantly rising consumption norms.[31] As time passed, however, the inherent contradictions of this project made themselves felt. Where neoliberalism's dismantling of social protection was intended to impel the non-capitalists towards redoubled work efforts, it gave rise to an ever more unequal distribution of the social product, limiting effective demand and causing the productivity of the economy as a whole to stagnate or decline. For many of those dependent on the sale of their labour power, this meant that more and more effort was required to preserve what they already had gained, while what they could gain with a given effort became less and less. Progress disappeared into a distant future or became individualised, dependent on redoubled effort, privileged starting conditions, and the accidents of fortune. Now, even subsistentialist withdrawal into a traditionalist, static mode of life required greater exertion, including a watchful readiness to adapt oneself obsequiously to constantly and unforeseeably changing markets and competitive conditions, at a high risk of failure and with no guarantee of a good end.

No one really knows how the current *revolution of sinking expectations* might be ended. To bet on promises of capitalist progress, for

30   Michel Foucault, *The Birth of Biopolitics: Lectures at the College de France, 1978–1979*, London: Palgrave Macmillan, 2008.
31   Colin Crouch, *The Strange Non-death of Neoliberalism*, Cambridge, UK: Polity Press, 2011.

example in connection with the so-called digitisation, seems risky to say the least; digitisation is politically marketed not as a beacon of hope but as a 'challenge'. Nor does a rhetoric of blood, sweat, and tears, as an encouragement to 'painful structural reforms', kindle any enthusiasm when there is no credible prospect of a shining future after the end of the hard times. Exhortations to the many to be satisfied with less, which may be more topical than ever against the background of the environmental crisis, but also of geostrategic deglobalisation and the war, can hardly expect to receive much of a hearing in view of increasing distributional inequality in favour of the few. The same was already true of neoliberal exhortations to join in altruistic pro-capitalist enthusiasm over calculations by the World Bank and others, according to which, as a result of neoliberal globalisation, fewer inhabitants of the planet than ever had to make do with less than \$1.90 a day, which was claimed to mean that they had been 'lifted out of abject poverty' by capitalism.[32] Human needs cannot be determined absolutely but only in relation to particular local conditions of life and work – not to mention that prosperity depends not only on individual income per capita but also, and presumably predominantly, on collective goods such as access to clean water and health care, hygienic waste-disposal, freedom from corruption and violence, an equitable education system, and the like. The dawning suspicion that the limits to growth in a capitalist accumulation economy might have drawn nearer combines, for more and more people, with a sense that living and working are getting ever more burdensome, and life ever more restless and insecure. Increasing effort for declining returns raises the question of when the costs of life under capitalism will finally outweigh capitalism's benefits for the mass of ordinary people. Small wonder that the mood became so sour and that acts of defiance such as those by the 'Yellow Vests' or the friends of lignite mining can increasingly be observed.

---

32   According to the World Bank's definition, \$1.90 a day in 2011 prices is the threshold below which people are in 'extreme poverty'. In 1800 (at a time when the dollar did not yet exist), some 80 percent of the world's population are alleged to have lived in extreme poverty while, by 2015, after more than two centuries of capitalism, their share is said to have fallen to only 20 percent. Other estimates, by the UN for example, arrive at just 10 percent for the same year. There is agreement among those performing calculations of this type that the number of people in extreme poverty, defined and measured as above, has fallen recently, allegedly from around 2 billion in 1980 to less than 1 billion in 2015 (see 'Extreme Poverty', wikipedia.org).

Politics in stagnant neoliberal capitalism has got stuck, as it no longer knows how to legitimise not just capitalism but also itself: by invoking happy prospects of renewed growth or by preaching anti-materialist sermons demanding a return to a simpler life, which, in practice, would mean water instead of wine for most and champagne for the happy few. Under the mixed economy of the post-war past, capitalism derived its legitimacy from a political promise of a pacified social existence in the lee of creative destruction, untroubled by its storms. Social stability rested on widely shared 'fictional expectations' of a life in quasi-retirement outside the rat race of capitalist progress, a life under a non-capitalist capitalism, or a not-really-capitalist capitalism – on fictional expectations of liberation from the pressures of markets and competition, alongside the fictional expectations associated with money and credit, investment, innovation, and consumption that Jens Beckert has so impressively analysed.[33] Even before the latest crises that put an end to the neoliberalism of the New World Order, capitalism had become, for a growing section of its domestic servants, a *capitalism without transcendence*, entirely self-referential, lacking any perspective beyond itself: *capitalism pure and simple*, thoroughly secularised, capitalism with nothing else, bare of any promise of, or hope for, a non-capitalist future.

---

33 Jens Beckert, 'Capitalism as a System of Expectations: Toward a Sociological Microfoundation of Political Economy', *Politics and Society* 41, no. 3 (2013), 323; Jens Beckert, 'Capitalist Dynamics: Fictional Expectations and the Openness of the Future', MPIfG Discussion Paper 14/7, Max Planck Institute for the Study of Societies, Cologne (2014); Jens Beckert, *Imaginierte Zukunft: Fiktionale Erwartungen und die Dynamik des Kapitalismus*, Berlin: Suhrkamp, 2018. Expectations, that is, of a stabilised, non-market-driven future existence as pensioners, crystallised around the prospect of 'retirement' with an old-age pension. The only way of life that has remained beyond capitalism is the life of the pensioner, and defence of retirement seems to have become the last form of anti-capitalist struggle among most ordinary people in the rich capitalist societies. One subjects oneself to the iron rules of life in the service of capital accumulation until the age of, say, sixty-two or sixty-five, to be from then on entitled to retire and 'enjoy life' while still young enough to do so. Seen this way, it is not hard to discover why pensions are, in the jargon of American politicians, the 'third rail' of politics today – the rail that carries high-voltage electricity: *touch it and you are dead*. The long and drawn-out history of cautious and mostly vain attempts to reform the French pension system, from Alain Juppé to Emmanuel Macron, is one example of this among many others. The public pension system as the last remaining object of anti-capitalist desire and militancy: the utopia of a life of truth in a false society.

6

A Dual Crisis II: Democracy

I come now to the second structural root of the political tug of war in this age of waning neoliberalism, the conflict between, on the one hand, the attempted neutralisation of democracy at the level of the nation, its desocialisation and liberalisation (see fig. 5, p. 51) in favour of supranational mercato-technocracy, and, on the other hand, the counter-movement triggered by that process, a 'populist' defence of democracy as a plebeian, egalitarian protection against the political unleashing of a new wave of accelerated capitalist modernisation and rationalisation, aimed at ending the secular stagnation of a demo-cratically softened capitalism. Numerous concepts are available to characterise this historical situation: the transition to a 'market-compatible democracy' (Angela Merkel), where the market is a world market and the democratic state is a price taker in the broadest sense; the associated bourgeoisification (*Verbürgerlichung*) of democracy, at the cost of its plebeian-popular dimension; the uprooting of public policy from the societies affected by it, in the course of the shifting of decision-making onto international organisations and institutions far away from the grass roots and immunised against electoral pressures; and, not least, the trivialisation of popularly accessible politics by its separation from questions of economic distribution and its trans-formation into culturalist moralising. In the following, I will briefly summarise how the present conflict over democracy and its function in global capitalism is related to the stalemate over political scale between internationalisation and renationalisation.

States between Democracy and Globalism

Contrary to what is often asserted, neoliberalism is more than just a catchword for everything one dislikes.[1] It is a long-established concept, in existence for almost a hundred years, and it has a precise historical and political significance, being directed against the nation-state's claim to self-determination, not only in relation to other states but also, and above all, in relation to the world market.[2] Neoliberalism originated in the two decades after 1918, following the collapse of nineteenth-century liberalism in the First World War and the replacement of the defeated empires by sovereign nation-states.[3] The aim of neoliberalism as a political movement and a trend in economic theory was to fight against the tendency of nation-states to intervene politically into the liberal capitalist market economy, which was founded on private property and was regarded as essentially international. Its leading figures were the Austrian economists Friedrich Hayek and Ludwig von Mises, whose political ambition amounted to nothing less than the restoration of the pre-1914 world economy, based on an international gold standard and conceived as entirely barrier free. They were the intellectual antipodes of Karl Polanyi, also present in Vienna in the

---

1   The amount of literature on neoliberalism, and on the term's precise meaning, has become almost unmanageable. There is a range of definitions stretching between two poles: a culturalist one (Michel Foucault, *The Birth of Biopolitics: Lectures at the College de France, 1978–1979*, London: Palgrave Macmillan, 2008) and a political-economic or structuralist one (for example, David M. Kotz, *The Rise and Fall of Neoliberal Capitalism*, Cambridge, MA: Harvard University Press, 2015). An incomplete selection includes Wendy Brown, *Undoing the Demos: Neoliberalism's Stealth Revolution*, Cambridge, MA: MIT Press, 2015; Grégoire Chamayou, *La société ingouvernable: Une généalogie du libéral-isme autoritaire*, Paris: La Fabrique, 2018; Colin Crouch, *The Strange Non-death of Neoliberalism*, Cambridge, UK: Polity Press, 2011; Pierre Dardot and Christian Laval, *The New Way of the World: On Neo-liberal Society*, London: Verso, 2013; Gérard Duménil and Dominique Lévy, *Capital Resurgent: Roots of the Neoliberal Revolution*, Cambridge, MA: Harvard University Press, 2004; Martijn Konings, *The Emotional Logic of Capitalism: What Progressives Have Missed*, Stanford, CA: Stanford University Press, 2015; Martijn Konings, *Capital and Time: For a New Critique of Neoliberal Reason*, Stanford, CA: Stanford University Press, 2018; and Quinn Slobodian, *Globalists: The End of Empire and the Birth of Neoliberalism*, Cambridge, MA: Harvard University Press, 2018.

2   Slobodian, *Globalists*.

3   For a recent account, see Robert Gerwarth, *The Vanquished: Why the First World War Failed to End, 1917–1923*, London: Allen Lane, 2016.

1920s, with whom they debated in newspaper articles and scholarly publications.

The history of neoliberalism is a part of the history of political economy in the twentieth century, the 'age of extremes'.[4] The dream of a return to the liberalism of the pre-war era came to grief in the first half of the century with the rise of communism, fascism, and (social) demo-cratic New Deal capitalism – three post-liberal variants of modern industrial society which were all at each other's throats. Nor did old liberalism return, at first, after the inferno of the Second World War. On the contrary, for three decades, its advocates had to hibernate as exotic outsiders. In spite of them, a system of national economic and social-political autonomy, inspired by John Maynard Keynes, grew up in the 'West', resting on an international trade and currency regime ruled over more or less benevolently by the United States under the sign of the Cold War and as a follow-up to the New Deal. In this era of 'embed-ded liberalism' – of liberalism embedded in society rather than society in liberalism – a political order took shape in the countries in question which I suggest we consider as the 'standard model' of post-liberal, state-administered 'democratic capitalism'.[5] Its versions varied from country to country; but what they all had in common was a national government formed according to the principle of majority rule through reasonably free elections, whose legislation needed the consent of a parliament elected similarly in a reasonably free manner, and whose executive acts were subject to legal control in one way or another, and were observed by an, again, reasonably free and independent press which could describe itself, with halfway good reason, as the country's 'fourth power'. Among the pillars of this arrangement were solidly organised mass parties, ideally two 'people's parties', one of the centre-right, the other of the centre-left, together reflecting the dominant classes in capitalist industrial society, not exactly but only approxi-mately, which was supposed to render them capable of compromise and incapable of civil war. Governmental authority could shift from centre-right to centre-left and back, which constituted an effective deterrent

---

4   Eric Hobsbawm, *The Age of Extremes. A History of the World, 1914–1991*, New York: Pantheon, 1994.
5   John Gerard Ruggie, 'International Regimes, Transactions and Change: Embed-ded Liberalism in the Postwar Economic Order', *International Organization* 36, no. 2 (1982), 379–415.

against one of the two sides forgetting about the class compromise that underlay post-war democracy; at the same time, it also allowed for a swing of the political pendulum between more or less progressive, in the sense of 'decommodifying', social policies, which made possible a step-wise improvement, compatible with economic growth, in the position of the lower classes.[6]

Although this is readily overlooked in present-day liberal discourse, the standard model also included interest groups (preferably comprehensively organised), which typically represented labour and capital. Among them were strong trade unions with a quasi-constitutional right to regulate wages and working conditions by collective contract, aided if needed by a legally guaranteed right to strike. Unions and employers also participated, in ways that varied from country to country, in the administration of the institutions and funds of the emerging welfare state, financed by expected constant increases in productivity. Their participation made them jointly responsible for the welfare state's financial health but also put them in a position to protect the contributions of their members from a state ever in search of revenue, and, not least, it helped them safeguard their organisations in a variety of ways. The class organisations of labour and capital – the trade unions and employers' associations – together formed a second, 'corporatist' level of government beneath the government of the state as established by the parliament.[7] Its significance for the stability of post-war capitalist democracy was that it institutionalised, meaning both licenced and regulated, distributional class conflict, freeing the state and parliamentary democracy from the direct involvement in problems that all too easily overwhelms its capacities.[8]

---

6   Gøsta Esping-Andersen, *Politics against Markets: The Social-Democratic Road to Power*, Princeton, NJ: Princeton University Press, 1985.

7   Gerhard Lehmbruch, 'Liberal Corporatism and Party Government', *Comparative Political Studies* 10 (1977), 91–126; Philippe C. Schmitter and Gerhard Lehmbruch, eds, *Trends Towards Corporatist Intermediation*, London: Sage, 1979; Gerhard Lehmbruch and Philippe C. Schmitter, eds, *Patterns of Corporatist Policy-Making*, London: Sage, 1982; Wolfgang Streeck and Lane Kenworthy, 'Theories and Practices of Neo-corporatism', in Thomas Janoski et al., eds, *A Handbook of Political Sociology: States, Civil Societies and Globalization*, New York: Cambridge University Press, 2005, 441–60.

8   It is a fact worth noting, and also highly revealing, that trade unions and employers' associations are almost never mentioned in present-day 'democratic theory', although they were absolutely indispensable for the – temporary – embedding of capitalism in the

Politically, too, the welfare state of democratic capitalism was far from completely liberal. After the unconditional capitulation of Nazi Germany and the successful incorporation of the West German rump state into the newly established capitalist world system, only one of the two historical enemies of Western democracy, fascism and communism, was still in existence. Where Communism was weak, as in West Germany, owing to its relocation to the German Democratic Republic, its organisations could be banned. The situation was similar in the US, where the persecution of Communists had already started shortly after the end of the war and went on reach its climax in the 1950s and celebrate lasting successes under Joseph McCarthy and his supporters. At the same time, the CIA organised and financed a multifaceted international cultural offensive against the Communist enemy. In countries where Communism was deeply rooted in the party and trade union system, it was necessary, at first, to live with it. In Italy, in particular, but also in France, this involved locking mass Communist parties out of the constitutional spectrum by threats of military intervention, as well as using financial means to break up Communist-controlled national trade union federations.[9]

Nevertheless, and within these limits, the situation that emerged in the region under Western rule after the Second World War facilitated a

---

political system of post-war democracy. Their absence is glaringly apparent in historical retrospect. What calls itself democratic theory today has largely forgotten, if it has not repressed, the fact that under capitalism, democracy needs not only a right to discuss but also a right to strike. Hardly anyone still talks of what was long regarded as self-evident: the need for the power imbalance between labour and capital to be neutralised, at the workplace as in politics, through labour law and 'industrial democracy', involving the legally embedded self-organisation of workers which, among other things, relieved parliamentary democracy, through collectively bargained temporary compromises, from conflicts of interest and problems of distribution which are impossible to solve through discussion (Stein Rokkan's 'second tier of government'; see Stein Rokkan, 'Norway: Numerical Democracy and Corporate Pluralism', in Robert A. Dahl, ed., *Political Opposi-tions in Western Democracies*, New Haven, CT: Yale University Press, 1966, 70–115). There is no clearer evidence of the vulgar idealism of a large part of modern democratic theory than its complete neglect of material economic power relations. This, too, is an aspect of the move from a social to a liberal version of democratic theory (see fig. 5, p. 51).

9   I mention this to remind the reader that in post-war capitalism, democracy was not an autopoietic system of non-hierarchical (*herrschaftsfrei*) discourse, drawn after long deliberation by free citizens from a store of models for the good life, any more than it had been in the aristocratic slaveholder societies of Athens, Rome, and Virginia. Democracy as a system of non-hierarchical deliberation is best imagined when those who do the work are excluded from participation.

form of peaceful coexistence between capitalism and democracy which, until then, had been regarded as impossible. Capitalist democracy was held together as a marriage of historical convenience by the peace formula of Keynesian economic theory, which redefined democracy as a *force of capitalist production*: a government electorally obliged to the interests of the wage-earning majority, in alliance with institutionally fortified trade unions, ensured a continuous downward redistribution which, according to the economic wisdom of the time, distilled from the experience of the world economic crisis of the inter-war period, was necessary to reliably maintain effective demand at the level required to produce growth and full employment. A capitalism tamed by democratic politics and trade unionism could thus appear, for a certain time and for its practical purposes, as having been transformed from a *class society* into a state-administered *collective prosperity cooperative*, technocratically fine-tuned towards a stable economic and social equilibrium by a democratically sensitised government machinery under pressure from a working class whose readiness to compromise and cooperate was indispensable to the reinstatement of capitalism after 1945.

Of course, this arrangement lasted no longer than three decades. In the 1970s, all over the Western world, it started to crumble, although this was not always noticed immediately. The precise cause was and continues to be disputed, which is hardly surprising when it comes to such a complex and politically fateful process. One factor of obvious significance was the rise in workers' expectations of the ability and willingness of the owners and movers of capital to pay, which became apparent in the worldwide disturbances of the late 1960s. Capital, which had become used to its role as an infrastructure of production, now awoke and rediscovered itself as a class. The initial expression of the conflict over distribution which flared up again as a result was the worldwide inflation of the 1970s, combined with an equally worldwide profit squeeze, followed by stagnation and unemployment, which were manifestations of a 'loss of confidence' on the part of 'capital'.[10] By then, at the latest, capital began its search for an exit from the subservience to national social democracy in which it had had to spend the Trente Glorieuses. It was a search which, very soon, would issue in so-called globalisation.

---

10   Robert Brenner, *The Economics of Global Turbulence: The Advanced Capitalist Economies from Long Boom to Long Downturn, 1945–2005*, London: Verso, 2006.

The impact of globalisation on the relation between capitalism and democracy was, first and foremost, to alter the power relations between capital, its owners and managers now internationally mobile, on the one hand, and political democracy, still stuck at the national level, on the other – and, by implication, between capital and labour, the latter dependent both on the former and on democratic politics. In the decades which followed the watershed of the 1970s, ever-new escape routes opened for capital out of its role as an object of social democratic husbandry, into the immense wilderness, untouched by democratic interference, of the free world market. Societies and states which were unwilling to let go of what they had long regarded as 'their' capital now had to adapt themselves, after the anti-authoritarian euphoria of the 1960s, to another *revolution of rising expectations*, this time coming from the opposite side of the economy. With this began the era of neoliberal 'reforms' aimed at revitalising capitalism on its own terms – deregulation, the opening of markets, free trade, Bill Clinton's 'end of welfare as we know it': less state, more market, and austerity without end.

Globalism against Democracy

Thus, democracy as egalitarian political intervention into the economy fell into discredit: first among the elites, who saw it as technocratically 'under-complex' in view of the 'heightened complexity' of the world in general, liable to overburden state and economy, and politically corrupt because it was unwilling to teach citizens 'the laws of economics', as rediscovered by the neoliberals. According to them, growth does not come about through redistribution from above but, to the contrary, from below: at the lower end of the income distribution, through more powerful incentives to work by the abolition of minimum wages and cuts to social security benefits, and at its upper ranges, in contrast, by improved opportunities for profit-making and higher pay, assisted by lower taxation. I have described the underlying process as a transition to a new, *Hayekian* growth model, destined to replace its *Keynesian* predecessor as part of the neoliberal revolution.[11] As with any economic doctrine,

---

11   Wolfgang Streeck, *Buying Time: The Delayed Crisis of Democratic Capitalism*, 2nd ed., London: Verso, 2017, 110–12.

both must be understood as camouflaged presentations of political constraints and opportunities arising from a historically contingent distribution of power, dressed up as manifestations of natural laws. The difference is that in the Hayekian world, democracy no longer appears as a productive force but, on the contrary, as a millstone around the neck of economic progress, for which reason the spontaneous distributional activity of the market needs to be protected from democratic interference by Chinese walls of all kinds or, better still, by replacing democracy with global governance.[12]

Much analysis has centred on the way the standard model of democratic capitalism began to disintegrate with the advance of globalisation.[13] Over the course of roughly two decades, since the disappearance of Soviet Communism, neoliberalism has celebrated an astonishing comeback: Hayek, long laughed at as a sectarian cult leader, won over towering shapers of world affairs such as Keynes and Lenin. Hayek's thought experiment – on a system in which private property would receive international protection and global market freedom would rank above national policies, on liberalisation through identical legal orders in formally sovereign states ('isonomy'), on the inevitable economic liberalisation in heterogeneous international federations,[14] on a prohibition of state interventionism through international competition law, and the free movement of goods, services, capital, and human beings as a means to the economic neutralisation of the nation-state – had penetrated deeply not just into the thinking of economists and international institutions but also of national governments and political parties, which began to share the suspicions of themselves that public choice theory had raised.[15] Until it was demystified

---

12   For a representative example of the rapidly growing literature on the inadequacy of liberal democracy in a supply-oriented economic world, see Daniel A. Bell, *Beyond Liberal Democracy: Political Thinking for an East Asian Context*, Princeton, NJ: Princeton University Press, 2006; and, more generally, Jason Brennan, *Against Democracy*, Princeton, NJ: Princeton University Press, 2016, with a passionate argument in favour of 'epistocracy' (the rule of the knowledgeable) as an alternative to democracy.

13   Wendy Brown, 'Neo-liberalism and the End of Liberal Democracy', *Theory and Event* 7, no. 1 (2003).

14   Streeck, *Buying Time*, 97–103.

15   James M. Buchanan, *Public Principles of Public Debt: A Defense and Restatement*, Homewood, IL: Richard R. Irwin, 1958; James M. Buchanan, 'Politics without Romance: A Sketch of Positive Public Choice Theory and Its Normative Implications', *IHS-Journal* 3 (1979), B1–B11.

by the Great Recession, neoliberalism thus became the ruling political-economic doctrine of modern capitalism: the utopia of a self-regulating global capitalist market economy, in which national politics was limited to the establishment of free markets, the implementation of flexible adaptation to them, plus, perhaps, the folkloristic conservation of local cultural and political traditions.

The forward march of the globalist-neoliberal growth model was paralleled by a gradual erosion of the standard post-war model of democracy.[16] Since the end of the 1970s, there had been a remarkable decline in participation in elections of all kinds in all capitalist democracies. This was particularly so among those at the lower end of the distribution of income and life chances – those who actually had the greatest need for a politics of social protection and redistribution. At the same time, political parties registered a dramatic fall in their membership, irrespective of any institutional differences. The same applied to trade unions, which, since the end of the 1980s, were seldom in a position to make use of their right to strike with any prospect of success.[17] As far as the party system is concerned, the established state-upholding parties of the centre increasingly withdrew from the society of their voters into the apparatus of the state, as political scientist Peter Mair has shown, and the creeping *statification of the parties* had its counterpart in a *privatisation of civil society*. The main driving force in this was the factual compulsion (*Sachzwang*), derived from globalisation, to govern 'responsibly' – in other words, the actual or pretended lack of political alternatives to the expanding neoliberal *pensée unique* of the so-called Washington Consensus.[18] In the same way as trade unions

---

16   See Armin Schäfer and Wolfgang Streeck, 'Introduction', in Armin Schäfer and Wolfgang Streeck, eds, *Politics in the Age of Austerity*, Cambridge, UK: Polity, 2013.

17   'Trade Union Dataset', OECD.Stat, data extracted on 4 January 2020. With the exception of Italy, where union density remained roughly at 35 percent, it declined in all Western European countries in the two decades between 1998 and 2018, falling in Sweden from 92.6 to 65.6 percent, in Britain from 30.1 to 23.4 percent, in Germany from 25.9 to 16.5 percent, in the Netherlands from 23.9 to 16.4 percent, and in Spain from 17.9 to 13.6 percent. OECD, 'Industrial Disputes', September 2017.

18   Peter Mair and Richard S. Katz, 'Changing Models of Party Organization and Party Democracy: The Emergence of the Cartel Party', *Party Politics* 1, no. 1 (1995), 5–28; Peter Mair and Richard S. Katz, 'The Ascendancy of the Party in Public Office: Party Organizational Change in Twentieth-Century Democracies', in Richard Gunther et al., eds, *Political Parties: Old Concepts and New Challenges*, Oxford: Oxford University Press, 2002, 113–35; Peter Mair, 'Representative versus Responsible Government',

which want to preserve their members' jobs can put forward only moderate demands, if any, political parties which want to rule their states, now embedded in the world market, cannot let themselves be influenced too much by their members (in Mair's words: *responsibility* comes at the price of *responsiveness*).

The final disintegration of the standard model coincided with the accelerated globalisation of the 1990s. For the sake of brevity, I limit myself to sketching out just four aspects of this process, which appear to be characteristic features of the liberal involution of capitalist democracy. What is involved here is a specific shift in the interests and attitudes represented by the centre of the democratic political system, the formation of a corresponding pattern of political supply and demand, and increasing conflicts over the status of the nation-state with respect to rising interests in the restoration of a politics of protection and redistribution.

(1) In the political systems of the post-war standard model, the conservative parties of the 'centre-right', which were in continental Europe often of a Christian Democratic orientation, had the task of reconciling social traditionalism with capitalist modernisation. This became increasingly difficult under the pressure of globalisation. It was not just that the end of Communism meant the disappearance of bourgeois conservatism's antithesis, whose existence had facilitated the reconciliation of traditionalism with capitalism. In addition, the new competitive pressures on centre-right parties made them abandon their balancing act between progress and preservation and take sides with the creative destructionists and cultural modernisers in the name of national competitiveness. (One example among many is the politically encouraged transition to a social structure of universal labour market participation, which severely weakened society's receptiveness towards a conservative family policy.) All of this made growing sections of the culturally conservative electorate politically homeless.

(2) A corresponding development took place within the mainly social democratic parties on the other, left half of the political centre. The accelerated opening of national economies had taken out of their hands the most important instrument in their political toolbox, Keynesian

MPIfG Working Paper 09/8, Max Planck Institute for the Study of Societies, Cologne, 2009; Peter Mair, *Ruling the Void: The Hollowing of Western Democracy*, London: Verso, 2013. On the Washington Consensus see pp. 190, 229.

economic policy in its post-war iteration. The same can be said of the rapid rise in state indebtedness after 1970 and the fact that in open international markets, the costs of a nationally based de-commodifying social policy risked becoming a competitive disadvantage.[19] If they wanted to be involved in globalisation, or saw it as unavoidable, they could follow a Third Way to adapt to the new borderlessness. If the conservative parties of the centre had evolved into the managers of capitalist progress, their social democratic counterparts now became its facilitators, guarantors, and propagandists by enthusiastically telling their voters about the light of renewed prosperity at the end of the tunnel of globalisation – although, of course, they would have to pull their socks up to get there. In Germany, for example, the idea was that they reinvent themselves as individual entrepreneurs – if need be, with state funding. Or it was explained to them that the modern epoch required an 'investment'- rather than a 'consumption'-oriented social policy, to prefer flexible adaptation over early retirement; and that international solidarity now meant international competition in open markets. This, too, did not go down well; while the achievers among their supporters felt represented in part – only in part, though, as a good proportion of them went over to the new Green parties of the centre-left – the losers of globalisation, who found all of this too much to deal with, deserted the banner of social democratic modernisation.

(3) By entering the united front of globalism, the centre-right and the centre-left both lost their political identity, however vaguely defined. In the process of adaptation to the world market, the democratic politics of the post-war period changed from the long-term pursuit of different

---

19   Adam Przeworski has put together an impressive summary of the problems faced by social democracy in the decades of globalisation: 'Slow growth, inflation, unemployment, large fiscal deficits, and balance of payments crises did not leave socialist governments much room to manoeuvre. The Maastricht Treaty, which went into effect in 1993, was intended to be a solution to these problems, but it came at the cost of tying the hands of social democrats behind their backs: with a limit of 3 percent on annual deficits and of 60 percent on the ratio of debt to GDP, Keynesian stimulation was nearly impossible, and increased social expenditure tightly circumscribed. As the right moved to the right, the left moved even farther to the right, and the economic policies of the centre-left and the centre-right became almost indistinguishable. Social democrats embraced liberalisation of capital flows, free trade, fiscal discipline, and labour market flexibility, abstained from counter cyclical policies and from using most industrial policies.' 'From Revolution to Reformism', *Boston Review*, 28 January 2021, bostonreview.net.

models of an ideal society – a paternalistic-hierarchical model on the one hand and an egalitarian classless model on the other – into a succession of pragmatic, short-term reactions to constantly and unpredictably changing market conditions. Politics and policies became less ideological than ever, devoid of perspective and therefore mutually indistinguishable. Thus, democracy could turn into post-democracy, on the one hand entertaining voters as passive spectators and, on the other, bringing in spin doctors and public relations specialists to design their policies.[20] Voting behaviour – both the intentions counted on by electoral strategists and the choices of the voters themselves – changed accordingly: it was no longer oriented towards a collective social ideal, a common future for which to strive jointly, but decoupled from class positions and ideologies, reacting to the moment rather than to a future goal. Hence, voter fluctuation between parties increased while the old parties of the standard model were less and less able to count on the stable backing of an established support base.

(4) The pragmatic depoliticisation of policy produced by globalisation, particularly in the sphere of political economy, and the emergence of a uniform market-conforming economic policy ended the structuring of party-political conflict along the capital–labour axis as it had shaped political differentiation and integration in the standard model.[21] It was replaced by a new line of cleavage, which crisscrossed the client structure of the old party system, between a shrinking majority who felt by and large represented in post-democratic politics, and a growing minority who found themselves excluded. Among other things, this found expression in a fall in voter turnout and a high degree of electoral volatility, as well as a in dramatic decline in the trust of citizens and their expectations in politics and parties, across all groups. In the years of internationalism and its crises, another cleavage crystallised between a national and an international orientation of perceived political interests. Those who, in one way or another, felt they had gained from globalisation found themselves at home in the narrowed band of Third Way politics. Among globalisation's economic and cultural losers, on the other hand, who did not find themselves represented by the reorganised political centre, there

---

20 Colin Crouch, *Post-Democracy*, Cambridge, UK: Polity Press, 2004.
21 Gerhard Schröder in 1997, before he became chancellor two years later: 'There is no right or left but only modern or outdated economic policy.'

developed a long unarticulated and politically submerged preference for a restoration of the political autonomy and capacity of the nation-state. That preference was increasingly available to be mobilised by parties and movements oriented towards a nationalism of the right or the left and excluded as 'populist' from the constitutional spectrum.

Democracy against Globalism

The 2008 crisis marked the end of the heyday of neoliberalism. Too much had been promised, too little delivered. Now, doubts about democracy, if not about capitalism, began to grow also among ordinary people, who rediscovered and reconstituted themselves politically in manifold forms and colours, as protesters as well as voters. A loss of stability and trust, an ever more unequal distribution of ever more slowly growing wealth, and economic stagnation despite demanding structural change, along with increasing cultural insecurity and deprecation of those left behind, gave rise to plebeian popular counter-movements from below, which were greeted with horror and condemned as 'populist' by the post-democratic neoliberal regime. Whether they grew out of the experience of globalised everyday life or were opportunistically fomented by new political operators, what they had in common was and remains a deep distrust for all kinds of 'opening up' with uncertain event, from free trade to migration, accompanied by a rediscovery of local solidarity and local justice, on a regional, national, and class basis, in all imaginable combinations. Already in the years before the crisis, globalisation – the euphoric perspective of both capital hard pressed by the welfare state and a left converted to the Third Way – had been the subject of protest; afterwards, via a multitude of detours, it effected a rapid re-politicisation of a political life which, for a while, had been at a standstill, culminating in a fundamental dispute, more or less clearly articulated, over the correct and rightful location in society of politics, democracy, and solidarity.

Today, in all the countries of OECD capitalism, the surviving remnants of the standard model of post-war democracy are being rediscovered and put to use as institutional resources for popular resistance against accelerated capitalist and cultural modernisation and the politically disempowering structural change driven by globalisation.

What this amounts to is a bitter struggle over the future character of statehood: centralised and unified to safeguard globalisation or decentralised and subdivided to prevent its further advance, elitist or egalitarian, (petty) bourgeois or plebeian? In the years before COVID, the outlines began to emerge of a reversal in the downward trend of political participation, with an increase in protest and more frequent strikes.[22] The parties of the standard model, whose voters and members had by then largely deserted them, and their media outlets in the public sphere of post-democracy had only little to do with this. In fact, they fought against the new wave of politicisation with the full arsenal of instruments at their disposal – propagandistic, cultural, legal, institutional – often unintentionally putting wind in the sails of those they had declared to be enemies of the state.

The dynamic of this development is evident from the reversal, during the 2000s, of the long-standing decline in electoral participation (fig. 17). Before that, voter turnout in the European democracies had been falling, continuing a long trend which had started at the end of the 1960s.[23] This was most pronounced at the lower end of the social and economic spectrum. In the mid-2000s, however, there was a rise in turnout of about three percentage points, accompanied by a rapid increase in the average voting share of so-called right-wing populist parties, from 11 to 17 percent. Among the additional voters were probably not just supporters but also opponents of the new opposition: while the parties of the neo-right, favoured by the political and economic circumstances of neoliberal post-democracy, were first able to mobilise apathetic or disgruntled non-voters, their success then helped the old and new parties of the centre, in turn, to mobilise, if not new sympathisers, then at least the opponents of their opponents. This, of course, does not alter the fact that the reversal of the long-deplored retreat of large parts of the electorate from politics – a retreat for which the parties of the centre were anything but free of responsibility, as much as they deplored it in public – predominantly stems from the rise of the new right-wing parties, diagnosed by the incumbents as un- or even anti-democratic. Liberal commentators felt compelled by this inconvenient

---

22   Donatella Della Porta, *Social Movements in Times of Austerity: Bringing Capitalism Back into Protest Analysis*, Cambridge, UK: Polity, 2015.

23   Schäfer and Streeck, 'Introduction', 10–17.

Figure 17. Electoral participation and voting share of 'right-wing populist' parties, 1985–2015

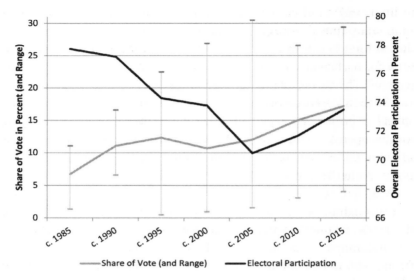

Sources: European Election Database; IDEA Voter Turnout Database; data issued by national institutions; author's calculations.

turn of events to switch from a participatory to a revisionist theory of democracy, according to which high electoral participation is an expression of political discontent and a concomitant of political radicalisation, endangering rather than strengthening democracy.[24]

Post-globalist Democracy?

Three decades of neoliberal political-economic centralisation and unification have changed Western democracies at their core: electoral turnout declined, as did centrist political parties; trade unions lost members and political status; and new right-wing parties, and currents within parties of a 'populist' sort, have eaten into centrist conservatism, sometimes including traditional social democracy. By 2023, the new

---

24   Classically, Seymour Martin Lipset, *Political Man: The Social Bases of Politics*, Garden City, NY: Anchor Books, 1963 [1960].

opposition had, in all Western countries, turned into a more or less influential political force to be reckoned with, in some even becoming an informal or formal partner in government, sometimes even as its dominant political force. This holds true for the United States and the United Kingdom as well as for Italy, France, Austria, and the whole of Scandinavia, let alone Poland, Hungary, and Eastern and Central Europe generally. Whatever may divide the new right-wing nationalists, what they have in common is that they oppose internationalisation and the centralisation and integration of governance that come with it, bringing into the open and politicising a line of conflict in capitalist democracies inherent in the New World Order of global neoliberalism and related to its demise in the 2010s.

Today, pressures for local self-rule – for decentralisation of governance through the restoration of national sovereignty – and the question of how to respond to them are a central issue of policy and politics in national and international political and economic contexts. Political forces that insist on the sovereignty of their nation-states – in relation to other imperial states, as well as to international organisations dominated by these and to global or continental free markets – can, in principle, claim that they are defending an indispensable condition of national democracy, even if they want it only for themselves and not also for their opponents. Those trying to preserve the liberal democracy of the neoliberal period tend to underestimate the power of the opposition to it, while overestimating the ability, political as well as technical, of supranational organisations and imperial hegemonic countries to govern politically and economically. Neoliberal democracy had been unable to prevent a profound loss of confidence in its institutions on the part of citizens, which is another dramatic long-term development of the three centralist-neoliberal decades. Nor was neoliberal centralism able to create and support national or international institutions capable of stabilising a global market economy; as markets failed, neoliberal politics, which had placed its bets on their infallibility, was bound to fail as well.

The neoliberal revolution had thoroughly shredded the political and social order of the post-war compromise, ruling out a simple return to it. This makes it all the more necessary to understand the exact causes of the failure of supranational centralism, in order to understand the possible contours of post-globalist and post-neoliberal democracy. Only in this way can we hope to fill the political gap left by neoliberalism with a functional equivalent for the standard model of the post-war era. Just like its predecessor, a post-globalist model of – decentralised – democracy must be embedded in an accommodating international order, one that respects local political autonomy and national state sovereignty as a fundamental condition of democracy in society and economy. Here, lessons can be learned from the fate of the European Union on the fragility of internationalism, the limits of supranationally centralised governance, of integration as unification – in short, on the futility of attempts, more or less well meaning, to relegate to the dustbin of history the nation-state as the site of distributed sovereignty. This is why the next chapter will be devoted to a review of the condition of the EU at the end of neoliberalism and the beginning of post-globalism. What can be studied here are the forces of resistance to a hierarchical-technocratic supranational politics of scale that had, before the war in Ukraine, driven apart member states supposed to grow into a United States of Europe. Moreover, the way the reins were tightened again and centralisation was restored in the course of the war suggests that supranational unification of sovereign nation-states is best pursued with the help of a common enemy as external and an imperial state as internal unifier: an imperial state capable of defining or even creating a common international security problem to be collectively addressed at a supranational level under imperial leadership – a matter of life and death, quite different from a voluntary renunciation of national sovereignty for economic prosperity and cosmopolitan comfort, and extremely dangerous to boot.

PART III

States and State Systems

7

Integration and Differentiation

No state ever exists by itself; 'the state' only exists in the plural form and in the company of other states. Democracy, in turn, exists only within states, and its existence depends on its state's internal constitution as well as its external relations. States, and the systems of states to which they belong, unify the diverse societies they rule and organise, or divide them up; they either integrate or differentiate. How this happens, how unity and diversity are related and allowed to express themselves, determines not just the stability of the state but also the possibility of democracy. In this chapter, I will attempt to identify some parameters of this relationship, which is all too often neglected in democratic theory.

Gibbon: Unity or Diversity?

Halfway through his monumental work *The History of the Decline and Fall of the Roman Empire* (1896–1900 [1776–1789]), Edward Gibbon, the eminent historian of the ancient world, reaches the point towards the end of the fifth century at which the Western Roman Empire expired.[1] Before he finally turns his attention to Byzantium, which

---

1 On Gibbon, see 'Edward Gibbon', wikipedia.org. The following paragraphs are based in part on my Adam Smith Lecture in Jurisprudence, given in 2018 at the University of Glasgow: Wolfgang Streeck, 'Reflections on Political Scale', *Jurisprudence* 10, no. 1 (2019), 1–14.

would last another thousand years, Gibbon pauses to look back over almost four centuries of Roman history and reflect on the lessons that might be learned for the instruction of present and future ages from the 'awful revolution' he had described.[2] After all, says Gibbon, 'it is the duty of a patriot to prefer and promote the exclusive interest and glory of his native country; but a philosopher may be permitted to enlarge his views, and to consider *Europe as one great republic*, whose various inhabitants have attained almost the same level of politeness and cultivation.'[3] Gibbon, by the way, was both a patriot and a European: he was for some time a member of the British House of Commons, though he never made a speech there, and of the Board of Trade, but he spent many years of his life in Switzerland, writing not just in English, which he mastered with incomparable elegance, but also in French. Indeed, according to an apocryphal source, he almost decided to write his masterpiece in that language.

Could such a tragedy as the collapse of the Western Roman Empire have also occurred in early modern Europe after the end of the Middle Ages? 'We may inquire, with anxious curiosity', writes Gibbon, 'whether Europe is still threatened with a repetition of those calamities which formerly oppressed the arms and institutions of Rome.' In answering this question, Gibbon shows himself to be a contemporary of the Enlightenment, someone who believed in the ultimately irreversible march of historical progress, despite his occasional penchant for melancholy irony. Gibbon offers three reasons why 'our general state of happiness, the system of arts, and laws, and manners, which so advantageously distinguish, above the rest of mankind, the Europeans and their colonies', can never be essentially injured. Firstly, the barbarian tribes, which penetrated into the Roman Empire in ever-repeated waves of conquest, had themselves become sedentary, as a 'happy consequence of the progress of arts and agriculture': 'Instead of some rude villages thinly scattered among its woods and morasses, Germany now produces a list of two thousand three hundred walled towns; the Christian kingdoms of Denmark, Sweden, and Poland have been successively established', and

---

2   Edward Gibbon, 'General Observations on the Fall of the Roman Empire in the West', in *The History of the Decline and Fall of the Roman Empire*, vol. 6, ed. John Bagnell Bury, New York: Fred de Fau & Co., 1906, chapter 38, 287–98, available at the Online Library of Liberty, oll.libertyfund.org.

3   Emphasis added.

even Russia 'now assumes the form of a powerful and civilised empire'. There were no longer hordes of barbarians wandering through Europe as in the time of the Great Migration. At most, there were a few 'Calmucks or Uzbecks', who could not seriously threaten Europe. Nevertheless, 'unknown dangers' might *'possibly* arise from some obscure people, scarcely visible in the map of the world', as had happened in the sixth century, when the Arabs, who 'had languished in poverty and contempt' for so long, began to conquer the world, after Mohammed had 'breathed into those savage bodies the soul of enthusiasm'.

Gibbon's second reason for European optimism is similar to his first. Their victorious wars, he says, enabled the Romans to make advances in culture and civilisation which undermined their ability to educate 'a race of soldiers'; this forced them to rely on barbarian mercenaries who later destroyed their state from within. Since then, however, there have been changes in military technology: 'Mathematics, chemistry, mechanics, architecture, have been applied to the service of war', and whoever wanted to win a war would not get very far now with martial valour alone. Science and technology are required instead, replacing military virtues and accelerating their decline. 'Cannon and fortifications now form an impregnable barrier against the Tartar horse; and Europe is secure from any future irruption of barbarians; since, before they can conquer, they must cease to be barbarous.' With this, Europe has become militarily invincible, despite having been demilitarised by civilisation, because the dependence of its potential conquerors on scientific and technological progress of their own compels them to become just as civilised and therefore just as incapable of making war in the old way as the Europeans.[4]

---

4 Gibbon thought that serious wars *within* the post-Roman state system of Europe were even more unlikely, because of the continent's division into a multitude of small independent states, which held each other in check, thereby maintaining an equilibrium within the system. In the worst case there would be 'temperate and indecisive contests' that would restrain European forces from larger undertakings. What Gibbon did not foresee was the impending replacement of small monarchies or republics by a few large states with imperial ambitions, accompanying the expansion of the capitalist mode of production during the nineteenth century. Still less could he have imagined that the slackening of the martial spirit brought about by civilisation would come with a development of techniques of destruction which made it possible to wage large-scale wars increasingly without human participation, or at least without any physical risk for the participating personnel.

Seen from today, the most interesting of Gibbon's arguments against
the possibility of a new 'decline and fall' of Western European civilisation is the third one, where he compares the political organisation of the
Europe of his time with that of the Roman Empire. Rome, he says, was
too big and too centralised. For one thing, 'the servile provinces, desti-
tute of life and motion, expected their safety from the mercenary troops
and governors who were directed by the orders of a distant court'; this
made them vulnerable. Moreover, in the Roman Empire 'the happiness
of a hundred millions depended on the personal merit of one or two
men . . . whose minds were corrupted by education, luxury and despotic
power'. All this had now changed, and the following key passage of the
text is worth quoting in full:

> Europe is now divided into twelve powerful, though unequal king-
> doms, three respectable commonwealths, and a variety of smaller,
> though independent states: the chances of royal and ministerial
> talents are multiplied, at least, with the number of its rulers . . . The
> abuses of tyranny are restrained by the mutual influence of fear and
> shame; republics have acquired order and stability; monarchies have
> imbibed the principles of freedom, or, at least, of moderation; and
> some sense of honour and justice is introduced into the most defec-
> tive constitutions by the general manners of the times. In peace, the
> progress of knowledge and industry is accelerated by the emulation of
> so many active rivals.

The division of state sovereignty between small political units, Gibbon
suggests, makes states and state systems more stable and more favourable to progress, and simultaneously more peaceful and more able to
defend themselves, than when they are combined together and centralised. In a state system where governmental power is decentralised,
misguided political decisions in one state only harm a part of the population of the system as a whole; the other states can insulate themselves
against their consequences. Another advantage of a decentralised system
is that it benefits from distributed intelligence; this makes it possible to
try out and compare different answers to similar problems, after which
the best solutions can be adopted by everyone. As a general illustration
of the superiority of divided state sovereignty in 'Europe as one great
republic', where variety is defended by internal borders but also kept

within limits by a common cultural legacy – what present-day systems theorists refer to as requisite variety – Gibbon makes use of a military thought experiment.[5] If, he writes, 'a savage conqueror should issue from the deserts of Tartary he must repeatedly vanquish the robust peasants of Russia, the numerous armies of Germany, the gallant nobles of France, and the intrepid freemen of Britain; who, perhaps, might confederate for their common defence'. Here, too, the divided Europe of Gibbon's day appeared superior to him to the civilisation of antiquity, otherwise so worthy of respect.[6]

Gibbon's issue in looking back on the 'awful revolution' of the fall of the Western Roman empire is, at its core, nothing other than the proper scale of territorial political organisation. Which political order is better for a region such as post-Roman Europe? Should it be unified and inclusive or subdivided? How should one draw the boundaries of sovereignty at which internal relations and institutions end and are replaced by international ones? Which social relations and transactions should be internalised by states and dealt with as internal matters, and which externalised and treated as foreign affairs? Gibbon's perspective on the political scale of states and state systems looks promising also with respect to current questions about the proper relationship between domestic and inter-state relations within encompassing architectures of sovereignty: consolidated or subdivided, integrated or differentiated, centralised or decentralised, ruled vertically or horizontally. Particularly useful in this respect is Gibbon's distinction between the European cultural space, understood as the totality of the national societies that emerged from the Western Roman Empire, and the European state

---

5   The phrase 'requisite variety' was coined by W. Ross Ashby (1903–1972), a psychiatrist and biochemist who also worked as a neuroscientist and was one of the pioneers of cybernetics. Ashby's 'law of requisite variety' states that 'for a system to be stable, the number of states that its control mechanism is capable of attaining (its variety) must be greater than or equal to the number of states in the system being controlled.' Quoted in John Naughton, 'Ashby's Law of Requisite Variety', response to annual question '2017: What Scientific Term or Concept Ought to Be More Widely Known?', edge.org.

6   It seems relevant in this context that Gibbon spent a large part of his life in Switzerland – a small state at the centre of the Western European state system and indubitably European in character, which, in order to accommodate the multicultural composition of its population, was divided into still smaller highly autonomous self-governing federal subdivisions. Before Gibbon started his magnum opus, he was working on a 'History of the Liberty of the Swiss', a project he subsequently abandoned.

system that organises it. The themes that this distinction brings to the surface include the distribution of sovereign authority within state systems; the accommodation of diverse societies by means of dispersed sovereignty; the relationship between cooperative and hierarchical coordination between and within a state system's member states, between international order through power and authority on the one hand and shared interests and a common culture and mutual observation on the other; the forms and results of competition between neighbouring states with common cultural roots; the limits of the integration of diverse societies or, put differently, the minimum level of cultural commonality or a shared 'way of life' required to ensure the cohesion of a state system, and the like.

Two and a half centuries after Gibbon, we observe a severe crisis in the project of economic and political 'integration' between the states which share the former territory of the Western Roman Empire, a project which was conceived as the precise opposite of Gibbon's plea for a Europe with dispersed rather than unified sovereign authority. In the language of its advocates, 'integration' means 'an ever closer union among the peoples of Europe', embodied more or less explicitly in a unified state organisation comprising Europe as a whole, with the United States of America often invoked as a model.[7] A broad movement of opposition to this has arisen, aimed at winning back control over each nation's collective destiny after it had drifted upwards and away. Restoration of control is to be achieved, if not by returning to smaller units of political sovereignty, then at least by re-empowering those units – by fighting not just a future European superstate but also the already-existing structures of unified and centralised rule not only at the European level but also within some of the states comprised by the European state system.

In what follows, I shall examine the questions of political scale raised by Gibbon from a historical-institutionalist rather than a presentist technical economics perspective. My concern – unlike that of the economic literature on the subject, which is not abundant but is, in parts,

---

7   The formula first appeared in the preamble to the Treaty of Rome (1957) which established the European Economic Community. Later, it was repeated again and again at various points in the succession of European treaties expanding on the Treaty of Rome.

highly stimulating – is not to establish a normative-prescriptive theory of the proper size of a state; to do this would suggest that it was possible to develop and apply a general formula for the optimal division of the world into reciprocally connected sovereign political units.[8] Nor is it my intention to contribute to a *positive-economic* theory of state and inter-state structures which see these as the result of a collective social pursuit of economic growth or efficiency – rather than as a (possibly inadequate) arrangement for the democratic embedding of a capitalism conceived as fundamentally crisis free and capable of continuous improvement. Instead, I shall begin with some simple quantitative parameters of the global state system after 1945, starting with the initially surprising circumstance that the increase in worldwide economic 'integration' was accompanied by *an increase and not a reduction* in the number of sovereign ('nation-') states that make up the global state system. After this, I relate the high and growing demand for state sovereignty that is expressed in this increase to the achievements of present-day sovereign states in internal and external social integration. In particular, I propose that we should see current demands for the decentralisation of large states and state systems in the context of a changed political economy of the capitalist world system, in which conflicts between classes can be fought, superficially but no less momentously in their political consequences, as conflicts between nations within the state system or between substate regions within states. I illustrate this context with a historical-institutionalist reflection on current separatist tendencies endeavours in Scotland and Catalonia compared with Germany, where the nation-state appears to be largely immune to regional separatism.

After that, I return to Karl Polanyi's 1945 article, mentioned above in chapter 1, in which he examined the prospects for the construction of a democratic political economy in Europe under the conditions of the international state system that had emerged from the Second World War. Polanyi's approach supplements the concept of the state system I

---

8   See, above all, Alberto Alesina, Enrico Spolaore, and Romain Wacziarg, 'Trade, Growth and the Size of Countries', in Philippe Aghion and Steven N. Durlauf, eds, *Handbook of Economic Growth*, vol. 1B, Amsterdam: Elsevier, 2005, 1499–542; and Enrico Spolaore, 'National Borders and the Size of Nations', in Donald A. Wittman and Barry R. Weingast, eds, *The Oxford Handbook of Political Economy*, Oxford: Oxford University Press, 2008, 778–98.

have drawn from Gibbon in that it adds the political-economic dimension of the relationship between democracy and capitalism – a theme
which could not yet play a role in Gibbon's time. It also, for reasons just
as obvious, offers a more precise fit to the conditions of present-day
Europe and the European process of integration and centralisation,
providing what I believe is a useful analytical framework for understanding the European political deadlock between neoliberal centralism
and democratic decentralisation, as it had evolved before the war in
Ukraine. Towards the end of the chapter, I shall introduce a distinction,
compatible with Polanyi, between confederal and imperial inter-state
systems, that lays the groundwork for my claim, to be developed in the
next chapter, that the forced integration of a state system with the aim of
amalgamating it into a single state cannot in the present world any
longer, and particularly in Europe, produce anything other than an
inter-state empire – or, more precisely, a would-be- or quasi-empire
committed to neoliberal convergence and therefore condemned to
failure in the longer term.

The Contemporary State System: A Survey

Since the end of the Second World War, there has been a constant
increase in the number of states in the global state system (fig. 18).[9]
The division of global society into sovereign states continued during the
era of accelerated 'globalisation' which began in the 1980s, so that they
now cover almost the whole of the earth's surface; in the six decades
between 1950 and 2010, the number of sovereign states more than

---

9   Similar Egbert Jahn, 'Die wundersame Vermehrung der Nationalstaaten im
Zeitalter der Globalisierung', in *Politische Streitfragen*, Wiesbaden: Springer, 2014,
13–31. As always, there are cases where classification is difficult. Is the part of Palestine
controlled by the Palestinian National Authority, based in Ramallah, a state, or even a
sovereign state? And what about Abkhazia? On the other hand, all doubtful cases
concern very small states, or non-states, and even if they were included, this would not
greatly affect the numerical outcome. Of the 91 sovereign states counted for 1950, only
60 were members of the United Nations. Among the non-members were Mainland
China, the German Federal Republic, and the German Democratic Republic. Of the 202
sovereign states in 2002, 192 belonged formally to the UN, ruling out any doubts about
their formal sovereignty under international law.

doubled.[10] The majority of them are small; their average population in 2010 was 34.0 million, as against 27.9 million in 1950. This was an increase of 22 percent, far less than the increase of 174 percent in the total population of the world. Owing to the extreme differences in size among the members of the state system, average population figures present a distorted picture of the reality of global small-statism: the median – the midpoint of the distribution of states by population size – was always below the arithmetic average. Today, despite a rise since 1980, it is no larger than 7.1 million, almost the same as it was in 1950.[11]

Figure 18. The global state system

	World population in millions	Sovereign states	Population per state in millions	
			Average	Median
1950	2,536	91	27.9	7.0
1960	3,035	120	25.3	6.3
1970	3,700	159	23.2	4.8
1980	4,458	177	25.9	4.9
1990	5,372	185	28.9	5.1
2000	6,143	202	30.4	5.6
2010	6,957	202	34.0	7.1

Sources: 'World Population in Millions': United Nations, World Population Prospects 2019, population.un.org. 'Sovereign states': the figures comprise members of the United Nations ('Growth in United Nations Membership', un.org), and other sovereign states ('List of Political Entities by Century', wikipedia.org). 'Population per state in millions (average and median)': Author's calculations, based on the United Nations Demographic Yearbooks and the World Bank World Development Indicators. If no data were available for the year in question, data for neighbouring years were used. The following alternative sources were used for some years in order to fill in gaps in the data: South African Police Service (for 1990); Statistisches Bundesamt (for 1980); US Census Bureau: International Database (for 1950). 1950 population statistics for the USSR were taken from E. M. Andreev, *Naselenie Sovetskogo Soiuza, 1922–1991*, Moscow: Nauka, 1993.

---

10   The most recent members to join the United Nations were East Timor, Montenegro, and South Sudan (Jahn, 'Die wundersame Vermehrung der Nationalstaaten', 7).

11   In other words, of the 202 states that exist today, half have a population smaller than 7.1 million.

Why this remarkable increase in the number of sovereign states since 1945? One reason is the end of colonialism. The colonial empires of the UK, France, Belgium, the Netherlands, and other states disappeared from the map during the reorganisation of the global state system after the Second World War. New, formally independent nation-states emerged, most of them constructed on the model of their former colonial rulers. Whereas in 1945 an estimated 703 million people still lived in mainly European colonies, five years later their number had already shrunk by more than half; in the 1990s, it had finally fallen to zero (fig. 19). One driving force in decolonisation was the United Nations, which early on set itself the goal of completing a globally encompassing state system. Another was the United States, which had always seen itself as a non-colonial and anti-colonial power and expected its global influence to increase with the dissolution of the European colonial empires into sovereign nation-states. In addition, there were the local national liberation movements, which the Soviet Union saw as allies in the worldwide struggle between capitalism and communism. Thus, the 1950s and 1960s became the great age of the emergence of independent states all over the world. A second wave followed after 1990, with the collapse of the multinational USSR

Figure 19. Population under colonial rule

	Number of people, in millions
1945	703
1950	324
1960	245
1970	223
1980	154
1990	168
2000	0
2010	0

Sources: Our World in Data, 'People Living in Democracies and Autocracies, World', ourworldindata.org; and A. Wimmer and B. Min, 'From Empire to Nation-State: Explaining Wars in the Modern World, 1816–2001', *American Sociological Review* 71, no. 6 (2006), 867–97.

and its empire in Eastern Europe, along with the associated dismemberment of multinational Yugoslavia. Just as in the case of decolonisation, the splitting up of the East European state system into individual sovereign states proceeded sometimes peacefully and sometimes accompanied by violence; the Balkan wars of the 1990s contrasted with the quiet subdivision of Czechoslovakia between Czechs and Slovaks, which was accomplished in an atmosphere of mutual amity.[12]

It is noteworthy that in the eventful three-quarters of a century since the end of the Second World War, there are almost no attempts, and no successful attempts, to combine two or more sovereign states into one, leaving aside German unification, which can certainly be considered a special case.[13] Some may still remember the project of a United Arab Republic, consisting of Egypt and Syria; the common state, founded in the name of pan-Arab unity, only existed for three years, from 1958 to 1961, and it broke up over the conflict between Egypt's ambitions for centralisation and Syria's preference for federalism.[14] Even among states with greater affinities than Egypt and Syria, voluntary unions have never been seriously planned, never mind accomplished; nothing is known of any desire by Italy, Spain, and Portugal to form a state called Mediterranea Latina, or by Sweden, Denmark, and Norway to create a Greater Scandinavia.[15] The European Union is not a counter-example,

---

12   On the latter, see Ivan Gabal, 'Czechoslovakia: The Breakup and Its Consequences', in Wojciech Kostecki et al., eds, *Transformations of Post-Communist States*, London: Palgrave Macmillan, 2000, 110–32. For a comparison between the dismemberments of the Soviet Union, Yugoslavia, and Czechoslovakia, see Valerie Bunce, 'Peaceful versus Violent State Dismemberment: A Comparison of the Soviet Union, Yugoslavia, and Czechoslovakia', *Politics and Society* 27, no. 2 (1999), 217–37.

13   After three decades, whether it was 'successful' continues to be a subject of passionate debate.

14   Elie Podeh, *The Decline of Arab Unity: The Rise and Fall of the United Arab Republic*, Brighton: Sussex University Press, 1999.

15   'In no case did there emerge from the populations of the French, British, Spanish, Portuguese, Dutch, Russian or Ottoman empires nation-states which tore down the boundaries between provinces with different legal status in the imperial state structure and replaced them with a common national state, whether centralised or federal' (Jahn, 'Die wundersame Vermehrung der Nationalstaaten', 16). A nation-state did arise after an extremely bloody struggle for independence in Algeria, an area which, according to the French view, had been incorporated into the territory of France; if one wishes, one may call this an example of failed multicultural integration. This category probably also includes Ukraine, which – or parts of which – had since the end of the tsarist and Habsburg empires resisted incorporation into both Poland and Russia. What

even though it was sometimes, particularly in Germany, seen as a first step on the way to an amalgamated and unified European state with integrated sovereignty. In actual fact, none of the member states entered the EU or its predecessors with the intention of giving up their national sovereignty; this includes the Federal Republic of Germany, which was in fact still semi-sovereign when it joined.[16] Their objective was rather the opposite: to defend their sovereignty, to recover it, or to realise it to the fullest extent. This goes without saying for the 'Kleinstaaterei', the small-statism of the three Baltic republics of Estonia, Latvia, and Lithuania. Having recovered their independence from the Soviet Union and Russia, they did not, for a moment, think of joining together to form a United Baltic Republic. Even if, as is sometimes asserted, the EU is all about a pooling or sharing of national sovereignty, ultimately this serves to maintain it, approximately in the same way the management of a business may agree to share its power with a works council in order to hold on to it.[17] In any case, it is exclusively the member states, as the 'masters of the treaties', which decide over their union's further development under a self-imposed rule of unanimity.[18]

What are the reasons for the high demand for state sovereignty on the part of small territorial societies and for their evident aversion to abandoning it once it has been achieved? One might well be that modern international law, under the pressure of the United Nations, gives better

---

is at stake in its present war with Russia, with the support of the 'West', is the preservation of a national sovereignty it achieved for the first time after 1990, accompanied by the domination within the country of the Ukrainian over the Russian ethnic group in particular. Going to war for national sovereignty would have been regarded, until the Russian invasion, as culturally retrogressive and politically illegitimate by Western, and particularly by German, globalists.

16   Peter J. Katzenstein, *Policy and Politics in West Germany: The Growth of a Semisovereign State*, Philadelphia: Temple University Press, 1987.

17   William Wallace, 'The Sharing of Sovereignty: The European Paradox', *Political Studies* 47 (1999), 503–21.

18   This point will be addressed in more detail below, when we deal with differences in size and power within 'Europe', particularly in the context of the relation between neoliberal capitalism and democracy. An appropriate concept to use here, as I shall argue, is that of 'empire'. As regards democracy in the context of the European institutions, the principle expressed classically by Jean-Claude Juncker continues to apply: 'There can be no democratic vote against the European Treaties' (interview, *Le Figaro*, 28 January 2015). Similarly, and also classically, see Wolfgang Schäuble's statements to Yanis Varoufakis in Yanis Varoufakis, *Adults in the Room: My Battle with Europe's Deep Establishment*, London: The Bodley Head, 2017.

protection to the sovereignty of states than ever before, so that it offers small states in particular a form of protection against the claims of larger neighbours and big empires; this makes it more attractive to organise states on a small scale. That guarantees of protection under international law do not always work was shown by the invasion of former Czechoslovakia by the Warsaw Pact countries under the leadership of the Soviet Union, which gave rise to the 'Brezhnev Doctrine' of the 'limited sovereignty' of socialist states, and also by numerous 'Western' interventions in countries such as Iran, Serbia (under the heading of a 'further development' of international law in the direction of a duty of the 'international community' to protect citizens against their own state, called a 'duty to protect'), Iraq, Syria, Afghanistan, and Libya, among others.[19] But this does not mean sovereignty, at least as a rhetorical and legitimating resource, is not demanded above all when a nation does not have at its disposal sufficient military means to defend its interests, particularly its independence. Palestine is one example. There, the Palestinian Authority, which is restricted to functioning as if it were a creature of Israel, although it is called 'autonomous', has attempted for many years to achieve international recognition as a state. It has failed for several reasons, the most important one being that the Israeli occupation authorities rightly fear that they would no longer be able to do as they wish in the occupied territories if their occupation regime were transformed into a relationship between two states.

While statehood promises autonomy towards the external world, internally it offers the possibility of democracy; therein lies the second ground for its legitimacy. Put briefly, the relationship between democracy and sovereignty is such that sovereignty without democracy is possible but the reverse is not. It is possible for states which have claimed and achieved a monopoly of the legitimate use of force within their territory to fall into the hands of warlords or drug cartels, which oppress the societies they rule as states and squeeze them dry as criminals. But, in principle, such states can be returned to democracy, in extreme cases by revolution, so long as this is not made impossible by outside imperial powers.

---

19   See, most recently, Philip Cunliffe, *Cosmopolitan Dystopia: International Intervention and the Failure of the West*, Manchester: Manchester University Press, 2020, on so-called 'humanitarian interventions' and the permanent state of war they have caused.

Figure 20. The number of democratic states

	Democracies according to . . .					
	Polity IV		Vanhanen/ Polyarchy	Varieties of Democracy	Democracy/ Dictatorship (Cheibub)	Boix- Miller- Rosato
	All	Full				
1950	23	18	35	25	38	35
1960	34	21	47	29	55	43
1970	34	19	48	38	40	41
1980	40	20	51	41	52	54
1990	54	27	78	57	70	71
2000	79	31	116	87	109	107
2010	92	31	n. d.	98	118	117

When to count a state as democratic is a subject of dispute, and over the years, political scientists have developed indicators for distinguishing democratic from undemocratic states, both in absolute terms (Is a state democratic? Yes or no?) and on a graduated scale (Is it more or less democratic?). Figure 20 presents the results of five classification attempts of this kind side by side; Polity IV and Vanhanen/Polyarchy classify states according to their level of democratisation, the other three distinguish between democracies and non-democracies. Details are irrelevant at this point; it is what the six time series have in common that is important. Five of the surveys include all democracies; the sixth only counts the subgroup of what it calls 'full democracies'. Among the former, the proportion of states ranked as democracies has risen more or less continuously since 1950, from an average of 34 percent across all five indicators for the 91 states counted in 1950 to 54 percent for the 202 states counted in 2010. Whatever lies behind these numbers in individual cases, the similarity of the values ascertained and the uniformity of the trend observed over time confirm the assumption that states, unlike the privately, mainly American-owned giant companies which today dominate the global economy, cannot always turn down demands for democratisation, which today emerge precisely in reaction to the domination of the world market by oligopolistic mega-companies.[20]

---

20   For example, the five internet giants, Alphabet, Amazon, Apple, Meta, and Microsoft, also referred to as the Big Five, somewhat in analogy to the Seven Sisters of

More difficult to estimate than the number of democracies is the number of 'failed states' – in other words, states which can no longer fulfil their function of preserving law and order, and which exist as territorial rulers only on paper.[21] 'Failed states' are neither sovereign nor capable of becoming democratic. The two main reasons why a state becomes dysfunctional are civil wars, often kept going by foreign imperial powers as proxy conflicts, and military interventions from outside which have failed to achieve their original objective of 'regime change' and transformed an orderly situation into anarchy. Examples include African states such as Somalia, the Congo, Libya, and Niger, and Central

Figure 21. Failed states

	Sovereign States	Failed States
1950	91	3
1960	120	10
1970	159	25
1980	177	30
1990	185	31
2000	202	27
2010	202	22

State failure is divided into three categories: political and ethnic wars, hostile regime change, and genocide/politicide. The figure represents all countries in which one of the three kinds of state failure is observed.

Source: Center for Systemic Peace, PITF State Failure Problem Set, 1955–2018, systemic peace.org.

---

the twentieth century (referring to the seven largest oil companies). In 2018, the Five had a total turnover of $1.5 trillion. This was slightly below the GDP of Indonesia, which had the sixteenth-largest economy in the world, and it equalled the combined GDP of the 101 economically smallest countries (out of a total of 191). If the Big Five were a single economy, their combined GDP would rank fourteenth in the world. An even starker picture would emerge if, for example, the ten largest companies in energy, finance, and food were added.

21 Surprisingly often, they owe their condition to military interventions by the 'West', under the leadership of the United States – as for example Libya, Iraq, and Afghanistan – interventions in the name of a post-authoritarian, American-led, rules-based, and democratic global order.

Asian ones like Afghanistan. How many currently existing states are dysfunctional in this sense depends in large part on the definition that is applied. In any case, figure 21 shows an increase between 1950 and 1980 in the number of states classified as dysfunctional, parallel to the rise in the total number of states but steeper in relative terms. After another thirty years, the number of failed states had fallen, from thirty to twenty-two, despite the continued increase in the total number of states – a fall from 17 to 11 percent in the total number of states.

What is close to impossible is to give a statistical presentation of the fact that state systems are less egalitarian than they should be under international law. I refer to groups of states with an asymmetrical distribution of power, and the dependency resulting from it, as 'empires'; the states that belong to them are formally equal in sovereignty, but some, namely those at the centre, are more sovereign than the others. The boundaries of 'empires' are often unclear; their precise demarcation must have been easier during the Cold War than it is today. At that time, two rival blocs of states, coupled together by imperial means, confronted each other: the Communist 'Eastern bloc' led by the USSR and 'the West', dominated by the US. Independent from both was a 'Third World' of Non-aligned nations, organised in 1961 on the initiative of Yugoslavia, Egypt, India, and Indonesia.[22] I shall return, at the end of this chapter, to the tension between state sovereignty and imperialism, in relation to present-day state systems and in the light of its relationship with capitalist globalisation; but, first, a few more remarks on the sociology and political economy of the so-called nation-state.

Metamorphoses of the Nation-State

The essence of the post-neoliberal stalemate is a blockade of politics between national and global systems, due to the fact that the battle over the future of the nation-state in an increasingly interconnected economic world has yet to be decided. In the discourse of a cosmopolitanism which sees itself as non- and anti-national, especially in Germany, it is

---

22   The Non-aligned state grouping continues to exist but has become less significant with the end of the Soviet empire. In 2012 it had 120 nominal members; there do not appear to be any more recent figures.

regarded as a foregone conclusion that 'the nation-state' had not only outlived its usefulness – all 'important problems', it is claimed, could be solved 'only internationally', leaving open precisely how and, above all, by whom – but also its ethical justification, in view of 'its' bloody history of internal dictatorship and external bellicosity. In this section, I shall briefly summarise why this view of history is not just oversimplified but also misleading.

First, the emerging nation-states of nineteenth-century Europe did not go to war against other nation-states but predominantly against the dynastic, and therefore strictly anti-nationalist, empires of their time, which were often the first to resort to arms to resist their disintegration into a multitude of small bourgeois 'people's states' (*Volksstaaten*, which was then the German translation of 'democracy', also used by Marx and Engels.) European nationalism was as much a liberation movement externally as it was a bourgeois-liberal democratisation movement internally. Its militarism was directed less against other nationalisms within the European state system – unless, like revolutionary France, it was attacked by the powers of the old regime, or nation-state formation was supressed by other, already-existing nation-states – than it was against the non-European outside world, when the new nation-states tried, with varying success, to become colonialist 'world powers', emulating of the activities of their dynastic predecessors in the early modern epoch. Therefore, leaving aside the not-inconsiderable group of the remaining enthusiasts of multinational empires such as the Ottoman and Habsburg Empires,[23] the bad reputation of the nation-state stems above all from the period after the First World War, when the victors, led by the US and France, proceeded to divide the defeated empires into nation-states according to the principle of 'national self-determination'.[24] In doing this, they looked for state borders which would also be national

---

23 With regard to the latter, see the 'pan-European' Otto von Habsburg, *Die Reichsidee: Geschichte und Zukunft einer übernationalen Ordnung*, Vienna: Amalthea, 1986, and the largely Austrian anti-nationalist economists who set themselves the goal of nothing less than the restoration of the economic liberalism of the Danubian monarchy in the form of a global neoliberal order (Quinn Slobodian, *Globalists: The End of Empire and the Birth of Neoliberalism*, Cambridge, MA: Harvard University Press, 2018). To that extent, the anti-nationalism of the present has a pro-imperialist past; as I shall later argue, it also has a pro-imperialist present.

24 Robert Gerwarth, *The Vanquished: Why the First World War Failed to End, 1917–1923*, London: Allen Lane, 2016.

borders, assuming, as a matter of course, just as the nations that they had liberated from the imperial 'prisons of the peoples', that nations had to be conceived as ethnic units.

As is well known, what might be described as a first attempt at global governance ended in large-scale ethnic cleansing and racist dehumanisation on a scale hitherto unthinkable. Nation-states were to be organised from above, their boundaries coinciding with those of nations, conceived, and conceiving themselves, as communities of biological descent. But almost no nation-state is ethnically homogeneous, nor can it be, unless it wants to be a dwarf state, and particularly if it is to emerge on the territory of a former multinational empire with an interspersed settlement structure, as for example in the Balkans. To paraphrase a bon mot falsely ascribed to Otto von Bismarck, nation-states (and laws) are often like sausages: it is better not to know how they are made. Before the Second World War, when repression was easily available for national unification, states could build nations instead of being built by them, in France more successfully than in Yugoslavia.[25] National wars (France under Napoleon, Germany under Bismarck – though in the latter case, due to the inheritance of the Old Reich, it was evident from the outset that only a federal state could emerge, not a centralised one) – and civil wars (the United States above all) were also helpful in establishing national unity, as was a good slap for schoolchildren who spoke their regional language in class. In the Second World War, then, the tensions between the imperial ambitions of various large nation-states that did not feel comfortable in a world ruled by the Anglo-Americans, together with the aggressive potential of culturalist and racist myths, used to legitimate internal repression and external expansion, resulted in a worldwide bloodbath of a previously unimaginable magnitude.

Today, three-quarters of a century after the end of the Second World War, the distinction between nation-states and nations should be firmly established, at least in Europe. *Nations*, or peoples, are historically grown *communities of experience and communication*. Their collective memories, laid down in a common language, establish collective identities, supported by inevitably 'monocultural' affective ties, built up from childhood, to a territory, a mother tongue, a dialect, a form of music, a

---

25   See, like many others, Eugen Weber, *Peasants into Frenchmen: The Modernization of Rural France, 1870–1914*, Stanford, CA: Stanford University Press, 1976.

diet. The more they are distinguished from their neighbours by them, the more they see themselves, and are seen by their neighbours, as particulars – Westphalians and Rhinelanders less than Tiroleans and Italians. *Nation-states*, in contrast, are *institutions*, constituted not necessarily by descent but by political and social struggles and rights of citizenship gained through them, including rights to democratic participation. Nation-states and nations are related, but they are almost never coextensive; almost everywhere there are exist non-identical linguistic, ethnic, or cultural enclaves, even if ethnic majorities are often unwilling to recognise this, or even refuse to do so at all. Moreover, boundaries between nation-states are almost always more or less arbitrary, and groups which feel themselves to be a nation, and want to be regarded as such, may find themselves in a nation-state which does not seem to them to be theirs, and therefore strive to establish a state of their own. Scotland and Catalonia are not the only examples of more or less powerful separatist tendencies in multi-ethnic European nation-states; I shall soon revisit them in more detail.

One means of preventing secessions from a multinational nation-state which is often, though not always, effective, is a federal constitution – the formula of success in Switzerland with its four ethnic groups, in Belgium (until now) with three, in Canada (since the 1970s) with two, and (until now) in India with its twenty-eight member states and twenty-three official languages.[26] In the years of peace after 1945, many European nation-states learned their lesson from the catastrophes of the inter-war period and responded, for the sake of internal harmony, to internal ethnic diversity with decentralisation and constitutionally guaranteed autonomy instead of denial and oppression, while, at the same time, keeping the peace with their neighbours by recognising their mutual historical boundaries and renouncing territorial claims – even where ethnic communities were split apart by state borders,[27] as for

---

26 Jahn, 'Die wundersame Vermehrung der Nationalstaaten'.

27 As laid down in 1975 in the Helsinki Final Act, by which the Conference on Security and Cooperation in Europe (CSCE) was set up. In the Final Act, the signatories committed themselves to respect their equal sovereignty, together with human rights, the inviolability of frontiers, the peaceful settlement of disputes, and non-intervention in the internal affairs of other states. The Organisation for Security and Co-operation in Europe (OSCE), which replaced the CSCE two decades later, took over the Final Act as its legacy.

example in Tyrol, also called Alto Adige, or the German-speaking enclave in eastern Belgium.[28]

However, federal constitutions were not the only, and probably not the most, important reason why the multinational nation-states of Western Europe have been spared for so long from separatist tendencies, especially since the delegation of rights to self-government can also produce the reverse of the intended result, by providing an institutional basis for secessionist movements and parties (about which I shall say more later). In this context, it is necessary to look again at the standard model of Western post-war democracy, which institutionalised class division as the most important line of social conflict, thereby pushing ethnic differences into the background or the underground. National trade unions and industrial umbrella organisations as well as a party system divided between a centre-right and a centre-left for everyone – for instance, for Spaniards both Castilian and Catalan – turned class conflict into a vehicle of nationwide social integration, even where parties and interest organisations wisely took account of regional diversity, ethnic or otherwise, by establishing appropriate organisational subdivisions for the legitimate articulation of subnational special interests.[29]

Just like the standard model of post-war democracy, and together with it, this arrangement has not withstood the triumphant progress of neoliberal internationalism. The transformation of the welfare state into a 'competition state', which acts as local enforcer of the unrestricted world market, has put a premium on collaboration between labour and capital, at the national and enterprise level.[30] But, under the neoliberal configuration, unlike the corporatist system of post-war democracy, this

---

28   In the poisonous atmosphere of Germany's nation-state 'discourse', it is advisable to point out that nothing in the above excludes the possibility of hybridisation at the boundary between two national communities. Indeed, it happens normally, without being a harbinger of full convergence. See today the case of the excellent cuisine of South Tyrol in which, after a (by and large) happy conclusion to a tragic history of conflict, dumplings and pasta are joined amicably, to everyone's advantage.

29   On integration through conflict, see Lewis Coser, *The Functions of Social Conflict*, Abingdon: Routledge, 1956.

30   See, among many others, Bob Jessop, 'From the Welfare State to the Competition State', in Patricia Bauer, ed., *Die Europäische Union: Marionette oder Regisseur? Festschrift für Ingeborg Tömmel*, Wiesbaden: VS Verlag für Sozialwissenschaften, 2004, 335–59.

does not take place on the equal footing of collective-conflictual negotiation but under the hegemony of capital, which has the last word, guaranteed by its property rights, over what is best for the competitiveness of 'the economy' and therefore for 'all of us'. Integration into classes through conflict is thus replaced by integration through competitive pressure into collaborative partnerships of diverse kinds, not only in the enterprise but also in the region.[31]

The formation of local competitive partnerships may produce or strengthen tendencies towards political independence from the nation-state; in extreme cases, this can put the territorial integrity of a multinational nation-state in question. There are various mechanisms which can contribute to this. In a more or less completed world market, the ability of a central state to redistribute internally between strong and weak regions is reduced. Internationally successful firms, at home in successful subnational regions, can resist national taxation in favour of lagging regions by pointing to the need to preserve their achieved competitiveness by large investments and competitive profits. As convincingly argued by Alberto Alesina et al., the indispensability of the national market for subnational regional economies declines as the national market becomes absorbed into the world market; national political integration loses attraction where it can be replaced by international economic integration without any downward redistribution through taxation.[32] Moreover, traditional non-economic – one might say subnationalist – motives for withdrawal and separation will, in open world markets, no longer be kept in check by economic interests.[33]

31   See, on this, Wolfgang Streeck, 'Von Konflikt ohne Partnerschaft zu Partnerschaft ohne Konflikt: Industrielle Beziehungen in Deutschland', *Industrielle Beziehungen* 23, no. 1 (2016), 47–60.

32   Alberto Alesina and Guido Tabellini, 'A Positive Theory of Fiscal Deficits and Government Debt', *Review of Economic Studies* 57, no. 3 (1990), 403–14; Alesina, Spolaore, and Wacziarg, 'Trade, Growth and the Size of Countries'. Note that the regional separatist parties of Scotland and Catalonia insist that, after their exit from their current (multi-)nation-states, they wish to remain members of the European Union, or in the case of Scotland, rejoin it – not, of course, to give up the sovereignty they have just won but to retain access to the European internal market. That market membership has a price in terms of national sovereignty has as yet played no role in the discussion – just as little as, in the case of Catalonia, the fact that the EU will admit a new member only if all existing members agree to this, which would include Spain.

33   There are analogies here in the relationship between nation-states and international organisations. The neoliberal nationalists among the advocates of a British

It is not just prosperous regions that can be tempted to cut the ties that bind them to a multinational state, form a sovereign nation-state of their own, and try their luck at an independent existence. Underperforming regions may arrive at the conclusion that they cannot count on any effective national redistribution in their favour within a 'competition state' driven by world market imperatives. Economic disparities between regions, measured in terms of income per capita, did in fact increase between 2000 and 2016; but it is not possible to establish a direct link between this and openly separatist political tendencies.[34] Where, in the past, the capacity for regional redistribution was not particularly strong, the higher overall growth that prevailed at the time tended to conceal this and to curb inter-regional distributional conflicts. But at present, high growth cannot be counted on. Apart from that, regional relative deprivation also occurs as a result of inadequate public investment in the national infrastructure connecting town and country as well as of worsening demographic conditions outside often booming urban centres; in income statistics, both are reflected at most indirectly.[35] Peripheral regions which have given up hope for anything more than symbolic support from the central government might turn to demanding a redistribution of jurisdictional authority, as a substitute for redistribution of resources. This could go as far as a push for substate or small-state autonomy, to enable them to identify and develop their special advantages, outside of nationally imposed restrictions, as a way of becoming more competitive internationally.

---

withdrawal from the EU never tire of declaring that, in view of the size and easy accessibility of the world market for a country free from the restrictions of European institutions and closely allied with the US as a door opener, membership in the EU is dispensable.

34   According to the OECD, regional disparities in income per capita decreased slightly between 2000 and 2016 in Finland, Portugal, Austria, and Ireland, where they were already low. In France, Greece, the UK, Poland, Hungary, and Turkey, where they started at a higher level, they increased considerably during this period. A differentiated assessment for Germany is found in Michael Hüther, Jens Südekum, and Michael Voigtländer, eds, *Die Zukunft der Regionen in Deutschland: Zwischen Vielfalt und Gleichwertigkeit*, Cologne: Institut der deutschen Wirtschaft, 2019. The situation is most dramatic in Italy. See OECD, *OECD Regions and Cities at a Glance 2018*, Paris: OECD Publishing, 2018.

35   On this see Julie Froud et al., *Foundational Economy: The Infrastructure of Everyday Life*, Manchester: Manchester University Press, 2018. For eastern Germany, see Chantal Mouffe, *On the Political*, Abingdon: Routledge, 2005; Steffen Mau, *Lütten Klein: Leben in der ostdeutschen Transformationsgesellschaft*, Berlin: Suhrkamp, 2019.

Centrifugal tendencies – politics-of-scale calls for federal decentralisation, regional autonomy, or sovereign statehood – are likely to be particularly troublesome to large states because their internal ethnic, cultural, and economic heterogeneity can be expected to be greater than that of small states, other things being equal. A centralised state finds it more difficult to deal with regional cleavages than with – comparatively simple – class divisions; as a rule, regional patterns of conflict are more complex than the binary line of division between the two main classes of capitalist society: labour and capital. In addition, conflicts between regions, unlike the conflict between classes, cannot be institutionalised by relocating them to a second, corporatist level of government, disburdening the state and allowing for bargained compromise. When even large states are no longer able to offer their regions access to their national markets as an incentive to national-state loyalty, because their national economies have become merged into the world economy, political repression is often the only instrument left for the defence of multinational cohesion and governing capacity when faced with escalating subnational claims for scarce national resources and jurisdictional independence. This could be one reason why in the heyday of globalisation around the turn of the century, several multinational states shifted to more authoritarian methods of government – for example, India, Turkey, the Philippines, Brazil, Russia, and indeed, in a different scale-political and geostrategic condition, the United States, with its political society split into two hostile camps.[36]

---

36   China is an interesting example. According to almost all outside observers, it is ruled in a more authoritarian fashion by its present president, Xi Jinping (in power since 2013), than under his predecessors. Having had the Chinese constitution changed, Xi can remain in office for life, and his 'Thoughts' must be studied by party members just as those of Chairman Mao had to be. A main part of his programme is the unconditional defence of the territorial integrity of the Chinese state. This does not just refer to Tibet, Hong Kong, and the Uighur 'Autonomous Region' of Xinjiang, but also to Taiwan, whose reincorporation into the mainland Xi has declared his central aim in life. Since the end of the civil war, the government of Kuomintang-ruled Taiwan has agreed with the Communist government on the mainland, if on nothing else, that there can be only 'One China', and that the only issue was which is its legitimate government, the Kuomintang in Taipei or the CCP in Beijing. After mainland China turned capitalist in its own distinctive way, the Kuomintang declared itself ready to agree with the CCP on using their common 'One China' doctrine as a vehicle for national reunification. The result, however, was that it lost its majority to a party whose supporters consider Taiwan, integrated into the world market, as part of 'the West' and resist reunification with the

Statehood and the Constitutive Particularism of Human Socialisation

There are many reasons why a large unitary state that joins different societies together into a single unit in a universalistic fashion is incapable of functioning, or can function only if supported by repressive political power, which is a precarious basis in the long term. They all lead back to the constitutive particularism, or pluralism, of human socialisation, which I should now like to examine more closely because it is fundamental to my argument.[37] In contrast to other animals, who inhabit a closed 'world' limited to their own species, humans are *weltoffen*, or 'open to the world'.[38] What kind of world they will live in is not yet decided when they are born. The organic substrate on which humanity grows is largely uninstructive; the *differentia specifica* of the human species is its lack of natural specificity. No other animal appears in such a variety of forms as the human animal: a human baby, whenever or wherever it is born, can grow up as a Tibetan monk or a Greenland whale-hunter, as a Philippine fisher, an African camel nomad, a Scottish labour lawyer or a New York taxi driver, even as a Rhinelander or a Westphalian, *and still remain a member of the same species.*[39] Everything, or pretty well everything, that characterises humans in their respective

---

mainland. The new Taiwanese nationalism, which has replaced the Chinese nationalism of the Kuomintang and led to considerable tension with the People's Republic, must be seen in the context of the conflict over Hong Kong. There a population which is similarly integrated with the world market disputes, or attempts to dispute, the prospect held out by the Beijing government of the territory's definitive incorporation into the People's Republic after 2047, when its special status and its autonomy expires.

37   This is in line with writers like Chantal Mouffe (*On the Political*) and Dani Rodrik (*Has Globalization Gone Too Far?*, Washington, DC: Institute for International Economics, 1997), who make this the starting point of their critique of 'globalisation'.

38   The concept derives from the German tradition of philosophical anthropology, going back as far as Johann Gottfried Herder. It occupies a central position in the thinking of Max Scheler, Arnold Gehlen, Helmuth Plessner, Martin Heidegger, and, outside of Germany, Jean-Paul Sartre. Common to all its usages is the notion of the human species as one of 'deficient beings' (*Mängelwesen*) who, lacking in instinct, have to create their rules themselves collectively because nature will not do this for them.

39   A newborn child of the Cro-Magnon people, who inhabited Europe for some 40,000 years, from the last Ice Age until roughly 12,000 years before the Common Era, would grow up inconspicuously in a present-day family and blend into 'modern' society without difficulty.

shape could also be different, depending on the society into which an as-yet-unformed person enters. This is what Aristotle means when he speaks of man as a *zoon politicon*: a social (*not* political) animal, who, as Marx notes following Aristotle, 'can only separate himself in society', where 'separate' means 'become an individual'.

The unimaginable diversity of forms which is characteristic of humanity is 'natural' only to the extent that human nature has handed over the realisation of its respective manifestations to the process of socialisation; this is what renders human existence a *social* and not (just) a biological fact. The socialisation of a human individual proceeds in historical space and time under the influence of fellow human beings socialised into contingent cultural traditions and institutional orders. Characteristic of these is that, in their local contexts, they congeal into distinct societies which, under modern conditions, can more or less easily constitute themselves as (nation-)states. There is no need here to examine the source of the differences between societies and to account for them in each individual case; adaptation to geographical conditions certainly plays a role, as does the limited reach of human action, experience, and praxis. Other factors would include 'accidental' events at historical turning points now far in the past, the, always debatable, authoritative interpretation of inherited cultural values, and traditions in general which can always be revised and revitalised, although never in their entirety, and in most cases only with the means provided by the tradition itself. What is important here is that however contingent the institutionally crystallised, identity-forming substance of a society, its 'way of life' (which is not, as just pointed out, biologically determined), once it exists in the world, cannot easily removed from it. Contingent yes, but not disposable at will.

It is important to understand what this does *not* mean. It does not mean, to begin with, that identities, individual as well as collective, are set in stone. The historical forms humanity takes are always in a state of flux, socially and individually. No identity, no way of life, is without its contradictions or so firmly fixed that it cannot be changed by coming into contact with other identities and ways of life; to that extent even the socialised human being, like the institutionally integrated society, remains capable of change and therefore of development. Human beings can learn, more or less successfully, to live in another society than 'their own' and to get along within it, without feeling excessively 'other' or suffering from too much 'homesickness'. Of course, different individuals and societies are differently suited to secondary socialisation and integration, and, even in the best case, an element of strangeness, identifiable on both sides, almost always remains.[40] One can argue over what is more changeable, cultural habitus or institutional structure, as long as one does not forget that the contingent character of socialisation does not mean, inversely, that its constructions can be remodelled at any time, by cultural imperialists coming from outside.[41] History brims with examples of adopted identities being defended to the death – including that of the defender. Outsiders – people whose equally contingent identity happens to be different – may regard it as senseless, or even utterly insane, when someone would rather starve or allow themselves to be tortured and executed than eat pork. But when people find it incompatible with their dignity to value their life over their identity, what is being defended is not so much the latter – which after all is not 'natural' and therefore not the only possible one – as their autonomy *in relation to it*: their right, themselves, to determine whether and in what direction they want to change, *according to principles that are a part of their identity*.

The same applies to societies, and probably to even a greater degree. Societies are complexes of institutions which have historically grown together to become interdependent, often but not always bundled together, formalised, defended, and revised within states and by them. As such, they are more or less well adjusted to their social and natural environment, the limits set by it, and the opportunities it offers. The institutions more or less coherently combined in a given society demand compliance from their members, sometimes, but not always, backed up by a state with a monopoly of the use of force. Members, in turn, identify more or less with the society to which they regard themselves, and are regarded by others, as belonging. For them, 'their' society is, in normal and stable situations, a repository of reliable, obvious truths, a reservoir

---

40   Very few people would be able, like the Pole Józef Teodor Nałęcz Konrad Korzeniowski, later Joseph Conrad (1857–1924), to emigrate to a foreign country and became one of its greatest writers in his adopted language.

41   But this is exactly what is assumed by integration enthusiasts, particularly in Germany, as if societies consisted only of positive laws that can be changed by decree at any time, and did not also include informal relations, identities, and continuities to which individuals are emotionally committed. Habermas himself, as noted earlier, repeatedly refers to 'ways of life' which need to be defended, and are defended even where they are considered illegitimate by progressive identity technologists.

of routines one can and should follow without question, routines which 'people like us' can use to manage our daily lives – which are not free from contradictions but pragmatically compatible with each other. Institutions so crystallised, reciprocally nested in unique geographical and temporal configurations, are also subject to change, but, like the individuals formed by them, they have for this programmes of their own, which they prefer to externally dictated one-size-fits-all formulas.[42]

To sum up, the constitutive particularism of social life does not render multinational statehood impossible, provided the social diversity covered by its overarching structure remains within limits. The more varied the societal landscape covered by a multinational nation-state, the more precarious that state becomes. Beyond a certain level of differentiation, the only solution is decentralisation – or, if this is not desired, force, to the extent that it is available. Particularly when cohesion is sought through decentralisation, much, if not everything, depends on institutional subtleties and details, the manifold ramifications of which cannot be investigated here. There must also be a good measure of 'statecraft', of *virtù* and *fortuna*, skill and luck, if a heterogeneous structure is to be put together and held in place. In the following, I propose to illustrate the complexity of the problem *ex negativo*, as it were, looking at two examples of actually existing regional secessionism within two established multinational states, the United Kingdom and Spain, and one case of *non-existent* separatism in Germany, where regional separatism failed to arise. The examples, I argue, show how complex and historically improbable the institutional conditions are for a stable naturalisation and the prevention of subsequent self-denaturalisation of diversity in a modern nation-state. As mentioned earlier, similarly strong *upward* tendencies out of the nation-state, in the direction of a supranational superstate, are nowhere to be seen; it is differentiation, not integration, that nation-states need to contain politically, and can contain only under favourable conditions.[43]

---

42   Vernon Bogdanor, *Beyond Brexit: Towards a British Constitution*, London: I. B. Tauris, 2019, offers an impressive reconstruction of the crystallisation of local institutional traditions into a uniquely configured nation-state, which, owing to this complex internal interdependence, stubbornly retains its character through all the changes it undergoes.

43   The war in Ukraine set the seal on the failure of the Russian attempt, as far back as Stalin, to integrate the Russian empire more or less forcibly through russification,

Excursus I: Scotland and Catalonia

Scotland and Catalonia are the two European nations in which sub-nation-state nationalism has found its strongest recent expression.[44] In a fascinating book, the British historian John H. Elliott has traced their common features back to the fifteenth century.[45] Spain and the United Kingdom were historical monarchies which grew by conquering neighbouring regions and later expanded into colonial world empires. Their internal unity was always fragile. Long centuries filled with conflicts and disappointments over the right and just relationship between the central state with its citizens, on the one hand, and the provinces and their ethnically more or less diverse inhabitants, on the other, have left behind a rich stock of constantly reinterpreted traumatic memories on both sides, which colour their mutual relationship right up to the present. Scotland in the United Kingdom and Catalonia in Spain are only the most extreme cases of a conflict between centre and periphery which is present in other regional nations as well: for example, Wales and Northern Ireland in the United Kingdom, Andalusia, Galicia, and the Basque Country in Spain.[46]

What are the particular characteristics shared by Catalonia and Scotland that make the drive towards separatism so strong there at present?

------

aimed not least at denying rival powers such as Germany access to its territory. From the Russian point of view, Ukraine's present endeavour to build a sovereign nation-state of its own is tantamount to an attempt at secession, with the help of foreign powers. Today, the United States occupies the place of Germany in this scenario. Whereas Germany hoped to annex Ukraine as the 'granary of the Reich', the US sees the country as a building block in a ring of states stretching from Asia to Northern Europe encircling Russia.

44   Leaving aside Belgium, where, despite economic success, the Flemings continue to feel exploited and undervalued by the Walloons. The (multi-)national state of Belgium seems to be held together only by its large public debt, which nobody knows how to divide, and the city of Brussels, which is largely francophone but located in the Flemish part of the country.

45   J. H. Elliott, *Scots and Catalans: Union and Disunion*, New Haven, CT: Yale University Press, 2018.

46   By which I mean: nations, perceived as such by themselves, that have not achieved a nation-state of their own but are governed within a multinational nation-state that may contest their claim to full nationhood, as it would ultimately imply a claim for full nation-statehood. Many Scots, Welsh, and Irish speak in this sense of four nations comprised by the United Kingdom, including the English (many of which, identifying with the United Kingdom as a whole, reject the perception of themselves as a subnational nation in a multinational nation-state like the three others).

Elliott reports how in both countries a long history of conflict over integration and autonomy, over squandered and stolen sovereignty, nourished collective feelings of discrimination and marginalisation on the emerging nation-state periphery. Associated with these were collective memories of missed historical opportunities which could be activated at any moment, in which the central state – Castile in Spain, England in the United Kingdom – with its people figures as a permanent adversary, acting openly or in the background, and aiming to humiliate those on the periphery and rob them of their freedom.[47] In times of economic prosperity, the desire for independence increased, giving rise to a feeling of confidence that one could go it alone. This was so in Scotland during its industrial heyday in the nineteenth century, and in Catalonia at the end of that century when it became the centre of Spanish industry and the driving force in the country's cultural modernisation, and then again in Scotland during the oil boom of the 1980s and 1990s. But it also grew in times of economic crisis, during which the feeling could and repeatedly did emerge in the two provincial nations that the central government could have prevented the crisis, or at least lessened its impact, but was less concerned about the periphery than about its own regional or ethnic base – just as it laid hands on the wealth of the two provinces during periods of prosperity, for example when the British government took control of Scotland's North Sea oil, with the belief widespread among Scots that they could have made better use of the proceeds than the English.[48]

---

47   Particularly traumatic for Scotland was the Darién adventure: an attempt, at the end of the seventeenth century, to create a Scottish colony in present-day Panama, as the first step to a Scottish colonial empire which would compete with the English one. The enterprise was conducted by a joint-stock company especially set up for the purpose, in which the population of Scotland had invested their savings – between one-quarter and one-half of the liquid capital available in the country. It failed, or, as one might say today, it crashed. Among the reasons for this catastrophic outcome were the refusal of the Anglo-Scottish crown to stand by the colony, as well as the hostile manoeuvres of the (English) East India Company, which could not really be expected to welcome Scottish competition. In the end, Scotland was faced with state bankruptcy. A few years later, in 1707, it had to agree to the *Act of Union* with England, by which England took over Scotland's national debt and incorporated the country into a customs union with its own colonies.

48   Financial subventions to the periphery by the central government, of the kind that in the case of Scotland have regularly flowed from Westminster to Edinburgh since the nineteenth century, with the explicit aim of taking the political wind out of the sails

Still, according to Elliott, all this is not enough to explain why separatist forces in both would-be states became so popular and powerful in the 1990s. As far as Scotland is concerned, Elliott points to the end of the British Empire in the second half of the twentieth century. Like the collapse of the Spanish Empire approximately a hundred years earlier, this necessitated a redefinition of the role of the British state in the world, including a rethinking about its internal structure. Scotland, the Scots, and, not least, Scottish regiments had played a disproportionately large part in administering and defending the empire, from which they also profited economically. A further factor was Britain's turn towards Europe, leading to its integration into the European internal market which took the place of the free trade zone of the vanished empire. There also was the international peace order based on the Western alliance after the Second World War, under which a state, at least in Europe, did not necessarily need to be large to defend its right to national self-determination. All of this culminated in the inclusion of the European market in the course of 'globalisation' in the developing world market, which once again cast doubt on the role of the nation-state, in Britain as in Spain, and not only because it made even access to a large national market appear economically unnecessary.[49] As Elliott points out, as a result of denationalisation, 'old institutions were everywhere being questioned by voters who had had enough of governments that appeared incapable of finding answers to the challenges of globalisation, economic crisis, the power of supranational companies and organisations, and widespread social inequality.'[50] Elliott continues: 'Separatism appeared to

---

of the demand for autonomy, have been unable to eliminate the suspicion of the Scots that they are being exploited. A similar phenomenon can be seen in the former GDR, many of whose citizens see themselves as victims of West German robbery, which the financial transfers under the 'Rebuilding the East' (*Aufbau Ost*) scheme are simply aimed at concealing. Exactly the same argument could be expected if financial transfers within the EMU from Germany to Italy were to become normal.

49   As mentioned above, for a while both the Catalan and the Scottish separatists hoped to remain in the EU, including its Monetary Union, or, in the Scottish case, to rejoin the EU as full members, once they would have left their respective nation-states. The 'nationalist' exit of Britain from the EU has had the paradoxical consequence that the Scottish separatists could combine their own 'nationalist' exit from the United Kingdom with a desire to continue as members of the multinational EU: supranationalism to promote nationalism. In a more general sense, this is an art the established member states of the EU also master.

50   Elliott, *Scots and Catalans*, 267.

offer an easy answer to those who felt they had lost control over their lives. Independence would allow them once again to be masters in their own house.'

Elliott suggests yet another reason why regional separatism in Britain and Spain – two monarchies and former colonial empires assembled around a hegemonic central state – should have become so powerful in reaction to 'globalisation'. Both democratic post-Franco Spain and Europe-oriented postcolonial Britain had tried since the 1970s to take the wind out of the sails of regional demands to be released from their respective multinational states by granting their subnational regions ever more powers of self-government within them. Far from containing regional separatism, however, 'devolution' in Britain, just as constitutional guarantees of Catalonia's status as an 'autonomous community' in Spain, actually consolidated it, as the institutions of regional self-government conceded from above soon became a basis of power for separatist movements from below. This was so, in particular, during the decades of accelerated internationalisation, when the traditional parties of the centre-left and centre-right lost popular support, in Britain and Spain as in other capitalist democracies.

In both Catalonia and Scotland, this resulted in a takeover of the newly created representative institutions by regional parties. Thus, in Scotland, support for the Conservatives 'collapsed' in the 1980s under Thatcher, while the same happened to support for the Labour Party in the 2000s under Blair, which made it possible in 2007 for the Scottish National Party to become, in effect, something like a Scottish regional state party.[51] In Catalonia the same had happened earlier when the social democratic Spanish Socialist Workers' Party (PSOE) and the conservative People's Party (PP), the two pillars of the Spanish party system after Franco, were driven out of the regional parliament, having to make way for Catalan regional parties. In both regions today, movements whose radical wings, which aim at full sovereignty, enjoy the support of at most half the electorate are able to speak for the whole population of their part of the country thanks to their control of the regional executives. According to Elliott, in the long history of the two states-in-waiting, this makes their separatist projects more promising than ever.

---

51 Ibid., 266–7.

There is no simple answer to the question of why devolution in Scotland and autonomy in Catalonia have sharpened rather than mitigated the conflict over national unity. It is noticeable that unlike, for example, in Canada, where in the 1970s a radical federalisation of state institutions successfully pacified the separatist movement in Quebec, in Spain and in the United Kingdom the historical central states, Castile and England, remained exempt from complete federalisation, as a result of which the constitutional edifice that emerged became asymmetrical.[52] In Canada, by comparison, strict attention is being paid to ensuring that the English-speaking part of the country does not appear privileged in any respect. Further clues to understanding the centrifugal tendencies in multinational states and state systems may be found by looking at Germany, in an effort to explain why in that country there is not, and has not been, a similarly virulent separatism as in Catalonia and Scotland.

Excursus II: Germany in Comparison

As such, there has been no lack of separatism in German history – not in the Rhineland and not, above all, in Bavaria. That, unlike Scotland and Catalonia, separatist tendencies have not become stronger in the last three decades cannot be explained by the absence in both regions of a separate language. Like Bavarian in Bavaria, Celtic languages have long since gone out of everyday use in Scotland (as also in Northern Ireland and Wales), but this has not stood in the way of the advance of Scottish (and also Northern Irish and Welsh) separatism. In Germany, as in Britain, speech is coloured by dialect, and this has given rise to mockery or even discrimination against the speaker, but there is no comparison with the suppression of the Catalan language by Castilian

---

52   In the United Kingdom, there are different devolution regimes for the four parts of the United Kingdom. While a regional parliament was conceded to Scotland, Wales, and Northern Ireland, England alone is ruled by the Westminster parliament which is responsible for the United Kingdom as a whole. While the UK Parliament is dominated numerically by England, it includes Scottish, Welsh, and Northern Irish MPs, who were at the time of writing predominantly members of their regional parties. In Spain, every autonomous or semi-autonomous region negotiates its status individually with the central government in Madrid.

central governments, particularly under Franco. In the mainly Catholic Rhineland, separatism was not fuelled by language either; the dominant factor here was the religious conflict with Protestant Prussia, which culminated at the end of the nineteenth century in what is known as the kulturkampf. Elements of it still survived into the years after the First World War, as represented by the Rhenish League (Rheinbund). Konrad Adenauer, mayor of Cologne at the time, was suspected throughout his life by his opponents, above all the more Protestant-oriented Social Democrats, of having worked after the 1918 defeat for a separation of the Rhineland from the Reich, possibly even with the aim of joining France (in spite of its constitutional laicism). After 1945, that problem was resolved, among other things, by the division of Germany, which made the Catholics the majority of the West German Federal Republic; this found its political expression in the merging of the Catholic Centre Party (Zentrumspartei) into Adenauer's Christian Democratic Union (CDU) which united Catholics and Protestants and managed to lead the West German government without interruption from 1949 to 1969. There was also the influx into the territory of the Federal Republic of around 10 million refugees and expellees from Germany's eastern provinces and the German Democratic Republic (GDR), adding to the roughly 40 million that had survived the war in the West. The new arrivals broke up the more or less closed, homogenous regional societies and were intent on integration rather than separatism.

As far as Bavaria is concerned, it had long resisted entering the emerging Prussian-led German nation-state, until Bismarck used the bankruptcy of King Ludwig II – compare Scotland in 1707! – to buy the country in by offering it financial relief. Even so, anti-Prussian resentment over the loss of state independence persisted in Bavaria; it was not a coincidence that Hitler began his career in Bavaria with the Munich beer cellar putsch of 1923. After the Second World War, fear prevailed in the Bavarian member state of the young Federal Republic of the powers of an excessively centralised federal government; that is why in 1949, 101 of the 174 members of the Bavarian Diet, following a recommendation by the Bavarian state government, voted against the Grundgesetz, the provisional constitution of the new West German state. Later, the initially strong and openly separatist Bavaria Party (BP) was driven into insignificance by the Christian Social Union (CSU), with the help of an ingeniously exploited peculiarity of the West

German party system. This made it possible for the CSU to set itself up as both an independent political party and a 'sister party' (rather than a provincial branch) of the CDU – an arrangement under which it put forward candidates exclusively in Bavaria while the CDU, in return, refrained from participating in Bavarian elections, whether for the state or the federal parliament (Landtag or Bundestag). The result was a strong position for the CSU both in Bavaria, where it monopolised the conservative side of the political spectrum, and in the Federal Republic as a whole, where, from Adenauer to Merkel, the CDU was unable to form a government without the CSU. As a federal party, the CSU thus secured a grip on the federal budget in Bonn and later in Berlin – for example through the Ministry of Transport, which it customarily occupied as the third coalition party – which, in turn, enabled the CSU as a regional party, which ruled Bavaria for many years with an absolute majority, to convert its federal state from a land of poor peasants into the richest territorial state in the Federal Republic in an unprecedented process of modernisation, while, at the same time, defending its distinctive cultural and political character and identification (often referred to as 'laptop and lederhosen').

Things were also made easier by the fact that Bismarck had conceived the German nation-state right from the outset as a federation, in line with a tradition that reached back to the Middle Ages, and that he had excluded Austria – the, if primarily ceremonial, central authority in the Old Reich since 1648 – from participating in the foundation of the new one. As a result, the German Reich, unlike Spain or the United Kingdom, was not put together through the feudal attachment of additional nations to a monarchical core state but was based from the outset on a constitution. That constitution was, it is true, initially monarchical, and there was in fact a powerful hegemonic state, Prussia; at the same time, however, the new German nation-state was constituted as an all-German Reich and not an extension of Prussia, in which the Prussian king, while serving as German emperor, stood side by side with the rulers of the other member states, who occupied a position of formal equality. In addition, there was the institution of the Bundesrat, a second chamber in which Prussia was in principle no more than one member among others. Even this configuration might possibly have led at some point to conflict between centre and periphery; but, unlike Britain and Spain, the German monarchy had in 1918 to give way to a new republican constitution cast from a single mould, which replaced it as the unifying link between the peoples of the Reich. Later, after the short-lived imposition of a single centralist superstate by the Nazis, those who drew up the West German constitution were able – and were also obliged, owing to the demands of the Allies and the division of Germany – to resort to specifically German traditions of federalism, in particular the Bundesrat with its powerful role for the member states in national government. The dissolution of Prussia by the Allies in 1945 also ensured that the formal egalitarianism of the new German federal constitution could no longer be annulled de facto by one all-powerful member state. It is true that German federalism did, and does, allow responsibilities and tasks to migrate upwards to the national level, against, in particular, Bavarian resistance, which was sometimes successful and sometimes not; but this always happened with the agreement of the Bundesrat, *hence of the Länder as part of the national government.* Lately, demands by federal states for more autonomy seem to be on the rise; to the extent that this is so, they may be seen as the – watered-down – German equivalent of the separatist tendencies evident elsewhere in Europe.

Of more recent origin is the increasing cleavage between the five federal states which emerged in 1990 from the GDR and West Germany, which, in the course of reunification, incorporated them in the Federal Republic as *neue Länder* (new states). Like in Scotland and Catalonia, there seems to exist in the former GDR something like a collective trauma, to do with the loss of more or less sovereign independence and a feeling of cultural disparagement by the majority society. As in Bavaria and Scotland, here, too, the newly incorporated part of the country depended on economic renovation in the course of being taken over; initial feelings of gratitude quickly gave way to a sense of having fallen into foreign hands, especially as, with time, economic convergence came to a standstill – which did not ease the suspicion of having been betrayed, and the feeling of being looked down on.

It is worth noting that in the last few years, a separate party system, different from that in West Germany, has begun to take shape in the *neue Länder*, much like in Scotland and Catalonia. The Social Democratic Party of Germany (SPD) and CDU, the traditional parties of the centre-left and centre-right in the Federal Republic, are losing support, while the party of the left (Die Linke), the successor of the communist Socialist Unity Party (SED) and for a short time an East German regional party, has collapsed as well, probably because of its increasingly West German orientation. This gives Alternative for Germany (AfD) the hope of moving, as a new regional party, into the centre of a new East German party system. It seems unlikely, however, that the consolidation of the latter will support separatist movements as strong as those in Scotland and Catalonia, where they have far-deeper historical roots and were virulent long before the collapse of the old party system. Moreover, the former GDR was divided at unification into five federal states eager to maintain their autonomy, while the AfD is a *German* nationalist party, not an East German nationalist one.

What can be learned from this for the difference, and perhaps the choice, between small- and large-statism? First, that institutions are as important as they are tenacious. Moulded by formative events at critical turning points, and in place over long stretches of historical time extending far beyond the horizon of those who have created them more or less intentionally, they are an inheritance that societies can reject only with difficulty, at the price of unforeseeable risks for their stability.[53] Multinational states wishing to defend their unity are either supported or obstructed by the foundational history of their institutions; it is not in their power to simply get rid of it. Unforeseen events or new developments may help, but only in conjunction with a historical institutional substructure which they can modify but never clear out of the way. As far as the cohesion of its nation-state is concerned, Germany has, exceptionally, been lucky with its history, unfortunately, perhaps, for its neighbours; whereas Spain and Britain have been unlucky with theirs, as was apparent at the latest by the end of the twentieth century, when the politics of globalisation put the integration of large states to the test.

What holds for the *avoidance of separatism* holds also, inversely, for the *enforcement of integration*. *Imperial* integration, dictated by powerful core states, is unstable, particularly when the use of force is out of the question. *Federalist* integration seems more promising, but only when institutional traditions do not stand in the way and the states that are to be united can share in the federal government in the framework of a participatory pluralism; how much integration this leaves depends on the circumstances as much as on the skill of the unifying elites. *Monistic*,

---

53   Stephen D. Krasner, 'Sovereignty: An Institutional Perspective', *Comparative Political Studies* 21 (1988), 66–94.

unitary state integration takes a long time to grow – in France it took centuries[54] – and when it is imposed rapidly, in a revolutionary manner, on a social landscape riven with pluralistic fissures, as happened in Italy during the Risorgimento, there is a danger, if not of separatism then of partial ungovernability.[55]

---

54   Alexis de Tocqueville, *The Old Regime and the French Revolution*, New York: Anchor, 1983 [1856].

55   In Germany, the United States is often invoked as a counterexample, a model for the voluntary unification of a number of diverse states into a single large democratic state, and a beacon lighting the way to the longed-for coalescence of the European nation-states into a future 'United States of Europe'. This ignores, firstly, how little consolidated and how relatively similar the thirteen British (and only British!) colonies in North America were, which declared their independence in 1776 and joined together in 1788 to form a federal state. Secondly, the establishment of a strong federal state – the US-American 'Hamilton Moment' – was only possible against the opposition of a democratic grass-roots movement which was deeply entrenched in some of the states. Opponents rightly suspected that the aim of Alexander Hamilton and the 'Federalists' was to ensure the continued dominance of a 'democracy-sceptic' aristocracy by way of constructing a large centralised state – a project that they tried in vain to prevent by putting forward the rival project of a confederate rather than federal state structure (Dirk Jörke, *Die Größe der Demokratie: Über die räumliche Dimension von Herrschaft und Partizipation*, Berlin: Suhrkamp, 2019, 66ff). Thirdly, the other states of the US that later were included in the federation – in other words, the great majority of today's member states – were founded from above by the central government after 1788, through the conversion of the 'territories' established by it into states that never had the option of refusing to join the Union. That same option was also denied to what are today called the 'Native Americans' and in Canada the 'First Nations' (!); their assigned form of political organisation was not a federal state, located on the traditional territories of which they had been deprived, but the reservation. And, fourthly, by the middle of the nineteenth century, the differences in economic interests on the North American conti-nent had grown so serious, owing to the boom in the slave economy and the plantation system, that the country could only be kept together by an anti-secessionist civil war. That war lasted for four years, from 1861 to 1865, was conducted with a ferocity regarded until then as unthinkable, and ultimately resulted in the deaths of 700,000 men on the battlefield and in the prisoner-of-war camps operated by both sides. The north-ern states of the Union, led by President Abraham Lincoln, had two objectives. One was to end the divisive tendencies which had developed on the question of extending the slave system to the new federal states which were being created in the west. The other was the establishment of a single large unified state to rule over the whole of the North American continent, which implied the expulsion of the Spaniards and Mexicans from the southwestern region. That same large unified state also rid itself of potentially ungovernable diversity through a sustained policy of ethnic cleansing, which lasted until the early twentieth century and liquidated the continent's original inhabitants in a genocide with millions of victims. It was only around the time of the First World War that a fully integrated nation-state in the modern sense, still with pronounced

'Taking Back Control'

If we take Polanyi's remarks on the situation of the UK in 1945 as our starting point, we can use his conceptual equipment to illuminate the politics of Brexit, that complex configuration of interests and expectations regarding the European Union which has disrupted not just the EU but the British party system as well. 'Taking back control', the slogan of the 'leavers', can mean two things: Britain's emancipation from the shackles of the neoliberal European superstate's 'four freedoms', which bind the country to a constitutionally embedded international market economy and stand in the way of any attempt to plan its 'foreign economy' (the slogan's *left* version), or, conversely, to offer the country the opportunity to associate itself with the boundless globalism and universalism of the United States, at least until Trump came along (the *right* version; for a schematic overview see fig. 22). While left-wing leavers expected that winning back control would result in a return to a social democratic management of the economy in a smaller political entity than supranational Europe, the objective of their right-wing fellow leavers was to protect the country against any possibility, however remote, that the EU might subject the political economy of its member states to democratic interventionism. Both schools of Brexit supporters wanted to restore national sovereignty, but with opposite aims: one wanted to be able to domesticate market forces through national politics, while the other wanted to join a universal market system, led by the US, in which the balance of trade was left to adjust itself, enforcing 'structural reform' where appropriate, in pursuit of neoliberal policies on a global rather than a merely European level. While neoliberal Brexiteers saw the EU as a potential supranational welfare state, with

---

oligarchical tendencies, grew out of this maelstrom. Even then, the country remained divided between North and South, as had been the case since the Civil War, with the dominant North compelled, for the sake of national unity, to be so considerate for the Southern 'way of life' that the part of the population descended from the former slaves remained unable, right up to the present day, to gain full citizenship, despite their continuing struggles for 'civil rights': a failure of 'integration' if there ever was one. That, despite all this, the US continues to be put forward as a case of peaceful and democratic combination of a multitude of heterogeneous small states and their societies (with the debt-financed COVID Recovery and Resilience Facility of the EU being celebrated as the EU's 'Hamilton Moment') is a breathtaking example of historical amnesia.

Figure 22. Complex: British positions on membership in the European Union

		Against	In favour
Left	Pre-Thatcher	Resistance to state regulation of labour relations	Economic modernisation
	Post-Thatcher	Winning back a socialist option	Protection against neoliberal austerity
Right	Nationalist	Defence of national sovereignty; balancing from outside	Europe as a new British Empire; balancing from inside
	Neoliberal	Neoliberal globalisation preferred over neoliberal Europeanisation	Competitive pressure on British state and economy

globalism offering a way out, their fellow campaigners on the left regarded the EU as a supranational market state invented to rule out anything that resembled national economic planning.

The picture is complicated further by another right-wing leave faction, oriented towards nationalism rather than neoliberalism. For them, recovery of national sovereignty was to facilitate the country's return to a foreign policy of maintaining a balance of power on the European continent, and of preventing from outside the emergence of a continental unifier, keeping Britain free for all manners of special relationships with its former colonies all over the world, including the US. Their position is not always easy to distinguish from that of the nationalist remainers, intent on warding off from within a German, French, or Franco-German continental hegemony, or even, as presumably under Tony Blair, on establishing the United Kingdom itself as the leading power in continental Europe. There were also neoliberal motives among the right-wing opponents of Brexit, which had to do with the presumed advantages of the internal European market for the British economy, in particular the 'four freedoms', which were hoped to expose British businesses and, above all, British workers, to international competition in a way that would, presumably, improve their productivity.[56] Remarkably, left remainers, at the

---

56 Not to be forgotten is the hope for judicial oversight at the European, or, derived from this, the national level over the British Parliament, which is not bound by a

same time, expected the EU to provide protection to member-state political economies against totalitarian neoliberalism. The result was an unstable alliance on the side of the remainers between, on the one hand, the project of an elitist market society, which would preserve the power and status of an old capitalist-colonialist ruling class – in Polanyi's words, 'reactionaries' who 'still hope that it is not yet too late for Britain's own system of foreign economy to be changed back so that it may fall into line with that of America' – and, on the other hand, the post-neoliberal hope for a return to an egalitarian mixed economy, administered by a sovereign democratic nation-state.

Polanyi's real theme, of course, was not Britain but the opportunities opened up or closed off by the international state system of his time for the European countries to jointly build an economic and social order which would take to heart the lessons of history, in other words overcome liberal capitalism by democratising it. Three-quarters of a century later, in the age of expiring neoliberalism, the same theme is again reasserting itself in contemporary form, as the question of the possibilities of development of a European state system stuck fast between two contradictory tendencies: towards political-economic centralisation on the one hand and decentralisation on the other; in the direction either of a global neoliberal capitalism or a regionally regenerated democratic state interventionism; between neoliberal superstatism and democratic nationalism; between economic universalism and economic particularism. Here, we can make use of a further analytical perspective offered by Polanyi: the connection he established between the structure of the European state system, with its opportunity for integration through 'regional planning,' and the structure of the world system, for Polanyi a product of historical contingency characterised by the relation between two global power centres, one capitalist and the other communist. According to Polanyi, regional planning – a cooperative economic regime of neighbouring sovereign and democratic nation-states – requires that no existing state system should endeavour to gain, or succeed in gaining, the upper hand over the others, so that there should be a balance of power between them allowing for a pluralism of coexisting particularisms.

---

constitution in the European sense, in case it might at some future point fall into the hands of a left Labour majority.

Here, it needs to be pointed out that, after the demise of the Soviet Union and the Eastern bloc, a balance of power of this kind had ceased to exist, as a result of which the Western European state system organised itself to move towards the formation of a neoliberal, large-scale centralised market state, incorporated into the global empire of Western capitalism. Now, with the appearance of China on the world stage, the gap which the collapse of the Soviet Union had left in Polanyi's trinity of world powers is beginning to close. Along with the exhaustion of American hegemony and the possible return of a worldwide balance of power, this makes it possible – and indeed, if one follows Polanyi, necessary – to resume the discussion about the future of the European state system. Of particular interest in this connection must be the current attempts to turn the EU into a supranational superstate by militarising it and thus, if in no other way, to decide the conflict between globalism and democracy in favour of the former and at the expense of the latter. In the following section, I shall conclude my examination of the structural parameters of state systems by introducing what I consider a centrally important distinction between two modes of international order: horizontal-confederational and vertical-imperial.

Confederation or Empire?

In his book *Friedensprojekt Europa?* (Peace project Europe?), sociologist Hans Joas refers to two eminent social theorists of the inter-war period, Otto Hintze and Carl Schmitt, to ideal-typically distinguish between two models of international order.[57] Both Hintze and Schmitt, as many others after 1918, were concerned with the conditions for a restoration of stability in a fundamentally anarchic international environment, the one in a voluntary and confederal way, the other with hierarchical and authoritarian means. Comparing them can help us achieve greater conceptual precision on the structural parameters of state systems and, following Polanyi, connect them with their political economy under conditions of globalisation.

Joas's interest in Hintze as a theorist of international relations stems from Hintze's reflections on the prospects for an international peace

---

57 Hans Joas, *Friedensprojekt Europa?*, Munich: Kösel, 2020.

regime to rule out a repetition of the catastrophe of the First World War. As a historian and social scientist, Hintze had argued early on that one should not underestimate the cooperative and associative roots of social order – horizontal and unforced solidarity among equals – in favour of exclusively vertical structures of domination. Free and equal individuals, per Hintze, are able to associate in cooperative solidarity, thereby making their subjection to authoritarian power unnecessary as a requirement for social order. This, Hintze argued, was true not just for individuals but also for states, to which Hintze ascribed the ability to achieve peaceful cooperation from below by joining together voluntarily, without the need for directions from above.[58] It seems obvious to associate Hintze's idea that states can cooperate as neighbours while respecting each other's freedom and sovereignty with Polanyi's conception of 'regional planning.'

As the opposite pole of Hintze's *Föderation*, Joas presents the model of an order enforced by an *empire*, as represented by Carl Schmitt, for whom it offers the only realistic solution of the problem of international stability.[59] Empires, according to Schmitt, develop out of the differences in power that are unavoidable in state systems; they secure peace insofar as and as long as the states that command hegemonic power are able to authoritatively discipline the weaker states whose pursuit of their special interests might create discord. In empires, states rule over states, or, in an older version, peoples rule over peoples, irrespective of formally equal sovereignty, by using a variety of ways of securing obedience: soft ideological, less soft economic, and, in the last resort, hard military ones.[60] A rough criterion for distinguishing between confederations and

58   Otto Hintze, 'Föderalistischer Imperialismus', in Gerhard Oestreich, ed., *Otto Hintze, Gesammelte Abhandlungen*, vol. 2, *Soziologie und Geschichte*, Göttingen: Vandenhoeck & Ruprecht, 1964, 210ff.

59   Better read as 'Konföderation', in Jörke's sense (*Die Größe der Demokratie*), to avoid confusion with a 'federal' superstate.

60   It was entirely in line with Schmitt that in 1940, a year after the war had begun so well for Germany, an author who would later achieve high office in the Federal Republic speculated in the journal *Die Hilfe* about 'a German claim for leadership in a European order'. In its service, he wrote, international law was faced with 'the inspiring task . . . of finding an elastic terminology . . . to soften the hard concept of sovereignty'. The author in question was the later president of the Federal Republic, Theodor Heuss. It cannot be said that 'European law' (in German: *Europarecht*) has failed to continue working on this 'inspiring task'. The quote, above, comes from an (obviously well-informed) letter to the editor in the *Frankfurter Allgemeine Zeitung* (25 September 2020, 29). The

empires is that while countries can leave a confederation at will, they cannot as easily leave an empire (or a federal state).[61]

An empire, according to the historian Jürgen Osterhammel, whom Joas quotes, is 'a territorially extended, hierarchically ordered body politic of a polyethnic and multireligious character, whose coherence is ensured by the threat of force, through administration, indigenous collaboration and the universalist programmes and symbols of an imperial elite'.[62] In a more historically specific and less analytical, but

---

interest expressed by the arch-liberal 'Papa Heuss' in a 'softening' of sovereignty – always the sovereignty of others to wit – tends to develop in the centre of every empire, including a liberal or neoliberal one: 'The main enemy of neoliberalism', as of any other imperial project, 'is the sovereignty of the people' (Chantal Mouffe, personal communication to the author). On the (in this context) far-from-irrelevant prehistory of the 'European project' in the 'Third Reich' and in the Second World War, and its lasting impact at the start of the post-war process of 'European integration' which culminated in the EMU, see Perry Anderson, *Ever Closer Union? Europe in the West*, London: Verso, 2021; Hans Werner Neulen, *Europa und das 3. Reich: Einigungsbestrebungen im deutschen Machtbereich 1939–45*, Munich: Universitas, 1987; and Antoine Vauchez, *Brokering Europe: Euro-Lawyers and the Making of a Transnational Polity*, Cambridge, UK: Cambridge University Press, 2015.

61 The unified-state character of an empire is informal (the states attached to or included in it remain sovereign on paper and retain the right to secede). An empire would become formalised only to the extent that its peripheral states would be incorporated into the central state. However, this does not mean that it would be as easy to exit from an empire as from a confederation of states. Among the operators of the European Union, Brexit was and is regarded as, unfortunately, (still) legal but nevertheless illegitimate, which is why they believed they were entitled to use all possible means to make it difficult. States which, unlike the (perhaps soon disunited) United Kingdom at the time of Brexit, are members not just of the EU but also of the EMU (the European Economic and Monetary Union) will find it much harder to exit, particularly if the EU is not accommodating; after all, to make membership in 'united Europe' irreversible was one of the political objectives of the common currency. Under certain conditions, hegemonic states may prefer an empire over a single integrated state, because after full integration their core population may find itself in a minority position; see the problem Israel faced with the formal annexation of the West Bank and Gaza before the military destruction of the latter, if not the former, in the war that began in October 2023. For the elites of peripheral states, a hegemonic but not completely integrated regime could have the advantage that they would not themselves have to suspend democratic forms of government domestically if that turned out to be necessary for 'political stability', and instead could let it be imposed by an external power. International elite management within an empire, as a lesser form of single-state unity, may be preferred by both sides on account of the possibility of sharing the burden of legitimation and exploiting the advantages of functional differentiation.

62 Jürgen Osterhammel, 'Europamodelle und imperiale Kontexte', *Journal of Modern European History* 2, no. 2 (2004), 172–3.

more pointed and, in a cynical way, more normative mode, the concept appears in Schmitt, who developed it under Nazi rule.[63] Schmitt's concern was not just with the domestic nature of empires but also with their external relations, in which what is at issue is the establishment and defence of boundaries as well as the assertion of interests. The aims that evolve in this sphere, according to Schmitt, dictate imperial domestic policy insofar as the imperial powers have to have a free hand in arranging the internal order of their empires for their convenience – as when the United States not only closed its South American 'backyard' to other powers with the Monroe Doctrine but also, with an unlimited entitlement to intervention, opened it for itself. Peace ensues, according to Schmitt, if and only if each empire recognises the spheres of influence of all others, with empires mutually conceding to each other the right to organise their respective territorial spaces as they wish, according to their own requirements; the international equilibrium resulting from this would rule out wars, or at least make them unlikely.[64]

Schmitt's concept of empire does not preclude the possibility that a power-based hegemony will take a legal form and thereby be both formally legitimated and disguised. Empires consisting of formally sovereign states can constitutionalise themselves through international organisations, thereby to varying degrees incorporating cooperative features. As Joas shows, Hintze, for his part, in his critique of Weber's sociology of domination (*Herrschaftssoziologie*), reached the conclusion that it was not only possible but also necessary to supplement relations

---

63   Carl Schmitt, 'Völkerrechtliche Raumordnung mit Interventionsverbot für raumfremde Mächte: Ein Beitrag zum Reichsbegriff im Völkerrecht', in Günter Maschke, ed., *Carl Schmitt: Staat, Großraum, Nomos: Arbeiten aus den Jahren 1916 bis 1969*, Berlin: Duncker & Humblot, 1995 [1939], 269–341.

64   Schmitt's ideal of an international system governed by a limited number of empires with equal rights, which tolerate each other's way of conducting their regional affairs without universalist ambitions to shape the world – a pluralist world system, in other words – does not seem drastically different from Polanyi's post-war model of mutually independent world regions determining their respective internal arrangements themselves. One difference is that Polanyi sees the United States as habitually expansionist and by no means continentally isolationist, as implied by the Monroe Doctrine. Even more importantly, Polanyi, unlike Schmitt, sees the possibility of a cooperative and egalitarian system of sovereign non-imperial states in at least one of the three zones that emerged from the Second World War, namely in a Western Europe still, even after the end of Britain's domination of the world, led by Britain led, in turn, by a Labour government.

of domination with confederative relations of cooperation, so as to stabilise them; for him, in that sense, confederation and empire were not firmly fixed, mutually exclusive alternatives. Sovereign states can, in fact, engage in contractually agreed cooperation by handing over areas of competence to jointly established authorities, thereby evoking the appearance that all member states are equally subordinate to a collective supra-state system of government; Hintze would perhaps have described this as a combination of confederal and imperial elements of government, of a cooperative-associational and hegemonic-hierarchical pole of international order, hoping that the imperial element would gradually be pushed aside by the confederal element.[65] Development can, however, also proceed in the opposite direction, and formally free treaties can become unequal in practice when the less powerful party has no choice but to sign them; in such cases the confederal exterior serves to gloss over the imperial core.

The possibility of transitions between confederation, empire, and superstate federalism is of particular significance in the case of the European Union. Here, the distinction between differently ordered state systems appears also as a historical sequence, in the development of the European Economic Community into the completed internal market of 1992 and the Monetary Union of 1999 – a process in which the EEC-EC-EU became less and less confederal and more and more imperial, while regarding itself as on the path to a kind of federalist superstate. Functionally and technocratically legitimated in terms of an appropriate 'upwards' delegation of 'tasks' to common institutions, Europe increasingly became the instrument of imperial rule of the stronger over the weaker member states, either through central EU institutions or bypassing them. Distinctions of this kind will be useful for gaining a more precise view of the Polanyian alternative between, on the one hand, a return of the EU to a confederal system of sovereign states and, on the other hand, its present condition as a fragile quasi-empire stuck between small-statism (*Kleinstaaterei*) and mega-statism (*Großstaaterei*), at an intermediate stage on the road to an, ultimately ungovernable, European single state.

---

65   Hintze, 'Föderalistischer Imperialismus', 215.

The Dimensions of States and State Systems

As stated at the outset, 'the state' only exists in the plural, as a state among other states, a member of a *state system*. No state exists in isolation, even a 'Westphalian' one; state sovereignty is, as such, a relation between states and, for that reason, anything but monadic or sufficient unto itself. State systems, in turn, sit on fissured territorial landscapes of socialisation and communalisation, and differ according to their horizontal and vertical articulation. The structure of state-territorial authority interacts with the pluralism of the socialisation that underlies it, which it reflects to a greater or lesser degree, but hardly ever maps it congruently. The structure of a state system is not determined by the structure of the social system on which it is based: binary demarcations are always arbitrary, owing to the fluid transitions that characterise the real world.

There are similarities and connections between the dimensions of state systems and of states (fig. 23). The division of state systems into states – many small ones versus a few large ones – corresponds to the division of states into regional subunits; in both cases, the issue is one of a politics of scale, in terms of power politics, economic efficiency, and social-psychological identity. And, just as the vertical construction of a state can be more regionalist or more centralist, so also can state systems either locate sovereignty at the national level or centralise it supranationally. The pluralism of human socialisation, together with the technical limits to the management of complexity, places limits on both

Figure 23. The dimensions of states and state systems

		States	State systems
	Horizontal	Many small vs. a few large subunits (regions, federal states)	Many small vs. a few large member states
Dimension	Vertical	Centralised vs. decentralised government	International superstate vs. nation-state sovereignty

the centralisation of states and the transfer of state sovereignty to international organisations, empires, or superstates – limits that can be extended, at most, by the use of force.

The historical dynamic of the state systems of today must be understood in the context of the pressure towards denationalisation and globalisation exerted by contemporary capitalism in its crisis of stagnation and of the reciprocal relationship between capitalist accumulation and state institutions, both national and international. Here, the essence of the matter is the vertical dimension of states and state systems, in particular, their degree of universalism and centralisation in response to a denationalised capitalism's demand for convergence. The struggle over the relation between market, economy, and capitalism, on the one hand, and society, on the other, is at the same time a struggle over the structure of the state system and vice versa; capitalist globalisation comes up against the proper dynamic of the relation between state structures and their underlying societies. Whoever wants neoliberalism must want globalisation and Europeanisation; whoever wants globalisation and Europeanisation wants neoliberalism, whether they know this or not; whoever wants the market to be embedded in democratic politics must oppose the globalisation of the state system and, with it, global governance. This conflict does not take place on a tabula rasa but in a historically grown state system in which the march into global convergence of the ways of economic activity has come to a standstill in the cul-de-sac of conflict-ridden and crisis-prone empires.

As institutions, state systems are more than the sum of their member states and the decisions these take for themselves. They, in fact, determine, organised or not, normatively or factually, the limits and possibilities for the development of the individual states belonging to them, reaching deeply into their political economy. Polanyi's 'regional planning', agreed between neighbouring sovereign states, presupposed a particular configuration of international politics, specifically an equilibrium between great powers unable or unwilling to strive for global hegemony, ruling out global unification of a universalistic kind. Polanyi's world-spanning historical institutionalism, which conceives of states and regional groups of states as elements of a global state system, makes possible a historical account of the political-economic paths of development, particularly in the European state system, that are emerging in the twilight of neoliberalism, and of the strategies pursued within and with states in the conflict between globalism and democracy. Not least, it allows us to recognise, in the present condition of the world, a historical window of opportunity in which a recovery of democratic control over the economy can at least be attempted.

Empirically, it emerges that the increasing density of inter-societal relations – the growing 'global' interdependence – precisely does not provoke a desire for inter-state integration but, to the contrary, calls forth an insistence on differentiation both within states and between them, as well as within international organisations. Localism and regionalism, separatism and nationalism, today have the same origin: the issue is always the maintenance and restoration of the capacity of identifiable communities for collective action through a decentralisation of decision mechanisms and government jurisdictions – resisting a worldwide, allegedly inevitable neoliberal transformation, both economic and cultural, and rejecting the imperative, associated with integration and centralisation, for societies to let go of their former national economies striving for entry into the world beyond their borders. The more the pluralism of human ways of life is questioned by global processes of standardisation, the more it comes to the fore in its defence; as a result, the state system may tend to become more fragmented and pluralistic rather than more integrated and centralised. Progress towards a centralisation of states or state systems, whether through a vertical, upward transfer of responsibilities or a horizontal amalgamation of individual states or substate regions, is nowhere to be observed, while the opposite is true for movements in the direction of differentiated autonomy.

8

The European Union: From Neoliberal to Geopolitical Integration

If the history of the European Union began with the European Economic Community (EEC), which went into operation in 1958, it has by now lasted almost two-thirds of a century, in which it several times changed beyond recognition (fig. 24). It started out as a six-country alliance jointly administering two key sectors of the post-war economy, coal and steel. Among other things, this made it possible for France to forego another occupation of the Ruhr Valley, Germany's key industrial district at the time, like the occupation between 1923 and 1925 which had contributed to the rise of German revanchism after the First World War. In the wake of the industrial conflicts of the late 1960s, and following the accession of three more countries – the United Kingdom, Ireland, and Denmark – the EEC turned into the European Community (EC). Dedicated to industrial policy and social democratic industrial reform, the EC was to add a so-called 'social dimension' to what was on the way to becoming a common market. Later, in the course of the neoliberal revolution and after the collapse of Communism, what was then renamed the European Union became both a container for the new nation-states in the East about to join the capitalist world, and an engine of neoliberal restructuring, supply-side economics and New Labourism in, at its peak, twenty-eight European countries, embedded in the emerging American-dominated, unipolar global order after the end of history.

Figure 24. The evolution of the European Union

Organisation	Year	Members	Treaty
EEC	1958	6	Rome
EC	1967	9	
	1986	12	SEA
EU	1993		Maastricht
	1995	15	
	1999	15	Amsterdam
EMU	*1999 (2024)*	*11 (20)*	
	2003	15	Nice
	2004	25	
	2007	27	
	2009	27	Lisbon
	2013	28	
	2021 (Brexit)	27	

The European Union of the three decades after 1990 was a regional microcosm of what on the world scale came to be called hyperglobalisation, a place where the transformations of the capitalist economy and its state system were bound up with each other more than anywhere else. In fact, the EU became, in a significant way, a smaller-sized, continental model for the integrated global capitalism that was the ultimate objective of those subscribing to the 'Washington Consensus' of the time.[1] It featured a borderless internal market for goods, services, labour, and capital; rules-based economic governance upheld by a uniquely powerful international court, the European Court of Justice (ECJ); and a common currency, the euro, managed by the equally powerful European Central Bank (ECB). The arrangement closely matched the Hayekian idea of an international federation deliberately designed to be unable to engage in discretionary economic policy: an almost perfect approximation to what Hayek had called isonomy, meaning identical market-liberal laws in all states included in a supranational state system.[2] In the 2000s, after the euro had become the common currency, the

---

1   On the Washington Consensus, see Sarah Babb and Alexander F. Kentikelenis, 'Markets Everywhere: The Washington Consensus and the Sociology of Global Institutional Change', *Annual Review of Sociology* 47, no. 1 (2021), 521–41.

2   Friedrich A. Hayek, *The Constitution of Liberty*, Chicago: University of Chicago Press, 1960.

no-longer-political economy of the EU was ruled by a politically steri-lised combination of technocracy – the ECB and the European Commission – and what might be called nomocracy – the ECJ – under an (in practice unchangeable) de facto constitution, consisting of two effectively unreadable treaties among twenty-eight countries, each of them entitled to veto any change.[3] Anchoring the whole construction in the global financial system dominated by the United States, the treaties provided for unlimited capital mobility, not just within the Union but also across its borders.[4]

That this arrangement suffered from what came to be euphemisti-cally called a 'democratic deficit', even in a limited liberal, formalist sense, did not go unnoticed. Indeed, among insiders in Brussels, the joke is often heard that with its current constitution, the EU would never be allowed to join itself. In recent years, efforts were made by the European Commission and, in particular, the so-called European Par-liament to fill the democratic gap with a politics of common 'values' to be enforced by the EU on member states – of, basically, human rights in contemporary Western interpretation as a substitute for the politics of the political economy that had become excluded from the politics of the Union. Above all, this included re-educational interventions in the countries of the former Soviet empire to convert governments, parties, and people to Western European liberalism – not just economic but also social, if need be – by withholding part of the fiscal handouts that were to support the countries' transformation into bona fide market-economies-plus-capitalist-democracies. Increasingly, this culminated in a crusade against so-called 'anti-Europeans' of all sorts, identified by

---

3   In reference to the Treaty on European Union (TEU) and the Treaty on the Functioning of European Union (TFEU), the former also called the Maastricht Treaty (effective since 1993), the latter the Treaty of Rome (effective since 1958), both of which have been amended many times – for example, by the 2009 Treaty of Lisbon. In May 2005, a proposed 'Constitution of the European Union' failed in a French referendum after 55 percent of voters rejected it. The turnout was 69 percent. The failure was attrib-uted by political operators, in part, to the French government having made the mistake of distributing a copy of the treaty, hundreds of pages long and impossible to understand for non-specialists, to every French household.

4   According to Article 63 of the TFEU, 'all restrictions on the movement of capital between Member States and between Member States and third countries shall be prohibited', the same applying to 'all restrictions on payments', again both 'between Member States and third countries'.

social scientists and political spin doctors as 'populists' – a top-down educational programme, the mandate for which was derived from ever more extensive (and indeed intrusive) interpretations of the declaratory sections of the Treaties.[5]

In the 1990s, in particular, the EU became a showcase and proving ground for neoliberal political economy. Behind the scenes, the opaque institutions of the EU's multilevel political system were utilised by the declining parties of the old centrism and their disabled governments as something like a shunting yard for moving political responsibility opportunistically from the nation-state to the supranational quasi-state and back, a construction sold to 'pro-Europeans' as a new, better kind of statehood, both more effective and more ethical. At the same time, the de facto centralisation and depoliticisation of the Union's political economy; the 'rule of law' as the rule of an all-powerful court; the formally rules-based but, in practice, more and more discretionary economic policy of the European Central Bank; and the sanction-supported attempts at re-educating traditionalist European societies in European 'values' inserted a hierarchical centre/periphery dimension into the Union, making it increasingly resemble a *liberal empire*, in both an economic and a cultural sense, the latter as legitimation for the former.

Europe as Battleground and Place of Desire

Nothing has been more carefully avoided in EU Europe, during the decades of its continuous hardening as a neoliberal economic regime, than debates over the so-called *finalité* of the 'European project' – over the final goal of integration and the architecture of a future European

---

5   Article 4, 1. The TEU states that, 'in accordance with Article 5, competences not conferred upon the Union in the Treaties remain with the Member States.' According to Article 5, 1, 'The limits of Union competences are governed by the principle of conferral. The use of Union competences is governed by the principles of subsidiarity and proportionality.' The Commission and the European Court of Justice are trying to get around treaty restrictions on their competences by trying to derive specific powers for themselves from general clauses, like for example in Article 2 of the TEU: 'The Union is founded on the values of respect for human dignity, freedom, democracy, equality, the rule of law and respect for human rights, including the rights of persons belonging to minorities. These values are common to the Member States in a society in which pluralism, non-discrimination, tolerance, justice, solidarity and equality between women and men prevail.'

state, if that it was to be. Beneath the surface of the integration process, there had grown up a liberalisation machine which, while penetrating ever more deeply into the societies of Europe, was dressed up as a non-political economic and legal techno-bureaucracy serving self-evident common interests beyond partisan quarrels, leaving the political shape of the future Europe to expert insight into the evolving requirements of capitalist development. One reason was that it was clear to all that any discussion of the kind of state 'European integration' was to produce – a superstate or a super-market, unity or diversity, central government or decentralised cooperation, democracy or technocracy, a federation of states or a federal state – would have risked bringing the integration process to a standstill, owing to insurmountable differences between the nation-states involved, not least on their own role in the European state system.

As a result, for a long time, the respective next steps towards what was called integration were justified as momentarily unavoidable pragmatic, quasi-technical reactions to objective needs defined as such according to contemporary neoliberal doctrine, instead of being legitimated as advances in the direction of an identifiable common goal. This all the more assured that institutional change would move, as it were blindly, in a neoliberal direction, without need to disclaim any of the manifold contradictory and incompatible fantasies associated with 'Europe' in public rhetoric. Thus, a political-economic construct could emerge which, like a political mollusc, could take on any desired shape in the perception of 'pro-Europeans' of whatever descent, above all in regard to its future. At the same time, internally, underneath a chameleon-like surface, the Treaties engineered an 'iron cage' (in Weber's sense) whose true nature remained hidden behind a veil of ideological incantations.

In the longer term, of course, this did not prevent ever-deeper 'European' interventions into national societies, unintentionally but inevitably setting off what was seen by the operators of the integration project as a dicey and therefore undesirable 'politicisation' – known after 2008 as 'populist' politicisation. An early attempt to constitutionalise integration came to grief when a draft constitution, passed after long deliberation and impossible for normal people to read, and enigmatic in particular with reference to its intention and purpose, was rejected in several referenda, one of them in France. In typically Brusselian manner, it was nonetheless subsequently put into effect via the back door, as a 'constitutional treaty' sold as an update to the existing treaties, once again without laying down a final goal for the 'ever closer union of the peoples of Europe.'[6]

As a result, a situation came about in which the non-committal character of the programmatic objectives of the 'European project', combined with the depoliticisation of its pragmatic purposes, made it possible for the EU to be converted from a battleground between contending political-economic interests in state and democracy into an otherworldly place of desire, refashioning the conflict over the evolving architecture of the European state system under neoliberal-ism as a *Kulturkampf* for European 'values' – re-education taking the place of redistribution, in line with the liberal refashioning of democracy (see fig. 5, p. 51). Rather than the 'how' of the new Europe, which everyone could imagine as they wished after the political neu-tralisation of its technocratic substructure, it now became the 'whether', and with it the 'how much', of 'Europe' that stood to debate: whether someone was 'for Europe' and its 'values' or not, for supranationalism or nationalism, as a pro- or as an anti-European. In this way, contrac-tually cemented neoliberal 'Europe' could become a post-materialist object of collective identification, particularly for the new liberal-internationalist centre, offering an upward escape from the self-inflicted political deficiencies of neoliberalism, through an identity politics fight-ing nationalism as a retrograde political habitus – 'Europe' as vision and dreamland, politically-economically depleted but emotionally and sentimentally enriched.

The price to be paid for dematerialising 'Europe' by evading argu-ments over its destination was and continues to be a complete blurring of the issue at stake. This can be seen when, like with the most neoliberal of the neoliberals, the desirable political structure after the end of the European nation-state is no longer described as a state, leaving open its precise nature. Here is Habermas, for instance: 'The federal state is the wrong model. A supranational, but *trans-state*,[7] democratic political community that permits *joint governance* also satisfies the conditions of

---

6   An expression used repeatedly in EU documents and resolutions. Note that it refers to the 'peoples', not 'the people', of Europe.

7   In German: *überstaatlich*. See Jürgen Habermas, *Im Sog der Technokratie*, Kleine Politische Schriften 12, Berlin: Suhrkamp, 2013, 154.

democratic legitimation', presumably ending the 'legitimation crisis' of capitalism diagnosed by the same author a few decades earlier.[8] Note that elsewhere, Habermas invokes as a reason for a centralised and unified Europe the need for the 'European way of life', presumably the same from Hammerfest to Agrigento, to be defended by an army equipped and commanded by his future European rather-not-state.[9] How a 'trans-state democratic political community' should operate and command a highly lethal organisation like a continental army remains an unanswered question.[10] Equally unclear is the precise nature of Habermas's 'European way of life', in particular its relationship to the various national ways of life which have already made their home in Europe.[11]

The reinterpretation of 'Europe' as a place without qualities but of desire makes it possible to demand a 'European solution' for any arising problem, shifting responsibility upwards to the European marketocracy

---

8   Jürgen Habermas, *The Lure of Technocracy*, Cambridge, UK: Polity, 2015, 99–100.

9   See the appeal signed by Habermas for the creation of a 'European army', quoted earlier and discussed in more detail below, under 'Integration by Militarisation?'

10   In Habermas's EU of the future, 'all political decisions are legitimised by the citizens in their dual role as European citizens, on the one hand, and as citizens of their respective national member states, on the other' (Habermas, *The Lure of Technocracy*, 100. How this might facilitate the successful conduct of a war – against China, Russia, or Boko Haram, all presumably enemies of the 'European way of life' – remains a mystery.

11   One could also ask, for example, whether a German, French, Romanian, Swedish, or indeed a Scottish, Bavarian, or Catalan 'way of life' can exist at all from the political integration perspective, and why they do not deserve to be defended just as much as, or more than, the 'European' one. In any case, a European way of life which is supposed to subsume national ways of life as distinct as the Danish and the Bulgarian will inevitably be defined more generally (one could also say: more superficially) than its manifold national subvarieties. And if the German, the English, or any other national ways of life promote a bad kind of nationalism and therefore must be absorbed in, or subordinated to, a European way of life, why should the latter, especially when it bears arms, be immune from producing a bad European nationalism? After all, a 'unified Europe' would be large enough to be tempted to participate in various new versions of the *great games* played by the former empires (see, on this point, the interesting comments of Moritz Rudolph: 'Eurofaschismus: Wer gegen ihn ist, könnte für ihr sein', *Merkur* 73, no. 843 [2019], 90–4). One could also ask how a 'European way of life' could be defined specifically enough to inspire the soldiers of a European army to put their lives on the line to protect it – unless, of course, what is envisaged as a 'European army' is from the beginning a force of mercenaries specialising in the physical elimination of non-Europeans using the latest long-distance technology.

and technocracy whenever those responsible in national politics cannot, or will not, exercise it themselves: 'Europe' as a solutionist's solution for everything – from economic growth to public finance, from migration to internal and external security, from the financial crisis to the climate and COVID crises. In practice, in the uniquely impenetrable European multilevel institutional undergrowth, shrewd politicians operating at the interface between national and supranational politics have learned to move between doing nothing at the national level in the name of 'European integration'; blaming 'Europe' for the failure of national policies; or presenting to their national constituents the policies they favour as prescribed by 'Europe', thus immunising themselves against democratic resistance at home. All of this takes place in front of spectators who have to make do without any intuitive understanding of the meaning of what they see and of the rules that govern it. Citizens can, perhaps, understand the politics of their own country, through the national political system's capillary roots connecting it to their respective 'ways of life', to the extent that post-democracy and technocracy have not already disposed of them. But, in relation to Brussels and its brand-new, synthetic, expert-run institutions, divorced from people's daily life and devoid of tradition, one can only deliver European-identitarian declarations of loyalty combined with pious hopes for whatever one finds morally desirable. Knowledge of what is and is not happening in Brussels's sealed council chambers, or understanding of what the communication specialists in charge are letting the world outside know about it, is reserved for those who have become insiders through hard conformist work.[12]

Nevertheless, or precisely for that reason, the European Union succeeded in establishing itself in broad circles of liberal-cosmopolitan European society as an ideal political system, as an alternative to the old Europe of nations and classes, its present imperfections happily forgiven in view of its future virtues – a wonderland of post-industrial and post-materialist, indeed post-political and post-capitalist politics, driven by values instead of power, home to citizens rather than classes, with

---

12   On the language of 'Europe', see Francisco Seoane Pérez, *Political Communication in Europe: The Cultural and Structural Limits of the European Public Sphere*, Basingstoke: Palgrave Macmillan, 2013; on the peculiarly 'pro-European' role of 'Euro-journalism', see Martin Herzer, *The Media, European Integration and the Rise of Euro-journalism, 1950s-1970s*, London: Palgrave Macmillan, 2019.

problems instead of conflicts and pragmatic solutions instead of rigid ideologies. What had made this possible, or was to have done so, was the de-economisation of domestic politics through a constitutional hand-over of the European political economy to denationalised economic and legal institutions and experts, together with a denationalisation of international politics and society, both of which as yet incomplete but certain to be fully realised in a not-too-distant future. All of this exerted a magnetic attraction on those harbouring a free-floating desire for something new, a nonpartisan – in fact, non-plebeian – way of settling crises through conflict-free cooperation, a world in which the wish has power, emancipated from constraining traditions and the burdens of history, and untainted by the disasters of the past – a desire, it may appear, for an innocent European subsection to the US's New World Order of 1990 at the 'end of history': 'Europe' as a euphoric idea, as the fictional expectation, indeed, of a second United States of America, as longingly imagined by Goethe at the end of his life, a little more than three decades before the American Civil War, the bloodiest war of the nineteenth century and the first modern war in history:[13]

> America, you have it better
> than our continent the old
> No ruined castles
> Nor basalt
> Your mind is not troubled
> In time alive
> By useless memories
> And futile strife.[14]

---

13 Jens Beckert, *Imagined Futures: Fictional Expectations and Capitalist Dynamics*, Cambridge, MA: Harvard University Press, 2016.

14 In German: 'Amerika, du hast es besser / Als unser Kontinent, das alte, / Hast keine verfallene Schlösser / Und keine Basalte. / Dich stört nicht im Innern, / Zu lebendiger Zeit, / Unnützes Erinnern / Und vergeblicher Streit.' J. W. Goethe, 'Den Vereinigten Staaten', in 'Zahme Xenien', chapter 9, *Gedichte: Nachlese*, 1827, author's translation.

Before Ukraine: Critical Fault-Lines, Impending Failure

Empires are at a congenital risk of overextension, in territorial, economic, political, cultural, and other respects. The larger they get, the more it costs to keep them together, as centrifugal forces grow with internal diversity and the centre needs to mobilise and spend ever new and ever more resources to contain them. After the global financial crisis of 2008 and its spread to Europe, the EU and its monetary union began to fracture along several dimensions, their economic, ideological, and coercive capacities for maintaining the integration of 'Europe' increasingly overtaxed. On the EU's western flank, Brexit was the first case of a member state leaving a Union that ideologically considers itself permanent. Many factors contributed to the outcome of the Brexit referendum, and they have been widely debated. One major reason (less spectacular but certainly of major importance) why British membership proved unsustainable was a profound incompatibility of the British de facto constitution – in particular its parliamentary absolutism – with Brussels-style rule by judges and technocrats. Another was the inability, and indeed unwillingness, of the Brussels neoliberal bureaucracy to do something about the long-standing neglect by British governments of the creeping disintegration of their country's social fabric as a consequence of neoliberal austerity.

Turning to the south, traditional national ways there of doing capitalism proved incompatible with the one-size-fits-all prescriptions of the EMU and its internal market, leading Italy, in particular, down a path of prolonged economic decline. Attempts to turn the trend around, either through 'structural reforms' in line with neoliberal prescriptions as part of a centralised, rules-based economic policy, or through the European Central Bank and the European Commission bending the anti-interventionist rules governing the EMU, with silent toleration by the French and German governments, failed dismally. By 2023, at the latest, it had become clear that even the EU's debt-financed COVID Recovery and Resilience Facility (RRF), and the fiscal subsidies it was to provide to Italy, will not solve Italy's problems with the EMU either.[15] Among

---

15   The RRF was set up in July 2020 to dispense €750 billion to member countries, proportionate to the losses they were found by the European Commission to have

other things, the Italian case proved that a supranationally centralised regional policy aiming at economic convergence, with sovereign states as regions, is even less likely to be successful than regional policies within a nation-state.

Furthermore, on the Union's eastern periphery, countries carry a historical legacy of cultural traditionalism, political authoritarianism, and nationalist resistance against international interventions in their internal life, the latter reinforced by their experience with the Soviet empire. Efforts to spread Western European mores and tastes to these societies, especially when accompanied by threats of economic sanctions (as with the Union's so-called 'rule of law' policies), predictably called forth popular 'populist' opposition and resentment among citizens and governments against what was perceived as attempts to deprive them of their newly recovered national sovereignty.[16] Conflicts on the European Council, the body uniting the heads of state and government of member countries, over cultural issues – the moral utopia of cultural unity engineered by technocratic rule – went as far as Western political leaders more or less explicitly urging their Eastern colleagues, in particular from Hungary and Poland, to leave the Union if they were unwilling to abide by its 'values'.[17] Combined with the threat of

---

suffered from the COVID-19 pandemic. Italy was to be the leading beneficiary, with €192 billion (€69 billion in grants, the rest in – very long-term – loans). This was the first time that the EU was allowed by its member states to take up debt; the fund is entirely debt financed. To get a sense of its effective magnitude, note that Germany, responding to American complaints over it not spending enough on defence, set aside in early 2022, in a matter of a few days, a debt-financed special fund of €100 billion for upgrading its military – more than half of what the entire country of Italy is allocated by the Recovery and Resilience Facility, to be spent over seven years. If there was in the 'European Parliament' something even resembling a parliamentary opposition, the RRF – its origin, construction, and administration – would be an unending subject of public inquiry and controversy.

16   On the politics of the 'rule of law' issue, see Wolfgang Streeck, 'Ultra Vires,' *New Left Review Sidecar* (blog), 7 January 2022, newleftreview.org; Wolfgang Streeck, 'Rusty Charley,' *New Left Review Sidecar* (blog), 2 November 2021, newleftreview.org.

17   At an EU summit meeting in June 2021, the Dutch prime minister, Mark Rutte, under pressure at home over illegal punitive measures taken under his watch by government authorities against welfare recipients, mostly immigrants, told his Hungarian counterpart, Viktor Orbán, that Hungary had to exit from the EU unless the Hungarian government withdrew a law that was to ban schools from using materials seen as promoting homosexuality. From a Reuters report: 'Several EU summit participants spoke of the most intense personal clash among the bloc's leaders in years . . . "It was

economic sanctions, this amounted to nothing less than thinly veiled attempts to bring about a regime change in culturally diverse fellow member countries.[18]

More fault-lines, both old and new, exist at the centre of the liberal empire, reflecting the fact that the European Union never had a member state powerful enough to be its hegemon. Instead, there were and are two leading countries, Germany and France, neither of which could and can dominate the Union alone. Nor can they dominate the Union together, 'in tandem', an oft-used euphemistic metaphor for France and Germany together promoting European unity. While each would need the other to organise and lead Europe, there is no agreement between them on what its integrated structures, interests, and policies should look like.

Up to a few years ago, Franco-German differences were seen as essentially deriving from the differences between their national 'varieties of capitalism', France cultivating a tradition of statist dirigisme and Germany sticking to its post-war invention of a 'social market economy'. More recently, especially after Brexit, equally deep differences in foreign and national security policy came to the fore. While they already existed in the 1960s, they were thrown in sharper relief, first by the end of the bipolar world after 1989 and then by the fact that, with Brexit, France became the only EU member state with nuclear arms and a permanent seat on the UN Security Council. Because France is unwilling to share either with Europe, meaning above all Germany, Germany's nuclear dependence on the United States, which keeps roughly 38,000 troops on German soil, together with an uncounted

---

really forceful, a deep feeling that this could not be. It was about our values; this is what we stand for," Rutte told reporters on Friday. "I said 'Stop this, you must withdraw the law and, if you don't like that and really say that the European values are not your values, then you must think about whether to remain in the European Union.'"

18   Another, rarely studied, division among EU member states is that between countries that are and are not members of the EMU. According to the Treaties, all EU member states except Denmark are supposed to join the euro as soon as their economy meets the conditions of EMU membership. This rule, however, has never really been enforced, and joining EMU effectively remained a decision for each member state to take for itself. The United Kingdom, for example, while comfortably satisfying the criteria of accession, under Blair and Brown resolved, after some back and forth, to keep its own currency, which in the end made it easier for it to exit from the EU. Today, Bulgaria, the Czech Republic, Denmark, Hungary, Poland, Romania, and Sweden are not in EMU. Regardless of this, they participate fully in EU monetary policy-making as the Maastricht Treaty assumes as a matter of course that all EU members will also be in the EMU.

number of nuclear warheads, effectively stands in the way of what multiple French presidents have called 'European strategic sovereignty', meaning a transfer of geostrategic competence to 'Europe' in line with French national security doctrine and under French leadership. Moreover, while France had traditionally strong interests in West Africa and the Middle East, German national interests, as they relate to Europe, focus on Eastern Europe and the Balkans. As a result, disagreement on fundamental issues, although carefully and often skilfully concealed, was and still is endemic between the two would-be riders of the imagined French-German European 'tandem'.

More Unity through Less Unity?

Before the Ukraine war, there were, in principle, two opposite approaches to resolving the impasse over the future of the European Union and preventing its disintegration. One would have been the pursuit of more unity through less unity, of retrenchment of the Union, if not territorially, then functionally, making a little less close the 'ever closer union of the peoples of Europe'. Among others, it was the American sociologist Amitai Etzioni who had for some time advocated *less* integration as way to *more stable* integration.[19] This was reminiscent of older concepts of an integrated Western European state system as a Europe *à la carte*, a Europe of 'variable geometry', or even de Gaulle's 'Europe of fatherlands'. What these had in common was a vision of a regional state system on the model of a cooperative rather than an empire, as recently outlined by Hans Joas in an important book on Europe as a 'peace project'.[20] In it, Joas referred to a debate on the possibilities of international peace between Carl Schmitt and the German historian Otto Hintze in the 1920s and 1930s. Schmitt believed that peace in a world region could be assured only by a regional imperial power at its centre, imposing its order on a periphery of dependent states, essentially with the way and the means it saw fit. Schmitt's real-world model of a viable international order in this sense was the American hemisphere under the Monroe Doctrine. Arguing against him,

19   Amitai Etzioni, *Reclaiming Patriotism*, Charlottesville: University of Virginia Press, 2019, 142ff.

20   Hans Joas, *Friedensprojekt Europa?*, Munich: Kösel, 2020.

Hintze, who had studied the German tradition of cooperative associations (*Genossenschaften*), insisted on the possibility of an international system organised through voluntary cooperation within a framework that obliged participating countries to recognise each other's sovereignty. This model came close to that of the 1648 Peace of Westphalia, after the Thirty Years' War, with the creation of what was later named the 'Westphalian state', embedded in a system of loosely coupled inter-state relations without a dominant central power, imperial or federal.

What would a European Union of fatherlands look like if it ever had been given a chance? Obviously, it would provide for more local, in the specific sense of national, autonomy, rather than insisting on political and economic uniformity among member countries – a state system with less centralised and less hierarchical institutions and more space for democratic national self-determination. The European Commission would be something like a platform for technical support of projects of international cooperation, jointly chosen and voluntarily agreed between member states in different configurations. For this, the Commission would have to give up its aspiration to grow into a pan-European supranational executive; the same, mutatis mutandis, would apply to the EU Parliament if it was needed at all. Also significantly reduced would be the role of the European Court of Justice: it would cease to be a constitutional legislator in disguise, in charge effectively of everything it (or its integrationist clientele) chooses for it to be in charge of, with the power to intervene almost at will in national states, national law, and national politics. In some ways, a decentralised EU of this sort might resemble the Nordic Council formed by the Scandinavian states in the 1950s. Its members were (and remain) Denmark, Finland, Iceland, Norway, Sweden, the Faroe Islands, Greenland, and Åland. The Nordic Council knows no equivalent to the European Court, the EU Parliament, or the European Commission. While member states keep borders open among themselves, each continues to have its own economic and social policies, very much in the spirit of Polanyi's 'regional planning' and far from the centralism the EU tried to impose on its members in the course of its neoliberal turn.[21]

---

21   According to its website, 'The Nordic Council of Ministers is the official body for inter-governmental cooperation in the Nordic Region. It seeks Nordic solutions wherever and whenever the countries can achieve more together than by working on their own.'

In political practice up to 2019, still firmly under the spell of the neoliberal recipe to save the capitalist political economy by hyper-globalising – or hyper-continentalising – it, a rollback of integration in order to preserve it was always an unrealistic project, if it ever was any-one's project at all. It might have had a chance in the event of a catastrophic breakdown of the EMU, caused, for example, by a state bankruptcy of Italy, as a reconstruction project after an institutional collapse rather than as a reform policy to prevent such collapse. Under existing rules, then as today, more unity through less unity would have required a fundamental revision of the Treaties, requiring agreement by all twenty-seven post-Brexit member states, some of whose assent would have to be approved by popular vote. The practical impossibility of a meaningful revision of the Treaties – and, with it, of the de facto consti-tution of the Union – may be understood as an intended feature of a mode of European supranational state-building planned to be irreversi-ble, in the same way as, and together with, the historical transformation of state-administered social democratic capitalism into its globalised neoliberal incarnation.

Institutional inertia also stood in the way of ending the deadlock in the European politics of scale in the opposite direction, by moving 'upwards' towards more, rather than 'downwards' towards less, unifi-cation and centralisation – by a further tightening of integration, after somehow breaking the resistance which it had met from below as the neoliberal era unfolded. That resistance was not limited to an increasingly strong 'populist' opposition. As much as the EU's member states liked the EU as a depository for problems they could or would no longer address, let alone solve, when it came to their remaining, economically cleansed sovereignty, they were unanimous in protecting it against supranational expropriation. What seemed to be on the book for the EU as the 2010s drew to an end, therefore, was a long period of institutional deadlock and uncertainty, of provisional fixes of arising problems, of improvised muddling-through amid rising distributional and other conflicts between member states – a political crisis sequence accompanying the economic crisis sequence of the neoliberal era, with a prospect of short-term gains for skilled players of multilevel politics, exploiting the rich opportunities it offered for organised irresponsibility, at the price of long-term institutional decay.

Integration by Militarisation?

A third potential way out of institutional stagnation was suggested by a group of retired German politicians from both major parties, led and presumably inspired by the philosopher Jürgen Habermas. Among them was Friedrich Merz, a sidelined long-time rival of Angela Merkel, then chairman of the board of Blackrock Germany, who was surprisingly resurrected in 2022 to be Merkel's successor as leader of what by then had become Germany's main opposition, the Christian Democrats. In October 2018 the group issued a public appeal titled 'For a Europe based on solidarity: Let's get serious about the will of our Constitution, now!'[22] Among other things, the group urged the creation of a European army ('We demand a European army'), given that 'Trump, Russia, and China' were 'testing ever more severely . . . Europe's unity, our willingness to stand up for our values together, to defend our way of life'. To this there could be 'only one answer: solidarity and the fight against nationalism and egoism internally, and unity and common sovereignty externally'. Setting up a European army was to be a first step towards a 'deeper integration of foreign and security policy based on majority decisions' on the European Council. Remarkably, the group argued that this did not require 'more money' as 'the European NATO members together spend about three times as much on defence as Russia'; all that was needed was an end to national fragmentation, which would make for 'much more defensive power without additional money'.[23] (No reason was given why 'more defensive power' should be required, in view of the fact that Western European countries, as mentioned by the group itself, by far outspent their closest and most likely enemy.) Moreover, according to the appeal, 'since Europe's defences are not directed against anyone, the creation of a European army should be linked to arms control and disarmament initiatives', an effort in which Germany and

---

22   Hans Eichel et al., 'Für ein solidarisches Europa – Machen wir Ernst mit dem Willen unseres Grundgesetzes, jetzt!', *Handelsblatt*, 21 October 2018, handelsblatt.com. See above, 'Europe as Battleground and Place of Desire', pp. 192ff.

23   SIPRI, the Stockholm International Peace Research Institute, reported Russian military spending in 2018 to amount to $62.4 billion. The UK, France, Germany, and Italy, the four largest European NATO members, together spent $175.2 billion, 2.8 times as much as Russia.

France, 'the founding states of Europe' [*sic*], should take the lead. The United States, which had in the preceding two decades systematically dismantled the global arms-control architecture inherited from the Cold War, was not mentioned.

Like 'more unity through less unity', European state-building through militarisation, somewhat reminiscent of the Prussian model, never had a chance.[24] This was in spite of the fact that on the surface, when its proponents pleaded for a 'common sovereignty' for Europe, they were obviously catering to the French taste, as expressed in Macron's 2017 Sorbonne speech, a day after Angela Merkel's last re-election.[25] Also, by listing more than one potential enemy against which Europe was to be defended, the appeal did not preclude something like European equidistance to Russia and China, on the one hand, and 'Trump', on the other, in line with the French vision for a desirable global order. Moreover, not just as the United States, but also NATO was never mentioned, let alone its new doctrine, adopted in the spirit of the New World Order, which extended its mission to worldwide 'out of area' operations including, presumably, humanitarian interventions in fulfilment of the neocons' proclaimed 'duty to protect'. In addition, in arguing that the new European army would not require higher defence spending, given the European NATO states' vast outspending of Russia, the appeal implicitly rejected the American demand that European NATO members, especially Germany, should increase their military expenditures to 2 percent of GDP – which, for Germany in 2018, would have meant an increase of more than 60 percent.[26] Note that the first time NATO had, under US pressure, discussed the 2 percent target was at a summit meeting in Prague in 2002 – the same meeting at which the alliance opened accession talks with Bulgaria, Estonia, Latvia, Lithuania,

---

24   As the French statesman Count Mirabeau allegedly put it in 1786, the year Frederick II of Prussia died: 'Other states have an army; Prussia is an army that owns a state.'

25   'In Europe, we are seeing a two-fold movement: gradual and inevitable disengagement by the United States, and a long-term terrorist threat with the stated goal of splitting our free societies . . . In the area of defence, our aim needs to be ensuring Europe's autonomous operating capabilities, in complement to NATO.' See 'Sorbonne Speech of Emmanuel Macron – Full Text/English Version', *Ouest-France*, 26 September 2017, international.blogs.ouest-france.fr.

26   According to Statista, Germany in 2018 spent 1.2 percent of its GDP on its military, amounting to $44.7 billion. Had it spent 2 percent, as asked by NATO, it would have spent the equivalent of $74.5 billion, $12.1 billion more than Russia.

Romania, Slovakia, and Slovenia and confirmed its open-door policy for Eastern Europe, including Georgia and Ukraine, against strong Russian objections.

Even more importantly, the document failed to address the issue of nuclear arms – not least, one might assume, to allow the German Greens of the time to join the cause. Of course, had the project ever been taken up by the German government – Germany being committed to not having nuclear arms, and indeed forbidden from having them under the Nuclear Non-proliferation Treaty of 1968 – it would have entailed the risk of having to exchange US for French nuclear protection. That risk would have seemed as unacceptable in Germany as was the idea in France of sharing its nuclear arsenal with 'Europe', meaning Germany under a European flag. Underlying this was the question of the extent to which a European army would be, or would be obliged to be, integrated in the command structure, and complement the 'capabilities' of NATO – its 'interoperability' with the military of the United States. As the Bundeswehr had, since Germany's rearmament in the 1950s, been fully integrated in NATO, the US would obviously have insisted on any European army, particularly its German contingent, to be integrated with NATO as well.

Moreover, had the appeal for a European army touched upon the nuclear arms issue, it would have become obvious that, superficial similarities notwithstanding, it was incompatible with core elements of the French European project of security and strategic sovereignty.[27] Like the US, France had long wanted Germany to spend more on defence – which the appellants explicitly declared unnecessary. In the French view, rather than adding to American transatlantic power, increased German military spending was to fill the conventional arms gap in the French armoury, caused by the high costs of France's nuclear force, enabling a French-led 'Europe' to better serve French ambitions in Africa and the

---

27 This alone raises serious questions about the basic political competence of the politicians who signed the appeal, including, in addition to Friedrich Merz, a former federal finance minister, Hans Eichel. A philosopher may perhaps be forgiven for expressing his desire for a castle in the air which, as he could easily have found out, would never be more than a figment of his imagination – although when serious issues are in play, such as nuclear bombs, such negligence is likely not just to set a bad example for others but also to mislead what philosophers call 'political discourse'. Coming from political leaders, past or present, however, chatter like this is outright irresponsible, apart from indicating deep contempt for the citizens being addressed.

Middle East. For European strategic sovereignty of this kind, some sort of détente with Russia would be helpful: a Eurasian settlement that would, however, be at odds with American expansion into the Russian periphery, more than perhaps with Russian expansion in the French-European periphery. For the US, the overarching aim was and remains to integrate the former Communist countries of Eastern Europe into an American-led 'West'. By making Europe, through NATO, take a hostile position towards Russia, it would also make it dependent on its alliance with the US, helping it maintain the unipolar world of George H. W. Bush. For France, to the contrary, a European army was of interest precisely to the extent that it would extract Europe from the close embrace in which the United States was holding it, not least by promising nuclear protection to non-nuclear Germany.

The effort to unify Europe by militarising the EU was, from the beginning, bound to fail. Shortly after the appeal had been published, it was forgotten; outside of Germany, it was never even noticed. All too obviously, the project bore the mark of the German obsession with submerging the German nation-state in a supranational European state, whatever the cost, as a side effect submerging all other European nation-states with it. The appeal also refrained from presenting an enemy, a *Feind*, who might have served as an external unifier standing in for an internal one; Russia was not considered for the role, rightly given its (correctly noted) military inferiority. (Only four years after the appeal, the Ukraine war was claimed to require a life-and-death defence of 'European values' against Russia, suddenly designated as a Schmittian 'existential enemy' ready to move on from Ukraine to conquer Western Europe as a whole.)[28] In fact, military considerations, to the extent that the appeal included any at all, were entirely subordinate to a 'European project' aimed at dissolving the European nation-states into a supranational European superstate: a European army to advance European integration rather than fight an enemy. Nobody in Europe, however, except for hardcore German 'pro-Europeans', was dreaming the German dream of costless European military power used for the non-military promotion of 'ever closer' European unity – a dream that saved its dreamers from having to deal with common-sense questions like, for example, who was to call the European army's shots, the president of the

---

28   Carl Schmitt, *Der Begriff des Politischen*, Berlin: Duncker & Humblot, 1932.

European Commission or the twenty-seven heads of state and government assembled in the European Council?

All of this became irrelevant in 2022 with the Russian invasion of Ukraine, which brought back, in new form, the issue of the European army. Suddenly, the militarisation of Europe was driven not just by one external unifier but by two, one named 'Putin', the other the United States – which, in a way, was an internal unifier as well, through its transatlantic European presence via NATO. Here, there was a crisis not of 'European integration' but of war and peace, caused by an, according to an impressively effective Western speech regime, 'unprovoked' attack on a European country by an evil empire reborn. It was in this context, through the international military hierarchy of NATO, that the US – standing in for the cowardly Germans, the egocentric French, and the imaginary German-French or French-German 'tandem', managed to organise a centralised military and political response to the Russian advance, forging 'Europe' together above and beyond the conflicts and divisions that had in the past stood in the way of its centralised unification. After all those years of stagnation and incipient disintegration, there was now finally a robust reason for standing united, forcefully represented by a strong leader, although outside Europe, with sufficient power to impose centralised discipline on the Western European state system. Now military integration was driven not by the friends of integration for its own sake but by the US-controlled NATO command. Rather than advancing *European* strategic sovereignty, now European unity was to be subservient to *American* strategic sovereignty, in the continuing American battle over the inclusion of ever more former parts of the Soviet empire in a New World Order conceived as a global extension of the American sphere of interest, under something like a universalised Monroe Doctrine.

After Ukraine

War is the ultimate stochastic source of history, and, once it is underway, there is no end to the surprises it may bring. Still, even though the war in Ukraine seems far from over, it has put an end, at least for the foreseeable future, to any vision of an equal-sovereignty, cooperative state system in Europe. It also seems to have dealt a death blow to the French

dream of turning the liberal empire of the European Union into a strategically sovereign third global power – a sovereign state, or superstate,
independent from and credibly rivalling both a rising China and a
declining US. The Russian invasion of Ukraine seems to have answered
the question of the post-neoliberal European order by reinstating the
model, long believed to be outdated, of the Cold War: a Europe united
under American lead, serving as a transatlantic bridgehead for the US in
its confrontation with an existential enemy, then the Soviet Union and
now Russia. Inclusion in a resurrected, remilitarised 'West', with new
functions as a European subdepartment of NATO – that is, of the American defence establishment – seems to have saved, for the time being, the
EU from the destructive centrifugal forces that beset it before the
Zeitenwende, without altogether doing away with them. By restoring
the West, the war for a time neutralised the various fault-lines along
which the EU had been crumbling, while catapulting the US into a
position of renewed dominance over Western Europe, including its
international organisation, the European Union.

The reintegration of the West under American dominance settled the
relationship between NATO and EU in favour of a division of labour
that firmly established the primacy of the former over the latter. In an
interesting way, this healed the rift between continental Europe and the
United Kingdom that had opened in the wake of Brexit. As NATO rose
to supremacy, the fact that it includes the UK together with the leading
member states of the EU restores a prominent European role for Britain
through its special relationship with the United States. How this affects
the international status of a country like France was illustrated by an
agreement in 2021 between the US, the UK, and Australia – the AUKUS
pact – under which Australia cancelled a 2016 deal with France to
purchase French diesel-powered submarines. Instead, it committed
itself to developing nuclear-powered submarines together with the US
and the UK – an event that served to show the French the limits of a
French-led EU as a global power.

The rise of NATO as a dominant force in the Western European state
system implied a decline of the European Union to the status of a NATO
civil auxiliary, subservient to American strategic objectives – and not
exclusively in Europe. The US had, since the 1990s, imagined the EU as
something like a training ground for future NATO members, especially
those neighbouring Russia, like Georgia and Ukraine, but also the West

Balkans. The EU, for its part, insisted on its admissions procedures, which include lengthy negotiations on national institutional and economic conditions that have to be met before formal accession. Among other things, this was to limit the burden the new member states would place on the EU budget and ensure that their political elites would be sufficiently 'pro-European' not to raise unmanageable problems for European-level centralised, techno-marketocratic governance. To the US, given the urgency of its geostrategic objectives, this appeared overly pedantic, if not obstructionist. Indeed, it had especially been France which resisted an all-too-liberal 'widening' of the Union, afraid that it might stand in the way of its 'deepening' à la Française.

From an American perspective, the EU is ideally conceived as a civil subsidiary of NATO on the European continent, with the task of integrating peripheral countries into the Western alliance and grooming them politically and economically for NATO membership. Burden-sharing between the US and European countries assigned to the latter the provision of economic incentives for new states in the East to join the West and helping them build the economic base for their political and cultural Westernisation, for example through EU 'structural funds' securing within aspiring member states social stability, in a Western-liberal-democratic sense. With the Ukraine war, that vision of the EU as a pep-up prep school for future NATO members is increasingly becoming reality. Any negotiated settlement of the war is likely for some time to preclude an accession of Ukraine to NATO. In compensation, fast-track admission to the EU could be offered, not least because it would secure funds for repairing the damage caused by the war – funds that the US is unlikely to be willing or able to afford. It seems likely that France will not be able much longer to block the accession to the EU of Albania, Bosnia and Herzegovina, North Macedonia, Montenegro, Kosovo, and Serbia, and ultimately, of course, Ukraine. Depending on how the war develops, there may even be some membership-like affiliation in store for Georgia and Armenia, all of them in an expedited procedure, not just making significant demands on the EU's budget but also shifting the Union's political centre of gravity both to the East and further to the Far West – meaning the United States.[29]

---

29 In preparation, France suggested the introduction of a sort of second-class membership for new admissions – making for a 'Europe of different speeds' – while

Apart from having to hold out a prospect of membership for countries of American strategic interest on the eastern periphery of Western
Europe, the EU, and the European Commission in particular, continues
to be in demand as an agency for planning, coordinating, and monitoring European economic sanctions against Russia and China. Sanctions
imply a deep reorganisation of the far-flung supply chains of the neoliberal age and the New World Order, to fit the less integrated and more
decentralised multipolar world that is about to emerge, with its emphasis on economic security and strategic autarchy. Having, for some time,
been an engine of globalisation, the EU will, as a result, in important
respects, have to devote itself to deglobalisation – something that, until
a short time ago, would have been considered a leftist absurdity. Paring
supply chains would seem to be less a function of politics than of technocratic expertise, which is difficult enough given the high degree of
economic interdependence inherited from hyperglobalisation. Still,
which sanctions are to be imposed on whom remains of great political
interest to national governments, acting under the watchful eyes of both
their constituents and their now-principal international organisation,
NATO, as directed by its strongest nation-state, the United States. Thus,
while industrial policy may experience a renaissance under US-ordered
deglobalisation, this is unlikely to benefit the EU and its project of cen-
tralising political-economic governance in Europe. It is true that NATO
does not have the necessary economic expertise to assess the effects of
sanctions on Russia, on the one hand, and on Western Europe, on the
other; however, as it has turned out, the EU does not possess it either.

What is not to be underestimated, though, is that the EU will be
assigned by the US and NATO a major role in the generation of international public money for rebuilding Ukraine after the war ends. The same
holds for the provision of financial support to countries on the European periphery that are lining up for accession to the EU and, ultimately,
NATO. The capacity of the EU to serve as a receptacle for a new kind of
public debt that is politically less conspicuous than at the national level –
as in the case of the above-mentioned Recovery and Resilience Fund

---

Germany is thinking about a reform of majority voting on the council, which would
make it impossible for small countries to veto decisions, in particular on the EU's
foreign policy. Neither proposal looks like it could find the necessary support among
member states, and discussions on the subject can be expected to continue.

(RRF), a first materialisation of the Commission's NextGenerationEU (NGEU)[30] – is likely to be permanently and extensively drawn upon for mobilising European contributions to the long-term non-military costs of the war. (Experience suggests that the American contribution will end with the military hostilities.)[31] This will exacerbate the fiscal crisis of the capitalist-neoliberal state. To cope with it, in addition to credit in capital markets, special services of the ECB will be needed, as used in the fight against 'secular stagnation' and, later, the pandemic – like the purchasing of government debt from private investors as a form of indirect state finance, in circumvention of the Treaties.

Liabilities Old and New

The new functions assigned to the EU as a result of the Ukraine crisis, and in the course of its subordination to NATO, are far from resolving its old problems; in fact, they exacerbate and add to them. On the EU's western flank, as noted above, the United Kingdom has, via its close alliance with the US via NATO, returned to the European theatre with a vengeance, although more like a deputy of the US than as one member state among others. In the south, there is no reason to believe that NATO's new European supremacy will help improve Italian economic performance; on the contrary, the higher costs of energy and the shortened supply chains are likely to impose an additional burden on the Mediterranean economies. While they are certain to demand compensation from the EU's rich member states, these will in turn be preoccupied with raising their defence spending in line with ever-increasing NATO demands, not to mention underwriting the accession of new EU member states on their way into NATO. Competition for

---

30   One of the fancy labels that the EU keeps inventing, only to forget them a short time later – adding to the confusion over what is and is not going on in Brussels.

31   For example, in February 2022 the Biden administration confiscated half of the frozen assets of the central bank of Afghanistan, deposited with the New York City branch of the Federal Reserve, to be set aside for the survivors of 9/11 and their lawyers. The impounded funds amounted to $3.5 billion. A few weeks later, an international donor conference, organised by the UN together with Germany, the UK, and Qatar, tried to raise $4.4 billion to help end mass starvation in Afghanistan, after the American departure under Taliban rule. Only $2.44 billion were contributed by the forty-one nations that were in (virtual) attendance; the US was not among them.

EU subsidies, in particular out of the so-called 'Cohesion Fund', will be more intense, not least because of new, war-related needs of Eastern member states – for example, the hosting of Ukrainian refugees and the absorption of Ukrainian agricultural exports.[32] Plans to cut financial assistance to countries with insufficient respect for the 'rule of law' will become obsolete as cultural conflicts between 'illiberal' and 'liberal' democracy are eclipsed by the geostrategic objectives of the US and NATO.

As the costs rise of what is called in Brussels 'cohesion', paid for by the rich Northwest while the economic disparities between the latter and the South continue to widen, a shift in political power inside the EU is under way in favour of the Union's Eastern-front states. Western cultural education exercises have begun to appear petty in the face of millions of refugees arriving in a country like Poland, with the US having little reason to pressure its Eastern European allies to cater to German or Dutch liberal sensitivities. Efforts to make economic support for post-Communist countries conditional on their adherence to 'democratic values' will come to very little as long as the United States is satisfied with their adherence to NATO and their willingness to fight the pro-Western good fight. As the US is preparing to let the Ukraine war last – which is only logical if the goal is regime change in Russia, or, in any case, a permanent weakening of Russia as a state – a country's preparedness to host American troops must take precedence over the fine print of democratic conditionality. In an EU turning, for an as-yet-uncertain number of years, into something like a supranational military auxiliary service, its Eastern-front states are likely to dominate the common political agenda. In this, they will be supported by the US, with its geostrategic interest in keeping Russia politically, economically, and militarily in check and isolated from Western Europe. Ultimately, this may result in the US, acting through its Eastern European allies and NATO, effectively taking the place of the Union's would-be dual hegemon, the French-German tandem.

With time, whether the war ends or, more likely, drags on, an EU subordinate to NATO will become dependent on the bizarre domestic

---

32   The EU Cohesion Fund supports member states with a GDP per capita of below 90 percent of the EU average, 'to strengthen the economic, social and territorial cohesion of the EU'.

politics of a declining great power, the United States, readying itself for a global confrontation with a rising great power, China. Nowhere in Western Europe today is the question seriously being asked what will happen either if Donald Trump is re-elected in the 2024 presidential election – which seemed increasingly likely in the winter of 2023/24 – or some ersatz Trump is elected in his place. Even with Joe Biden or some moderate Republican, the short attention span of American imperial policy, now a conveniently suppressed memory in Europe, will always be a present danger. Iraq, Libya, Syria, and Afghanistan document the American penchant to exit if liberal-capitalist 'nation-building' for some reason fails to work, leaving behind a lethal mess that others must clean up if they are interested in upholding a modicum of international order at their doorsteps.[33]

Beyond Superstate and Empire

The European Union has always been in flux, evolving over a sequence of intermediary stages from an instrument of cooperative 'regional planning' (Polanyi) for six neighbouring nation-states to the post-democratic technocracy and marketocracy of the neoliberal era. In the final years of the post-1990 New World Order, with twenty-eight members, the EU had entered into a period of institutional stagnation, a standoff in a tug of war between forces of centralisation and decentral-isation, with tendencies towards gradual disintegration, functionally or even formally. In part this was because the 'uniting of Europe' began to extend to areas of national economic, cultural, and political life that member states would or could not hand over to supranational rule; or it was due to differences in national interests emerging precisely as a result

---

33   One explanation that is too rarely invoked for the stunning negligence with which the United States enter into and exit from military adventures is the location of the United States on a continent-sized island, far away from those parts of the world, including Europe, where its political class might feel a need to deploy its troops and finish off a handpicked enemy. Whatever it does or does not do there, it has no conse-quences for the US at home. When things go wrong, the US can retreat to its home base, where nobody can follow it. Wishful thinking, lack of local knowledge, sloppy planning, and perhaps more than anything else a highly flexible tailoring of international strate-gies to domestic public sentiments pose an enduring risk for anyone entrusting the United States with representing them in international politics.

of integration working out differently in different countries.[34] Together with territorial expansion, these and other developments had given rise to ever more internal diversity that began to critically overstrain the governing capacity of the Union.

By the late 2010s, a desperate attempt by a group of German pro-Europeans had failed to unite Europe on a Prussian model of sorts, with state-building preceded by army-building. Alternative approaches to preserving and, indeed, reviving the EU as an international organisation by less, rather than more, integration never stood a chance; they were blocked by the complexities of the Treaties – the acquis communautaire – the technicalities of the common currency and, importantly, a lack of confidence, on the part of member states' political classes, in their capacity to govern their countries. This rendered almost irresistible the lure of the manifold opportunities for national political elites to use the EU's multilevel polity as a depository for problems with which they felt unable or were unwilling to deal, such as the regulation of uninvited immigration. There was also the sacrosanct moral status of 'Europe' among a new, allegedly 'post-materialist' middle class, as well as the divergent imperial interests of the EU's two biggest countries, Germany and France. It was in this situation, after the Union had had to leave the management of the COVID-19 pandemic essentially to its member states, that with the war in Ukraine a new kind of centralisation began in the Western European state system – one that was geostrategic, under the leadership of a non-European power, the United States, embedded in NATO as a transatlantic international organisation devoted, unambiguously, to 'the continuation of politics with other means' (in Carl von Clausewitz's German, 'die Fortsetzung der Politik mit anderen Mitteln').

Will the United States be able to keep a – further expanding – European Union together, centralised, unified, focused on defeating a common enemy, the old and new internal cleavages closed or papered over, bridged or suppressed, with national self-will disciplined by external pressures from both friend and foe? Even if the struggle over a *new* New World Order will move to the next theatre, the North Pacific – as it probably will – the United States will continue to have need for a united Europe as an ally and will, therefore, do its best to prevent the war in Ukraine being settled one way or other. There is no guarantee, however,

---

34   Ernst B. Haas, *The Uniting of Europe*, Stanford, CA: Stanford University Press, 1958.

that the old war and the new enemy – China – will appear threatening enough to European countries to make them continue following American leadership, at the expense of national interests. Then, the old differences among Germany, France, Italy, Poland, Hungary, and others may again come to the fore – differences that, unless somehow suppressed, will, as in the past, stand in the way of supranational integration of the European state system.

Within Europe, as the United States moves on to new venues in pursuit of its self-assigned historical mission to replace authoritarianism with democracy worldwide, it will become the task of Germany – having assumed, on American prodding, the role of single leader of the EU – to keep the Ukrainian war going by keeping the Ukrainian state and its government alive in its confrontation with Russia. US and British promises of an early defeat of Russia, effected especially by American and European economic sanctions, having proven fatally wrong, it will be Germany that will be left holding the bag, under supervision by the United Kingdom, the traditional linchpin of European transatlanticism. For the UK, just as the US, a prolonged Ukraine standoff will be preferable to a peace settlement; it will keep Europe, both Eastern and Western, allied under Western leadership and lock Germany into NATO and 'the West', in particular precluding any improper German tête-à-tête with France. In fact, the way things looked in early 2024, Russia may not be interested in peace anymore either, having defeated the US-led attempt to demolish its industrial base and force on it a Western-dictated regime change. Now, having learned from Angela Merkel and François Hollande that the Minsk negotiations were not meant seriously and were just a ploy to buy Ukraine time to build up its military, Vladimir Putin may feel he can, and indeed has to, turn the tables and destroy Ukraine as a viable nation-state – by waiting for its citizens to rebel against the ultra-nationalist government or leave the country forever, and for its oligarchs to relocate to New York or London – as well as discredit the EU as a viable international organisation.

Concerning the latter, Germany as internal unifier, left to its own devices by the United States, will, sooner or later, be overburdened by having to be the leading power of the European Union. While it is, nominally, the EU that will carry the burden of supporting Ukraine, in effect it will be its strongest and most Americanised nation-state that has to do the job. Given the limited capacity of other EU member states to support the Ukrainian state, Germany may have to double its defence budget in a very short time, not to mention significantly raising its contribution to the budget of an EU newly enlarged by several poor countries, above all Ukraine. It seems inevitable that this will call forth domestic opposition, in a country with a crumbling physical infrastructure, a failing educational system, an expensive programme of environmental transformation, rising costs of energy, and a prospect of rapid de-industrialisation.

Germany's foreseeable failure to sustain a Ukrainian nation-state under continuing military pressure from Russia will allow the US and the UK to shift the blame for the disaster of their Ukrainian strategy to 'Europe', as led by its most powerful state. It will also not bode well for the project of a unitary, centralised, hierarchically governed European superstate, the 'Gaullist' alternative to a Europe content with being a transatlantic extension of the US. Prospects for Schmittian regional hegemony, which would both provide for internal stability and allow for the external projection of power, would appear bleak given Germany's limited governing capacity. Facing Europe's deeply rooted national diversity of interests and capacities, European states may therefore, at some point, find themselves forced to think about other ways of asserting their interests in the world outside Europe – unless they want to be content with representation by a US where at the time of writing a return of Donald Trump to power seems likely. If 'Europe', in one way or other, wants to have a voice in a future multipolar world, or perhaps even wants to make a contribution to its emergence, it must learn to organise itself, neither as empire nor as superstate, but as a cooperative association of sovereign nation-states, acting on their interests, sometimes on their own and sometimes in alliance with others – as a Europe, again, of 'variable geometry' embedding itself in a global alignment of non-aligned countries, detached from the US until, perhaps, the latter will be ready to join it as one country among others.

Learning from Europe

The European Union may be considered the site of the most advanced historical experiment to date, exploring, on a smaller, continental scale, the prospects of the globalist utopia of a denationalised, unified, integrated, and centralised world political-economic order. The auspices for the experiment to succeed must have seemed overwhelmingly promising. Nowhere would the conditions for a voluntary merger of polities and sovereignties, for an escape from the provincialism of nation-states, have appeared more favourable than in Western Europe, a region where states and societies after the Second World War seemed like true birds of the same feather: liberal-democratic, capitalist with a human, social democratic face, joined in the same military alliance and, for decades since the early post-war years, accustomed to cooperating with each other on a wide range of subjects in a wide variety of ways.

But when, in the late 1980s, a new wave of economic and political 'European integration' began, building on the institutional foundations of the European Economic Community and the European Community, it ended, less than half a century later, in failure: nothing like a superstate, not even something like a functioning empire, on the most welcoming testing ground for a transition from sectoral cooperation between sovereign states to state sovereignties amalgamated into one integrated sovereignty, of state or empire. Rather than giving rise to a United Europe, the history of the European Union in its latest, neoliberal phase produced a state system stuck in a tug of war between forces of centralisation and resistance to centralisation, demonstrating the limits, apparently insurmountable, of unity in political orders, in the architectures of states as well as state systems.

With hindsight, we can understand what was, and is, at work here. In short, the more encompassing a political system, the more internally heterogeneous it becomes, and high internal heterogeneity makes integrated governance, where one size must fit all, inevitably technocratic, bureaucratic, mercatocratic – in other words, undemocratic. The result of this is a loss of legitimacy on the part of the centre – the central government of a superstate or the hegemon of an empire – accompanied by local opposition, expressed in claims for autonomy, a restoration of local sovereignty, for less integration and more local self-determination, for internal federalism or external independence.

The dysfunctions of over-integration that have brought the uniting of Europe to a standstill and are about to undo its 'globalist' progress from the neoliberal era are of two sorts: either functional and technical, or social and political. In functionalist-technical terms, overcentralised government tends to be overburdened by the variety of, in a general sense, local problems and contingencies that arise differently in its different constituencies, often as a result precisely of central policies meant to apply equally throughout the integrated political jurisdiction. In social-political terms, the political centre of a highly heterogeneous compound political community, superstate, or empire cannot always do justice to the often-conflicting traditional values and ongoing collective choices among its constituencies, fuelling desires for independent political representation and self-government. Also, as centralised government confronting high local heterogeneity fails to attend to locally specific (as distinguished from general) problems or demands, it may, as a consequence, asymmetrically benefit some of its subunits at the expense of others, setting off conflicts among local communities, or between them and the central power.

Moreover, hypercentralisation across too many diverse political localities is likely to give rise, in a centralised superstate, to a new political-managerial class expropriating national political classes of their power, or in an international empire to a hegemonic nation-state lording it over the other nation-states by assuming the role of internal or, for that matter, external unifier – or, as in the EU, to a combination of the two. Under such conditions, problem overload – excessive 'complexity' – and the social disconnectedness of governing political classes or states may shade into one another. Also, rather than fight each another, local and central political elites may conspire to exploit the complexities of a multilevel polity to cover up its political and technical ungovernability, or their own incompetence, or the generally unruly nature of capitalist democracies, by moving problems in need of address back and forth between national and supranational institutions to avoid having to actually address them.

As the drawbacks of centralisation make themselves felt more and more, pressures from below for a restoration of political sovereignty at the local level of a multilevel governance regime – superstate or empire – are likely to return and grow, setting in motion a movement against centralisation and for decentralisation, blocking further centralisation and calling forth debates about the costs of centralism (examined in the next chapter) and the possibilities and benefits of decentralised government with distributed sovereignty (discussed in the tenth and final chapter).

PART IV

Beyond Globalist Centralisation

9

Mega-statism and Its Limitations

Is escape upwards out of the post-neoliberal stalemate possible? I will argue in this chapter that it is not. Integration, centralisation, and unification are often recommended as technocratic 'solutions' to problems, as political and moral imperatives. But they are overestimated, in both respects, and they have long since reached the limit of their usefulness. Centralist unitary regimes are hard to construct and difficult to hold together; their political stability and technical capacity deteriorate with increases in the scale and heterogeneity of the world they govern. Universalism confronts particularism, the suppression of which consumes resources. Pervasive centrifugal tendencies grow as integration progresses. If the conversion of diversity into unity crosses a certain threshold, resistance becomes too great and integration grinds to a halt.[1] The result is a crisis of the institutions, today characterised by a reciprocal deadlock of capitalist universalism and social particularism, of globalism and democracy.

---

1 Amitai Etzioni, *Reclaiming Patriotism*, Charlottesville: University of Virginia Press, 2019. A book by Giandomenico Majone (*Rethinking the Union of Europe Post-Crisis*, Cambridge, UK: Cambridge University Press, 2014), subtitled 'Has Integration Gone Too Far?', applies this idea to the EU. Majone, who has published foundational research on the EU and was for a long time a defender of its integration model, concludes, taking into account the EU crisis following the global financial crisis of 2008, that the EU's eventual transformation into a superstate (however federalist) is now an untenable idea 'in a union of twenty-eight members at vastly different stages of socio-economic development, with different geopolitical concerns, and correspondingly diverse policy priorities' (322).

Neoliberalism, the stagnation and foreseeable end of which is the subject of this book, presents itself as cosmopolitanism, and as the universalist conquest of particularistic narrow-mindedness. Its aim is the abolition of differences in a worldwide community that no longer recognises nations but knows only individuals with their common human inclination, in the words of Adam Smith, 'to truck, barter, and exchange one thing for another'.[2] Neoliberal political economy, which reached its zenith in the New World Order dominated by the United States after 1990, unleashes 'market forces' not only within states but between them and beyond their borders, by means of a reorganisation of states and state systems – with the aim of dismantling them. Its utopia is a world without statehood, which naturally fails, of course, because free markets depend on states for their enforcement and defence. Neoliberal government policies seek to ensure that the worldwide integration, or unification, of markets and economies ('convergence') advances continuously, based on the dogmatic premise, or perhaps just the bold assertion, that a unified market in a unified economy benefits all participants equally, no matter how different they may be. In a perfect world, this would amount to a unified global state, a *single state* or world superstate, politically and institutionally inaccessible to 'populist' demands coming from below, and as such predestined to stand guard over a globally unlimited authoritarian liberalism. The trouble with this is that the existing states and the citizens living in them refuse to yield, meaning only second- and third-best solutions are available as intermediate stages on the way to utopia. Yet, in truth, these are the only possible choices in a social world contaminated by its historicity.

Here is where so-called global governance enters the scene: the use of the existing state system to simulate a unified authoritarian-liberal superstate, by means of summit conferences, expert commissions, depoliticised authorities in the form of democratically unaccountable central banks, and similar institutions, all set within the framework and on the basis of an international state system configured as voluntary ('liberal') and egalitarian ('multilateral'). However, this too is a castle in the air; in reality, it functions only as the instrument of a

---

2   Adam Smith, *An Inquiry into the Nature and Causes of the Wealth of Nations*, Oxford: Oxford University Press, 1993 [1776].

globally expanding process of capitalist accumulation, to the extent that it displays the characteristics of an empire. I will discuss this in detail later in this chapter, where I will show that the need for imperial international rule as a second-rate substitute for supranational statehood exists even in the European Union, which has progressed furthest on the path to an authoritarian-liberal superstate – though its advance has now come to a halt.

The Contradictions and Limits of Neoliberal Globalisation: Eight Theses

(1) States, at least when more than one exists, are, in principle, the natural enemies of neoliberalism, which is necessarily globalist. States have boundaries, and their policies can be made to serve territorially rooted and therefore particular interests; they can be used to support interests that would be unrealisable through the market – or, according to the market's logic, could not be realised by honest means. These are the interests of the losers, who want to become winners after the fact by political manoeuvres.

(2) However, as long as it remains impossible to replace particularistic, politically influenced state authority with a general set of rules locked in globally and immunised against plebeian pressure, states (and state authority) will still be indispensable for neoliberalism. Capitalism, especially global capitalism, is not a natural but a social system. It does not fall from the sky and does not remain in existence automatically but, rather, must be established and then defended against those who oppose it. This requires politics – politics of the state.

(3) Neoliberalism and globalism, despite their pretended rejection of state involvement, are nevertheless dependent on statehood. They must admittedly restructure it to fit their own requirements, so as to prevent the social particularism which underlies all states and and endangers the universalism of the global market. A reorganisation of this kind, however, is fraught with risks that may flare up at any time. As long as a state is reliant on a minimum level of democratic legitimation, it cannot be ruled out that populists and nationalists may gain influence within it. Denationalisation requires strong states, but these must not fall into the wrong hands. Liberalism, if it is to survive, must therefore be

'authoritarian', as Carl Schmitt demonstrated conclusively on the eve of the Nazis' *Machtergreifung*.[3]

(4) As we have seen, growing worldwide integration is accompanied by an increase in the number of states and thus a more differentiated international state system, along with a growing demand 'from below' for state independence. The progress of the neoliberal project therefore depends on its success in synchronising ever more states and welding them together, if not formally then at least functionally, into a single giant state for neoliberal purposes. This requires a general opening up of their societies, an effective abolition of their borders, a harmonisation of their domestic legal arrangements (described by Hayek as 'isonomy'), and a quasi-constitutional guarantee against the volatility of electoral majorities through a political system designed to impede as much as possible the authorisation of egalitarian and redistributive policies. Neo-liberal globalisation means overcoming the stubborn resistance of the participating states by means of a comprehensive process of institutional convergence.

(5) The restructuring of a state for neoliberal purposes, aimed at depriving social interests of the power to conduct market-correcting policies, requires a high degree of capitalist statecraft. This is particularly true if the political systems of the nation-states to be modified and incorporated are constituted democratically. As the experience of recent years has shown, there is no guarantee that demands for protection on the part of a nation-state can be suppressed in good time on every occasion. The use of democratic states in particular for the implementation of a unified global – or even continental – system of government can falter at any time. The recent history of the European Union documents that such regimes, even if they are firmly institutionalised in quasi-constitutional form, are extremely fragile; not even in the EU can it be assumed that 'Eurosceptical' movements hostile to the market and to integration will be permanently excluded from national political power.

(6) State systems linked to neoliberalism present themselves ideologically as multilateral, non-discretionary, rules-based international

---

3   Carl Schmitt, 'Gesunde Wirtschaft im starken Staat: Mitteilungen des Vereins zur Wahrung der gemeinsamen wirtschaftichen Interessen in Rheinland und Westfalen (Langnamverein)', *Neue Folge* 21, no. 1 (1932), 13–32; Wolfgang Streeck, 'Heller, Schmitt and the Euro', *European Law Journal* 21, no. 3 (2015), 361–70.

orders entered into voluntarily by contract. This is consonant with liberalism's notion of itself as the natural condition of a society of rational human beings untouched by the intervention of power-hungry political actors, motivated and rewarded by shared prosperity and collective security. But rules-based multilateralism alone can only exceptionally, if at all, enforce and guarantee the conformity of the internal arrangements of sovereign states; and, in the long term, it certainly cannot drive the expansion of a capitalist order from its centre to a periphery that is to be pushed ever further into the background and, at the same time, reorganised to bring it into line with capitalist requirements. Uniformity among formally sovereign states cannot be lastingly and reliably ensured without the power-based relations of inter-state rule. If a unified market system cannot be established on a single-state basis, or outside the state (by something like global governance), it must be achieved by means of a hierarchical international order, resting on supranational institutions or asymmetrical power relations, or – and this is typically the case – on both at once.

(7) International integration beyond a certain level, even if it is integration into a liberal order, therefore requires imperial structures. These structures presuppose an imbalance between a hegemonic power and other states more or less dependent on it, thus forming the basis of a differentiation between centre and periphery. Today's capitalism, now expanding globally, has historically always been based on a hegemonic state order characterised by a continuous outward extension of its borders by means of state power.[4] Even where capitalism has relied on the utopia of rules-based (and therefore egalitarian) multilateralism for its political legitimacy, as an international system it was always marked by an asymmetrical distribution of power – accompanied by an unequal division of imperial costs and revenues, and a considerable use of ideological, pecuniary, and military instruments.

(8) Empires, including neoliberal capitalist ones, are typically unstable: they depend not only on the superiority of their hegemonic

---

4   This thesis lies at the core of the so-called world-systems theory of capitalist development, to be found in the work of Immanuel Wallerstein (*The Modern World-System I: Capitalist Agriculture and the Origins of the European World-Economy in the Sixteenth Century*, New York: Academic Press, 1974; *World-Systems Analysis: An Introduction*, Durham, NC: Duke University Press, 2004), and Giovanni Arrighi (*The Long Twentieth Century: Money, Power, and the Origins of Our Times*, London: Verso, 1994) among others.

power – the power of the centre – and the degree of conviction carried by their legitimating 'narrative' but also on their cost/benefit ratio, especially in the eyes of the hegemonic power itself and its citizens. One cause of imperial instability, as mentioned earlier, is the increasing cost of maintaining the empire in the face of stagnant or falling hegemonic seigniorage; another is the tendency of empires to overextend themselves and thereby heighten the complexity of the problems the centre must solve, to such a degree that its capacity to govern is overburdened.

To summarise: neoliberal mega-statism (*Großstaaterei*) can assume many forms. The abolition of statehood in favour of technocracy or rule by the market – the establishment of a global *non-state*, as it were – was never a real possibility. Nor is a *world state* on the agenda. An attempt was made to link together a number of small states, which remained formally sovereign, through uniform legal systems, and to establish a kind of *unified sovereignty* through the World Trade Organization or the European Union – a point to which I shall return later. But this configuration proved impossible to expand beyond a certain level of integration; there was no route from there to the non-state, or the world state. Instead, the process remained stuck at a precarious intermediate stage on the road to empire, proclaimed as a *liberal international order* (or, LIO) – meaning a multilateral and rule-bound order, but based in actual fact on the vigorous extension of the hegemonic central state's legal order to all others. It was a *neoliberal imperial order* (or NIO) as a *would-be single state*, to extend the play on words.

Here, and in the next chapter, I shall discuss the limits to the neoliberal dissolution of boundaries and, consequently, any breakthrough at the top, out of the stalemate between globalism and democracy, with reference to two developments: firstly, the stalling at the second stage of globalisation, so-called hyperglobalisation; and secondly, the impasse of European integration, pursued as the dissolution of European nation-states within a neoliberal superstate. In each case, the result was a profound institutional crisis, both politically and in terms of the technique of government, after global governance had proved incapable of replacing statehood, and the superstate had shown it was in no position to replace the nation-state.

Globalisation beyond the State

There has always been unease about 'globalisation'. Yet it was only with the transition to neoliberal 'hyperglobalisation' that articulated oppositions developed worldwide, from below in the South, and from within in the North. These were not merely demands for the correction of excesses but also programmes for explicit *deglobalisation*; to this day, most are based on the ideas of Keynes and Polanyi in one way or another. The Turkish American economist Dani Rodrik, professor of international political economy at Harvard Kennedy School of Government, made significant contributions here. In 1997 he published a short book, *Has Globalisation Gone Too Far?*, under the imprint of the Washington, DC–based Institute for International Economics, a hotspot of the 'Washington Consensus'. A neoliberal manifesto calling for a market-driven international development policy, its tenor is reformist insofar as Rodrik identifies problems that might hinder the desirable progress of globalisation if they are not solved politically – as was, in principle, entirely possible at the time the book was written.[5] He describes three such problems in successive chapters as expressing 'tensions' between free trade and 'social stability' or 'social cohesion'. He itemises them as, first, conflicts between groups with differing opportunities to profit from international mobility; second, friction between the institutions of the societies engaged in opening up to each other in the course of globalisation; and, third, disputes over the extent of social protection required as the political price for economic liberalisation. According to Rodrik, only if means are found to ease these tensions will it be possible in the long run to oppose 'populist' demands for economic

---

5   The Washington Consensus is a list of ten macroeconomic prescriptions for combating crises in developing countries; it was drawn up in 1989 by a British economist, and the IMF, the World Bank, and the American Treasury secretary urgently recommended its application to the affected countries. The list represents a summary formulation of the neoliberal market fundamentalism of that time, with its stress on the need for an opening of the economy to the outside world, economic liberalisation, and a strengthening of 'market forces' within the countries in question. It was controversial from the outset, and by the turn of the millennium at the latest it turned out to be largely useless, as it was unenforceable. Wikipedia offers a good introduction for non-experts: 'Washington Consensus', wikipedia.org.

protectionism and to prevent economic integration from causing social disintegration.[6]

Rodrik's book concludes with a series of proposals and exhortations that could only appear as unorthodox against the background of the period's free market euphoria – the second wave of globalisation, as it were. Economists, he said, should become more engaged in the debate over the tensions between social stability and globalisation, in order to 'clear up the misunderstandings that opponents of trade often propagate. Keeping the debate honest and grounded on solid empirical evidence is a natural role for economists [sic]'.[7] They should, furthermore, speak out in support of the idea that countries which are in principle willing to engage in 'greater [international] harmonisation of domestic policies' should '[be able to] selectively delink from international obligations when these obligations come into conflict with domestic norms or institutions'.[8] Trade unions should ensure that national institutions promote labour mobility; governments should seek compromises between national particularities and openness to the outside world, and expand their social security systems instead of complaining about 'unfair' trading conditions; and international organisations should offer individual states more opportunities to move away from 'unconditional multilateralism'.[9] Rodrik's programme amounted to a combination of Polanyi's warnings of a liberal desocialisation of markets with Keynes's ideas of a global order stabilised by permitting exceptions.[10]

Almost a decade and a half later, in 2011, Rodrik published a second, and longer, book on the same subject, which cut far more decisively against the grain of mainstream economics. Its title, *The Globalization Paradox: Why Global Markets, States, and Democracy Can't Coexist*, indicates a primary concern with clarifying the role, the social place,

---

6　As a cautionary example, the book refers to the Republican politician Patrick Buchanan, who made repeated attempts to run for the presidency of the United States in the 1990s. Buchanan can be seen, in retrospect, as a comparatively civilised precursor to Donald Trump, in that he not only rejected free trade – in particular the North American Free Trade Agreement (NAFTA) – but also global US military interventions. Dani Rodrik, *Has Globalization Gone Too Far?*, Washington, DC: Institute for International Economics, 1997, 69–85.

7　Ibid., 73–4.
8　Ibid., 73.
9　Ibid., 77, 77–81, 81–5.
10　Ibid., 71–2.

and the practical feasibility of the state actions he had previously recommended for identifying and dealing with the 'tensions' arising from globalisation. It is striking the degree to which events that had occurred since the publication of *Has Globalization Gone Too Far?* caused the author to lose patience with his fellow experts, and with 'hyper-globalisers' in politics and business. Rodrik includes himself expressly in his criticism; he too underestimated the problems at the time, because he had not detached himself sufficiently from the basic assumptions of the discourse on economic globalisation. A few months after the publication of his book, the economies of Thailand, Indonesia, and South Korea collapsed in the 'Asian financial crisis'. Casualties of 'a massive international financial whiplash', they were soon joined by Russia, Brazil, and Argentina, along with the Nobel Prize–winning hedge fund Long-Term Capital Management.[11] As much as these events may have contributed to the earlier book's success, Rodrik commented in 2011, it was ultimately undeserving of the plaudits it received: it dealt exclusively with the international trade in goods and had deliberately ignored the financial markets. This is why he had therefore subsequently turned to researching financial globalisation. In 2008, together with a co-author, he had completed an article for the International Monetary Fund entitled 'Why Did Financial Globalization Disappoint?', which attempted to explain 'why unleashing global finance had not delivered the goods for the developing nations'. The world financial crisis broke out shortly afterwards: 'Once again I had missed the bigger event unfolding just beyond the horizon.'[12]

Crises like that of 2008, Rodrik continues, would have been entirely predictable if economists, himself included, had been prepared to break from the groupthink of their discipline. In a remarkable mea culpa, he writes:

---

11   Dani Rodrik, *The Globalization Paradox: Why Global Markets, States, and Democracy Can't Coexist*, Oxford: Oxford University Press, 2011, ix. Long-Term Capital Management (LTCM), with Nobel Prize–winning economists Myron S. Scholes and Robert C. Merton on its board of directors, was founded in 1994 to commercialise their revolutionary mathematical methods for determining the value of derivatives. The fund collapsed after the Asian Crisis of 1997 and the Russian Crisis of 1998, and had to be recapitalised by fourteen major banks, to the tune of $3.6 billion, under the supervision of the Federal Reserve. It was dissolved in the year 2000. The collapse of LTCM was the first big financial crisis of the era of hyperglobalisation to have a direct impact on the United States and other Western countries.

12   Ibid., xi.

Hubris creates blind spots. Even though I had been a critic of financial globalisation, I was not immune from this. Along with the rest of the economics profession, I too was ready to believe that prudential regulations and central bank policies had erected sufficiently strong barriers against financial panics and meltdowns in the advanced economies, and that the remaining problem was to bring similar arrangements to developing countries. My *subplots* may have been somewhat different, but I was following the same grand narrative.[13]

Following 2008, however, economists too began to doubt the governability of a neoliberal globalisation which left everything and everyone to market forces; questions about the distribution of output and protection against possible crises were now raised by the architects of hyperglobalisation themselves. As a response, Rodrik proposed an alternative arrangement based on 'two simple ideas':

First, markets and government are complements, not substitutes . . . Markets work best not where states are weakest, but where they are strong. Second, capitalism does not come with a unique model. Economic prosperity and stability can be achieved through different combinations of institutional arrangements in labor markets, finance, corporate governance, social welfare, and other areas. Nations are likely to – and indeed are entitled to – make varying choices among these arrangements depending on their needs and values.[14]

---

13   Ibid., xii.

14   Ibid., xviii. The preface to *The Globalization Paradox* concludes with a three-page section under the heading 'Economists Are Human Too'. It argues that, like all human groups, economists are subject to a collective 'heuristic bias', which can – and in this case must – be overcome if they want to do good, as is indeed possible. Nevertheless, these comments were not sufficient to prevent Rodrik's ouster from the 'guild'. In the preface to his next book, *Straight Talk on Trade: Ideas for a Sane World Economy*, Rodrik recounts how he once asked a well-known economist to endorse *Has Globalization Gone Too Far?*: 'The economist demurred. He didn't really disagree with any of the analysis but worried that my book would provide "ammunition for the barbarians". Protectionists would latch on to the book's arguments about the downsides of globalisation to provide cover for their narrow, selfish agenda. It's a reaction I still get from my fellow economists' (ix). In the meantime, doubt has penetrated the highest circles of the 'guild', especially the American milieu, reaching even the likes of Paul Krugman, who has long been an intransigent free trader. In this respect, rational argument may have contributed to Trump's ascent to the US presidency in 2016. See Michael Hirsh, 'Economists on the Run', *Foreign Policy*, 22 October 2019, foreignpolicy.com.

In the central chapter of his book, Rodrik develops his plea for an economically and politically diverse form of globalisation in a discussion of what he calls 'the political trilemma of the world economy' – 'pick two, any two'.[15] It consists in the fact that of three different situations – profound economic integration in the mode of hyperglobalisation, the nation-state as the dominant form of political organisation, and democracy as the mode of producing collectively binding decisions – only two can be realised at any one time (see fig. 25, p. 236). Thus, hyperglobalisation and a system of nation-states are only compatible if one is ready (or can be forced) to abandon democracy. Rodrik describes this configuration as 'a golden straitjacket', adopting the expression used in a popular economics book written at the end of the 1990s that advocated neoliberal globalism, and which called for a renunciation of democratic politics by ceding political decisions to global governance – the only remaining secure path to economic prosperity.[16]

Rodrik uses the example of 1990s Argentina to show that such an approach could at best work only temporarily; the 'golden straitjacket' might very rapidly turn into an iron one.[17] Argentina adopted neoliberal globalisation policies overenthusiastically, subjecting itself in effect to a monetary gold standard by anchoring its currency to the US dollar, and thereby falling into the austerity trap described by Polanyi. In theory, stabilisation of the national currency should have rehabilitated the Argentinian economy. But in practice, the sacrifices it imposed on the population, which were supposed to be limited to the short and medium term, encountered increasing resistance. Rodrik, unlike orthodox economic theorists, viewed this development not as a contingent political – in the sense of non-economic – accident, but as an endogenous component of any attempted transition to deeper, more denationalised economic integration. This, in turn, affects the technocratic durability of neoliberal globalisation as a series of economic policies, because popular resistance influences other interested parties, particularly the financial markets: 'Democratic politics casts a long shadow on financial markets . . . Investors and creditors grew increasingly skeptical that the Argentine Congress, provinces, and ordinary people would tolerate austerity policies. In the end, the markets were

---

15   Rodrik, *The Globalization Paradox*, 185–206.
16   Thomas Friedman, *The Lexus and the Olive Tree*, New York: Farrar, Straus and Giroux, 2000.
17   Rodrik, *The Globalization Paradox*, 184–90.

right. When globalization collides with domestic politics, the smart money bets on politics.'[18]

The nation-state stands in the way of deeper globalisation, insofar as the latter must reach across borders and into countries so as to align their institutions to its requirements. As hyperglobalisation, globalisation demands the denationalisation of national institutions to achieve their reciprocal harmonisation; according to Rodrik this applies, among other things, to labour markets and employment, business taxation, market regulation, and industrial policy.[19] It is to be expected that the establishment of institutional convergence in service of greater internationalisation will always meet with resistance, to be overcome politically, most reliably by the neutralisation of national democratic politics wherever this affects the relation between economy and society. Those who still call for democracy must look for it 'higher up', to a sphere above the nation-state level. But the aspiring democrat is now faced with the second leg of Rodrik's trilemma, where hyperglobalisation and democracy come together in a global federalism of a more or less centralised world state. Rodrik finds this scenario just as unrealistic as the tacit acceptance of neoliberal global governance by the citizens of upwardly dissolving nation-states – what is assumed in the conventional economic models.

Rodrik does not leave the matter there. Whereas other economists recognise the impossibility of creating a federalist world state as a disagreeable, but merely contingent and empirical fact, so as to bemoan it in the hope of a brighter future, Rodrik sees the world state as not only unrealistic in practice but normatively undesirable: it is the embodiment of a universalism that fails to do justice not only to the complexity of the problems in need of solving but also to the legitimate peculiarities of territorially based societies – a universalism which seeks to reduce rather than to respect complexity, or diversity:

There is simply too much diversity in the world for nations to be shoehorned into common rules, even if these rules are somehow the product of democratic processes. Global standards and regulations are not just impractical; they are undesirable. The democratic legitimacy

---

18   Ibid., 188.
19   Ibid., 190–200.

constraint virtually ensures that global governance will result in the lowest common denominator, a regime of weak and ineffective rules. We then face the big risk of too little *governance* all around, with national governments giving up on their responsibilities and no one else picking up the slack.[20]

What remains is the choice between the nation-state in a straitjacket imposed 'from above' and a nation-state with democracy 'from below', the former *with* far-reaching globalisation, the latter *without*. Rodrik's position on this question is clear: 'Democracy and national self-determination should trump hyperglobalisation. Democracies have the right to protect their social arrangements, and when this right clashes with the requirements of the global economy, it is the latter that should give way.'[21] For Rodrik, as for Polanyi before him, the determination of society's needs, and of the way of life and the basket of goods appropriate to it, can never take place solely through markets and under their pressure to adapt but must also, and primarily, be determined through the medium of democratic and participatory politics. Such needs cannot be determined by the unintentional aggregation of individual preferences happening behind the backs of the people involved through the invisible and inherently mysterious algorithm of the market, and certainly not according to the stipulations of the giant firms dominating the market. They must, rather, be determined by collective agreement through public discussion and collective reflection. But this requires a minimum level of the sort of shared political-cultural self-understanding and awareness of the problem at hand that can only grow and become habitual within the institutional framework of a nation-state.

A further requirement is sovereignty of the nation-state, without which any democratic decision-making would be in perpetual danger of irrelevance. Where these conditions are met, and only here, can ways of life emerge and endure that elude the dictatorship of the lowest market price and the lowest marginal cost, because they can consider qualitative costs and benefits other than those measurable in monetary terms. The Bretton Woods regime inspired by Keynes (fig. 25) – that is, the historic compromise between national democracy and global free

---

20   Ibid., 204.
21   Ibid., xix.

Figure 25. Dani Rodrik's trilemma

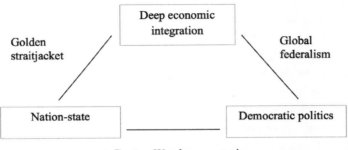

THE POLITICAL TRILEMMA OF THE WORLD ECONOMY

Source: Rodrik, *The Globalization Paradox*, 201.

trade – offers itself as a model for a global system in which democracy at a national level is enabled by limiting global integration. For Rodrik, its contemporary renewal is the order of the day.[22]

Global Market Economy and National Democracy

World trade, measured as the share of exports and imports in the world's total GDP, has increased sharply almost every year since the 1970s, from 27 percent in 1970 to 61 percent in 2008, the year of the global financial crisis (fig. 26). As a consequence of the latter, it collapsed dramatically in the following year, by almost 9 percent. By 2011, it had returned to the 2008 level, where it has remained since, albeit with downward fluctuations, but without ever surpassing its 2008 record. Global capital flows have followed a similar trajectory. According to the McKinsey Global Institute (fig. 27), in the 1990s, they rose from roughly a trillion dollars to 3.8 trillion, accounting on average for 5.3 percent of global GDP. They then increased during the four years 2003–07 from $3.6 to $12.4 trillion, comprising an average of 11.5 percent of global GDP over the years 2000–10. During the financial crisis in 2008 and 2009,

---

22   See chapter 10 for more on Keynes and his understanding of democracy as a countervailing force to the economisation of social life.

Figure 26. World trade as a percentage of world GDP

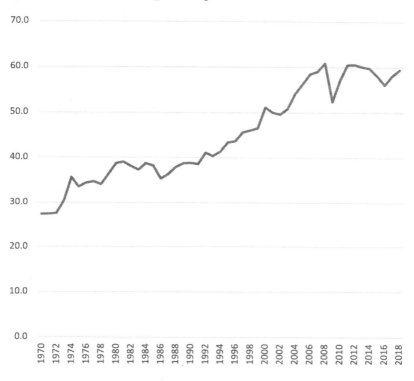

World trade is defined by the World Bank as the sum of all national imports and exports as a percentage of world GDP

Source: World Bank Open Data, 'Trade (% of GDP)', data.worldbank.org.

they fell back to the level of the early 1990s and, since then, have hovered around a value of approximately $5 trillion, tending downwards.

Global capital flows are hard to calculate, and the methods for doing so are controversial. One way of learning more about their dynamic is to examine the international capital flows of what is still the biggest economy in the world, that of the US (fig. 28). US gross capital flows began to rise sharply at the beginning of the 1990s, interrupted briefly by the first financial crisis and the terrorist attacks of 11 September 2001, and climbing from under 5 percent to around 22 percent of the nation's GDP. After 2008, there was a dramatic decline, which brought capital flows down to 8 percent by 2018, roughly a third of the peak of a decade earlier. In the summer of 2020, there were still no figures on the

Figure 27. Global Cross-border capital flows, 1990–2016, in US$trillion

Global cross-border capital flows have declined 65 percent since the 2007 peak

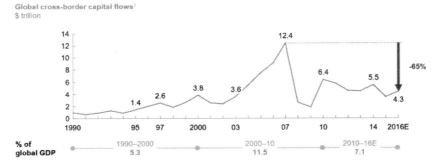

1   Gross capital inflows, including foreign direct investment (FD), debt securities, equity, and lending and other investment.

Source: Susan Lund et al., *The New Dynamics of Financial Globalisation*, McKinsey Global Institute, 2017, 1 (IMF Balance of Payments; McKinsey Global Institute analysis).

impact of the global COVID crisis on world trade and capital mobility, but further declines are to be assumed with some certainty.

The break in the trend that took place in 2008, and the subsequent stagnation in world trade – though, admittedly, starting from a high point – are reflected in the decay, or even the collapse, of the international institutions whose task it should have been to extend the globalisation of the economy. I will discuss two such institutions in more detail here: the World Trade Organization (WTO) and the Transatlantic Trade and Investment Partnership (TTIP) planned between the EU and the US. Different as they may be, the crises that afflict them, as well as other similar institutions of global governance, have the same cause: the change in world trade and its relation to the nation-state in the transition from globalisation to hyperglobalisation, and the resistance this provoked in the participating countries. The unwillingness of the US to continue bearing the international overhead costs of the global trading regime as a benevolent hegemon also belongs in this context, because its national political costs, in the shape of globalisation-driven de-industrialisation and social division, have for some time exceeded the regime's benefits, if not for American capital, then at least for the majority of American voters.

It is not my intention here to revisit the specialist discussions which have for decades held the attention of legions of experts and non-experts

Figure 28. United States, gross international capital flows, three-year averages, 1990–2019, as a percentage of US GDP

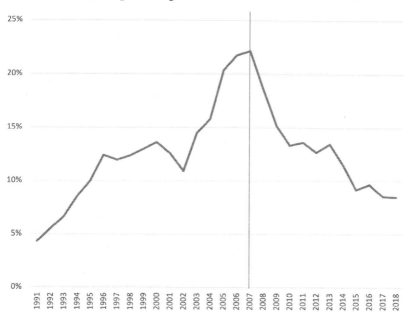

Gross capital flows are calculated from the sum of inflows and outflows. They comprise direct investments, portfolio investments, financial derivatives, and other investments. No gross flow data could be calculated for financial derivatives and central bank reserves.

Source: IMF Balance of Payments and International Investment Position Statistics, World Economic Outlook, April 2020, and author's calculations.

both in the WTO and the TTIP. They have, in any case, hardly achieved anything, in any direction, because very few people could (or would) follow their arguments. What finally tipped the scales was the deep distrust which had accumulated over the years among the citizens and voters of the member states of the WTO and the prospective partners of the TTIP towards anything that looked like a transfer to global governance of responsibility for their livelihood and way of life. The WTO emerged in 1994 at the instigation of the US, then the sole global superpower, from the so-called Uruguay Round of the General Agreement on Tariffs and Trade, and was intended, by means of new trade agreements, in principle, to extend global free trade to all sectors of the economy. Additionally, it was to advise those countries seeking to join, to settle disputes among member states (if possible, authoritatively), and to assist in harmonising the legal systems of participating countries – formally in accordance with collectively established international norms, but in actual fact with the Anglo-Saxon legal systems of the US and UK in particular.[23]

The WTO still exists as the most important subsidiary organisation of the United Nations on paper, with no fewer than 164 member states and a sprawling secretariat in Geneva. But it finds it increasingly difficult to carry out its mission. The WTO has been less and less successful in obliging its member states to integrate international law into their national laws, so as to achieve global legal uniformity. The same is true of its mandate to prevent special regional agreements among its members, such as the EU or the Southern Common Market (Mercosur), and instead to enforce rules that apply equally to all member states. As the failure of the so-called Doha Round has shown, free trade agreements for services, 'intellectual property', and agricultural products are more difficult to negotiate than for manufactured goods; but it is precisely the first three that are of particular interest to the largest member state by far, the United States, and its world-beating financial, cultural, software, and agricultural industries.[24] In the 1990s, resistance to further steps towards general liberalisation grew; there was an increase in demands for national or sectoral protection from international competition and for exemptions from free trade rules, and not only for so-called developing countries. As time went on, such demands were expressed ever more emphatically. This tendency reflected a growing appetite on the part of states to organise their external economies in a more sovereign and individual manner, in cooperation with selected partner states and according to their own requirements. As a

---

23   This was in addition to the competitive pressure on law as a factor of location (on this see Johanna Stark, *Law for Sale: A Philosophical Critique of Regulatory Competition*, Oxford: Oxford University Press, 2019) and the global lobbying of Anglo-American law firms to incorporate the laws of their home countries into national legal systems. Katharina Pistor, *The Code of Capital: How the Law Creates Wealth and Inequality*, Princeton, NJ: Princeton University Press, 2019.

24   The Doha Round was launched by the WTO in 2001 in order to extend existing free trade agreements to new areas and to make the global free trade regime attractive to emerging powers of increasing importance like Brazil, India, and South Africa. The subjects under discussion included agricultural subsidies in the rich industrial countries, patent rights, particularly for therapeutic drugs, and, as a concession made by the wealthy 'West', special rights for economically less developed countries. The negotiations stretched out over one and a half decades and were finally broken off in 2016, without result.

result, the WTO became progressively immobilised until it was put into an induced coma by Donald Trump, who entered office as an avowed protectionist and bilateralist. In 2019, the US refused to approve the appointment of new members to the WTO's Dispute Settlement Body, officially in protest of the continuing classification of China as a developing country and its associated trading privileges burdening American foreign trade.[25] As a result, the WTO was, and remains, incapable of performing its most important function by far – the only one for which it had been given the right to make binding decisions for its member states.

However, it was not only the US under Trump and other nation-states intent on preserving their sovereignty and special interests that challenged the WTO's mission. Social movements critical of globalisation, often represented by international NGOs, began to develop around the world in the 1990s and, through their resistance, were increasingly successful in setting limits to the US-driven globalisation agenda. Mass demonstrations of various kinds, notably held at successive major international conferences called to adopt new agreements on trade and investment, occasionally led to situations reminiscent of civil war, typically as a consequence of heavy-handed interventions by local police, as in Seattle in 1999 (the 'Battle in Seattle') and Genoa in 2001. The driving forces of this resistance included, and continue to include, movements of social and national liberation in the global South, such as the Zapatistas in Chiapas, Mexico, who organised an armed uprising in 1994 against the North American Free Trade Agreement (NAFTA), and other organisations of Indigenous peoples, as well as leftist political currents in developed and developing national societies.

---

25   It can be assumed that the United States' agreement to admit China to the WTO as a developing country was primarily due to pressure from the American consumer goods sector, which had become increasingly dependent on Chinese suppliers and on its own production facilities in China. See the case of the retail colossus Walmart, where Hillary Clinton served as a board member for several years (1986–92): Michael Barbaro, 'As a Director, Clinton Moved Wal-Mart Board, but Only So Far', *New York Times,* 20 May 2007. On 26 July 2019, Donald Trump posted the following now-famous tweet: 'The WTO is BROKEN when the world's RICHEST countries claim to be developing countries to avoid WTO rules and get special treatment. NO more!!! Today I directed the US Trade·Representative to take action so that countries stop CHEATING the system at the expense of the USA!'

In the second half of the 1990s, the Multilateral Agreement on Investment (MAI), pursued by the OECD, was also a target of worldwide protests, which set the pattern for later conflicts. Its eventual failure in 1999, formally due to the resistance of the French Socialist government headed by Lionel Jospin, whose wish to secure cultural exemptions for the French film industry, for example – 'respect for cultural differences' – had been ignored. The MAI's demise made clear to the participating states and governments of the capitalist West the unpopularity of both their mode of procedure and some of their most important objectives.[26] As a result, they were compelled to pursue their globalisation agenda with a guilty conscience, or at least in constant fear of domestic political conflict with militant and highly articulate social groups, and they therefore increasingly retreated from it. One of the high points of the emerging anti-globalist protest movement, which gained worldwide publicity, was the social forum held in Porto Alegre, Brazil, in January 2001, which, with over 10,000 participants from 117 countries, made clear the breadth and diversity of the currents critical of globalisation which had arisen during the previous decade.

TTIP was yet another example of what was at issue and what was opposed, of the intent, and – in the period of waning neoliberalism – of the end, or at least the stagnation, of the policy of capitalist

---

26 See 'Multilateral Agreement on Investment', wikipedia.org: 'The Multilateral Agreement on Investment (MAI) was a draft agreement negotiated in secret between members of the Organisation for Economic Co-operation and Development (OECD) between 1995 and 1998. It sought to establish a new body of universal investment laws that would grant corporations unconditional rights to engage in financial operations around the world, without any regard to national laws and citizens' rights. The draft gave corporations a right to sue governments if national health, labour or environment legislation threatened their interests. When [it] became public in 1997, it drew widespread criticism from civil society groups and developing countries, particularly over the possibility that the agreement would make it difficult to regulate foreign investors. After an intense global campaign was waged against the MAI by the treaty's critics, the host nation France announced in October 1998 that it would not support the agreement, effectively preventing its adoption due to the OECD's consensus procedures.' The official aim was to replace the patchwork of bilateral agreements for the protection of investment with globally standardised rules. Particular objection was taken to the secrecy of the negotiations and also to some of the subjects discussed, in that the latter involved interference in the autonomy of the relevant states in the regulation of their international economic relations and the foreign firms engaged in production and trade on their territories.

globalisation. TTIP was a regional free trade agreement between the US and the EU, meant to replace the failed global projects of the WTO, the finalisation of which had been delayed repeatedly by what were felt to be excessive demands on the part of the less developed countries. Here, too, I will refrain from discussing the economic merits of the plan, as it was debated passionately by experts of all sorts over many years, essentially on the basis of econometric predictions of future increases in prosperity.[27] The negotiations, which began in 2013, were shelved by the EU in November 2016, shortly after the election of Donald Trump; the reason for this probably had less to do with Trump than with the unexpectedly strong resistance on the part of the EU's member states.

One point of contention, not so much between the negotiating partners as between them and the population as a whole, particularly in Europe, was, as in the case of the MAI, the secrecy around the subjects under negotiation, the documents that were exchanged, and the interim results obtained – a procedure characteristic of global governance. Then, little by little, leaks by whistle-blowers made it possible to gain some insight into the subjects and aims of the negotiations, making it easy for the democratic opposition in countries like Germany and France to mobilise public opinion against the agreement. For instance, the US evidently asked to be allowed to retain its 'buy American' laws for government contracts, while similar exemptions were not to apply in Europe. Other points of conflict were health standards for agricultural products ('chlorine chickens', 'hormone steaks'), approval procedures for medicines, environmental and industrial standards, and workers' rights.[28]

---

27   Expert reports of this kind are, in any case, in a league of their own. The so-called Cecchini Report of the European Commission (Commission of the European Communities, *Europe 1992: The Overall Challenge*, SEC (88)524 final 1988) promised the citizens that the 'completion of the internal market' planned for 1992 would reward them with a wealth increase of 5 percent of Europe's GDP, and an average fall of 6 percent in the prices of consumer goods, as well as 'millions of new jobs' and an improvement of public finances amounting to 2.2 percent of GDP. The report includes no data on the prospective distribution of the increase in wealth between and within the participating countries. Only two years later, the European Commission calculated that the introduction of a common currency would have an additional impact of a similar magnitude.

28   It remains to be seen to what extent protectionist interests were behind the demands for higher standards for imported products. At that time, 'protectionism' – that is, the protection of home populations and their way of life from economic

On the institutional front, the proposals envisaged arbitration courts intended to replace ordinary national courts in disputes between firms and foreign governments. This gave rise to protests by prominent legal scholars, who feared an erosion of the rule of law. Equally contentious were provisions for the protection of investment that seemed to go even further than those in the failed MAI project; among other things, they included claims for damages by foreign investors if a country were to raise its labour market standards, and to thereby violate the 'trust' placed in it.

In relation to the EU, it became a serious issue whether the ratification of TTIP, once negotiated and signed – the sole negotiator for all the member states was the European Commission – should be done by the European Parliament alone, or by the parliaments of the member states as well; this was not a surprise, in view of the agreement's unclear constitutional status. This question also reflected the increasing gravity of the EU's internal problems and the growing desire of its members to preserve their national sovereignty. Ultimately, neither the American nor the European side thought there was any chance of bringing the agreement to fruition. In August 2016, the German minister of economics at the time, Sigmar Gabriel, declared the project a failure, primarily because it had become so unpopular with the German public that ratification by the Bundestag could no longer be expected, and its ratification by the European Parliament alone would have boosted so-called anti-European forces.

The trend towards global governance in matters of trade had been propelled by the leading capitalist countries after the collapse of Communism; its end was now brought about by protest movements and coalitions of a new kind, in part global in scale, though without the emergence of any alternative economic order. The march towards neoliberalism had, however, been halted by making its continuation less attractive to its supporters. Contrary to the wishful thinking of

---

subordination by 'free markets' – was widely regarded as unethical. Anyone who sought, or wanted to guarantee, protection against the 'free play of market forces' had to avoid any appearance of being in favour of 'protectionism' (on this, see Rodrik's experiences with his colleagues, mentioned earlier). Here, too, the COVID crisis and the war in Ukraine have contributed to a change of attitude, and not just when the issue was the production of vaccines or protective equipment for those employed in the medical profession.

Immanuel Wallerstein, no international mass anti-capitalist party arose along the lines of the People's Front of Porto Alegre, one capable of challenging the Davos front of capital in a final revolutionary struggle, to take place, at the latest, by the mid-twenty-first century.[29] The opposition to globalisation was too diverse for that, and the interests represented within it too varied. This is not to say that the diversity of the opposition, which was a source of strength in the struggle against neoliberalism, must prove to be source of weakness after its victory. After all, what this diversity mirrors is nothing other than the elemental way concrete politics is bound up with the concrete circumstances of settled peoples and nations – exactly the affiliation which has caused the failure of neoliberal globalism and would also cause the failure of a left-universalist globalisation, whatever form it might take.[30]

The most important common feature shared by the various groups which have brought neoliberal globalisation to a standstill, and from a practical standpoint the most productive one, is their desire to integrate into the emerging world society, after their own fashion and according to their local circumstances – a desire, in other words, for state sovereignty as the prerequisite for national democracy and for social self-determination, in a global context and in the crises and opportunities that arise within it. It is, therefore, no accident that where opposition against the neoliberal trade regime has been successful in the long term, this has almost always resulted from a defence of the national right to self-government – no doubt also because this is the issue on which it is easiest to find a compromise with those conservatives who have never strayed into the neoliberal camp (which is anything but conservative), and even with 'populists', insofar as they were and remain committed

---

29   Immanuel Wallerstein et al., *Does Capitalism Have a Future?*, Oxford: Oxford University Press, 2013, 35.

30   'All politics is local.' This expresses the wisdom, honed by experience, of the American politician Thomas 'Tipp' O'Neill (1912–1994), who was the speaker of the US House of Representatives between 1977 and 1987 and one of the last politicians in that country to be respected by both parties. In today's conflicts over globalisation, one can derive from it the hypothesis that the relevant line of international conflict, in contrast to Wallerstein's expectation, will initially not be a global *class struggle* between 'capital' and 'labour', but a *state struggle* for the defence and recovery of national political sovereignty and the opportunities for democratisation linked to it.

to genuine diversity and locally rooted social solidarity. If the struggles around the World Trade Organization, MAI, and TTIP have proved anything, it is, in my view, that salvation from the worldwide dictatorship of free markets, unfettered megafirms, and politically irresponsible techno-bureaucrats can be expected only from the revival and re-establishment of the nation-state's democratic and political capacity, both neutralised by neoliberalism. Without this, the world in the age of hyperglobalisation is threatened by a state monopoly capitalism with *states* but without *the state*, a globalised formlessness lacking constitutional responsibility and shaped by global US megafirms spared any controls on mergers (or anything else), acting as spiders at the centre of a web of worldwide 'value creation', or – a better term – chains of capital accumulation.

Unity from Above: Global Governance

Can the mixture of nation-states and global corporations that is today's global political economy be governed in such a way, even without a world state, that private capitalist profit-makers feel encouraged to no longer hide behind the social capital they control? And can an upward leap out of the rut of the unending stalemate of neoliberalism be achieved? Appropriate institutions would be required for this – institutions at a level of political decision-making above the manifestly irremovable nation-state, with sufficient power to act and assert themselves, so as to extend a universal regime to cover the wide variety of local systems and anchor it to the bedrock of social life. Are there institutions able to contain the systemic risks associated with globally integrated capital accumulation within acceptable limits, at least as far as they affect investors and their time frame? How deeply must they intervene into the affairs of existing states? And in the long term, how can non-, super-, or post-state institutions establish and safeguard a centralised order suitable for such purposes?

I do not propose, in what follows, to go through the full range of the various attempts to establish global systems and generally binding legal norms intended to eliminate, or at least tame, the particularistic stubbornness of local societies. Instead, I will limit myself to the recent past, the three decades since the collapse of the Soviet Union, during which the number of nation-states, as we have seen, increased by leaps and bounds and posed the problem of how the New World Order of George H. W. Bush could be constructed in accordance with the dramatically expanded horizon of capitalist globalisation. We have seen how states were able to assert themselves in the disputes over a suprastate, hyperglobalised trade regime, at least to the extent that the system's final institutional consolidation had already reached a standstill before the last two 'exogenous' crises. I will continue here by discussing, in succession and under the general rubric of global governance, three approaches to an internationalist elimination of national democracy in favour of transnationally institutionalised markets and global value chains. The first of these is already somewhat out of date, the second has survived on paper, and the third is brand new, allegedly deriving from what some regard as the 'lessons' of the 2008 global financial crisis and its aftermath. All three, I shall argue, have either long since come to grief, or are on the way to doing so, on the two principal obstacles to the establishment of a stable regime of global accumulation: the stubborn opposition of nationally organised democracy on the one hand, and the inherent ungovernability of an undivided and unbounded capitalism on the other, with its self-contradictory and ultimately self-destructive requirement that politics and society should serve as its facilitators and that it should itself produce endless and limitless profits.

Before expanding upon my three examples of global governance – there could well be others, owing to the inherent vagueness of the concept – I need to make some remarks about the general problems that affect centralised international systems. The ambition of all political regimes, whether states or empires, is to unify and centralise. But this finds its limits in the diversity of the world they wish to rule, and the instruments of power at their disposal. The greater the diversity, the less it is possible to achieve uniformity with the given instruments of power; and the greater the degree of uniformity desired, the greater the amount of power that must be employed to counteract the diversity that stands in the way. Resistance – demands for special provisions or self-government – must be argued against, bought off, or smoked out. But even when this is successful and the problem of power can be satisfactorily solved, it cannot be said that the uniform system subsequently adopted is necessarily an equally good 'fit' everywhere.

When centralists ignore diversity for the sake of enforcing uniformity, this can result in technical failures of government 'on the ground' and a corresponding accumulation of discontent in a metaphorical barrel that can overflow at some point; the use of force, even if at first successful, may contribute to this. The headquarters of centralism can be overextended, not only in social but also in material terms, and not only in relation to their instruments of power but also with regard to their means of cognition, their 'intelligence'.

There are more than enough instructive examples of centralist regimes' excessive ambition towards uniformity in relation to both the diversity of the territory they ruled and the power they possessed, and of the crises in which over-centralisation may culminate. As discussed in chapter 7, Edward Gibbon's explanation of the downfall of a Roman Empire which stretched from Mesopotamia to Scotland in terms of its dependence on a single continually overburdened centre, and the reasons he gave for the superiority of the decentralised Europe of his time over the giant civilisations of antiquity, provide the analytical model. When the Catholic Church, for example, rose during the Middle Ages to become a pan-European great power with claims to universality, it exceeded its capacity to govern. While it had succeeded, up to the fifteenth century, in using its theocratic and secular instruments of power to put down local secessionist aspirations, later on, after long and bloody conflicts in the century of the Reformation, it was no longer able to prevent territorialised subsocieties in Northern Europe from appropriating theological novelties to gain state recognition as legitimate local variants of European Christian culture. The process came to an end definitively in Germany and the Netherlands through the 1648 Treaties of Münster and Osnabrück. Today, the papacy is increasingly forced, as the central authority of a world church that developed in the wake of colonialism, to take into account in its politics and doctrine the various special conditions, claims, and interpretations of the world more or less faithfully represented by national bishops' conferences in, for example, Africa, Latin America, Asia, and Eastern and Western Europe; only in this way can it hope perhaps to prevent the institutional unity of Roman Catholicism from breaking apart over disputed matters such as celibacy, the ordination of women, or how to handle homosexuality or sexuality as such. Whether a revocation of its dogmatic and organisational claim to unity will in fact save the church as a Catholic – that is, all-embracing – institution, is today more than ever the decisive question for its worldly leadership.[31]

A second case, one more familiar to political scientists, was the Third Communist International, or Comintern. It too represented the failure of an over-centralised regime whose leadership based its claim to power on a globally uniform internationalist worldview. Its politics and organisation were grounded in the conviction that the historically impending communist revolution would inevitably proceed everywhere according to identical laws, those of 'Marxism-Leninism'. As early as 1920, under Lenin, the national Communist parties were transformed into local sections of the Comintern, all of which were obliged to follow the same political and military recipes, developed and prescribed by the strategists of the Moscow centre, who had an overview of the whole world. Thus in 1928, under Stalin, the so-called theory of social fascism was made compulsory for all member organisations, or, more accurately, sub-organisations. According to this theory, social democratic parties were to be fought as fiercely as fascist parties, because they were to be regarded as the allies of the latter in the fight against the Soviet Union. Then, in 1935, the social fascism (*Sozialfaschismus*) doctrine was replaced, again from above, by the Popular Front strategy. The catastrophic results are well known. Where the agents of the Comintern succeeded in committing the local Communist parties to the Moscow general line, they often suffered bloody and irreparable defeats in the struggles of the 1920s and 1930s. By contrast, national communist movements of the kind found in China were often able to bring their revolutions to a successful (albeit equally bloody) conclusion.[32]

---

31   See, among many others, Gerald O'Collins and Mario Farrugia, *Catholicism: The Story of Catholic Christianity*, Oxford: Oxford University Press, 2015.

32   Among those who recognised the self-destructive consequences of Moscow centralism early on was Antonio Gramsci, who as general secretary of the Italian Communist Party (PCI) insisted more than other Communist Party leaders that conditions in his country were sufficiently different from those in other countries to justify local divergences from the strategy prescribed from above, and which required the national party leadership to exercise more individual initiative and freedom of decision adapted to the situation. As a result, the PCI remained trapped in a permanent conflict between the 'democratic centralism' of Moscow and the particularities of Italy as a possible site of anti-capitalist revolution, as analysed by Gramsci. This led to the party's exclusion from political power until its dissolution after 1989 (Perry Anderson, *The Antinomies of Antonio Gramsci*, London: Verso, 2017).

Now, as far as a uniform neoliberal order of a supranationally globalised world and its economy is concerned, this requires institutions able both to eliminate and harness the existing system of nation-states according to liberal methods – to eliminate them as disruptive factors in the world market, particularly as representatives of local societies surrounded by the market, and to harness them as local mechanisms for implementing market requirements and combating discontent, as forward observers, informal collaborators, and so on. That such a regime cannot act as a state is already expressed in the name that has become generally accepted for what it is expected to provide. Not a world government – a term like that might provoke questions about its democratic credentials – but global governance: gentler than government, not necessarily tied to statehood like the latter, diffuse enough to appear less in need of democratisation, but all the more 'global', evocative of worldwide cooperation and co-optation on an amicable basis and of practically oriented, dispassionate 'problem-solving' – a dream image and utopia of rule by the reasonable and expert, finally freed from politics, a benevolent technocracy of problem-solvers.

'Governance', instead of 'government', is a way of describing a function which can be carried out by states but does not have to be, because it can also be performed without the coercive means of a sovereign state. It probably came into common use among political scientists in the late 1980s, in the course of the neoliberal revolution, and was taken over from the vocabulary of 'new institutionalist' efficiency theory, previously at the margin of mainstream economics, but which was then enjoying a revival, particularly in the form of transaction cost theory and the contract theory developed in connection with it.[33] According to this theory, governance emerges when prudent trading partners agree to submit to customised institutions of oversight and

---

33   In 2009 Oliver Williamson was awarded the Nobel Prize for Economics for his work on the subject, at a time of widespread, although short-lived, doubts about standard economic theory. On 'new institutionalism' and transaction cost analysis, see Oliver Williamson, *The Economic Institutions of Capitalism: Firms, Markets, Relational Contracting*, New York: Free Press, 1985; Oliver Williamson, 'The New Institutional Economics: Taking Stock, Looking Ahead', *Journal of Economic Literature* 38 (2000), 595–613. Like others, I used the concept of governance in the 1990s to analyse the performance of economic sectors (J. Rogers Hollingsworth, Philippe C. Schmitter and Wolfgang Streeck, eds, *Governing Capitalist Economies: Performance and Control of Economic Sectors*, Oxford: Oxford University Press, 1994), without looking too closely at what it implied.

arbitration, jointly set up, case by case, in the interests of efficient and trust-based execution of their contracts, in the course of a 'private ordering'. One context in which the concept became particularly relevant was the turn towards shareholder value in the theory and practice of the joint-stock company. As a result, the concept of corporate governance, until then buried deep in the economics literature, migrated into everyday language, where it came to describe a division of power and responsibility within corporations that enables 'the markets' to have confidence in the unwavering, because institutionally internalised, subordination of publicly listed companies to the claims and interests of their shareholders.

As it took hold in the globalisation debate of the 1990s, the concept of global governance was, and still is, used in connection with a number of institutions, including the WTO, with its claim to the authoritative arbitration of conflicts over trade. Ultimately, however, it seems to date to the occasional summit conferences of the largest economic powers of the 'West', first convened as the 'G6' in Rambouillet in 1975 at the invitation of the French president Valéry Giscard d'Estaing. With the addition of Canada, the group became the G7; in 1998 it expanded to become the G8 with the admission of Russia, until the latter was expelled in 2014 upon its repossession of Crimea. From 1999 onwards, an intermittent G20 summit was added, presumably to accommodate the rise of China. The G7, deliberately set up informally as a 'network' without bureaucratic infrastructure, was probably originally motivated by the wish of its European members to incorporate the United States into a jointly coordinated global economic policy regime following the end of the Bretton Woods system. Its founding was, moreover, likely also an attempt to pursue such international economic policy coordination outside of and bypassing the United Nations, given the increased danger of a takeover of the latter by a majority of former colonies, now sovereign states. Indeed, the so-called developing countries had attempted for a period, during the 1980s, to construct a 'New International Economic Order' (NIEO) around the UN, intended to end the domination of the rich industrial nations – a project with which the G7, which in 1985 accounted for 62 percent of the global economy but only 12 percent of the world's population, could hardly be in sympathy.

The G7 was an instrument for avoiding democracy, not only vis-à-vis the NIEO and the UN, but also in relation to the citizens of its member states. Summit conferences such as the G7 enable the participating governments to agree to binding measures for their countries – behind closed doors – that would otherwise be difficult to implement domestically. The same mechanism, described by political scientist Robert Putnam, among others, as two-level diplomacy, operates in the EU even more effectively, where it is routinely used in the format of the European Council.[34] Two-level diplomacy strengthens the position of national executives towards national parliaments and publics in a variety of ways, for example because it allows governments to assert, virtually irrefutably, that 'it is impossible to get any more' and that rejection of such a painstakingly negotiated compromise would damage the government's international prestige and weaken the country in the next round of negotiations. Summit meetings can thus be used by the assembled leaders to mount conspiracies against their respective electorates, as was the case in the 1990s in the EU, when the privatisation of state-owned post offices and telecommunications agencies was pushed through.

As far as the G7, in particular, is concerned, for a time the US sought to use it as an instrument of hegemonic regulatory policy, but with less and less success in the post-Clinton years (and, perhaps, increasingly diminished need, owing to the worldwide dominance of the US dollar and Federal Reserve). The annual meetings yielded correspondingly meagre outcomes, especially with respect to overcoming the financial crisis of 2008 and restructuring global financial markets. Of course, they were by no means cancelled as a result. The gatherings took place in different countries in turn, and the choice of date and venue depended, to a large extent, on electoral considerations. For the governments involved, they were a good opportunity to bring their own international importance to the attention of their respective publics. The final declarations were agreed on in advance; the more meaningless they were, the more laborious and costly were the conference arrangements and the security measures required, and the bigger was the crowd of journalists from all over the world, who had little else to do, given the lack of political substance on display, than to report on possibly violent demonstrations and on the facial expressions of the leaders during their

---

34   Robert D. Putnam, 'Diplomacy and Domestic Politics: The Logic of Two-Level Games', *International Organization* 42, no. 3 (1988), 427–60.

public breakfasts. Even the participating governments no longer spoke of global governance.[35]

Global Governance as Technocratic Utopia

Global governance as a non-governmental, post-political foundation of order on a world scale, and a way of cutting out the particularistic obduracy of democratic forces institutionalised in nation-states, will not disappear from globalism's programme simply because it has not materialised anywhere thus far. So long as it fails to become a reality, it will live on as an idea and an aspiration, as exemplified by a book by Helmut Willke, a student of Niklas Luhmann, and, at that time, according to his official job description, '*Professor für Global Governance*' at a southern German private university.[36] This book – from which I am taking my second example of what global governance can signify – bears the title *Demokratie in Zeiten der Konfusion* (Democracy in a time of confusion) and is intended to liberate the former from the latter, by abandoning any democratic claims incompatible with globalism, in particular plebeian participation and egalitarian redistribution. Willke aims to demonstrate the ways in which democracy can be made suitable for global governance so that, firstly, it causes no disruptions and, secondly, it improves the latter's 'problem-solving' ability.

How is that supposed to work? Willke's world is the 'knowledge society', not the trade union meeting; there are no strikes, only 'steering'. He does not speak of power and resistance, capital and labour, oligarchy and precariat, but he does have a lot to say about intelligence, in the sense used by the political scientists Karl Deutsch and Charles

---

35 The 'German' G7 summit was held in 2015 at Schloss Elmau, close to the Austrian border, in a luxury hotel inaccessible to demonstrators. According to figures released by the federal government, it cost around €113 million; but unofficial estimates of the cost ranged from €200 million to €360 million; some 17,000 police were deployed. The motto of the summit was: 'Think of Tomorrow. Act Together.' At the Hamburg G20 meeting two years later, which took place in the city centre, 31,000 police officers were mobilised to protect thirty-five delegations with 6,500 participants and 5,100 journalists. The police operation alone is said to have cost €85 million. If we leave aside the violent protests of the so-called anti-globalisers, an account of a meeting of this kind reads like a report of the proceedings of a Reichstag of the Holy Roman Empire.

36 Helmut Willke, *Demokratie in Zeiten der Konfusion*, Berlin: Suhrkamp, 2014.

Lindblom.[37] From this perspective, for democracy to continue to fare well, it must allow itself to be reorganised to accommodate an increased 'interdependence' between national and international problem-solving, between socially interdependent nation-states, and, as a matter of fact, between policy areas whose complex – because global – interaction creates unpleasant systemic risks.

Democracy, says Willke, must improve if it is to match its rivals, of which there are three: the Chinese dictatorship, the American community of money and religion, and, lo and behold, the European liberal market technocracy. Willke's proposed reforms aim to enhance the intelligence of democracy by emancipating it from its plebeian ties; through democratic empowerment of technocratic expertise and competence of the global knowledge society, the preservation of democracy is to be achieved by way of its de-democratisation. The model is the participation of civil society in specialised international organisations and institutions like the WTO, which have outgrown the nation-state and are immune to stultification from below.[38] The idea is to remedy the confusion of democracy with more, but this time a benign confusion, in the form of an 'intelligent combination' of democratic and specialised decision-making, where the former serves to enthrone the latter as legitimate ruler. His final conclusion, all in English: *smart governance, good governance, political restraint, best practice, communities of practice, epistemic communities, global law without a state* (as a model), *zero trauma* (as an objective), without *quick wins*, the disempowerment of the *median voter* and the *median official*, and so forth.

'Smart governance' also envisages participation, but it must be 'focused' and 'differentiated . . . according to standards of competence, involvement and professionally based sustainability'.[39] Inevitably, this involves a 'loss of formal democracy' of the 'one person, one vote' type. 'Concrete decision-making capacity' – 'the decision-makers know what they are doing' – is to replace the 'ignorance of most people', which is

---

37   Karl W. Deutsch, *The Nerves of Government: Models of Political Communication and Control*, New York: Free Press, 1963; and Charles E. Lindblom, *The Intelligence of Democracy: Decision Making through Mutual Adjustment*, New York: Free Press, 1965.

38   Willke, *Demokratie in Zeiten der Konfusion*, 14–16.

39   Ibid., 158.

'pervasive and unavoidable' under conditions of global complexity.[40] 'Ignorance', writes Willke 'leads to exclusion. This exclusion is democratic because it affects most people. The result will be a reciprocal and multi-layered dependence of specialists on a plethora of other specialists in relation to a wealth of other issues and problems.'[41]

As is so often the case when it comes to 'governance', difficulties arise with the role of the state. It is said to lack the competence to exercise authority, but even so it is to establish a framework by 'managing the context' and 'moderating sub-system discourse', as a 'core competence'.[42] Concretely, Willke appears to have in mind a constitution in which the parliament withdraws and delegates cognitively demanding matters to specialist communities of experts constituted as themed councils – 'carefully chosen for their competence and involvement' – which are then to make decisions with due regard for vertical and horizontal, and, naturally, also international, interdependences as well as strategic goals and global interests extending beyond the electoral term. This is not too far removed from Hayek's model of democracy, and, as in that case, questions of disbelief arise as to who might appoint the constituent assembly charged with adopting such a constitution, how it might look, closely followed by the question of the composition of the knowledge society's 'policy networks' that are to be entrusted with *governance* by the state and democracy.[43]

It is easier to conceive of a democratically empowered technocracy or, alternatively, a technologically transformed democracy, when, like Willke, and also Luhmann, one views social systems as communication structures devoid of people.[44] This approaches a revisionist theory of

---

40   Ibid., 157.

41   Ibid., 159.

42   Ibid., 111. This is especially the case since, according to Willke, 'the primacy of politics' continues to operate in relation to capitalism, and 'it lies in the hands of democracy to manage and regulate capitalism in such a way that it is compatible with fundamental democratic principles', even if this is 'by no means guaranteed . . . in practice' (101). This is, in principle, all that Willke's theory of global management by the knowledge society has to say about capitalism. By avoiding this subject, he, of course, makes the problem much less serious, or even defines it out of existence. This once again demonstrates, with desirable and commendable clarity, how fundamentally absurd it is to propose a theory of democracy without a theory of capitalism.

43   See Wolfgang Streeck, *Buying Time: The Delayed Crisis of Democratic Capitalism*, 2nd ed., London: Verso, 2017, 103–19.

44   Willke writes of a 'turn towards communication', by which Luhmann goes beyond Weber's theory of society: 'The society's internal rules and regulations form an

democracy, in which it is reduced to knowledge-based control exercised by chosen experts and relieved of any representative functions. If, as with Luhmann, social systems, by definition, have no members, it is hardly difficult to reconfigure them, nor is it difficult to refrain from doing so. From this perspective, defenders of an 'old European' idea, according to which societies consist of people who have a right to identify with 'their' society, appear to be anachronistic populists who, under conditions of globalism, can and must be rejected as premodern; their views cannot in any case be considered a reason for critical reflection on the detachment of larger-than-life global contexts from the living environment of actually existing members of society.

In fact, much suggests that a world society is *only* imaginable as a dehumanised one, because the world citizen who belongs to it must be a person without qualities – lacking characteristics beyond a general humanity, and therefore without *concrete* characteristics. Seen in this light, the theory of democratically licensed technocratic global governance found in Willke can speak only of *rules*, but not of *power* or *power relations*; it cannot speak of states in hierarchical state systems shaped by power, nor of interests. It is, instead, concerned solely with collective goods, but most certainly not with the individuals who can either be mobilised to obtain these or, alternatively, be deprived of them. Global governance thus becomes the theory of government, as if world society were nothing but the product of more or less successful management decisions, and not also, or indeed predominantly, the outcome of struggle and conflict.[45]

---

ironclad enclosure of unprecedented unattainability, which radicalises the system theory imagined by Max Weber by conceiving human beings not as a part of society but as its environment. It is one of the mysterious necessities of human life that a person has to enter a relationship with this society which confronts him as alien' (Willke, *Demokratie in Zeiten der Konfusion*, 154). Luhmann is quoted as having said that, after the above-described 'inherent dynamic of the social' (153) has been acknowledged, 'humanist and regionalist (national) concepts of society . . . are no longer able to provide satisfaction'. From this perspective, Luhmann appears to be the main sociological ideologist of globalisation, standing alongside its main economic ideologists Hayek and von Mises: their inherent dynamic of capital accumulation is his inherent dynamic 'of society', and the loss of control by human societies over their fate is ontologised enthusiastically. How democracy can or should be a subject of discussion after the expulsion of human beings from society remains a mystery.

45   Like conventional political science generally, Willke's theory of democracy does not refer to the centrality of the capitalist accumulation process for the politics and

Willke presents central banks as the prime example of independent regulatory agencies backed by specialist knowledge and shielded from populism. He holds that their purpose is to compensate for the cognitive overload suffered by ordinary people under the conditions of globalism. Yet these banks' catastrophic failure in the run-up to 2008 should have been fresh in his memory the year his book was published, in 2014. Apart from this example, one is left to speculate. Does Willke perhaps have in mind the *comitology* of the European Union, so highly praised for a brief period?[46] Willke's rescue of democracy as problem-solver comes at the cost of abandoning it as an anti-oligarchic appeals body and agency for egalitarian redistribution. The approach has the air of a determined attempt to pour out an unloved baby with the bathwater. 'Essentially', he says, 'this is all about advancing from a Pareto-optimal (negative) coordination to a Kaldor-optimal (positive) coordination'.[47] How exactly that is supposed to function is something one will only find out when democracy – as a protection of the small from the large, a permanent threat to company boardrooms, and a constant warning to order-givers of all kinds not to take their interests for everyone else's – has gone the way of all the sacrificed pawns of globalisation.

---

organisation of mature capitalist societies. Politics, for him, is the more or less effective and efficient provision of collective goods desired by everyone and from which everyone benefits equally – not the struggle over the relation between this and the profit requirements of capitalist expansion. The struggle is not with capital but with the prisoner's dilemma. Politics is the product of skill, not power; power is seen as an *instrument* of politics, not a *restrictive condition* of it.

46   On this, see Christian Joerges and Jürgen Neyer, 'From intergovernmental Bargaining to Deliberative Political Processes: The Constitutionalisation of Comitology', *European Law Journal* 3, no. 3 (1997), 273–99; Christian Joerges and Jürgen Neyer, 'Transforming Strategic Interaction into Deliberative Problem-Solving: European Comitology in the Foodstuffs Sector', *Journal of European Public Policy* 4, no. 4 (1997), 609–25; and Josef Falke, 'Comitology after Lisbon: What Is Left of Comitology as We Have Praised It?', in Christian Joerges and Carola Glinski, eds, *The European Crisis and the Transformation of Transnational Governance: Authoritarian Managerialism versus Democratic Governance*, Oxford: Hart, 2014.

47   Willke, *Demokratie in Zeiten der Konfusion*, 13.

Another Plan A

Failing elites and schools of thought increasingly unmoored from reality appear to have an unlimited capacity to always stay the course, especially during major crises, in the expectation that, somehow, in the next attempt at bashing their thick heads against a wall, they will emerge alive and intact. After the stagnation of state-sponsored mercatocracy – the rule of the market over a world society derived from it – and the bursting of the dream of global governance by summit meetings or sectoral cooperation between experts, the technocracy of central banks is now to take their place in neoliberal centralism's increasingly panicked vision of the future: instead of informal meetings of heads of state and consensual *comitology*, there is now the hard stamp of the money-printing press – the third version of global governance covered here.

The secret charm of the central banks as problem-solvers in times of political deadlock lies in the promise, initially projected onto them and later more or less appropriated by them, of a new kind of philosophers' kingdom, independent of elections and parties, purged of particular interests and ruled objectively. The fact that the central bank version of scientific economic and social management from above is based on a general theory claiming to be true endears it to a knowledge-society left that has become shy of democracy, but also renders it suspect to a status-conscious right – not least because of the utopian prospect of an unlimited and free supply of money hovering vaguely in the background of an expanded central bank regime. This would also mean an end to scarcity by way of a crisis-immune guaranteed basic income for all.[48] The new technocratic model is not supposed to function, like the market, behind the backs of the citizens but, rather, over their

---

48   This is now apparently a favourite idea of a growing number of Silicon Valley oligarchs, who are anxious about the purchasing power of the surplus populations sitting unemployed in front of their screens, on whose orders advertising revenues depend. If a basic income is provided and distributed synthetically ex nihilo by the central banks, as a form of 'helicopter money', the new superstar enterprises will even be able to cut expenditures on tax avoidance. A basic income also fits very well into an individualistic and consumerist model of a society able to do without collective goods, which have to be financed by taxes and potentially require democratic action. Daniel Zamora and Anton Jäger, 'Historicizing Basic Income: Response to David Zeglen', *Lateral: Journal of the Cultural Sudies Association* 8, no. 1 (2019).

heads – provided that the independence of the central banks is preserved as a historic achievement, and that they are allowed to derive their inscrutable decisions from a theory only comprehensible to insiders, and, incidentally, one subject to continuous advances yet always true, again and again.

Of course, one does not have to look very far to see that rule by the central banks – the next and until now the most ambitious technocratic Plan A to appear – would soon prove to be just as unstable under the pressure of reality as rule by the markets. After all, central bank technocracy is also aimed at neutralising the democratic nation-state – in Europe, where a single central bank is responsible for sixteen countries at once, even more so than elsewhere. A transfer of the as-yet-non-existent common European economic policy to the benevolent and rational dictatorship of the European Central Bank (ECB), especially in the hope that this would be irreversible once it happened, would amount to a travesty of the very political union that should have preceded the currency union – but could not have, for sound reasons of national politics. It is, overall, an absurd idea that a single, uniform, undivided, centralised government of experts could suffice to bring similar prosperity and equal justice to everyone everywhere in a social landscape as diverse as Europe's. In today's populist and anti-authoritarian society, respect for 'experts', especially those whose theories offer 'no alternative', is not very widespread anyway, and is getting progressively less so.

This does not mean that there are no supporters of the idea of curtailing a national democracy, seen as incompatible with globalisation, by transferring governmental functions to central banks independent of democratic control. One important advocate of this is the New York–based economic historian Adam Tooze, author of an impressive study of the 2008 financial crisis.[49] On the basis of a series of long exclusive interviews with members of the narrow circle of bankers and central bankers who were directly involved in crisis management at that time, Tooze concluded that it was thanks, above all, to the skilfulness and unflappability of his interlocutors that the civilised world did not perish. For Tooze, and for others who are convinced by his apotheosis of the authoritarian super-decision-makers – the same people who had

---

49   Adam Tooze, *Crashed: How a Decade of Financial Crises Changed the World*, New York: Viking, 2018.

previously allowed the crisis to unfold without doing anything at all –
this raises the question of whether it might not be possible to set more
permanent limits to the claims to power of the potentially populist plebs
by expansion of the formal responsibilities of the central banks than by
means of a neoliberal mercatocracy.

In concrete terms, Tooze appears to favour the utopia of a benevolently administered monetary and thus world-dominating exercise of
global governance by the *community* of the four or five largest central
banks, led collegially by the US Fed. According to Tooze, an extension
of the powers of the central bank could also be of great use to the
European Monetary Union, that unhappy empire stuck halfway
between the nation-state and the superstate, divided sovereignty and
unified currency, national fiscal and economic policy and supranational
financial policy. Tooze sees the EMU's malaise as finding expression,
among other things, in the conflict between the European Court of
Justice and the German Constitutional Court over the public sector
purchase programme (PSPP) of the European Central Bank. In an
article for the newspaper *Frankfurter Allgemeine Sonntagszeitung* on 5
July 2020 entitled 'A new role for the ECB', he recommended that in
order to protect the bank from being exposed once again to 'monstrous
attacks on its independence' as well as the 'blind fury and incompre-
hension expressed in the case brought before the German court', its
mandate should be extended to cover a wider field than the protection
of monetary stability required by the European Treaties. This would
legalise what has, since the financial crisis, become the established
practice of the ECB, having been factually and technically necessitated
by the changed economic conditions and the common goal of defending the euro, and thus immunise it against sovereigntist challenges
from below by German ignoramuses fearing for their savings or their
constitution, or both.[50]

Tooze recommends four specific changes to the ECB's mandate.
Firstly, and above all, central banks should henceforth be responsible
not only for monetary stability but for financial stability in general, to

---

50   The article in the *FAS* was intended as a political intervention and can therefore
be treated as the practical quintessence of Tooze's scholarly work ('cutting a long story
short'). A longer, but equally trenchant version can be found in Adam Tooze, 'The Death
of the Central Bank Myth', *Foreign Policy*, 13 May 2020, foreignpolicy.com.

achieve an 'all-round reduction in financial risk'. Asset prices should not be allowed to collapse, property values should be maintained, a loss of confidence which might end in panic selling should be avoided, and so on. The danger of inflation has, fortunately, been averted by the 'weakening of Social Democracy' and the coming of 'globalisation'; the imperative now is to stabilise the financial markets instead of the labour market. 'At the very least the ECB should have a symmetrical price stability mandate, in which the fight against recession and deflation should have the same weight as the outdated worry over inflation.' He continues: 'This would end any further debate over Draghi's 2015 bond-buying programme' – and also, one might add, over the rapid increase in economic and social inequality associated with the programme and with *quantitative easing* in general, as a consequence of securing (rising) share and asset prices through monetary and credit policy, without any trade union protection of wages at the lower end of the labour market.[51]

Secondly, according to Tooze, 'in order to adapt the ECB's mandate to the real situation . . . its responsibility for maintaining the Monetary Union must be formulated explicitly'. Primarily this relates to 'speculators . . . who are the enemies of the Monetary Union' and who

---

51   The ownership structure of government bonds, investigated for Italy by Tobias Arbogast ('Who Are These Bond Vigilantes Anyway? The Political Economy of Sovereign Debt Ownership in the Eurozone', MPIfG Discussion Paper 20/02, Max Planck Institute for the Study of Societies, Cologne, 2020), is also of interest in this respect. What precisely the 'stabilisation of the financial markets' is supposed to mean continues to be an open question. In the case of what Tooze regards as the urgent problem of deflation, the concern seems to be that with generally falling nominal price levels, debtors will no longer be able to meet their obligations and creditors will be ruined by debtors' insolvencies. A remedy could be something like a general central bank guarantee for trading securities, making them hypersecurities. This would correspond to the way in which the ECB's bond-buying programme already makes government bonds risk-free, and thus, with the private banking sector acting as the intermediary, maintains their liquidity as well as that of states which are already in principle over-indebted. The immunisation of the owners of assets and collateral against the collapse of their post-industrially financed business model, combined with the simultaneous rise in precarious and low-wage employment and increasingly unequal distribution, appears to be at the core of what Tooze's understands as the stabilisation of financial markets. What he describes as the 'liberal corporatism' of the 1960s and 1970s involved a 'divided and hesitant sovereignty' which sacrificed 'financial stability' in the interest of both 'better business conditions for entrepreneurs' and 'less unemployment for the trade unions'. Owing to the absence of trade union power and the constitutionally entrenched rule of the central banks, he adds, this situation will not be repeated.

'speculate on a collapse of the euro'. Although the details remain unspecified, they can be because, *thirdly*, the ECB is to be given 'overall responsibility for emergencies'; after all, one cannot 'foresee every eventuality'.[52] As 'we' have learned from Carl Schmitt, the sovereign is whoever commands a state of emergency; it is therefore amazing, or perhaps not so amazing, that the topic is only mentioned in passing in Tooze's work. We would probably be right to assume, however, that Tooze's reforms would also integrate into the ECB's legal arsenal the temporary interruption of an entire country's cash supply so as to bring its government back to economic reason, as was done in the case of Greece. *Fourthly*, and lastly, Tooze proposes that the ECB should additionally be given responsibility for the 'challenges of the Anthropocene' in view of the lessons of COVID, so that it can make 'the road to decarbonisation worked out by the European Commission . . . a binding obligation for all economic and financial authorities'. At first glance, this appears to be an unassailable 'motherhood and apple pie' demand, which the ECB itself attempts to use as an innocent way of introducing the idea of extending its field of responsibility.[53]

What, then, would such a 'dramatically' (Tooze) expanded mandate signify for the ECB's relationship with the parliamentary governments of the Monetary Union's member countries, and what consequences would both the mandate and the relationship have for the independence

---

52   See the following question from a participant in a German macroeconomic discussion forum, conducted under the Chatham House Rule permitting a speaker's words to be quoted anonymously: 'Who exactly were the speculators in the Greek crisis: the insurance companies which sold the bad bonds in the interests of their clients – or the hedge funds which bought them in the expectation of a bail-out? . . . It is depressing in itself to read an anti-speculation proposal of this kind from a prominent economic historian.'

53   The ECB would not be alone in this. Since June 2020, 'climate change' has been a part of the Bank of England's 'financial stability mandate'. This is likely more than just a friendly PR gesture towards the supporters of Fridays for Future. Against the backdrop of all central banks' insistence on their 'independence', their adoption of subjects previously reserved for democratic politics would, if successful, substantially hollow out the latter to the benefit of organisations that are (and wish to remain) institutionally shielded from electoral majorities. As far as climate policy as such is concerned, its handover to the central banks carries two implications, both dubious enough: firstly, that it is neutral as regards distribution, and secondly that it cannot be implemented adequately by democratic means. With the further rise in indebtedness as a result of the last two crises and inflation, different themes have of course now come to the forefront, possibly for a very long time.

of the central bank, on the one hand, and for the sovereignty of the member states or the European Union, on the other? Here, at one of the key points in his text, if not *the* key point, Tooze is as taciturn as he is superficial – so much so that the attentive reader perceives his intention, and, if the latter is not shared, can only be annoyed. The extended mandate, says Tooze, would 'simply reflect the position the central banks have created for themselves [!] in recent years'. And further: 'They [the central banks] are not fighting against the government' – who is 'the government' in the Monetary Union? – 'but side by side with it. The independence we [?] value includes freedom of judgment, protection from direct [?] political intervention and the independent authority to employ the instruments of monetary policy at the tempo the circumstances [?] require'. Tooze also recognises that the ECB would take over a considerable part of what today still belongs formally within the jurisdiction of elected governments. What they would then still retain he leaves unanswered. Indirectly, it is conceded that the central bank would exercise a discretionary governmental authority, which, under a still nominally democratic constitution, would somehow require legitimation; what Tooze has in mind here is a 'balanced' constitution, where 'the central bank would regularly give an account [?] both to well-informed public opinion [?] and to the European Parliament'. It should also be possible 'to contest [?] the bank's actions . . . before the European Court of Justice', though it remains unclear how well-informed could be distinguished from badly informed public opinion, what results would follow when the bank gave its account to the European Parliament and on what basis the bank's actions could be contested. Admittedly, the ECB's mandate ought not to 'rigidify once again after its re-definition into an untouchable taboo'. It should, rather, be 'regularly discussed and re-defined, if the circumstances and the political argument [?] require it'; who is to do this is not specified. This would, of course, only be really necessary if the ECB's 'general emergency responsibility' unexpectedly turned out to provide an inadequate basis for an expanded reinterpretation of its jurisdiction.

As he himself makes plain, Tooze's proposal amounts to a call to 'politicise' the ECB while, at the same time, maintaining its independence at the expense of majoritarian democratic institutions. In any democracy, the latter would have to hold a monopoly over discretionary political action. To the extent that politicisation implies something like accountability, this is minimised in Tooze's proposal by the shift away from electoral institutions capable of giving satisfaction to a 'well-informed' public, a 'parliament' – that of the EU, which is not empowered to take legislative initiatives – and an enthusiastically supranational de facto constitutional court operating without a constitution. Substantive questions remain unanswered, such as, for example, how the politicised use of conditionality relates to European protection of member states against a loss of their creditworthiness. Should the ECB be allowed to demand that eurozone states cut their budgets, abolish industry-level agreements, and remove heads of government whom it dislikes, as happened in the past, in return for the discretionary supply of fresh money? And can it apply conditionality with varying degrees of strictness, by imposing it on less favoured governments while neglecting it benevolently for others?

In the real world, a formal extension of the ECB's area of responsibility would only be possible with considerable political effort, if at all. But, according to Tooze, all that is involved is the legalisation of a practice that is well established despite its dubious legality – a practice not only tolerated but encouraged, even by the German government. Indeed, it is encouraged precisely because it takes place covertly or as part of a series of rescue operations according to the motto 'Necessity knows no law'. Tooze's aim is to protect these activities from obstruction by German chief justices and thus to dissolve the precarious hybrid of national and supranational jurisdiction by progressively depriving member states of their power at the top. Where 'we' might derive the necessary majority support for this is left unsaid; nor is there any consideration here of the (quite prohibitive) political risk that the amendment of the Treaties could wake the sleeping dogs of populism.

In any case, to an experienced power broker, a proposal like Tooze's must look like an embarrassing expression of intellectual overzealousness, which is better kept in check – especially as the German federal government can more safely ensure the de facto expansion of the ECB's mandate by appointing less scrupulous, 'pro-European' judges to the constitutional court at Karlsruhe. An initiative like the one proposed by Tooze would do a disservice to the painstakingly constructed politicised rule, not *of* technocracy but *through* technocracy, the 'technocratic façade' as it were. It is well meant but strategically misguided, because it would have the foreseeable result of burdening the technocrats of the central bank with the unfulfillable obligation to provide legitimation for decisions which, in their (capitalist) essence, can only be taken and secured politically behind the scenes of the imperial theatre.

There are two main reasons why central banks cannot take over from governments the business of governing in both domestic and foreign policy, or can only do so underhandedly. The first is that there is quite simply no canonical theory of monetary policy, if only because there is no canonical theory of money. In fact, money is probably the most mysterious and the most uncontrollable institution, not only of modern society but of every society in which it has ever existed.[54] Anyone seeking to achieve economic or social objectives with monetary policy is entering terra incognita and is in danger of triggering unintended side effects of potentially immense magnitude, from inflation to deflation, from capital glut to capital shrinkage, including also the invention of new forms of money by market participants who find official money unsuitable for their purposes. Money constantly alters its shape, always surprising even those who claim to know everything about it. That is probably one of the reasons why we are repeatedly instructed by retired central bankers in their memoirs that to run a central bank is not a science but an art, and that what is most important is to have the right 'instinct', trust and confidence-inspiring demeanour, or 'psychology'.[55]

Secondly, and simultaneously, central banks, particularly when they are supposed to be independent of the government of the day, are not anchored in the society and its politics, nor should they be. To the extent that they are rooted at all in any environment outside the state apparatus, it is the financial industry, because their 'psychological' instruments must have their main effect there; without a functioning and willing

---

54   On this, see, inter alia, Michel Aglietta, *Money: 5,000 Years of Debt and Power*, London: Verso, 2018; Geoffrey Ingham, 'O Sacred Hunger of Pernicious Gold! What Bands of Faith Can Impious Lucre Hold?', *Archives Européennes de Sociologie* 54, no. 1 (2013), 127–46; and Joseph Vogl, *The Ascendancy of Finance*, trans. Simon Garnett, Cambridge, UK: Polity, 2017.

55   See the memoirs of Mervyn King (*The End of Alchemy: Money, Banking and the Future of the Gobal Economy*, London: Little, Brown, 2016), Adair Turner (*Between Debt and the Devil: Money, Credit, and Fixing Global Finance*, Princeton, NJ: Princeton University Press, 2016), and Paul Volcker (with Christine Harper, *Keeping at It: The Quest for Sound Money and Good Government*, New York: Public Affairs, 2018), or the biography of Alan Greenspan by Sebastian Mallaby (*The Man Who Knew: The Life and Times of Alan Greenspan*, New York: Penguin, 2016).

financial sector that knows how to 'read' the central bank's policies correctly, monetary policy does not have the transmission mechanism it needs to make a difference 'on the ground'. More than anything else, central banks need to enjoy the confidence of the private money business. This is one of the reasons why many of them, above all the US Federal Reserve, are at least in part privately owned – a fact that both institutionally reinforces and expresses their special position as a bridge between the worlds of banking and government.[56]

Central banks, as already mentioned, are not anchored in the social world, the world which states and governments are obliged to enter by means of parties and trade unions, or police forces and secret services, or all of them together. Only these, each in their own way, can help to work through the inevitable disappointments that occur when governing involves the denial of expectations that are perceived as fair, in favour of others which are perceived in the same way, even if it is only a matter of the chronological order of their fulfilment. Where the legitimacy and urgency of desires cannot be decided by force, particularly when questions of distribution and the treatment of social inequality are at stake, there is a need for decision-making processes that appear to have, and can be regarded as having, an open-ended outcome. Alternatives are discussed *publicly* and are represented by different, contending factions of the political class, within the framework of institutions providing for an exploratory and competing formulation of the wishes and expectations of the concerned parties, and offering the opportunity to redeem unfulfilled promises by the replacement of the previously victorious faction with another. A central bank can do none of this, regardless

---

56   On the role of the central banks as intermediaries between private money and the state, see Vogl, *The Ascendancy of Finance*; as well as Wolfgang Streeck, 'The Fourth Power?', *New Left Review* 110 (March/April 2018), 141–50, commenting on Vogl. On the class or sectoral character of the central banks, see most recently Benjamin Braun, 'Central Banking and the Infrastructural Power of Finance: The Case of ECB Support for Repo and Securitization Markets', *Socio-Economic Review* 18, no. 2 (2020), 395–418; and Timo Walter and Leon Wansleben, 'How Central Bankers Learned to Love Financialization: The Fed, the Bank, and the Enlisting of Unfettered Markets in the Conduct of Monetary Policy', *Socio-Economic Review* 18, no. 3 (2020), 625–53. See also Clement Fontan, 'Frankfurt's Double Standard: The Politics of the European Central Bank during the Eurozone Crisis', *Cambridge Review of International Affairs* 31, no. 2 (2018), 162–82, on differences in the severity of the conditions set by the European Central Bank in relation to states, on the one hand, and financial markets, on the other ('the double standard').

of the increasingly frequent emphasis on the need for better 'communication' of monetary policy – something which, given the nature of central banks, can only be done unilaterally from above: not as dialogue, but only as proclamation, 'psychologically' instrumentalised in pursuit of a specific economic policy objective.[57]

The call for rule by the central banks is the last resort of the advocates of a mega-state. It is their latest Plan A for a centralist breakthrough out of the post-neoliberal stalemate, towards the replacement of democratic, 'populist' politics by clever, elitist technocracy. Brecht's verdict *'Geh'n tun sie beide nicht'* [Neither one will work] can be applied to this plan, along with its neoliberal market-before-state predecessor.[58] Whether it is supposed to be the market that dishes out justice to a society left at its mercy, or the macroeconomic wisdom of a fraternity of economists presented as being as omniscient as it is benevolent, if the uninitiated are called upon to make asymmetrical sacrifices in the interest of the common good whose definition they are expected to allow to be imposed on them by some market or theoretical forces – while they remain defenceless, idle, passive, and uncomprehending – sooner or later, they will make themselves heard, and the longer this takes the more pronounced the sound will be.

This is especially so given the overt class character of both mercatocracy and technocracy. In the latter case, that applies not only to the

---

57   See Benjamin Braun, 'Governing the Future: The European Central Bank's Expectation Management during the Great Moderation', *Economy and Society* 44, no. 3 (2015), 367–91; Benjamin Braun, 'Speaking to the People? Money, Trust, and Central Bank Legitimacy in the Age of Quantitative Easing', *Review of International Political Economy* 23, no. 6 (2016), 1064–92, on the growing importance of communicating central bank decisions. Also of interest in this context is the recent appointment of the German economist Isabel Schnabel to the executive board of the ECB. According to the *Handelsblatt* (11 February 2020) she intended to use this position 'to promote a better understanding of monetary policy in Germany. She told the Legal Research Society in Karlsruhe that . . . criticism of the ECB based on "half-truths and false narratives" was "dangerous, because it not only threatened confidence in the common monetary policy, but also European solidarity"'. According to *Die Welt* (23 October 2019), which described her as 'opinionated, talkative and above all a convinced European', she saw it as her task 'to acquaint the public with monetary policy more effectively than had been done before'. It was however important, tweeted Schnabel, 'to respect the independence of the ECB *and not to direct any expectations towards it*' (emphasis added).

58   'Ja, mach nur einen Plan! / Sei nur ein großes Licht! / Und mach dann noch'nen zweiten Plan / Gehn tun sie beide nicht.' Bertolt Brecht, 'Das Lied von der Unzulänglichkeit', from *Die Dreigroschenoper* (1928).

shift in objectives from combating inflation to stabilising the financial markets. As mentioned above, one of the core tasks of a central bank is to ensure the well-being of the private banks, on whose ability to function as quasi-public institutions – guaranteeing the supply of cash and credit, and the open-market policy of the central banks themselves – they depend. But, to the extent that the private banks are also capitalist enterprises aimed at making profits, central bankers must be able to sympathise with them in their difficult task of combining both functions. This means they must be able to turn a blind eye occasionally to financial 'innovations', and also generally develop an understanding for the exhausting balancing act performed by the financial industry, caught as it is between the interests of the general public and the requirements of the shareholders, between the public and the private sectors, and between maintaining infrastructure and profit-making. This is also very likely the reason why the managers of central banks are frequently recruited from the ranks of those who previously ran private banks – one example is Mario Draghi, previously the European director of Goldman Sachs, who rose to the position of president of the European Central Bank. Expectations that the crisis-stricken citizens of the old Western democracies could confidently renounce national politics and democracy in favour of institutions of this kind rests on nothing other than a forced optimism in denial of reality.

Global Governance as Liberal Empire

The phrase 'global governance' suggests rule without rulers, by gentle means, united by goodwill, expertise, and a sense of responsibility, set against a backdrop of summit meetings, expert panels, and climate and health conferences. Its invocation belongs to an understanding of politics in which institutions appear as the embodiment of shared values and agreed norms, where the focus is not on domination and distribution of and through power, but intelligent problem-solving, where one person's problem is also another's and not its solution, and where the goal is not profit but a good life for all. What is also conceived, as both a result and a prerequisite of global governance, is a 'liberal', hence multilateral and rules-based, international order, with its air of uniform free will and normative commonality – a group of sovereign states in egalitarian juxtaposition, which are ready, if the cause requires it, to bundle their sovereign powers into joint institutions organised on a basis of equality. In the world of global governance, there is no talk of capitalism, its inherent logic of accumulation driving it forward under its own laws, to be flouted only at certain risk, and which operates as a restrictive condition on political action and as a parallel motor of social development in addition to politics, with its logic of state and empire.

It is now well known how superficial and 'ideological', meaning subservient to political interests, this image is. In the state system of the liberal international order (LIO) constructed after the Second World War and fully established after the fall of the Soviet Union, there were and still are stark differences in power between a political and economic centre and its various peripheries, linked to the centre in varying degrees of closeness. It will be recalled that Karl Polanyi described precisely the dynamic of the United States as a post-1945 global power, aimed at expansion and, in principle, at world domination, and he was rightly concerned that it could thwart the prospect of establishing a pluralistic world order and, thus, of a non-aligned third way towards regional planning.[59] Materially, according to Polanyi, the imperial ambitions of the US state and American capitalism, interwoven to the point of indistinguishability, involved the extension of the American version of a capitalist economy – capitalism as Americanism – to the rest of the world and the unification of the world under the US as a world state and world government; this connection characterised the rise of the US empire as well as its stagnation and decline after its apparently definitive victory following 1990.[60]

The history of the international order since the 1990s must be understood against the backdrop of a gradual shift in the balance of power between the US and its small and medium-sized allies. The latter repeatedly used the American empire's self-description as multilateral and

---

59   See chapter 1.

60   On the origin and structure of the US empire after 1945, see, among many others, Perry Anderson, 'Imperium', *New Left Review* 83 (September/October 2013), 5–111; Perry Anderson, 'Consilium', *New Left Review* 83 (September/October 2013), 113–16; Paul A. Baran and Paul M. Sweezy, *Monopoly Capital: An Essay on the American Economic and Social Order*, New York: Monthly Review Press, 1966; and Leo Panitch and Sam Gindin, *The Making of Global Capitalism: The Political Economy of American Empire*, London: Verso, 2013.

rules-based to justify appeals to it to refrain from acting unilaterally and to coordinate its policy with its client states. The US, on the other hand, used the formulaic commitment of all sides to multilateralism and the application of agreed rules to legitimate its role as the hegemonic power in an empire which wanted, and needed, to be recognised as the democratic antithesis to the USSR. This did not mean that American governments were prepared to renounce their 'exorbitant privilege' of choosing freely between multilateralism, bilateralism, and unilateralism, whichever seemed appropriate.[61] It also did not mean that membership in the US-American empire was, or could be, completely voluntary, even if frank formulations of a claim to determine the fate of other countries, such as the Brezhnev Doctrine, were avoided.[62] And, finally: the US, liberal empire or not, did not shy away from using military force during its period of hegemony wherever it seemed appropriate, particularly when there was need to prop up pro-American states and governments whose loyalty it valued.

The United States' liberal empire and the multilateral, rules-based international order it stipulated were distinguished from the outset by a characteristic interaction of force and consent, two sources of power which sometimes complemented each other but also occasionally clashed. After 1990, the New World Order proclaimed by the US in connection with German reunification can be understood as a substitute for a unified neoliberal world state that was bound to remain a utopia, even after the end of the Soviet Union. An empire made up of still-sovereign individual states, but organised in terms of power politics in such a way that national sovereignty would no longer have any decisive significance, proved to be the only possible, if perhaps second-best, solution for achieving a centrally imposed unification of the world as the borderless place of unlimited global chains of capital accumulation and expanding horizons of growth. Before I address why this variant of

---

61   The expression was used by the French finance minister of the time, Valéry Giscard d'Estaing, and originally referred to the ability of the US to pile up unlimited dollar-denominated debts because the dollar was the international reserve currency.

62   There is reason to assume that, as late as the 1970s, an attempt by Italy or even West Germany to leave NATO would have been answered in the way the 'Prague Spring' was on the other side of the 'Iron Curtain'; at least, this was the fear frequently expressed by Enrico Berlinguer, the leader of the Communist Party of Italy, in the years before and after the murder of Aldo Moro.

neoliberal global integration must also be regarded as a failure today – why, in other words, the liberal international order, neoliberalised as it is, can no longer be considered a path towards a neoliberal mega-state in which the nation-state is either made irrelevant or completely removed from the scene – I should like briefly to indicate some general features of empires, in particular liberal empires, in the following eight points, all of which also apply to the currently disintegrating US empire and the European Union.[63]

(1) Like other forms of rule, inter-state empires are also under pressure to establish legitimacy above and beyond the underlying balance of power, so as to avoid overstraining their means of coercion. This may require that the centre declare its commitment to rules applicable to all states within the empire. In order to achieve the desired effect, the hegemonic power's self-imposed obligations cannot be exclusively rhetorical. How far the ruling power needs to go in this direction, and the extent to which it can, in an emergency, exempt itself from the rules that purportedly also bind it, depends on the balance of power, in particular on how dependent the other states and their political elites are on its goodwill and vice versa.

(2) A liberal empire prefers to control the states on its periphery, not by military occupation but with the aid of reliably well-disposed local governments that are ideally supported by the majority of the respective population. Imperial orders can be described as state systems based on inter-elite relations, whose hegemonic powers take a keen interest in the domestic politics of the other states belonging to the empire.

(3) It is generally true that hegemonic international powers, like domestic rulers, can only count on lasting support if they 'deliver' something to those they rule in return for a willingness to follow – whether this is order and security or bread and circuses. Even the barons of the Middle Ages, whose peasants were their serfs, paid for the tithes and hand services due to them by offering protection from marauding gangs or rival barons. Even the most powerful hegemonic state will have to provide something like good government if it wants to remain in the saddle in the long term, and the smaller the power

---

63 The following outline concentrates on the internal dynamics of imperial state systems and ignores their foreign relations and the interaction of these with internal policy. It was written before the war in Ukraine between Russia and the 'West'.

disparity between the centre and the periphery, the more the centre will have to provide.

(4) In an empire organised along liberal lines, 'values', or, more precisely, a hegemonic 'culture', count for more than they do in one founded on force – as in, for example, a colonial empire. There too, however, the rulers – and to some extent the ruled – found it important to define the centre's civilising mission to which they could refer. This was the not only the case in what was then called 'the free world', but also in the former Eastern bloc – after all, the Brezhnev Doctrine purportedly served to defend a higher level of civilisation attained under socialism, and to fall below it would have signified a step backwards in history. Values of this kind are particularly useful in socialising local elites, who, as agents of indirect rule, are expected to work from the periphery to ensure the empire's cohesion. The universities, academies, and other educational institutions belonging to the centre, especially in the field of high culture, play an important role here, comparable to that of the missionaries of the colonial era. Thus, for example, the universities of the United Kingdom and the United States function as indispensable mechanisms for preserving the cohesion of their respective empires as their historical shape changes; the same is true for France too, though to a lesser extent.

(5) For an imperial centre, there is a more or less explicit cost/benefit calculation to be made that balances the returns of hegemony in the form of tributes of all kinds, direct and indirect, against the costs of enforcing and maintaining its supremacy. Such calculations are complicated and must, from one case to the next, take into consideration quite diverse circumstances, often making them difficult to quantify. For the stability of an empire, however, the assessment and dynamics of costs and revenues may be of decisive significance for its central power. If costs rise without a corresponding increase in revenues, or if revenues fall without costs being reduced, empires arrive at a point where their dissolution is imminent.

(6) The costs and benefits of empires as asymmetrical international alliances between national elites must be considered in the context of the social structure of the countries involved. The advantages distributed within international coalitions of elites must be shared with non-elites according to national political balances of power; similarly, the costs incurred for imperial cohesion can, to varying degrees, be

passed on by the elites of a hegemonic power to non-elites. Empires can become too expensive for non-elites, even if they continue to be profitable for elites. As inter-elite alliances, empires must develop an interest in maintaining the cooperation of their populations by allowing them to share in the advantages of empire; under democratic conditions this can be expensive, occasionally prohibitively so.

(7) Just as important as the integration of Indigenous national non-elites is the cultivation of the impression that equal state sovereignty is enjoyed by every country, even those at the empire's periphery. Considerable symbolic efforts are required to ensure that the latter do not appear as vassals of the hegemonic power, and that cooperation with it looks like an alliance rather than a relationship of domination. 'Soft' power is essential here. On the other hand, hegemonic powers must have the fundamental option of dissolving peripheral governments which oppose them, for whatever reason, and replacing them with more favourably inclined allies. 'Intervention in the internal affairs' of other formally sovereign states thus becomes commonplace, albeit no less perilous. To keep the resulting conflicts in a latent state requires sensitive modes of behaviour and elaborate rituals, although these of course can never guarantee that symbolic offences will not occur occasionally, and that they will then have to be atoned for with great effort.

(8) Empires organised along liberal lines, unable to put an end to insubordination simply by dispatching their troops, suffer from inherent instability. Friendly governments at the periphery may fall out of power; the search for a reliable successor may take time or fail; the cost of hegemony may become too high for the non-elites of the leading state; the compensation demanded by the states at the periphery may exceed the financial resources of the hegemonic power; and the disparity between the power of the centre and the power of the periphery may change in favour of the latter if, for example, a competing power centre enters the market for political alliances. If a hegemonic power finds itself compelled to shift from indirect to direct methods of rule, mainly at the outer edges of the empire, as in the case of the numerous worldwide military interventions by the US since 1945, this may at some point become too costly for the population at home, particularly if an operation ends in defeat. In general, the stability of an imperial system can be expected to decline if its expansion leads to a growth in the hegemonic power's sphere of control, and an increase in the complexity of the

particular interests it must regulate along with the problems it needs to solve through government action.

Global governance in its imperial form, as the political order of a globally expanding capitalism with the US as the hegemonic power, has proved to be particularly unstable. By its very nature, a capitalist empire is under pressure to expand; but if it gives in to this pressure, its internal heterogeneity increases and, with it, the costs of maintaining its cohesion. At the same time, an empire organised on a liberal basis must, if possible, avoid the direct use of force. For this reason, it must be willing and able to satisfy the states at its periphery – or, more precisely, their elites – by granting them material advantages; this may, however, come at the expense of its own population. Even so, the pressure and the temptation to overreach by excessive expansion is very great. The US empire of the neoliberal era arrived at this point in the late 1990s, during the period of hyperglobalisation, when it attempted to incorporate Russia under Yeltsin and then, by admitting it to the WTO in 2001, China under Jiang Zemin. China's subsequent rapid emergence as an economic and geopolitical competitor was an unintended consequence of this, and it put an end to the short-lived hope of a genuinely global 'Western' empire.[64] Moreover, it raised the costs of imperial cohesion, because it gave the formally sovereign countries at the margins of the empire the opportunity to demand a higher price for their compliance with the 'West'.

The rise of China as a geopolitical rival to the US has finally rendered utopian any idea of global governance in a world-spanning Western capitalist empire, with the US at its centre, that might serve as a precursor or minimal form of a one-state world order. In the long term, however, no empire oriented towards a hyperglobalised world capitalism could have been stabilised anyway, because its ability to rule would have been systematically undermined by the need to conform with the requirements of capitalism. The cause for this is a thematic selectiveness, structurally and politically built into the liberal international order, particularly in its neoliberal imperial form. This made it possible, for example, to institutionalise global capital mobility but not to prevent tax

---

64   This also holds for Russia, though it was not until the 2000s, when it was already ruled by Putin, that the country understood it could only enter the 'liberal international order' at the price of its absorption by US hegemony.

evasion, to provide protection for 'intellectual property' but not against brain drain, to secure the US against terrorism but not the world against climate change, and so on. In the following, I will take a closer look at another reason for the dysfunctionality of an organised imperial world order as revealed by the COVID crisis: namely that its manifest destiny, the facilitation of cross-border capitalist expansion, does not permit a realistic calculation or efficient allocation of the costs of globalisation, and thereby condemns the global regime to structural irresponsibility.

COVID: The Long-Hidden Costs of Globalisation

It took some time before the political classes involved in capitalist globalisation realised, in the early 2000s, that globalisation, as long as democracy still prevails, requires compensation for the losers in its countries of origin – that if it is to be sustainable, it will tend to require not less but more redistributive social policies.[65] Promises of the kind given by Bill Clinton, Tony Blair, and Gerhard Schröder that the expected rising tide of prosperity will lift all boats equally, whether they be large or small, lose credibility when it turns out that the burden of adjustment to globalisation-induced structural change is concentrated on certain regions and classes.[66] Overcoming their resistance through compensatory policies – from unemployment insurance to assistance with retraining and regional economic development – is, and can only be, the task of the globalising nation-states; there are no institutions for this at the international level. Social justice, regrettably from the neo-liberal perspective, is still understood in relation to the social conditions under which injury has been suffered and reparation is demanded. The incurable parochialism of ordinary people – their unwillingness to

---

65   Among economists, as explained above, it was Rodrik, above all, who contributed to the dissemination of this realisation – or, rather, demand (see Rodrik, *Has Globalization Gone Too Far?*). A brief summary of the political science compensation thesis can be found in Duane Swank, 'Globalization', in Francis G. Castles et al., eds, *The Oxford Handbook of the Welfare State*, Oxford: Oxford University Press, 2010, 318–30. Geoffrey Garrett, *Partisan Politics in a Global Economy*, Cambridge, UK: Cambridge University Press, 1998, among others, was optimistic about the prospects for compensation, although this view is over a quarter century old.

66   'A rising tide lifts all boats' – a metaphor frequently employed by John F. Kennedy indicating that economic growth is ultimately of equal benefit to everyone.

rejoice selflessly in the relocation of their jobs to the capitalist periphery, so inappropriate to a cosmopolitan age – calls the nation-state into action, even if it had long hoped to retire from socio-political matters after rejuvenating itself with economics.

Admittedly, the capacity of the nation-states of the global North to make the necessary compensatory payments for the implementation of globalisation is constrained; indeed, it is constrained by globalisation itself, as is only to be expected under capitalist conditions. National businesses, architects of new global systems of production and distribution, face an equally global competitive pressure that limits the extent to which they can be taxed in their home countries; at any rate, they can make this claim, and, if they are not listened to, they can threaten to shift more and more jobs abroad. On top of all this, these firms gain as allies the workers they threaten with unemployment. Moreover, once the finance industry has been globalised (something which occurred in the phase of hyperglobalisation that came after 1989), firms also have at their disposal ample opportunities to transfer their profits to tax havens inaccessible to the authorities of their homelands.[67] Thus, the costs of globalisation, where they cannot be reduced by social policy 'reforms' or denied by creative non-accounting, are reflected in rising budget deficits and correspondingly increased government borrowing; this solidifies the unequal distribution of wealth, which in turn increases income inequality. Then, at some point, both the compensatory effect of social policy and the sustainability of government indebtedness reach a limit, measured by the fundamentally unpredictable degree to which the financial sector is prepared to refinance the debt at an affordable interest rate. This, in turn, depends on the ability of the state, whether democratic or not, to impose fiscal discipline, also known as austerity, on its own citizens.

The COVID crisis has now dramatically reminded us once again, after the Great Recession of 2008, of the artfully concealed costs of globalisation and of the dilatory failure to pay them.[68] Advocates of the

---

67   Gabriel Zucman, 'Global Wealth Inequality', *Annual Review of Economics* 11 (2019), 109–38.

68   See, on this, the report laid before the World Economic Forum ('Committed to Improving the State of the World') in January 2019 (!): World Economic Forum, with Harvard Global Health Institute, 'Outbreak Readiness and Business Impact: Protecting Lives and Livelihoods across the Global Economy', white paper, Geneva: World

'Third Way' wanted to end the financial crisis of the state by entrusting the creation and preservation of legitimately shared prosperity to private business and a globalised market, convincing themselves that both business and the market would finance themselves, so to speak. However, just as with the generation of electricity by nuclear power plants, hyperglobalisation could only appear profitable if it was allowed to impose a considerable part of its growing costs on states that were neither politically nor fiscally able to bear them permanently, and therefore postponed their payment by borrowing in the hope that they would somehow disappear. But that is precisely not what is transpiring.

Globalisation entails the construction of earth-spanning production systems and supply chains which, by exploiting differences in productivity and more efficient transaction and coordination technologies, can simultaneously reduce costs and prices, and increase profits. Yet the further globalisation progresses, the more businesses – and the societies they supply, employ, and finance, along with their states – grow to depend upon the seamless functioning of steadily expanding, continent-encompassing collaborative relations involving a division of labour, but also requiring careful maintenance.

Globally distributed operational systems are subject to many contingencies and are correspondingly crisis-prone; they need constant supervision, protection, and upkeep of a kind that can only be guaranteed by state authority. The risks associated with globalisation would have to be estimated and insured against, and the insurance premiums would have to be charged to the globalisers according to the principle that the polluter pays. But this would compromise the profitability of long production and supply chains, thereby damaging globalisation itself. To forestall the occurrence of crises, it would also be necessary to install two, three, or more backup systems, whose construction and

---

Economic Forum, 2019. The executive summary of the report reads in part as follows: 'With increasing trade, travel, population density, human displacement, migration and deforestation, as well as climate change, a new era of the risk of epidemics has begun . . . Potentially catastrophic outbreaks may occur only every few decades, but highly disruptive regional and local outbreaks, such as the 2014 Ebola virus crisis in West Africa, are becoming more common and pose a major threat to lives and livelihoods . . . Economists estimate that, in the coming decades, pandemics will cause average annual economic losses of 0.7 % of global GDP – a threat similar in scale to that estimated for climate change.' A year and a half later, the estimated losses would no doubt have been still higher.

maintenance would be equally expensive; these too would have to be financed by the originators of the process, making the real cost of globalisation visible and perceptible, and thus, as a secondary consequence, allowing societies to set statutory limits to it. If, despite this, a crisis did occur, fire brigades and emergency services of all kinds would have to stand ready to prevent, as far as possible, the harmful side effects from spreading to society as a whole, or at least to keep them under control – including those areas people had believed were safe, such as retirement and care homes.

The magnitude of the risk posed to human societies by globalised operational systems was shown by the financial crisis of 2008, when the long-term impact of the financialisation of the housing market in the US – a substitute for government social policy and poverty relief, aimed at raising the American underclass to middle-class status – was transmitted globally through the credit markets established by the financial industry. The crisis disrupted prosperity and employment all over the world and compelled states to pursue a policy of austerity which weakened many of them economically and made it impossible to govern some of them democratically.[69] Twelve years later, global capitalism's lines of communication became the transmission paths of a disease whose containment was possible only at the price of the next worldwide depression. The immense economic losses it caused might, if it were possible to draw up such an account, be entered on the debit side of globalisation, a process which was declared to be as inescapable as it was harmless and, above all, profitable to all parties, and which therefore, it was claimed, ought to be left to its own devices. Moreover, the states and governments which either accepted hyperglobalisation as a welcome destiny, or promoted it jointly with its authors, had been warned by two previous viral pandemics, SARS-CoV from 2002 and bird flu, H5N1, from 2004. This did not prevent them from merely looking on during that decade, in the spirit of unrestrained capitalism, while the big pharmaceutical firms grew ever larger and more profitable in the course of globalisation with the help of an internationally recognised right to 'intellectual property', and refused to produce vaccines against novel

---

69   The cost of insurance that beneficiaries of financial market liberalisation would have had to pay to the states involved as a prerequisite for their participation is beyond all imagination. The same can be said about the costs arising from the climate crisis.

pathogens because they were insufficiently profitable. This was probably because they feared being compelled to supply them at affordable prices during a crisis (in other words, they might be treated as part of the social infrastructure), or because there was too great a danger that possible epidemics might be suppressed by non-medicinal precautionary measures, thereby making unnecessary (potentially profitable) mass immunisations.[70]

There was the additional factor, which has in the meantime become widely known, that governments refrained from building up surplus capacities and stockpiles of items such as ventilators, protective clothing, and test materials which were not normally required.[71] Nor were any obstacles placed in the way of the pharmaceutical companies when they began to shift the sourcing of raw materials indispensable to the production of high-value medications abroad, above all to China, the new workshop of the world. This was the very country in which industrial production temporarily came to a halt owing to an epidemic that, to combat, urgently required the materials produced there and only there. The degree of dependence arising when an industry which ought to have been part of a local public infrastructure is converted into a global machine for making private profits is shown, among other things, by the row that broke out between the US and China in March 2020, when the Chinese government looked as if it were threatening to ban

70   Jürgen Kaube and Joachim Müller-Jung, 'Ein Patient ist kein Kunde', *Frankfurter Allgemeine Zeitung*, 12 March 2020, 11. See also Stephen Buranyi, 'How Profit Makes the Fight for a Coronavirus Vaccine Harder', *Guardian*, 4 March 2020, theguardian.com; Anis Chowdhury and Jomo Kwame Sundaram, 'Politics, Profits Undermine Public Interest in Covid-19 Vaccine Race', Inter Press Service, 26 May 2020, ipsnews.net. On the long-standing lack of interest displayed by the big pharmaceutical firms in the timely development of vaccines against new kinds of viruses, as seen in the SARS epidemic in China in 2002 and the MERS epidemic on the Arabian Peninsula in 2012 (which could have been offered and were called for but were not produced owing to lack of commercial interest), see Astrid Viciano, 'Was die Konzerne wollen', *Süddeutsche Zeitung*, 25 May 2020, sueddeutsche.de.
71   It may be that governments wanted to let sleeping dogs lie; during the earliest stages of the COVID crisis, it was seen as anathema, in Germany at least, to assert that there was even a distant connection between globalisation and the spread of the virus and the defencelessness of most national health systems. In the meantime, more chains of causality became visible, such as those involving the worldwide industrialisation of agriculture and the destruction of habitats previously untouched by human activity.

the export of certain medical supplies to the US if the Trump administration continued to maintain that COVID originated in China.[72]

Even to arm national health systems against the risks posed by globalisation would have been expensive – so expensive that it would have
called into question the profitability of globalisation of the scale attained
in the 1990s. Moreover, it would have slowed the progress of globalisation, to the extent that it was pursued as a profit-making endeavour. The
costs were then further increased by a failure to prepare adequately for
them when they came due. When the virus hit, it was followed by a
global collapse of economic activity the likes of which the world had not
seen since the 1930s; in April 2020, the economic damage was provisionally estimated to have amounted to €1.15 trillion, or 8.3 percent of
the European Union's combined GDP for 2019.[73] Included in this
were the loss of income caused by weeks of interruption to almost all
economic activities, the resulting loss of tax revenue, government subsistence allowances, and compensation payments of all kinds, and the
cost of repairing the damage incurred after the end of the various shut-
downs. The bill also includes the interest to be paid in the coming years
(and decades) on the dramatic increase in public debt, and with it the
reduction in public investment compelled by a renewal of a sustained
austerity programme aimed at generating an annual primary surplus –
all done to retain the 'confidence' of private lenders.[74]

---

72   'As the war of words between China and the US over COVID-19 heats up,
Chinese state media have raised the spectre of using Beijing's pharmaceutical leverage to
block critical components and supplies for dependent US drug companies and send
America into "the hell of a novel coronavirus epidemic"': Guy Taylor, '"Wake-Up Call":
Chinese Control of U.S. Pharmaceutical Supplies Sparks Growing Concern', *Washington
Times*, 17 March 2020, washingtontimes.com.

73   Estimate of the European Commission, according to the *Financial Times*, 7 July
2020. For comparison: the German federal budget for 2019 came to €362 billion. It was
expected that the EU as a whole would grow by 5.8 percent in 2021. Germany came off
best, with minus 6.3 percent in 2020 and plus 5.3 percent in 2021; France, Italy, and
Spain were expected to have shrunk by 10.6 percent, 11.2 percent, and 10.9 percent
respectively in 2020.

74   I have spelled out the political logic of what I call the 'consolidation state' in
several publications, most recently in Wolfgang Streeck, 'The Rise of the European
Consolidation State', in Hideko Magara, ed., *Policy Change under New Democratic
Capitalism*, London: Routledge, 2017, 27–46; and Wolfgang Streeck, 'A New Regime:
The Consolidation State', in Desmond King and Patrick Le Galès, eds, *Reconfiguring
European States in Crisis*, Oxford: Oxford University Press, 2017, 139–57. Fiscal consol-
idation means restoring the burden of debt to a level which gives creditors confidence

COVID and the Fiscal Crisis of the State: A Conjecture

Why did it make sense, indeed why was it even necessary, to hide the costs of hyperglobalisation and defer them to a distant future it was hoped would never arrive? Some clues emerge in a theory of the financial crisis of the state, as I suggested in my book *Buying Time*, following the work of Adolph Wagner, Rudolf Goldscheid, and James O'Connor.[75] According to those authors, there are good reasons for assuming that, under capitalism, the social cost of the accumulation of capital must increase in the long term. Cost increases affect many areas: collective expenditure on the general infrastructure of production and distribution, the training of workers, the deployment of scientific knowledge to increase productivity, insurance against possible damage and the cost of repairing it (for instance, to the environment), military guarantees for a periphery willing to supply and absorb goods, and the cultural legitimation of the capitalist mode of production and life by means of a suitable management of motivations and expectations politically able to neutralise the unequal distribution of the common product. At the same time, the states – the executive committees of nationally organised societies – appear to be losing their ability to redirect the growing demands of capital for the enabling services rendered by the societies it inhabits back to capital, or to charge capital for these services in the form of user fees or higher taxes. Those states attempting this have risked being abandoned by profit-driven

---

that the debt will be serviced and can be repaid; this level varies from country to country, according to the way relations of national political power and mobilisation are assessed. A widely recognised indication of adequate 'debt sustainability' is the regular annual generation of a primary surplus, meaning a budget surplus excluding the cost of servicing debt if debt reduction through economic growth cannot be expected. In the European Economic and Monetary Union, there is also the possibility of negative external effects arising between the member states; if a state can no longer fulfil its obligations to the capital markets, refinancing costs – including the interest due on new loans – may rise for all member states, not to mention the impact of these measures on national banking systems or even the possibility of the dissolution of the euro as a common currency. This is why member states find themselves compelled to monitor each other's budgets, albeit highly asymmetrically; the institutions created for this purpose (first and foremost the European Fiscal Compact, concluded after the financial crisis) reinforce the pressure already being exerted by the 'markets' towards austerity and consolidation.

75   See Streeck, *Buying Time*.

capital in favour of more generous sites of production. From this perspective, rising state indebtedness in the capitalist democracies (see figs. 12 and 13, pp. 86–7) can be understood as an attempt to obtain resources beyond the narrowing limits of taxation in an ever more international capitalism, so as to cover this same capital's mounting needs for equipment, maintenance, repairs, and subsidies.

The fiscal problems arising from the rising overhead of capitalist progress remind us of one of the first modern theories of public finance, the 'law of growing state expenditure', put forward by the German economist Adolph Wagner (1835–1917). Wagner never explained in detail why, in his view, the state's share of the national economy should increase continuously in the long term; he appears to have imagined a linear upward trajectory of social development, not only in economic but in cultural terms as well. It would be an ascent to ever-higher levels of what he called 'civilisation', inevitably linked to or presupposing a disproportionate expansion of state activity.[76] Wagner was anything but a leftist;[77] he was a leading figure in the Prussian professoriate, anti-Semitic enough to be admitted to its ranks, and belonged to the so-called *Kathedersozialisten* (socialists of the chair), a loose group of economists who supported state involvement in the economy and an active social policy. Detested by the liberals around Max Weber, they sided with the aristocracy and its bureaucracy and distrusted private liberal capitalism. Wagner was certainly not disturbed by the fact that his 'law' implied that at a future, higher level of civilisation, most, or even all, economic activities would be state affairs; he would have gladly resigned himself to a Prussian state socialism.

Since the 1990s, hyperglobalisation has updated the problem of the growing overhead costs of capitalism, now evident as an expansionary

---

76   Adolph Wagner, *Grundlegung der politischen Ökonomie* (Leipzig: C. F. Winter, 1879), pp. 727ff.

77   This was equally true of Schumpeter, but in 1918, in a remarkable public lecture, he predicted that there would be a transition to 'socialism' and that this would be a step forward for human civilisation: 'By and by private enterprise will lose its social meaning through the development of the economy and the consequent expansion of the sphere of social sympathy. The signs of this are already with us and it was inherent in the tendencies of the second half of the nineteenth century, whose perhaps final aberration was all that which culminated in the world war. Society is growing beyond private enterprise and tax state, not because but in spite of the war. *That* too is certain.' Joseph A. Schumpeter, 'The Crisis of the Tax State', in Richard Swedberg, ed., *The Economics and Sociology of Capitalism*, Princeton, NJ: Princeton University Press, 1991 [1918], 99–141.

pressure on state budgets. This applies both to the revenue side, where globalisation has facilitated tax evasion and forced tax reductions for businesses and high earners, and to the expenditure side – insofar as ever-greater risks have accumulated in the ungoverned and ungovernable spaces of denationalised and deregulated global capitalism, the coverage of which exceeds the resources of states competing for capital's attention, or even its allocation. To allow globalisation to continue, such risks therefore were to be downplayed and hidden as much as possible from public view. For a while, it sufficed to deregulate the finance industry for this purpose, so that states could borrow more from it, cumulatively above all – that is, so they could pile up debts they would never need to pay off. But then came the financial crisis of 2008–09. It showed that the attempted solution to the state's fiscal crisis by means of unleashing the credit industry was nothing other than a time bomb; a few people became richer, many poorer, some fell into absolute poverty, and private credit creation had to be supplemented with state money creation through central banks and finance ministries, using fiat currency, so as to prevent the collapse of private banks under the weight of their 'financial innovations'.

What the COVID crisis then brought to light was that serious precautions and adequate insurance against disaster in a hyperglobalised world economy would have required public resources on a scale that would have made globalisation unachievable on a national level, where states alone can exist. Since attempts to finance these measures in real terms would have led to the collapse of globalisation's business model, everything was left to chance; the result was the biggest collapse of the accumulation process in the history of capitalist crises.[78] It was for

---

78   From this point of view, the 2020–21 pandemic was by no means exogenous to global capitalism: it spread through precisely those channels of communication established for the ever-wider circulation of capital as a guarantee of continued accumulation. Persistent vulnerability resulted from the gross profit-driven negligence conditioned by this system. Incidentally, the crisis which followed 11 September 2001 was by no means external to the process of globalisation: the attackers came from the US protectorate of Saudi Arabia and were financed with oil dollars; they had lived and studied in Hamburg, had learned to fly in Florida, and had travelled to the US on the day of the attack. In this case, of course, the country affected, the US, subsequently invested heavily in precautionary measures against similar effects of globalisation. Between 2000 and 2019, the United States defence budget grew from $376 billion to $738 billion; the cost of the immense apparatus of the Department of Homeland Security must be added to this.

the states, long up to their ears in debt, to mobilise their ultimate
weapon – central bank money created out of nothing, on the basis of
their waning authority – to contain capitalism, the only remaining economic force in their societies, and thus to prevent it from going under,
and with it society and its entire order. Only by an extreme expansion
of the state economy, and the absorption of capitalism into a public
sector that was increasingly coextensive with the whole economy, was it
possible to defend the 'level of civilisation' achieved. This was, of course,
not a public sector based on the replacement of capitalist private property by public ownership, as in Wagner's work; instead, it was founded
on the magic of (as yet) unlimited state creditworthiness and the infinite
state production of money out of thin air.

This raises the question of how and whether it could even be possible
to effect the revival of the economy after COVID as one encompassing
the recovery of globalised private capitalism as such. If appearances are
not deceptive, the latter can only survive long term – given the growing
and inexorable increase in its reproduction and crisis costs – by means
of the continuous extension of financial credit through the help of that
most state-related of all state resources: the unlimited creation of money
covered solely by the state's coercive power.[79] Alternatively, one could
ask how the social cost of globalisation could be made sufficiently
visible, and its promoters sufficiently accountable, so as to make it

---

79   Fiat-money (see on this, among many others, Streeck, *Buying Time*; Streeck, 'A
New Regime') reveals the last secret of financialised capitalism by finally eliminating the
idea that society has a finite money supply. This can awaken feelings of envy among
those who – unlike the financial wizards and bank saviours for whom the magical
character of money has long been a matter of accepted reality – continue to believe
money is acquired through work, achievement, saving, and so on. The all-too-public
utilisation of fiat-money undermines the 'achievement society', its work discipline, and
its channelling of aspirations; if the *Marktvolk* (the people of the market) can receive an
unconditional basic income, why not the *Staatsvolk* (the citizens of the state) as well (see
Streeck, *Buying Time*, 80, on the distinction)? And, why only during the crisis, since
money could otherwise be created without further effort by the authority of the state? If
a shortage of money starts to be seen as a result of strategic tightening – if it is clear that
no one needs to make an advance payment for money to appear – the pro-capitalist
political centre will quickly have to find a way to bring the infinite supply of money to
an end, so as to restore the discipline of work and achievement, without which capital
cannot continue to be accumulated in private hands. This is the latest and perhaps the
most difficult challenge to face the democratic nation-state, in its distorted form as a
'consolidation state'.

difficult to evade responsibility or to use debt financing to defer these costs into the remote future. This scenario might result in a partial reversal of the globalisation process, or at least a moratorium on its further advance. Neither global governance nor imperial hegemony would be in a position to ensure the required transparency or to bear the necessary cost, not to mention the sense of responsibility needed for this to occur. But could the task perhaps be undertaken by nation-states with a restored capacity for action and democratic accountability?

10

Small-Statism and Its Possibilities

The neoliberal world republic has foundered on the resistance mounted by friends of the homeland, as has the neoliberal regional superstate, with its downgraded version of democracy as technocracy plus the rule of law. Together with the notorious instability of its lesser imperial substitutes, these developments ought to be reason enough to explore the possibility of a downward path out of the post-neoliberal stalemate, in the direction of decentralisation, local autonomy and responsibility, devolution, secession, sovereignty, and democracy 'on the ground'. Would this be a step back from today's world order, often described as multilateral and rules-based, but which is, in reality, increasingly imperially organised, and no longer liberal but, rather, neoliberal?

It is no accident that the most interesting contributions to the growing discussion over ways out of the political and economic crisis have as their subject the possibilities and prospects of a more or less orderly withdrawal from the unrestricted globalisation of the neoliberal era. The tight linkages built up during this period between merely apparent sovereign member states also impose painful adjustments on them. As we shall see later, so-called trade protectionism is no longer just an issue raised by outsiders, and the COVID crisis strengthened this development – as has the war in Ukraine, raging since February 2022. After the collapse of the WTO and failure of TTIP, there will probably be no further neoliberal-style global free trade agreements, excluding special national regulations and the elimination of national courts;[1] following the electoral victory of Donald Trump in 2016, none other than the aforementioned Larry Summers (see chapter 5), for many years the standard-bearer of the liberal establishment, issued a call for a 'responsible nationalism'.[2] Modern monetary theory (MMT), a heterodox macroeconomic theory that nevertheless attracts a surprising degree of attention, presupposes an autonomous nation-state with its own currency and flexible exchange rates.[3] The economic policies of small states with monetary sovereignty and prosperous economies, such as Denmark, Sweden, and Switzerland, are gaining renewed interest. Nationalism below the nation-state level, as found in Belgium, Spain, and the UK, encourages new thinking about federalism and the more far-reaching decentralisation of sovereign government authority. Communitarian and republican theories about patriotism as the prerequisite for a robust democracy, requiring a somewhat integrated society, command just as much attention, as do structural political reflections on the potential contribution of 'patriotic' capital – meaning one which is less footloose – to economic prosperity.[4] In relation to the politics of migration, discussion of the limits to the load-bearing capacity of host societies and the costs migration imposes on societies of origin is now beginning to rival the universalist-individualist discourse of a human right to unrestricted mobility.[5] And in global geopolitics, the failure of the American empire with its interventionism on behalf of the market economy and human rights, along with the rise of China – a country which has not traditionally aimed at world domination – may have opened the way to a genuinely

---

1   Dani Rodrik, 'What Do Trade Agreements Really Do?', *Journal of Economic Perspectives* 32, no. 2 (2018), 73–90.

2   Lawrence H. Summers, 'Voters Deserve Responsible Nationalism Not Reflex Globalism', *Financial Times*, 10 July 2016.

3   William Mitchell and Thomas Fazi, *Reclaiming the State: A Progressive Vision of Sovereignty for a Post-Neoliberal World*, London: Pluto, 2017.

4   Amitai Etzioni, *Reclaiming Patriotism*, Charlottesville: University of Virginia Press, 2019.

5   Paul Collier, *Exodus: Immigration and Multiculturalism in the 21st Century*, London: Allen Lane, 2013; Alexander Betts and Paul Collier, *Refuge: Transforming a Broken Refugee System*, London: Allen Lane, 2017.

pluralist global order with greater national autonomy and nation-building from below rather than outside and above.[6]

There are many objections to this view, and they are well worth considering. They must, of course, be evaluated in light of the experience of neoliberalism, globalism, an ostensibly rules-based multilateralism, and their respective promises. Will a decentralised, and therefore more strongly national, order be able to combat international terrorism? Here one would need to ask, in view of Afghanistan, Libya, Syria, and so on, whether these are not, in any case, tasks for the police rather than the military (and perhaps then to be done without resort to torture). Can a decentralised international order cope with migration? It has turned out, especially in the European Union, that conditions, interests, and options vary so much from one country to the next that standard regulations are constantly frustrated and, in practice, replaced by voluntary cooperation on a case-by-case basis at best, if at all. What about tax evasion, and the growing inequality that results from it?[7] Even a rena-tionalised community of states could not do worse in this area than the liberal international order, including the EU. Here, the focus must be on deglobalisation and a financial sector with stronger local ties, controls on the movement of capital, fixed rather than mobile capital, a remodelling of tax systems (so that they include, for example, taxes on inheritance and capital gains), and ultimately a new monetary system. The latter is a topic bound to be on the political agenda anyway, in view of the use of all manner of devious methods of money creation in the fight against secular stagnation and the associated rise of the central banks to positions of super-governments, even if it is only at great risk that politicians can deal with the bedrock of trust in today's money-governed societies. The same is true of the use of supra-national borrowing to deal with the COVID crisis and the rise of so-called cryptocurrencies.

As far as 'Europe' is concerned, the question to be answered is whether a Europe of nation-states, a Europe of 'variable geometry', a 'Europe à la carte', a 'Europe of fatherlands', one could also say motherlands – all terms that trigger gasps among centralism-inclined integrationists – would

---

6   Philip Cunliffe, *Cosmopolitan Dystopia: International Intervention and the Failure of the West*, Manchester: Manchester University Press, 2020; Perry Anderson, *The H-Word: The Peripeteia of Hegemony*, London: Verso, 2017, 117–44.

7   Gabriel Zucman, 'Global Wealth Inequality', *Annual Review of Economics* 11 (2019).

really make for more antagonism between the member countries than the present regime of an *ever-closer union*. Consider just how fractured the relationship is between Germany and countries like Italy or the Visegrád states. They all view the German (or perhaps Franco-German) centralism of the present EU with hostility and have to be placated from time to time with financial concessions, as in the case of the European Commission's NextGenerationEU (NGEU) instrument (not to mention the UK, which has now left after a long and hard struggle). It would seem reasonable, then, to try something else for once, even if the EU's quasi-constitution is deliberately written in such a way that it can only be changed with maximum political effort, if ever.

Simon: Decomposing Complexity

But what about the 'complexity' of a globally interdependent world, so frequently invoked? Here, as mentioned earlier, we arrive at Hayek's last and intellectually perhaps most effective weapon against the nation-state and its interventionist 'arrogance of knowledge'. As is well known, Hayek was not discussing the establishment of a governing world state; even such a state would be overtaxed by global complexity, and only the free play of market forces and the shared knowledge of self-interested parties seeking an advantage – that is, a free world market – could create order under such conditions. The only liberal political alternative to this would be a worldwide technocracy unaffected by democracy and independent of election results, something along the lines of the International Monetary Fund or a European Commission expanded to global dimensions, insofar as this is technically and politically possible. The supporters of both approaches, neoliberal and 'new liberal', forget that the system-theorist Herbert Simon has shown that complex systems can be made governable by division into subsystems, each absorbing a part of the overall complexity and handling it internally; the world, ungovernable as a single entity, can be divided into governable national societies, organised as states.[8] Simon's essay 'The Architecture of

---

8   Or, to put this in a less constructivist and more historical way, by retaining the existing division of the world into national societies (rearranged as necessary) so that the complexity to be governed remains manageable. Simon, who lived from 1916 to 2001,

Complexity' is particularly relevant to our topic of the feasibility of dividing sovereignty between nation-states and the advantages that result from this; his line of thought will be summarised briefly in what follows, and related to the subject of this chapter.[9]

(1) The systems Simon examines are architectures of *organised complexity* – as opposed to the disorganised, unstructured complexity, where only the methods of statistics and probability theory can be used.[10] Systems as architectures of organised complexity are described by Simon as 'hierarchical systems'; they are divided into subsystems, and these, in turn, may have their own subsystems, with the total number of subsystems growing layer by layer in a downward direction; systems at higher levels are more comprehensive than those at lower levels. 'Hierarchy' does not mean subordination; higher units may or may not have authority over lower units: 'For lack of a better term', writes Simon, 'I shall use hierarchy . . . to refer to all complex systems analysable into successive sets of subsystems.'[11]

(2) Systems are complex to the extent that they are 'made up of a large number of parts that interact in a non-simple way'. This makes 'the whole more than the sum of its parts': 'not in an ultimate, metaphysical sense, but in the important pragmatic sense that, given the properties of the parts and the laws of their interaction, it is not a trivial matter to infer the properties of the whole'.[12] Emergent effects of this kind create uncertainty not only for the external observer but also, insofar as they affect human action, for participants within the system, who must be interested in mitigating as much as possible the uncertain repercussions of events at the system level on their respective subsystems.

(3) The division of systems into subsystems can be operationalised by partitioning structural connections according to varying densities of interaction. In hierarchical systems of organised complexity, a distinction

---

first studied political and social science, then economics; he later became a successful mathematician and computer scientist. His most significant social scientific contributions date from his time as professor of administration at the Carnegie Institute of Technology.

9   Herbert A. Simon, 'The Architecture of Complexity', *Proceedings of the American Philosophical Society* 106, no. 6 (1962), 467–82.

10   On the distinction between organised and disorganised complexity, see Warren Weaver, 'Science and Complexity', *American Scientist* 36, no. 4 (1948), 536–44.

11   Simon, 'The Architecture of Complexity', 468.

12   Ibid. This is followed by a nicely paradoxical turn illustrating the impressive elegance of Simon's thought: 'In the face of complexity, an in-principle reductionist may be at the same time a pragmatic holist.'

is made between interactions within each subsystem and interactions between the subsystems: the former are more intensive, in the sense of being more concentrated, than the latter. And, the higher the intensity, the lower is the level in the hierarchy.[13] Simon demonstrates that this applies to administrative structures and corporate hierarchies, to organic substances ('Intermolecular forces will generally be weaker than molecular forces, and molecular forces than nuclear forces'),[14] as well as to gases and other physio-chemical systems, and he offers both an evolutionary-ontological and an epistemological explanation for this.[15] He bases the evolutionary explanation on the assumption that units of a system, at each level, only possess a limited capacity for the construction and maintenance of strong bonds, hence strong bonds to one partner or several partners make the formation of further such bonds unlikely. The critical variable would be 'the extent to which interaction between two (or a few) subsystems excludes interaction of these subsystems with others';[16] Simon cites as an example the limited number of free valences possessed by molecules. If all possibilities for strong bonds are exhausted, only weak bonds can be formed, and, by definition, these cross the subsystem's boundaries: 'One cannot, for example, enact the role of "friend" with large numbers of other people.'[17] However, according to Simon, it can be assumed that non-hierarchical, non-subdivided complex systems exceed the human abilities of observation:

> If there are important systems in the world that are complex without being hierarchic, they may to a considerable extent escape our observation and our understanding. Analysis of their behaviour would involve such detailed knowledge and calculation of the interactions of their elementary parts that it would be beyond our capacities of memory or computation.[18]

---

13   Ibid., 473–7.
14   Ibid., 474.
15   Ibid., 475–6.
16   Ibid., 476.
17   Ibid., 477.
18   Ibid. Simon concludes the discussion of this subject with a remarkable retraction: 'I shall not try to settle which is chicken and which is egg: whether we are able to understand the world because it is hierarchic, or whether it appears hierarchic because those aspects of it which are not elude our understanding and observation. I have already given some reasons for supposing that the former is at least half the truth – that evolving complexity would tend to be hierarchic – but it may not be the whole truth' (478).

It is not difficult to recognise such a non-hierarchical complex system in the world market invoked by Hayek and other globalists.

(4) Simon's most important concept, at least for our problem of the ability of nation-states to govern themselves in the face of global social complexity, is that of the *near decomposability* of hierarchically structured systems. A system is hierarchical if it consists of islands of high interactive density that can be demarcated clearly from one another. If their reciprocal interactions are negligible, they can be regarded as independent; the system to which they belong would then be decomposable. Yet, according to Simon, this is only a borderline case: normally, interactions also take place between the subsystems of a system, albeit to a lesser extent than within them, but nonetheless forcefully enough to hold the system as such together. A state of near decomposability is reached when relations between the subsystems are just sufficient to ensure this; two conditions apply here: '(a) the short-run behaviour of each of the component subsystems is approximately independent of the short-run behaviour of the other components; (b) in the long run the behaviour of any one of the components depends in only an aggregate way on the behaviour of the other components', thus not on the behaviour of specific individual subsystems.[19]

What can we learn from Simon and his 'architecture of complexity' about the potential for a system of self-governing nation-states under conditions of global interdependence? State systems are complex systems whose subsystems are states themselves; the world economy is a complex system of national economies. Here, too, interactions within subsystems are denser and more intensive than between them: both states and national economies, combined as nations, are embedded in and bound by the elementary particularism of human socialisation.[20] What distinguishes them from cells and molecules is that, as collective social formations that are subsystems of larger systems, they can make their internal and external relations the subject of collective decisions, hence of politics. Their reciprocal relations are governed not by natural but by human laws. Political communities can and must decide – and a failure to decide is also a decision – the extent to which they wish to

---

19   Ibid., 474. Accordingly, an imperially structured system would not be 'nearly decomposable', but egalitarian systems would be, in various ways.

20   See, on this, chapter 7.

shape their fate actively in self-chosen, selective cooperation with other political communities, or to accept it as an aggregated result of the interaction of other subsystems with each other and with the system as a whole. This choice translates into, among other things, the question of which functions a community would like to see fulfilled – or in what respect it can, wants, or must afford to be dependent on cross-boundary transactions and aggregate conditions occurring behind its back, and in what other respect it wants to prioritise its sovereignty instead, namely by creating the desired conditions internally and under its own jurisdiction. This is precisely the problem that, according to Polanyi, societies constituted as states must solve, want to solve, and can solve by shaping their foreign trade through regional planning.

Interactively consolidated subsystems of a global world society and economy, provided they have achieved statehood – to continue with Simon's approach – are by no means defenceless against the 'complexity' of the world market: the latter exists in the form of disorganised complexity and is located, in any case, at a lower aggregate level, in the world market, where it is not states that operate but businesses.[21] The world of states has roughly 200 members and as such is, in principle, manageable for all participants. Only when, in realising the neoliberal dream, states have been abolished, sidelined, or imagined away as market-distorters (or when states have done so to themselves or to each other) does the economic world become so complex, as with Hayek, that it can be declared a mystery to be marvelled at, but one best left to its own devices.

Globalisation, as one may reasonably understand it after reading Simon, is a political rather than natural occurrence entailing the de-differentiation of a structured complex system; how far it goes is decided by how states manage their borders, and whether they allow, encourage, or prevent them from becoming porous. Neoliberalism aims to eliminate, or at least disempower, the level of the system between the market and world society, and, by seeking to transform a hierarchical system into a non-hierarchical – or at least a less hierarchical – one, it creates precisely that disorganised complexity for which it then proposes the

---

21   Here, too, there are of course organising forces in operation, above all the gigantic multinationals with their highly consolidated global supply chains, detached from democratically active territorial communities and states. The question is whether politics should or must allow this, and on what grounds.

freely fluctuating world market as a solution – like an arsonist offering to put out his own fire. Economic globalisation is the shift in welfare production away from strong internal to weak external relations, planned or endured. In principle, deglobalisation would be just as viable as a shift of business relationships inwards, shortening instead of lengthening all manner of supply chains; nothing in Simon's theory of complex systems contradicts this. Both globalisation (the *removal* of boundaries, the obliteration of the difference between the internal and the external) and deglobalisation (the *restoration* of boundaries) are the result of political will and political power in the relation of the subsystems of the state system to each other – whether imperial or egalitarian – or, where contingently present, to hierarchical bodies endowed with authority at higher levels of the system.

Near decomposability in Simon's sense, with the scope for autonomy and the safety margins it enables, does not necessarily have to be thought of as the result of a benevolent institutional design coming from above. It may be brought about by the subsystems themselves, owing to the way their internal and external relations are constituted, to the extent that they possess the required freedom of movement or are able to reclaim it. Whether societies and their states favour long production chains stretching beyond their borders or short internal ones does not follow from any systemic necessities. There is a political choice between global coupling and national decoupling, and in reality, such choices arise constantly, much to the chagrin of the neoliberal globalisers. All-embracing non-sector-specific free trade agreements are in fact quite rare, and they mostly exist on paper; as we have seen, they are no longer concluded anyway. Products that derive from long, earth-spanning supply chains may be cheaper than equivalent domestic products; but low prices for consumers (and high profits for multinational companies and their shareholders) are not the only relevant interests so far as societies and states are concerned. For example, military security has always been an undisputed justification for trade restrictions. Moreover, after Trump, at the latest, no state can afford to disregard unemployment in its own country in the name of globalisation, if the former is the consequence of international undercutting and offshoring of production. Doubts are also increasingly being expressed as to whether societies should leave the task of supplying their national economies with credit to a globalised financial sector over which they have no control. And, during the COVID crisis of 2020, a widespread realisation seems to have dawned that it might have been a mistake to allow the pharmaceutical industry to source essential raw materials for urgently needed medicines *just in time* from a single distant country itself prone to crisis, so as to reduce costs to the public health system while increasing the industry's profits – instead of keeping them in stock for emergencies or producing them domestically, albeit at an inevitably higher cost.

Keynes: National Self-Sufficiency

That world society might become more governable by decoupling its national societies, and the same achieved for the world economy by disentangling its national economies, is not just an idea developed by general systems theory; it also has a place in the history of economic theory. In June of the fateful year 1933, when the New Deal began in the US and the Nazis took power in Germany, an article by John Maynard Keynes appeared in the journal *Yale Review*. Entitled 'National Self-Sufficiency', it was considered sensational enough to be announced separately the next day in the *New York Times*.[22] In it, three years before the appearance of his *General Theory*, Keynes publicly renounces the doctrine of free trade, which, as he writes, like most Englishmen, he had believed ten years earlier to be derived from 'fundamental truths' with which no rational person could disagree, and that it was nothing less than a moral law.[23]

At the centre of Keynes's 1933 reflections was the value of national autonomy in a globally integrated capitalist economy during a time of extreme economic and political uncertainty – a theme partly anticipating Polanyi's 1945 article on 'regional planning' (and there can be no doubt that Polanyi knew Keynes's article). Some of Keynes's essay points to the principles of the world economic order that would be established eleven years later at Bretton Woods, the conception of which he would take a leading part in planning, as is well known. This economic order, intended to reconcile national economic and political self-sufficiency

---

22   John Maynard Keynes, 'National Self-Sufficiency', *Yale Review* 22, no. 4 (1933), 755–69.

23   John Maynard Keynes, *The General Theory of Employment, Interest and Money*, London: Macmillan, 1967 [1936].

with international trade, was to become the institutional foundation of the post-war 'golden age' of state-regulated capitalism, until it began to disintegrate in the 1980s, at first gradually and then ever more rapidly under the onslaught of the neoliberal revolution.

Keynes begins by reminding his readers of the four promises of nineteenth-century liberalism and the international division of labour it engendered: the clear-sighted and rational approach to society, an end to poverty throughout the world, a facilitation of personal freedom by the abolition of privileges and monopolies, and the establishment of peace and economic justice among nations. Yet, with regard to the fourth point, Keynes remarks that doubts inevitably arise retrospectively. It is appropriate here to allow him to speak for himself, via a lengthy quotation indicating how close the economist Keynes was in 1933 to the views of the political economist Polanyi in 1945:

> But it does not now seem obvious that a great concentration of national effort on the capture of foreign trade, that the penetration of a country's economic structure by the resources and influence of foreign capitalists, and that a close dependence of our own economic life on the fluctuating economic policies of foreign countries are safeguards and assurances of international peace. It is easier in the light of experience and foresight to argue quite the contrary. The protection of a country's existing foreign interests, the capture of new markets, the progress of economic imperialism – these are a scarcely avoidable part of a scheme of things which aims at the maximum of international specialization and at the maximum geographical diffusion of capital wherever its seat of ownership. Advisable domestic policies might often be easier to compass, if the phenomenon known as the 'flight of capital' could be ruled out.[24]

If, according to Keynes, a liberalised world economy would actually lead to international peace, that would in itself be reason enough to support it. But this is not so, he says:

> I sympathize, therefore, with those who would minimize, rather than with those who would maximize, economic entanglement among

---

24   Keynes, 'National Self-Sufficiency', 757.

nations. Ideas, knowledge, science, hospitality, travel – these are the things which should of their nature be international. But let goods be homespun whenever it is reasonably and conveniently possible, *and, above all, let finance be primarily national.*[25]

Keynes's abandonment of nineteenth-century liberalism and his support for national economic self-sufficiency were linked to his disappointment with the capitalism of the period since the end of the First World War:

> The decadent international but individualistic capitalism, in the hands of which we found ourselves after the war, is not a success. It is not intelligent, it is not beautiful, it is not just, it is not virtuous – and it doesn't deliver the goods. In short, we dislike it, and we are beginning to despise it.[26]

Four reasons, in particular, drove Keynes to become an economic nationalist in 1933. *Firstly*, and most importantly, Keynes specifies the divorce of ownership from responsibility in modern corporations traded on the financial markets. This is already harmful within a single country, but when it crosses international borders, especially in times of crisis, it is completely unacceptable. Financially, it may pay for capital to invest in distant corners of the habitable earth where marginal returns or interest rates are highest, but 'experience is accumulating that remoteness between ownership and operation is an evil in the relations among men, likely or certain in the long run to set up strains and enmities which will bring to nought the financial calculation'.[27]

Secondly, says Keynes, a renunciation of national economic independence may indeed generate efficiency gains and cost reductions; but rarely are these large enough to outweigh the advantages of 'bringing the

---

25 Ibid., 758, emphasis added.

26 Ibid., 760–1. As Edward Fuller ('Was Keynes a Socialist?', *Cambridge Journal of Economics* 43, no. 6 [2019], 1653–82) has shown in his discussion of the authoritative biography of Keynes by Robert Skidelsky, Keynes was not a liberal concerned to save capitalism but a socialist who wanted to abolish it.

27 Keynes, 'National Self-Sufficiency', 758. Keynes mentions 'the part ownership of a German corporation by a speculator in Chicago, or of the municipal improvements of Rio Janeiro by an English spinster' (759) as examples of harmful economic internationalism.

product and the consumer within the ambit of the same national, economic, and financial organisation.[28] For example, the wealthier a country, the smaller the relative share of primary and manufactured products in the national economy compared with houses, personal services, and local amenities, which are not equally available for international exchange,

> with the result that a moderate increase in the real cost of primary and manufactured products consequent on greater national self-sufficiency may cease to be of serious consequence when weighed in the balance against advantages of a different kind. National self-sufficiency, in short, though it costs something, may be becoming a luxury we can afford, if we happen to want it.[29]

Keynes's *third* argument for economic nationalism is, above all, of a political nature, and its logic recalls not only Hayek's plea for free markets but also Gibbon's analysis of the superiority of a multistate system to one consisting of a single large state. Amid the crisis of contemporary capitalism, says Keynes, at a time when it was necessary to seek a new economic order to secure prosperity and peace, it was advisable to resist the universalism of free world markets, which, according to the wishes and conceptions of outdated liberalism, should lead to the best possible economic order, and to allow a variety of 'politico-economic experiments' in accordance with 'different national temperaments and historical environments'.[30] Russia, Italy, Ireland, and Germany had already begun to test new forms of economic activity, and even the US and the UK had recently started looking for ways to plan their economies. No one could know what would emerge from this:

---

28   Ibid., 760.

29   Ibid. This idea seems to be based on Keynes's conviction, developed in the 1920s, that capitalist societies, if they were rationally managed, would soon be in a position to cover their basic material needs, and that this would make further growth unnecessary, especially in industrial production. See John Maynard Keynes, 'Economic Possibilities for Our Grandchildren', in *Essays in Persuasion*, New York: W. W. Norton & Co., 1963 [1930]. Keynes did not foresee the consumer capitalism of the post-war period, which to this day, despite effective market saturation, sustains the high demand for all manner of industrial products, from SUVs to frozen pizzas; nor could he foresee the internationalisation of various services in the post-industrial era.

30   Keynes, 'National Self-Sufficiency', 761.

But the point for my present discussion is this. We each have our own fancy. Not believing that we are saved already, we each should like to have a try at working out our own salvation. We do not wish, therefore, to be at the mercy of world forces working out, or trying to work out, some uniform equilibrium according to the ideal principles, if they can be called such, of *laissez-faire* capitalism. There are still those who cling to the old ideas, but in no country of the world today can they be reckoned as a serious force. We wish – for the time at least and so long as the present transitional, experimental phase endures – to be our own masters, and to be as free as we can make ourselves from the interferences of the outside world.[31]

Under the circumstances of a general crisis, national economic self-sufficiency, Keynes continues, is not an ideal in itself but is directed 'to the creation of an environment in which other ideals can be safely and conveniently pursued'.[32] Keynes had therefore come to the conclusion, over the last few years, that countries at different levels of economic development needed different interest rates; but this would not be possible under a system of 'economic internationalism embracing the free movement of capital and of loanable funds as well as of traded goods'. Keynes adds:

We all need to be as free as possible of interference from economic changes elsewhere, in order to make our own favourite experiments towards *the ideal social republic of the future*, and a deliberate movement towards greater national self-sufficiency and economic isolation will make our task easier, in so far as it can be accomplished without excessive economic cost.[33]

Fourthly, Keynes hoped that the end to liberalism and the revival of economic nationalism, at least on an experimental basis, would lead to a political renunciation, rooted in national politics, of a universalist capitalist arithmetic dating back to the nineteenth century. In his formulation, everything was judged according to its *financial results* – that

---

31 Ibid., 761–2.
32 Ibid., 762.
33 Ibid., 763, emphasis added.

is, according to its value in terms of money as the universally tradeable commodity and thus its potential contribution to the accumulation of capital embodied in money, measured by 'what the financial reports are wont to call "the best opinion in Wall Street"'.[34] To an extent previously unknown in human history, resources went unused, owing to

> a system of financial accounting which casts doubt on whether their use will 'pay' . . . The same rule of self-destructive financial calculation governs every walk of life. We destroy the beauty of the countryside because the unappropriated splendours of nature have no economic value.[35]

Non-economic values, by their very nature, cannot be measured abstractly; they can only be experienced concretely, and can only be calculated in the context of a socially responsible public policy operating with criteria other than the profit-making opportunities of private individuals interested in increasing their monetary wealth:

> It is the conception of the Secretary of the Treasury as the chairman of a sort of joint stock company which has to be discarded. Now if the functions and purposes of the state are to be enlarged, the decision as to what, broadly speaking, shall be produced within the nation and what shall be exchanged with abroad, must stand high among the objects of policy.[36]

Keynes ends with a survey of the politics of his time, particularly in countries in search of economic self-sufficiency, among them Russia, Italy, and Germany. They have made many mistakes; Mussolini receives a fairly good report, while Russia is seen as a victim of disastrous incompetence.[37] As far as Germany is concerned, it is 'at the mercy of unchained

---

34   Ibid., 766.

35   Ibid., 764. Mass tourism, the economic exploitation of a natural world felt to be beautiful but which it will completely swallow up if it is not restricted by political regulation, did not yet exist at that time. Nor did the idea, obvious today, that tourism can also be a way of financing the now-necessary active rehabilitation of nature.

36   Ibid., 765.

37   One is reminded of Andrew Shonfield's enthusiasm, in *Modern Capitalism: The Changing Balance of Public and Private Power* (London: Oxford University Press, 1965), for the state-supervised industrial consortia founded under Mussolini, which he felt had contributed to the rapid growth of the Italian economy after 1945.

irresponsibles – though it is too soon to judge her'.[38] But when Keynes makes these criticisms, he does so as someone 'whose heart is friendly and sympathetic to the desperate experiments of the contemporary world, who wishes them well and who would like them to succeed', and 'who has his own experiments in view'.[39] The transition to a planned national economy is difficult; for one thing, the important achievements of the nineteenth century should not be discarded, and doctrinaire dogmatism, excessive haste, and repressive intolerance were hazards that could ruin everything:[40]

> The new economic modes, towards which we are blundering, are in the essence of their nature, experiments. We have no clear idea laid up in our minds beforehand of exactly what we want. We shall discover it as we move along, and we shall have to mould our material in accordance with our experience. Now for this process bold, free, and remorseless criticism is a *sine qua non* of success.[41]

---

38   Keynes, 'National Self-Sufficiency', 766. Keynes had predicted the collapse of the German state and the German economy as a result of the political and economic restrictions imposed on the country by the Treaty of Versailles (John Maynard Keynes, *The Economic Consequences of the Peace*, London Macmillan, 1919) and was therefore repeatedly suspected of being sympathetic to the German enemy, or even to German fascism. Keynes failed to see that economic self-sufficiency can also be sought through the conquest and subjection of other countries, as a form of imperial autarchy – for example, if the ambitions of other powers bar the independent route through 'regional planning'. A similar point can be made about Japan, another medium-sized power which was striving to achieve economic self-sufficiency through imperial autarchy.

39   Keynes, 'National Self-Sufficiency', 766.

40   There is, for example, 'a wide field of human activity where we shall be wise to retain the usual pecuniary tests' (ibid., 765).

41   Ibid., 768–9. Keynes leaves no doubt that his reorganisation of capitalism into 'the ideal social republic of the future' must be a gradual process: 'The economic transition of a society is a thing to be accomplished slowly. What I have been discussing is not a sudden revolution, but the direction of secular trend . . . The sacrifices and losses of transition will be vastly greater if the pace is forced . . . This is, above all, true of a transition towards greater national self-sufficiency and a planned domestic economy. For it is of the nature of economic processes to be rooted in time' (767).

Deglobalisation and Alternative Development

As is well known, Keynes was eventually able to contribute to the realisation of some of his 1933 ideas on a new international economic order,
in particular where they concerned a more socially oriented relationship
between national economies and world trade. The Keynes-inspired
Bretton Woods agreement of 1944 was followed by the long boom of
post-war democratic capitalism, then by the end of the Bretton Woods
system in 1973. After a few years of uncertainty, neoliberalism tri-
umphed both nationally and internationally: monetary and financial
stability replaced full employment, and globalisation replaced international trade. Keynes was forgotten or regarded as scientifically
outdated and politically defeated. In the 2010s at the latest, however, a
complementary term emerged to rival 'globalisation': 'deglobalisation'. A
bibliographical tally shows a steep rise in the number of publications on
the subject in the academic literature between 2016 and 2018 (fig. 29).

Figure 29. Publications on deglobalisation, 1993–2018

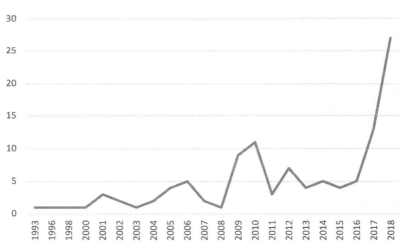

Source: *Scopus. Scopus* is a database operated by Elsevier since 2004. It includes 25,100
titles from more than 5,000 publishers. 'Publications' are defined here as articles, chapters
of books, conference contributions, and book reviews. Searches were made for the
following words in titles, headings and/or abstracts: 'de-globalization', 'deglobalization',
'de-globalisation', 'deglobalisation', 'Deglobalisierung', 'Entglobalisierung', 'démondialisa-
tion', 'desglobalización', 'des-globalización', 'desmundialización', and 'des-mundialización'.

Its visibility in politically activist publications is likely to have increased even more, and a further upswing in the wake of the COVID and Ukraine crises can be expected.

Current discussions about deglobalisation partly follow Dani Rodrik, but they also go beyond him in their critique of globalisation and their vision of the future. One prominent figure is Walden Bello, a social scientist and activist, educated in sociology and development economics at Princeton University, who, while directing a policy research institute in Bangkok, wrote the influential *Deglobalisation: Ideas for a New World Economy*, published in 2002.[42] In this book, Bello contextualises the critique of globalisation within a broader analysis of the crisis of postwar state-administered capitalism and its neoliberal transformation. He focuses, in particular, on global governance and its institutions, including above all the World Bank, the International Monetary Fund (IMF), and the World Trade Organization (WTO), organisations he describes as directed towards the interests and requirements of the US and its massive corporations – which, in the early 2000s, were a target of international criticism from below, and especially from the global South. For Bello, the so-called rules-based world economic order administered by these institutions is an instrument for subordinating national sovereignty, and thus democratic politics, to a uniform regime claiming universal validity: applicable to large and small nations, the rich and the poor, the North and the South, it is written and enforced by the rich North dominant in international organisations, with the US paramount. Globalisation at the end of the twentieth century, according to Bello, is a project for the promotion of large Western corporations. Global governance provides these corporations with profitable access to countries of the capitalist periphery aspiring to 'development'. As examples, Bello cites the treatment of debtor nations by the IMF and the structural adjustment programmes imposed on them, which regularly amount to a demand for opening the country in question to Western investment on market, or Western, terms.

Towards the end of his book, Bello examines a series of proposals circulating at that time for the reform of the international organisations driving globalisation. As one of the pioneers of the more radical

---

42   Walden Bello, *Deglobalization: Ideas for a New World Economy*, London: Zed Books, 2002.

critiques of this phenomenon, he concludes that the aim of globalisation's opponents can only be the abolition of these organisations. It is in
this context that Bello also refers to Rodrik, who, he says, advocates a
return 'to the original Bretton Woods system devised by Keynes . . . where
rules left enough space for national development efforts to proceed
along successful but divergent paths'.[43] It was not surprising that this
'global Keynesian' perspective 'resonated well with economists and technocrats from developing countries, the Asian economies which had
been devastated by the Asian crisis and the UN system' because the
UN system was well known as a refuge for Keynesians who had fled
'the neoliberal counter-revolution at the World Bank and universities'.
Bello adds:

> Some of the institutional innovations proposed by this school, such as
> a multi-tiered system of local, national and regional capital controls
> are definitely worth considering. Moreover, its advocacy for greater
> global space for the unfolding of distinct national strategies for devel-
> opment is certainly a step in the right direction. However, the
> Back-to-the-Bretton-Woods-System School fails satisfactorily to
> address the central questions. Can the World Bank, WTO and IMF
> really be transformed so as to allow such diversity to flourish? Are
> these institutions still the appropriate institutions of a system of
> global economic governance for an international economy built on
> different principles from those that now serve as its ideological
> pillars?[44]

The final chapter of Bello's book bears the title 'The Alternative: Deglobalization'. As with Rodrik, its emphasis is on the need for a system of
small states as a path to democratically controlled economic development in a fairly organised world economy. The prerequisite for finding
and pursuing this route, he says, is a break with the established pattern
of globalisation to date – in particular with institutions like the WTO,
set as they are on the continuation of neoliberal policies. The necessary
'rollback of free trade' could only be achieved through a reduction in the
power of the WTO. This would require a 'double movement' consisting

---

43   Ibid., 98–9.
44   Ibid., 99.

of, firstly, the 'deglobalisation of the national economy' and, secondly, 'the construction of a pluralist system of global economic governance'.[45] The 'deglobalisation' Bello envisages is not about withdrawal from the international economy but, rather, concerns a reorientation of economies away from production for export and towards production for the local market;[46] the internal rather than external procurement of investment capital, with the aim of becoming less dependent on foreign investment and financial markets; the redistribution of income and land to create more robust internal markets; the promotion of domestic cooperatives and of private and state enterprises to replace transnational corporations; and the implementation of the principle of subsidiarity in economic life by encouraging local and national production wherever possible at reasonable cost, for the sake of preserving community ties. It is a programme that could have been pulled right out of Keynes's 1933 *Yale Review* article.

Deglobalisation as empowerment of the local and national requires, secondly, a new and novel international order.[47] This, in turn, presupposes a significant reduction in the power of the Western corporations and the US, their political guarantor. The objective cannot, however, be another 'monolithic system of universal rules', even if these were to follow different, better principles, because such a system would be just as unable to 'tolerate and profit from diversity': 'Today's need is not another centralised global institution but the de-concentration and decentralisation of institutional power and the creation of a pluralistic system of institutions and organisations interacting with one another, guided by broad and flexible agreements and understandings.'[48]

To make it clear 'that the alternative to an economic *Pax Romana* built around the World Bank-IMF-WTO system is not a Hobbesian state of nature',[49] Bello points to the regime of the General Agreement on Tariffs and Trade (GATT), the predecessor of the hyperglobalisation pursued by the WTO. Echoing Polanyi and his conception of 'regional planning', Bello argues in favour of regional economic blocs, provided

---

45   Ibid., 112.
46   Ibid., 113.
47   Ibid., 114–15.
48   Ibid., 115.
49   Ibid., 116.

that – unlike the EU, Mercosur, and the Association of Southeast Asian Nations (ASEAN) – they do not become elite projects:[50]

> Trade efficiency in neoclassical economic terms should be supplanted as the key criterion of union by 'capacity building'. That is, trade would have to be reoriented from its present dynamics of locking communities and countries into a division of labour that diminishes their capabilities in the name of 'comparative advantage' and 'interdependence'. It must be transformed into a process that enhances the capacities of communities, that ensures that initial cleavages that develop owing to the initial division-of-labour agreements do not congeal into permanent cleavages, and which has mechanisms, including income, capital and technology-sharing arrangements that prevent exploitative arrangements from developing among trading communities.[51]

A pluralist global economic order would have to offer institutions 'dedicated to creating and protecting the space for devolving the greater part of production, trade and economic decision-making to the regional, national and community level'.[52] Tolerance of diversity would have to become the central principle of economic policy, and the most important task of regulatory institutions would have to be 'to express and protect local and national cultures by embodying and sheltering their distinctive practices'. The book concludes with a call for a 'more fluid, less structured, more pluralistic world', in which 'the nations and communities of the South – and the North – will be able to carve out the space to develop based on their values, their rhythms, and the strategies of their choice'.[53]

---

50   Ibid., 114.
51   Ibid., 117.
52   Ibid., 118.
53   Ibid., 118. A similar approach in relation to Africa is taken in Felwine Sarr, *Afrotopia*, Berlin: Matthes & Seitz, 2019. Like Bello, Kari Polanyi Levitt (*Die Finanzialisierung der Welt: Karl Polanyi und die neoliberale Transformation der Weltwirtschaft*, Weinheim: Beltz Juventa, 2020) believes that the most important problem for development economics is restoring the capacity of nation-states in the global South to act – that is, reversing hyperglobalisation and returning nation-states to their previous status, including their ability to cooperate and form coalitions autonomously, so as to enable regional and inter-regional planning.

Global Polycentrism

As early as the 2000s, deglobalisation ceased to be a utopian niche subject – unlike degrowth, at least in those days – and after the financial crisis, at the latest, the question of whether the level of uniform, mega-state, and non-state global integration could or should be reduced began to be raised openly by those who regarded themselves as belonging to the mainstream of right-thinking public opinion. Initially, melancholic and defensive contributions predominated, but these were soon eclipsed by criticisms of globalisation proceeding from a remarkable number of often-surprising points of departure. In 2012, for example, it was reported that the Economic Policy and Debt Department of the World Bank had done a study of the connection between world trade and climate change, in particular the carbon dioxide emissions blamed for it. In view of the parallel growth in global trade and in carbon dioxide emissions, the authors aimed to brand as 'protectionist' the environmentally minded, and perhaps obvious, call for restrictions on trade; they instead proposed certain measures against climate change that would not affect trade policy.[54] Two years later, in September 2014, the *Financial Times* ran a story under the heading 'The World Is Marching Back from Globalisation', where it was reported that the US – then under Barack Obama – had lost interest in a world order benefiting its rivals; at that time the main competitor was still Russia (ceded to Putin by Yeltsin, America's favourite); today, China has taken on this role.

The economic sanctions the US imposed on Russia that same year had the effect of propelling the retreat from globalisation already set in motion by the 2008 crisis. According to the *Financial Times*, the result was a progressive fragmentation of a world previously on its way to achieving harmonious unity; to make its case, *FT* furnished examples of an allegedly impending renationalisation of the financial industry, the end of the internet's global freedom from state interference, the collapse of the Doha Round, the emergence of regional instead of global trading systems, the foundation of a joint development bank for the BRICS countries (Brazil, Russia, India, China, and South Africa) independent

---

54   Harun Onder, 'What Does Trade Have to Do with Climate Change?', *VoxEU*, CEPR policy portal, 12 September 2012, cepr.org.

of the World Bank and Wall Street, the discontent of voters in the US over their worsening economic situation, and, in connection with this, the United States' abandonment of its role as guarantor of the multi-lateral system:

> The architect of the present era of globalisation is no longer willing to be its guarantor. The US does not see a vital national interest in up-holding an order that redistributes power to rivals . . . Without a champion, globalisation cannot but fall into disrepair . . . Globalisation needs an enforcer – a hegemon.[55]

Similar comments were made in Germany, though of course there the tone was more sentimental and contained a larger dose of anxious idealism. In May 2017, the news website *Der Spiegel* called for a 'new guiding principle' to replace a discredited globalisation. Banks and markets had collapsed in 2008, leaving behind a 'vacuum'; 'minor improvements' would no longer help; what 'the world' needed was 'a new leading idea. And, indeed, it is needed before populists of all hues fill this vacuum and set people at each other's throats. Time is running out.' The article listed all the social damage done by globalisation, par-ticularly in the US, and concluded: 'Thus the erstwhile myth has lost its power. What we need now is a big new idea.' A succession of econo-mists – including Rogoff, Piketty, Shiller, Akerlof, Stiglitz, Haldane, Schularick, Rodrik, and Mazzucato – are all briefly called into the ring, weighed up, and, for all their merits, found to be too lightweight:

> The search is on for a unifying formula, which should express the new idea: the *Leitmotiv* . . . It must not sound too crude, like the market-works-wonders formula. But it must at the same time be simple enough to get through to everyone.

The article ends by recalling the example of 'the US president Franklin D. Roosevelt, who issued a new slogan: the legendary [?!] New Deal', and adding: 'It is high time to learn lessons from this.'[56]

---

55   Philip Stephens, 'The World Is Marching Back from Globalisation', *Financial Times*, 4 September 2014, ft.com.
56   Thomas Fricke, 'Der neue New Deal', *Der Spiegel*, 13 May 2017, 68–9.

What these lessons should be was unclear, according to the newspaper *Frankfurter Allgemeine Zeitung* in its coverage of the World Economic Forum in Davos, even to those who ought to have known and were paid well for their expertise. 'Globalisation scepticism is on the increase among world leaders' ran the *FAZ* headline, primarily, as the article goes on to explain, because of increasing social inequality, unfair tax competition, and the climate crisis.[57] Three years later, in an interview with *Die Zeit* in March 2020, Joschka Fischer, formerly Germany's foreign minister and now an economic consultant, identified the rise of China as a further cause of the regrettable advance of deglobalisation. While a war between the US and China appeared unlikely, 'even so, their rivalry over technological domination will bring the unified world market to an end, I fear . . . The supply chains will no longer function as they did before.' The US, according to Fischer, had made the mistake of underestimating China, and it was now paying the price:

I keep asking the Americans: first you helped to make China what it is today, now you want to stop its rise. Did you knowingly support a strategic rival? What then was your plan? [Question from a journalist: 'What reply do you receive?'] Nothing . . . The Americans did not have a plan.[58]

Not long afterwards, the pandemic arrived and finally made the reversal of globalisation a legitimate topic for the political class. Even so, it was not true that the COVID crisis 'changed everything', as has been repeatedly claimed. Tendencies towards deglobalisation had already been in effect for some time when the virus entered the picture. Initially ignored and then invoked, they gradually gained attention even among academic social scientists who knew nothing, or wanted to know nothing, of their disciplines' Keynesian and Polanyian traditions. The pro-Brexit referendum and the election of Donald Trump were pre-COVID turning points which, even in the political mainstream, made it appear legitimate to ask whether hyperglobalisation might not in fact have been

---

57   Carsten Knop, 'Unter den Chefs wächst die Globalisierungs-Skepsis', *Frankfurter Allgemeine Zeitung*, 16 January 2017, faz.net.

58   Marc Brost and Xifan Yang, interview by Joschka Fischer, 'Statt aus den Fehlern zu lernen, eskaliert man diese noch', *Die Zeit*, 4 March 2020, zeit.de.

purely beneficial but also harmful – a question which would have to be taken seriously if Trumpism turned out to be more than just a political accident.[59] Trump openly and vociferously questioned the principle that the task of democratic politics in the world economy of financialised capitalism was to enable the latter to flourish by not interfering in its inner workings, and to protect its onward progress from being interrupted by borders of any kind. To the extent that the long-standing sole world power and the driving force behind the 1990s wave of liberalisation and globalisation began to abandon this approach in favour of a protectionist interventionism legitimated by democratic populism, the real emerging deglobalisation processes also gained interest among academic researchers. They could now ask what a deglobalised world economic order would, and could, look like; whether the horrific scenario of the 1930s – from autarchy to fascism, and from fascism to war – would inevitably repeat itself; and whether there might be less destructive escape routes out of deadlocked hyperglobalisation.

What paths towards deglobalisation could be discerned after the financial crisis, and even before COVID, based on the developments up to that point? Studies on this subject oscillate between the most varied disaster scenarios, both economic and political, and other approaches that advance the prospect of a renewed polycentric world system characterised by a plurality of governmental and economic arrangements – a replacement of the idealised uniformity of the US world empire after the end of the Soviet Union with variously structured regional divisions of the world. In German discussions, ideas of this kind are often associated with fear-ridden predictions of a world economic crisis set off by 'protectionism' and followed by a world war; there can be no world peace without a borderless single world market for German industrial products. But this view is not held everywhere, and in the literature on post-globalisation prospects one also finds reflections on the possibility of stable peaceful

---

59   The mantra of the World Bank that 'globalisation' has raised such and such percent of the world's population 'from deepest poverty' became a state-sanctioned catchphrase. This probably contributed to the fact that the devastation wreaked on the 'global South' by the free movement of capital and the new laws of 'intellectual property' long remained a subject restricted to so-called development economics, a field of research counted by 'proper' economists as part of 'people economics', and understood as not truly scientific given its surplus of real content. On development economics, see Polanyi Levitt, *Die Finanzialisierung der Welt*.

coexistence among different principles of politico-economic organisation. These do not rule out a non-hierarchical, non-imperial, cooperative structure of subsystems forming part of a global state system, and consisting of democratic and sovereign members – in a manner approaching what Polanyi envisioned in 1945.

Exemplary of the majority of academic literature on deglobalisation – politically value free and sympathetic to capital – is the prominent historian Harold James's 2018 survey, published under the title 'Deglobalization: The Rise of Disembedded Unilateralism'.[60] In it, globalisation appears in orthodox terms as a linear and progressive process, inherent to modern society – one that, to everyone's detriment, came to a halt after the financial crisis and has little chance of being restarted any time soon. Globalisation and hyperglobalisation are not differentiated; deglobalisation is described as the collapse of the tried and tested 'multilateral', 'rules-based' order organised by the US after the Second World War, and now causing a level of global disorder verging on anarchy. Around 2008, worldwide flows of trade and capital were at their zenith (peak trade and peak finance; see figs. 26, 27, and 28, pp. 237–9); among the reasons for their subsequent decline were increasing national restrictions on trade, and the shortening of global value chains owing to the shift in production back to industrialised countries, then facilitated by new technologies and aimed at maximising proximity to customers; this in turn led to a regionalisation of systems of international production.

But the main reason for deglobalisation, James tells us, was probably 'imperial overstretch', or the over-expansion and overloading of the US imperial system protecting globalisation – a fate that, according to James, befalls all empires eventually. Trump was only a symptom; Hillary Clinton, too, had spoken out against any further free trade agreements during the 2016 electoral campaign. Trump had been lifted to power by a social revolt and a 'localist impulse' comprehendible as a 'political-psychological reaction' to the complexity of the rules of global governance.[61] The G20 had also failed to make progress in developing a global regulatory framework after 2008, and this had led to a renationalisation of

---

60   Harold James, 'Deglobalization: The Rise of Disembedded Unilateralism', *Annual Review of Financial Economics* 10 (2018), 219–37.

61   Ibid., 232; 'One hypothesis is that there is simply a psychological reaction against too much globality' (214).

financial markets and a general shift away from multilateralism as well as from 'expert and scientific opinion'. As a result, John Ruggie's 'embedded liberalism' had finally been forced to give way to a 'disembedded unilateralism' for which *salus populi* was the *suprema lex*.[62] In the now-dawning post-hegemonic age, decisionism *à la* Carl Schmitt reigns, as reflected in James's discussion of national sovereignty found in foreign policy:

> The concept of sovereignty, as a political process that cannot be appealed against to an external agent, is reasserted. The main weakness of globalisation is seen as its simultaneous erosion of sovereignty with an augmentation of governance through international agreements, conventions and norms . . . Embedded liberalism is under attack because of a reaction against complex rules. Disembedded unilateralism, by contrast, derives rhetorical ammunition for changes in the domestic system from the (frequently mendacious) claim to speak for the good of the people and the principle of national sovereignty.[63]

Other articles published around this time on the topic of deglobalisation understand the causes in broadly similar terms, though they assess its consequences differently. Finbarr Livesey, whose essay focuses specifically on the industrial sector, maintains that he is seeing 'some elements of globalisation go into reverse' in the form of a shortening of global value chains (what he calls 'physical deglobalisation') – an increasingly pronounced tendency since 2008.[64] He argues this has been enabled by changes in production technology, especially the robotisation of industrial production, the resulting fall in the wage share of the cost of production, and thus the diminished competitive advantage of low-wage countries. Moreover, there are the advantages of producing consumer goods close to their target markets: such production allows

---

62   Although, of course, the *suprema lex* can only be the *salus mercatoris*. John Gerard Ruggie, 'International Regimes, Transactions and Change: Embedded Liberalism in the Postwar Economic Order', *International Organization* 36, no. 2 (1982), 379–415.

63   James, 'Deglobalization', 234–5.

64   Finbarr Livesey, 'Unpacking the Possibilities of Deglobalisation', *Cambridge Journal of Regions, Economy and Society* 11, no. 1 (2018), 177–87.

for greater responsiveness to rapidly changing customer requirements and avoids the disruption characteristic of longer transport routes emitting more carbon dioxide where customers, in any case, prefer more environmentally friendly local resource circuits. The relocation of production back to its highly industrialised countries of origin is also often accompanied by a deglobalisation of services and capital flows. Since between a half and two-thirds of world trade takes place within value chains, the significance for globalisation (and its potential cessation) of large companies' geographical decisions as shaped by international and domestic politics cannot be overestimated.

For Livesey, just how much the general attitude towards globalisation and deglobalisation has changed is shown by the difference between Tony Blair's rhetoric in 1998, when he presented globalisation as 'an irreversible and irresistible trend', and that of the then newly elected President Trump, who promised in his inaugural address almost two decades later to protect America's borders, adding: 'Protection will lead to great prosperity and strength.'[65] Unlike James, however, Livesey sees the possibility that a new and stable order might emerge from the reversal of globalisation, and that this would indeed be founded on a regionalisation of the world economy. Already today, the world is 'clearly more regionally based than the hyperglobalisation framing may lead many to believe.'[66] Global trade statistics – here, Livesey refers to the same data presented above in fig. 26 (p. 237) – obscure the fact that a considerable part of the trade in commodities takes place within specific regions of the world such as North America, Latin America, Europe, and Asia, rather than globally, and that this proportion has remained constant since the turn of the century (see the data on p. 184 of his article). In view of the deglobalisation he describes, Livesey concludes that the regionalisation of the world economy is likely to deepen further, 'on the path to some localisation for some types of manufacturing.'[67] Livesey's analysis would suggest that what is now referred to, more programmatically than realistically, as global governance may well be replaced by a multiplicity of different regional regimes as deglobalisation advances.

---

65 Ibid., 179.
66 Ibid., 183.
67 Ibid., 185.

A 2019 essay by Michael Witt reaches similar conclusions in examining the shape and impact of deglobalisation from the vantage of
international business economics.[68] As far as the facts of deglobalisation
are concerned, the author generally relies on the same observations
made by James and Livesey, supplemented by references to the fall in
foreign direct investment after 2008 as parallel to the tumbling volume
of trade.[69] Witt's principal aim is to highlight the importance of national
and international politics, not only for globalisation but also for deglobalisation.[70] He thus dissociates himself from the idea of globalisation
and hyperglobalisation as natural processes of economic development
arising automatically from economic necessity and entrepreneurial
strategy, irrespective of politics. For Witt, there are two rival theoretical
approaches to understanding international relations, 'liberalism' and
'realism', and they classify the causes and results of deglobalisation
differently.[71] Which theory one adopts also has consequences for the
strategies of internationally operating firms, argues Witt; the task of
international business economics is to clarify this.

From the perspective of 'liberal' theory, Witt continues, deglobalisation
is the result of domestic political resistance to further globalisation, just
as globalisation resulted from domestic political coalitions that supported
it. The now-predominant resistance, which is derived from the negative
experiences with globalisation's effects among growing sections of the
population, caused a partial abandonment of the institutions and practices of the globalised world before the financial crisis: 'International
institutions appear to be weakening, and domestic political interests seem
to have shifted to favour interdependence.'[72] The upshot has been a more
diverse and therefore more complex economic order, in which international trade relations and economic interconnections are selectively

---

68   Michael A. Witt, 'De-globalization: Theories, Predictions, and Opportunities
for International Business Research', *Journal of International Business Studies* 50, no. 7
(2019), 1053–77.
69   Ibid., 1058.
70   Ibid.
71   The terms were developed by US political scientists in the 1970s to differentiate
between a 'liberal' international politics governed by common institutions and universally applicable rules, as practised allegedly by the United States, and a coldly calculated
'Realpolitik', based on the right of the stronger, as practised by the Germans during the
Nazi period, the Soviet Union, or, at present, China.
72   Ibid., 1063.

built up and dismantled according to the dominant domestic political interests of the countries involved: 'The most likely outcome is a global-isation partnership in which different pairs or groups of countries provide for varying levels of interdependence between them. Geographically con-fined agreements are thus likely to gain in importance.'[73] Bilateral or multilateral sector-specific trade agreements are to replace global ones, as has been seen most recently since the decline of the WTO, while individ-ual countries attempt to reduce their dependence and increase their autonomy: 'Given diverse interests, it seems likely that variance in the extent and characteristics of economic openness will increase.'[74]

For 'realism', by contrast, economic internationalisation is the work of hegemonic nation-states possessing the means to build empires, within which economic interconnections can grow just as freely as within a state. The required international institutions are moulded, if not dictated, by the respective hegemonic power.[75] The highest form of globalisation would then consist of the incorporation of the world into the empire of a single state, and deglobalisation would, accordingly, be the result of the hegemonic power losing the ability to hold its empire together – in other words, present-day deglobalisation stems from the decline in US power and the parallel increase in China's. Witt illustrates both sides of this process with some impressive statistics.[76] How this will continue in the future is an open question, and, as things stand,

---

73   Ibid., 1065.

74   Ibid.

75   The archetype of foreign policy 'realism', in the American sense of 'Realpolitik', is the speech Thucydides attributes to the Athenians as they address the Melians. In it, Athens offers the Melians the alternatives of joining the league of cities under Athenian leadership, or being conquered and annihilated: 'For ourselves, we shall not trouble you with specious pretences . . . of how we have a right to our empire . . . since you know as well as we do that right, as the world goes, is only in question between equals in power, while the strong do what they can and the weak suffer what they must.' Thucydides, *History of the Peloponnesian War*, London: J. M. Dent, 1910, book 5, 89.

76   According to Witt, US economic strength peaked in 1999, when its GDP was almost three times as large (the factor was 2.9) as China's, then already the world's second-largest economy. In 2013 China had reached parity with the US, and by 2017 US GDP had fallen to 83.2 percent of China's. The evolution of defence spending is equally impressive. In 1992 US defence spending was nearly ten times that of France, which had the second-highest defence budget at the time. By 2017 China had replaced France in this second position, and the US defence budget was only two and a half times China's (Witt, 'De-globalization', 1063–4).

remains so. Like many others, Witt finds it possible to imagine a dual world order and world economy, with two empires sharing the globe more or less peacefully. But he also leaves room for the possibility that more than two regional blocs could emerge, each centred around a different hegemonic power, as for example India (he regards Russia and Japan as too small to be able to advance to a position of hegemony).

Leaving aside Witt's advice to global business, since it is of less interest here, the question still remains: Why does he insists on the sharp American distinction between 'liberal' and 'realist' explanations and visions of the future? After all, the withdrawal of the US from its role as global hegemon – which it only fully assumed in the course of hyperglobalisation after the 'end of history' in 1989 – was due not just to foreign but also domestic political causes, namely the neglect of the distributional consequences of economic liberalisation, and the de-industrialisation of the American homeland brought about by global financialisation. One can also ask whether 'liberal' and 'realist' predictions might not materialise simultaneously in the form of a plurality of regional systems, under which hegemonised blocs of states led imperially could coexist with state confederations associated in a liberal and voluntary manner. Regional empires *à la* Schmitt, in other words, could coexist with regional confederations of states *à la* Hintze, and united by sector-specific common interests rather than by hegemonic power.

Multipolarity, in the form of coexisting, differently structured regional subdivisions of the world system, is a perspective on the future which, as a 2018 essay by Stefan Link shows convincingly, can also be derived from a comparison between the deglobalisation of the 1930s after the Great Depression and the present deglobalisation following the 2008 financial crisis. Link's historical retrospective makes it clear that globalisation is more than 'the result of capital, goods and people seeking to transcend borders in a self-activating quest to put the world's resources to use where it was most efficient'.[77] Rather, it is an essentially political process, in which it cannot be assumed that 'collective economic actors (states, governments, or otherwise)' would 'always choose money-quantifiable welfare gains over considerations of status, dignity,

---

77 Stefan Link, 'How Might 21st-Century De-globalization Unfold? Some Historical Reflections', *New Global Studies* 12, no. 3 (2018), 343–65.

nationalism or perceived power differentials'.[78] Link demonstrates this by comparing the three phases of globalisation since the advent of capitalism: the *imperial* phase under the aegis of the British Empire; the *developmental* phase after 1945 under the leadership of the US, when the aim was to incorporate the defeated and war-ravaged countries into an American empire; and, finally, the *neoliberal* phase, which, from the 1970s on, shifted American economic dominance to services and finance; unlike in the 1930s, this established the US as the world's 'consumer of last resort'. Each of these phases, argues Link, was distinct, due to the respective interests and strategies of the dominant political powers:

> Measuring globalisation in terms of 'more' or 'less' integration misses much of the action. It is better to ask about the political architecture of different eras of globalisation: how do states, and domestic coalitions within them, attempt to engineer, and in turn respond to, shifts in the global division of labour? What strategies of engagement with foreign trade and capital have followed from these shifts? These questions apply to the hegemonic powers as much as to peripheral participants.[79]

The same can be said of deglobalisation. Neither in the inter-war period nor today can deglobalisation be understood as the displacement of natural economic reason by unnatural political irrationality; indeed, it was always, and still is, the result of a reorientation by the same political forces as had previously brought about, or participated in, globalisation. In the 1930s, according to Link, deglobalisation was not the *cause* of the world economic crisis but its *consequence*: it was a reaction to the steadily growing indebtedness of the capitalist countries to the US, whose protectionist trade policies made it more difficult for them to earn the

---

78 Ibid., 347. See, similarly, Elimma Ezeani, 'Comparative Advantage in Deglobalisation: Brexit, America First and Africa's Continental Free Trade Area', *Journal of International Trade Law and Policy* 17, nos. 1–2 (2018), 46–61, where she, in agreement with Rodrik, uses the example of Africa to show that specialisation according to the principle of comparative advantage need not be the objective of a country oriented towards 'development'. From a political point of view (as she notes on p. 46), it could be more advantageous to invest in acquiring a broad spectrum of assets. This theme is already present in Keynes, 'National Self-Sufficiency', as noted earlier.

79 Link, 'How Might 21st-Century De-globalization Unfold?', 356.

dollars they needed to service their debts. Here, Link presents a notably revisionist evaluation of the so-called drive towards autarchy of the time; its aim, he says, was never to seal off the countries in question from the world economy, but only to restore their economic room for manoeuvre and freedom of action:

> Invariably, what was at stake was economic independence – understood as the capacity to source strategic raw materials without interference, to determine the social structure of national economies, to break loose from international debt service and from the constraints posed by exhausted foreign exchange reserves, and to attain capacities for technological development under national control.[80]

Autarchy, according to Link, who quotes the eminent German sociologist Werner Sombart, is etymologically nothing other than self-rule, and an autarchic national economy is one which 'does not find it necessary to carry on foreign trade, but which imports and exports at free discretion what seems best for it'.[81] Independence, not self-sufficiency, was the goal of the push towards autarchy; it involved 'not simply "less" globalisation' but represented an attempt to 'fundamentally reconfigure it' in places where 'financial crises, balance-of-payments problems, over-indebtedness, and sustained breakdowns in credit relationships have frequently empowered domestic coalitions' seeking 'autarchy in the name of economic self-determination'.[82] Such coalitions, Link continues, 'then attempt to reorient their economies towards trade and investment relationships over which they are able to exert greater political control than previously'.[83] Again, the echoes of Keynes and Polanyi cannot be ignored.

The post-neoliberal deglobalisation of the twenty-first century – the end of 1989's neoliberal dream of a single, permanently integrated

---

80   Ibid., 358–9.
81   Ibid., 359.
82   Ibid., 360.
83   Ibid., 362. Relevant here is Peter A. G. van Bergeijk's observation in 'On the Brink of Deglobalisation . . . Again', *Cambridge Journal of Regions, Economy and Society* 11, no. 1 (2018), 59–72. He notes that in the 1930s, it was primarily states under authoritarian or dictatorial rule which sought to break from the global division of labour, but that now, conversely, deglobalisation tends to be pursued by democratic governments.

world economy, governed in a universalistic manner, never again to be segmented into states – shares a certain political character with the deglobalisation of the inter-war years but, for this very reason, also differs from it. After 2008, according to Link, central bank interventions and flexible exchange rates prevented a return to the protectionism of the 1930s. More importantly, the structure of the international economic division of labour had grown more balanced; disparities in development had lessened, and, with the rise of Asia, the world was no longer the periphery of a single centre. The more pronounced decentralisation of the global system of production and the resulting multipolarity of the global economy effectively increased its powers of resistance when compared to the first half of the twentieth century. At the same time, this dynamic deprived capitalism of its power to act as a Habermasian cunning of reason, historically destined to unify the world. Whereas in 2005 the US was still the largest trading partner of fifty-three nations, and China of ten, nine years later the figures were thirty-one for the US and forty-three for China.[84] Comprehensive dependencies were replaced by exclusively sectoral interconnections; as a result, withdrawal from the international division of labour was no longer required for the defence of one's autonomy. This also meant that there was no immediate threat to 'American dominance in key sectors such as finance, professional services, and Silicon Valley-type hi-tech'.[85] Link concludes by suggesting that the end-of-history thinking about globalisation, one based on the binary alternatives of Western best practices and a disastrous 'deglobalisation', is in need of revision. It might be time to 'take a deep breath and develop tolerance for the vision of a multipolar globalisation architecture . . . which accommodates a variety of world market engagements, perhaps even including strategic, development-oriented disengagement'. The historic norm, in any case, is 'separate multiverses . . . The prospect need not alarm us; we might even welcome it.'[86]

---

84   Link, 'How Might 21st-Century De-globalization Unfold?', 364.
85   Ibid., 365.
86   Ibid.

Disentanglement: COVID and the Supply Chains

In the autumn of 2020, there was general agreement in the financial press and in public discussion that the experience of the COVID pandemic would reinforce and accelerate tendencies, already in progress for some time, towards a shortening of international supply and value chains – or capital accumulation – that had emerged at the height of globalisation. Actual or imminent disruptions to global flows of commodities, especially certain inputs, illuminated the economic and social vulnerability caused by global interdependency, and businesses and consumers alike expected the state to respond. The state was thus given tasks only classifiable as aspects of 'regional planning'. Moreover, debates on whether the limits of globalisation had been reached (or exceeded) revealed more clearly than ever to a broad public the advanced degree of national economic and social global interdependence, and the risks associated with it.

The most immediate and obvious problem was excessively long, market-organised, and politically unregulated supply chains for medicines. Although these were ultimately produced in the rich consumer countries, it turned out that in a hyperglobalised economy they were often reliant on preliminary inputs originating mainly from Asian countries – often from China, but also India. When these countries were no longer willing or able to make shipments after the outbreak of the pandemic, certain medicines, such as the painkiller paracetamol, became scarce in the US and Europe; the provision of pharmaceuticals had been transformed from a social infrastructure into a commodity-producing commercial sector under the influence of market forces. The same applied to hospital equipment. Even a government such as Boris Johnson's found it was compelled, as was Donald Trump's administration in the US, to announce state measures to secure medical supplies. Such actions were plainly at variance with the maxims of a denationalised globalisation. As for the EU, it came under such pressure that member countries with stocks of hospital supplies were unwilling to share with those countries lacking them. Until then, the EU, which had repeatedly called for reductions in health spending, could do no more than urge 'solidarity', while states without supplies accused those with them of failing to adopt a European attitude.[87]

---

87   In the eight years between 2011 and 2018, the European Commission issued 301 specific recommendations for spending cuts to the twenty-eight member states of

Related problems emerged in other sectors, too. They were discussed from the point of view of reliability of supply and national security, often using the slogan or catchword of the year, 'resilience', meaning the ability to withstand conditions of crisis. Resilience became the aim of a wide array of, horribile dictu, protective interventions into free trade by businesses and governments, sometimes even acting together. It is, for example, assumed, as mentioned above, that industrial production will increasingly return to its countries of origin (*reshoring* as opposed to *offshoring*) through the application of robotics ('Industry 4.0'), resulting in the reindustrialisation of the global North.[88] At the same time, the automobile industry is endeavouring to obtain politically secure access to batteries produced abroad, or, alternatively, government subsidies for battery production at home; here, too, the state takes on the role of managing the national economy's external relations after a loss of confidence in the market.[89] Some very diverse approaches can already be observed in this connection, from Trump's appeal to Americans to buy only American goods in times of emergency, or perhaps at any time ('Buy American'), to the establishment of a cabinet committee in the UK to discuss a 'Project Defend', by which the government intends to achieve 'supply chain resilience', bearing in mind experiences with the pandemic, and to reconcile the country's national security with its ambition to 'be a global champion of free trade'.[90] According to newspaper reports, the issues to be examined range from the supply of pharmaceuticals to the question of whether to use Chinese technology for 5G wireless networks, and they include measures for the establishment of parallel supply chains, for diversifying the sources of supply, and for enabling sectors of British industry to ramp up production in an emergency, for example from 20 to 90 percent of the country's

---

the EMU, in the context of its efforts to fight 'macro-economic imbalances'. Sixty-three of these concerned health care, surpassed only by 105 recommendations of pension cuts. See Emma Clancy, 'Austerity Kills: EU Commission Demanded Cuts to Public Healthcare Spending 63 Times from 2011–2018', *Brave New Europe*, 29 March 2020, braveneweurope.com.

88   Deborah Winkler and Adnan Seric, 'COVID-19 Could Spur Automation and Reverse Globalisation – to Some Extent', *VoxEU*, CEPR Policy Portal, 28 April 2020, cepr.org.

89   Jack Ewing, 'The Pandemic Will Permanently Change the Auto Industry', *New York Times*, 13 May 2020, nytimes.com.

90   Christopher Rowland, 'Trump Order Requires Government to "Buy American" for Certain Essential Drugs', *Washington Post*, 6 August 2020, washingtonpost.com. Four years later, after considerable domestic turmoil in the politics of the UK, it is not clear what became of 'Project Defend'.

consumption. Also explored is the possibility of de facto seizure of production capacity for the purpose of redirecting it for the manufacture of essential goods.

The British situation is particularly interesting, owing to Brexit and the associated requirement to withdraw the UK from the European internal market and formulate its own national economic policy. If one reads the *Financial Times* more closely, it appears that 'Project Defend' means nothing less than a move away from the free trade obligations involved in EU membership, accelerated and conveniently legitimated by the pandemic.[91] Yet the special emphasis placed on the sourcing of medical supplies and on 'national security' vis-à-vis China's influence is calculated to conceal the significance of the other measures envisaged by the British government to intervene in the domestic economy, particularly its foreign relations, more deeply and extensively than it has done since the 1980s. These include identifying sectors in which close cooperation with the EU should be sought; using selective free trade agreements with countries like Japan; and shortening trade routes and value chains, and so on, employing 'reshoring' and other methods too. According to the *Financial Times*, at the first peak of the pandemic, the Tory government expected Brexit to give the country more freedom to 'use state aid to incentivise UK companies to make critical products, while ministers reserved the right to "force" them to onshore production of the most sensitive ones'.[92] The British state's greater freedom to conduct economic policy as a result of its exit from the EU, the article continues, should also be used, under the prospective 'COVID-19 recovery plan', to regenerate industrial production in the Midlands and the North of England – the parts of the country where, in the December 2019 election, the Conservatives had broken through the 'red wall' of the Labour Party's strongholds for the first time.[93]

---

91   George Parker and Daniel Thomas, 'UK Looks to Wean Itself Off Chinese Imports', *Financial Times*, 10 June 2020, ft.com.

92   Ibid.

93   The political-economic, as opposed to the sentimental, dimension of Brexit is illuminated by the fact that the industrial policy intentions of the British government and its abandonment of the neoliberal principle of 'market before state' were immediately attacked by the EU negotiating committee as a case of market distortion, to be prohibited by the exit treaty.

The many ways in which the epidemic experience influenced international trade flows – in the sense of shortening, or at least diverting them – is illustrated by the German pork industry. Germany is the third-largest pork producer in the world. At any time of the year, roughly 25.5 million pigs are being reared in Germany, one for every three inhabitants; circa 55 million pigs meet their death in German slaughterhouses every year. In the first six months of 2020, approximately 2.6 million tonnes of pork were produced in this way. A quarter of this amount was exported to China, roughly twice as much as usual, owing to an epidemic of animal disease there. In recent years, around 2.4 million out of the 5 million tonnes of pork produced annually has been exported.

A glimpse into how Germany's record production and export figures are achieved in a globalised economy was afforded by the first COVID months of 2020, when many members of the workforce of one of the leading German pork factories contracted the virus. Almost all were low-wage workers from Eastern Europe, receiving starvation wages for their fake self-employment as allegedly self-employed subcontractors. A large proportion of them were more or less obliged to pay high rents for their accommodation in tiny lodgings owned by their employers; this fact, and the miserable working conditions in the slaughterhouse itself, were blamed for their mass infection. The scandalous conditions prevailing in the industry had been known for years and had even attracted public concern now and again; but nothing had been done about the situation, no doubt partly because of the sanctity of Germany's export surplus. The high risk of infection posed by the affected workers, including to local inhabitants, changed that. At the same time, reporting on the meat industry's business model drew the public's attention to some of the more monstrous aspects of globalised industrial methods. It was asked, with varying degrees of vehemence, why the production of meat for a country like China, which was still half agrarian, had to take place in a densely populated, high-wage, highly industrialised country like Germany, at costs low enough to compete on the world market – therefore repressed mercilessly – and under such degrading conditions. The price paid for the competitiveness of the German exports is not only a considerable number of environmental problems, such as how to remove pig manure, but also the abomination of factory farming. All of this was a sharp contradiction of the fashionable tendency among more articulate consumers to prefer food 'from the region'. COVID could quite possibly strengthen this tendency, and that too would amount to a shortening of supply chains.

Incidentally, the sudden increase in Chinese demand for German pork was the result of the epidemic of African swine fever, which had forced the Chinese to destroy a large proportion of its pig stocks. Appropriately for a globalised world, African swine fever then spread globally. When it began to be suspected that it might have found its way into Germany's pigsties, China prohibited the import of German pork for a number of days. The largest German pork producer, in whose abattoir at Rheda-Wiedenbrück 25,000 pigs were being slaughtered and dismembered every single day before the advent of COVID, responded by commissioning a former German foreign minister (and also Willy Brandt's successor, for a time, as chair of the Social Democratic Party of Germany) to speak to the Chinese and put in a good word for the firm. That something of this nature could happen is, in the broadest sense, one of the risks of globalised life.[94]

The Keynes-Polanyi State: National, Sovereign, Democratic

The nation-state is the only institution capable of asserting the primacy of politics over the economy, or, indeed, the political primacy of society over capitalism in the face of hyperglobalisation.[95] Only in and through the nation-state could a renewed domestication, containment, and embedding of capitalism succeed, possibly followed in the future by its replacement with a less dangerous and more humane way of life. Only a sovereign nation-state can secure the borders needed to allow the ungovernable complexity of a global market and a global corporate economy to be partitioned into manageable subdivisions. And only a

---

94   'Gabriel war Berater bei Tönnies', *Süddeutsche Zeitung*, 2 July 2020, sueddeutsche.de. According to the report, Gabriel received a fixed fee of €10,000 per month; his job lasted for three months.

95   On this, see the already classical comments by Dani Rodrik, 'How Nations Work', in *Straight Talk on Trade: Ideas for a Sane World Economy*, Princeton, NJ: Princeton University Press, 2018, 15–47. See also Polanyi Levitt, *Die Finanzialisierung der Welt*, 314–22; Mitchell and Fazi, *Reclaiming the State*; and Ashoka Mody, 'Europe Cannot Escape Nationalism, Brave New Europe', *InsideOver*, 2 May 2019, available at briefingsforbritain.co.uk..

society bounded by national state sovereignty can be organised demo-cratically, so as to be able to generate a collective political will applying to all citizens and enforce it with legitimate authority – a will that counters capitalism's demand that society adapt to it, and that protects social existence, to some extent, from the unceasing turbulence of global markets and the unpredictable fluctuations in relative prices they gener-ate. Only a sovereign and democratic nation-state, in other words, can be the instrument of the protectionism (*Protektionismus*) that every society wishing to remain one needs.

The nation-state is small when compared to the totality of the world economy. That is why it can be democratic; the world, taken as a whole, is too big and too heterogeneous for democratic decision-making. A second structural condition of the nation-state is sovereignty, without which its democratically formed will cannot be put into effect; this in turn requires a non-imperial state system. As we can learn from Polanyi, domestic and foreign policy, internal structure, and external anchoring must be considered in their relation to each other. The larger and more centralised a state, the more difficult it is for its government to mobilise what Fritz Scharpf has called *input-legitimacy*, or democratic consensus. But large and centralised states also find it difficult to mobilise *output-legitimacy*, because they cannot react to local problems and requirements in a sufficiently differentiated manner. It is therefore generally impossi-ble for them to compensate for the input-legitimacy they cannot obtain by acquiring output-legitimacy through good government. States too large to be suitable for democracy also tend to be too large to be well governed; and states small enough for input-legitimacy are also small enough for output-legitimacy.

In what follows, I refer to the democratic and sovereign nation-state – small relative to its surrounding state system – as the *Keynes-Polanyi state*; it offers itself as the ideal type of a refuge and vehicle for a down-ward exit from the post-neoliberal stalemate. This state is characterised by internal institutions and external relations that provide it with a high degree of democratically intended autonomy both from the capitalist market and other states. The Keynes-Polanyi state remains at a friendly distance from its economic and political environment: friendly because it is fundamentally open to exchange and cooperation, and distant because it is interested in preserving the freedom of decision and action of its citizenry. The state aims to protect its politically represented citizens from every kind of involuntary dependency, and to guarantee their ability to form a political will of consequence – that is, to exercise state sovereignty.

The politics of a Keynes-Polanyi state is characterised by a specific relationship between the domestic and the external world, between internal and external relations, between transactions that stay within the state's borders and those that go beyond them, between domestic and foreign policy – this would be an answer to Herbert Simon's question about the correct balance between internalised and externalised complexity. Unlike the neoliberal state model, the Keynes-Polanyi state has a general preference for the greatest possible internalisation of economic and operational interconnections, even at the expense of economic efficiency, provided that this can be offset by non-material gains of greater value – here, one may recall Keynes, who held that states ought to liberate themselves from the dictatorship of the lowest marginal cost and cheapest price for the sake of non-monetary values. States on the Keynes-Polanyi model are protectionist in a strict sense, insofar as they are prepared to sacrifice economic values to protect non-economic ones, such as the minimisation of collective external dependency or the preservation of a minimum of social stability and continuity. Even if cross-border specialisation and capital mobility lead to a more efficient allocation of national resources, they may be undesirable for a Keynes-Polanyi state because they could cause an unacceptable level of dependence or, in capital markets, an unwelcome territorial separation of property ownership from responsibility. There is also the danger of imperialist interventions in other states to uphold investor interests. Both production and consumption, says Keynes, should take place in the same country if possible, so as to rule out international blackmail.

Keynes-Polanyi states form a cooperative-confederal, horizontally (rather than vertically) structured state system. Free markets are only suited for regulating foreign economic relations of these states if they can be shut down in the event of a failure to preserve national autonomy, or when it becomes necessary to secure the population's welfare. Negotiations on intergovernmental sectoral cooperation are conducted in such a way that autonomy of both sides is preserved. In macroeconomic terms, the autonomy of cooperating nation-states requires that they possess a currency of their own, ideally operating within an international exchange rate regime, but one that must be adjustable at the request of the parties involved, preferably in a regulated procedure. For Keynes, as for Polanyi, an international gold standard was therefore unacceptable because it might compel governments to undertake any necessary economic adjustments solely at the expense of the majority of their own populations, with destructive consequences for the democratic governability of the country.

The politics of Keynes-Polanyi states should reflect the fact that the national political economy is a result of fragile, historically and territorially localised compromises between capital and society, between the dynamic of capitalist accumulation and social existence. In Keynes's impressive formulation, nation-states that manoeuvre between capitalism and democracy are continuously in search of the 'ideal social republic', the most important feature of which is its non-identity with an ideal market economy.[96] (Polanyi describes the same search in more political terms: as a permanent conflict between the movement of capitalism and a social counter-movement, from which nationally diverse modes of existence emerge as intermediate stages of historical development.) The diversity of Keynes-Polanyi states, their necessary differentiation from each other, and their anti-hierarchical autonomy in relation to their state system are a result of the fact that the social compromises between capitalism and society they mediate cannot be negotiated and implemented in a uniform fashion but instead inevitably have an outcome that differs from one country to another, according to the interplay of internal and external conditions. The cultural identities formed as a result play a decisive role in identifying and measuring the society's non-material values – of an aesthetic, moral, and social kind – particularly in relation to collective decisions on what may (or may not) be economised, that is, approved for commodification and commercialisation. This is the precise demarcation in a compromise between the capitalist market economy and society. Trade-offs between non-material and material values created in the process of capitalist accumulation and quantifiable in money are not left to the dynamics of the market. Instead, decisions are made democratically and politically. The anti-globalist Keynes-Polanyi state must also be pro-democratic, so as to modify the respective national

---

96 Keynes, 'National Self-Sufficiency', 764.

armistice lines between capitalism and society according to changing circumstances.[97]

A central question in the tug of war between globalism and democracy is whether something is lost if, against the tide of the previous century's megalomaniac orthodoxy, the way out of the post-neoliberal impasse is sought in a movement downwards. This would be, in other words, a move towards a system of small, democratic, sovereign nation-states, and towards smaller political domains, with many small states instead of a few large ones, and with nation-states (instead of supranational states) enjoying dispersed and decentralised (instead of unified and centralised) state sovereignty. What does this say about how a deglobalised economy could function after the end of globalist neoliberalism?

Keynes-Polanyi states are, as just mentioned, small and form state systems where sovereignty is diffuse and decentralised instead of centrally concentrated. What can states of this kind do for their societies, and what can be expected from them in view of the current crisis of hyperglobalised neoliberal capitalism? The remainder of this chapter will be devoted to answering this question. A short examination of the economic and democratic performance of sovereign states that are small in relation to their state system will provide some initial indications. I will then look at the experiences of small European nation-states in the early phase of the neoliberal opening to the world market and the subsequent period of hyperglobalisation. Building on this, I will attempt to adumbrate the possible responses of small, sovereign, democratic

---

97   How such a state shapes itself and is related to other states is, by definition, its own affair, and will differ from case to case; it is impossible to overlook the numerous similarities between these proposals and the ideal developing country described in Bello, *Deglobalization*. What we can know for certain is what a Keynes-Polanyi state would *not* look like: namely, like a member country of the EMU, which has ceded its monetary sovereignty to an independent multinational central bank, thereby subjecting itself to a super gold-standard, and at the same time added its signature to a treaty that is practically unalterable and can only be terminated at great cost, if at all, according to which it must adhere to a debt limit of 60 percent of its GDP and a budget deficit limit of 3 percent a year, while also joining a free trade zone covering goods, services, capital, and labour. This zone, described as the 'internal market', includes a capital market in which capital controls are prohibited, not only internally but also in relation to the rest of the world. Disputes and matters of doubt are handed over to an international economic court not controlled by any democratic legislature, whose decisions are binding and can only be corrected by the court itself: a neoliberal dream.

nation-states to the crises of the present. I then discuss the question of whether small, democratic, sovereign nation-states are able to cooperate internationally in the production of global public goods, before concluding with an examination of the structural demands a system of democratic small states makes of the global or continental state system surrounding it.

Better Smaller

Are there reasons to assume that the small is inferior to the large – so much so that one would rather be large than small – even if that means having to come to terms with neoliberal or technocratic methods of mastering complexity? A comparison of the economic and political (and in particular democratic) performance of small or large states in terms of population will provide an initial reference. Firstly, as far as economic performance is concerned, there is no indication that large states are more successful than small ones, and therefore that an increase in a state's size as such brings economic advantages. Rather, the opposite is the case: if size makes any difference at all, it is negatively correlated with economic efficiency. One example among many is the average annual economic growth of the member countries of the European Union after the 2008 financial crisis, when the economies of the twelve small countries with less than 5.8 million inhabitants each, grew perceptibly faster, by an average 1.95 percent per year, than those of the six large countries with 38 to 83 million inhabitants (they grew by 1.34

Figure 30. European Union: Population size and average economic growth, 2009–2018

	Number of countries	Population (millions)	Average GDP growth, 2009–18
Large	6	38.0 to 83.0	1.34
Medium	10	7.0 to 19.4	1.31
Small	12	0.5 to 5.8	1.95

Source: Eurostat, Estimated Population, 1 January 2019; Real GDP Growth Rate.

percent per year; see fig. 30). Notably, larger size tended to coincide with considerably lower public debt (see fig. 31). I will not go into any further detail here, as it suffices for my argument that an upward leap in scale is not a recipe for economic growth and a downward leap does not necessarily have to be paid for with economic impoverishment, and so an adherence to decentralised sovereignty does not in itself risk impairing the prosperity of the national economies involved.

Figure 31. Correlation between population size and public debt, 36 OECD countries

	Pearson	Spearman
2018	0.36*	0.50**
2005	0.36*	0.53**

* Significant at the 0.05 level; ** Significant at the 0.01 level.

Sources: OECD Historical Population Dataset, IMF World Economic Outlook, October 2019.

No less important than growth is its distribution. If one looks beyond the EU to the OECD family of thirty-six highly developed capitalist states (the 'developed industrial countries'), one finds an unmistakable tendency for inequality in disposable income after taxes and transfer payments to increase with the size of a country (fig. 32), whether one measures the correlation cardinally by index value (Pearson) or ordinally by rank (Spearman). This correlation has become much stronger in the years of hyperglobalisation and since the financial crisis of 2008 – which is an argument in favour of the assumption that the increase in state size produced by the concentration of sovereignty in a superstate weakens the democratic redistributive capacity in crises (while it hinders the growth of redistributable wealth itself, as already shown). Even stronger evidence for this supposition emerges if the coefficients of inequality are calculated separately for large and small countries, and for gross and disposable income. This shows that the average coefficient of inequality in the group of smaller countries, already lower than in the group of large countries in any case, is much more strongly reduced by state intervention into the distribution of income than it is in the large countries (fig. 33).

Figure 32. Correlation between population size and economic inequality, 36 OECD countries

	Pearson	Spearman
c. 2017	0.45*	0.40*

* Significant at the 0.05 level. Economic inequality: Gini coefficient, disposable income.

Sources: OECD Historical Population Dataset, OECD Income Distribution Database.

Figure 33. Average levels of inequality (Gini coefficient) by population size

(1) Gross income (before taxes and transfer payments)

	2005	2017
Large	0.48	0.49
Small	0.47	0.46

(2) Disposable income (after taxes and transfer payments)

	2005	2017
Large	0.35	0.35
Small	0.30	0.29

(3) Redistribution effect

	2005	2017
Large	−0.13	−0.14
Small	−0.17	−0.17

All OECD countries. 15 large countries (with more than 15 million inhabitants); 21 small countries.

Sources: OECD Historical Population Dataset, OECD Income Distribution Database, author's own calculations. Gross income figures for Turkey: World Inequality Database; for Mexico: J. Scott, 'Redistributive Impact and Efficiency of Mexico's Fiscal System', *Public Finance Review* 42, no. 3 (2014), 368–90.

Dirk Jörke, who is mainly interested in the impact of country size on democracy, including 'social democracy', comes to a similar conclusion.[98] For twenty-one wealthy industrialised countries, he uses the findings of two studies undertaken by other authors to show that smaller countries (excluding the smallest: Jörke refers to 'medium-sized states' rather than small states) are more likely to qualify as 'social democracies', in relation to 'the level of social security, the institutionalisation of basic social rights, the social expenditure ratio, the employment rate, and also the involvement of the trade unions in the political process'.[99] Jörke rightly concedes that factors other than population size may also be involved – such as the extent of the territory rather than the size of its population, and the amount of ethnic diversity in the society, both of which have a negative effect on the amount of social democracy – and, with equal justice, comes out against a monocausal explanation. Theses like his, he says, cannot be 'proved, they can at most be made plausible'. After discussing various individual cases, however, he still reaches the conclusion that 'the assumption is in every case [very plausible] that an ambitious conception of democracy, centred on its two promises', namely participation and redistribution, 'can more easily be put into effect in medium-sized states' than in large ones.[100] In considering ways out of the post-neoliberal deadlock, one can conclude from this discussion that for states which have already implemented, or still wish to implement, an ambitious model of democracy, an upward shift in the political scale would very probably be accompanied by a regression to a less participatory and a less social level of democratic statehood.

Jörke's research programme aims to show that beyond a certain size threshold, such as that far exceeded by the EU, the character of democracy changes to such an extent that it transforms into something other than democracy. My purpose, on the other hand, is simply to show that the relatively small size of a state on the Keynes-Polanyi model in proportion to the surrounding state system does not have to come at the cost of a decline in economic performance or the quality of democracy;

---

98   Dirk Jörke, *Die Größe der Demokratie: Über die räumliche Dimension von Herrschaft und Partizipation*, Berlin: Suhrkamp, 2019.

99   Ibid., 103.

100   Ibid., 107.

on the contrary, there is every indication that, even in a hyperglobalised world market, smallness benefits a country both economically and democratically. Before examining what special reasons there might be for the superior *economic* performance of small countries and how this phenomenon manifests itself under the conditions of the present capitalist crisis, I would like to briefly discuss some of Jörke's arguments on the relationship between state size and *democracy*, insofar as they illuminate the expected influence of inter-state integration and mega-statism (*Großstaaterei*) on the quality of a state's democracy.

Jörke's thesis that participatory and redistributional democracy is only possible in smaller states, and cannot be scaled up, can be read in the context of a rich social scientific literature, according to which the size of a social entity is among the most important determinants of its structure. Following on from the difference between democracy in Greece and in Rome – with Greece standing for the polis and Rome for a world empire – and continuing with Rousseau, Montesquieu, and his own reading of the history of the foundation and development of the US after 1776, Jörke focuses primarily on two features of a political community that correlate with its size: the heterogeneity of its constituents and the character of its elite. Jörke refers, in particular, to Robert Dahl as a representative of the more recent political science literature on the subject. Dahl was still of the opinion in 1989 that globalisation both required and allowed a scaling-up of democracy, an 'optimistic diagnosis' that he subsequently abandoned.[101] As relayed by Jörke ten years later, Dahl held that international organisations are excessively heterogeneous 'as regards cultural identity, religion, language, historical experience, political conviction and economic performance', and that this 'makes the emergence of a common interest or any kind of public good appear extremely unlikely'.[102] For this reason, too, Jörke adds, elites form in such a way in large states that they are separated by profession, education, and income from ordinary citizens, and the larger the state, the wider the gap grows between them.[103] Jörke argues that this was, in fact, one of the aims of the American federalists around James Madison and Alexander Hamilton when they supported a strong central government:

---

101   Ibid., 109.
102   Ibid.
103   Ibid., 86.

they sought to strengthen the differentiation of elite representatives from those they represented and their interests.[104]

Just how democracy is diminished as the effective size of the state increases is shown in Jörke's chapter on the European Union, titled 'Liberal autocracy in Europe as a consequence of size'. It is among the best analyses of what is understatedly and misleadingly referred to as the 'democratic deficit' of the EU.[105] He then depicts two atrophied and minimal versions of democracy, namely 'deliberationism' and 'constitutionalism', offered strategically and euphemistically in the context of international organisations and of the EU as compensation for a loss of democracy.[106] Both, Jörke suggests, are linked by an elective affinity to

---

104   Jörke and others occasionally mention the various characteristics of small states that are conducive to democracy. These include a smaller number of internal dividing lines and veto points; an associated ability to negotiate compromises between conflicting interests more rapidly and simply; greater emotional identification of the citizens with the nation as a whole than with individual subgroups; and a shorter and more transparent path from political decision to implementation.

105   On this, see also Peter Mair, *Ruling the Void: The Hollowing of Western Democracy*, London: Verso, 2013, a book which continues to be worth consulting. The episode of the so-called 'suppertime consultation' may serve as an illustration of what counts in Brussels as the 'democratic deficit' and what is being proposed to overcome it. In spring 2018 the European Parliament, mainly under the pressure of its German members, voted to abolish the annual change from winter to summer time, if this was desired by 'the citizens of Europe'. To find out what the citizens really did desire, the European Commission conducted an online vote in July and August of the same year. In all countries apart from three, less than 1 percent of those eligible to vote participated; participation was highest in Germany (3.8 percent), Austria (2.9 percent), and Luxembourg (1.3 percent), for whatever reason. On 31 August the Commission announced that '84 percent' had voted to abolish summer time: 'The message is very clear: 84 percent do not want the clocks to change anymore. We will now act accordingly and prepare a legislative proposal to the European Parliament and the Council, who will then decide together.' As proof of the democratic responsiveness of the EU, the president of the Commission at that time, Jean-Claude Juncker, promised to end summer time before the European elections in 2019. Of course, neither the Commission nor the Parliament were entitled to act on this. The dossier was sent to the member states where it belongs, who tried, in a joint summit at ministerial level, to reach agreement on a uniform time system for Europe welcomed by all members states, from Latvia to Portugal. Before the pandemic, it was determined that decision was to be made at some point in 2021; of course, by the start of 2020, more serious matters overtook the issue, and it was forgotten.

106   Jörke, *Die Größe der Demokratie*, 146–59, 159–67. On this, see also Chantal Mouffe, *On the Political*, Abingdon: Routledge, 2005.

a specific supranational elite – one can also speak of a 'political class', as is traditional in Italy – owing its rise to the expansion of political jurisdiction and an attendant upward shift of governmental responsibility, along with the de-democratisation it entails.

It should be emphasised that Jörke is not misled by the argument that the efficiency of governments is improved by the expansion and centralisation of the state, and that there is therefore a trade-off between a democratic small-state system and effective state action. The experience of the years of hyperglobalisation has shown that precisely a lack of democratic legitimacy can provoke resistance to state action, making effective government impossible – as in the fate of neoliberal 'reforms' in France and Italy. Furthermore, centralised governments' unavoidable detachment from reality in relation to the heterogeneous problems faced by a mega-state can lead to a situation where its responses are ineffective and wrong. The consequence is a legitimacy deficit in the political system's output, just like those that arise when the market is left to govern complex situations in a neoliberal laissez-faire mode. Most importantly, however, one learns from Simon's theory of complexity that the governability of a world can be *increased* by decentralisation, since a complex system without subdivisions very quickly overburdens a centralised government.

'Economic Patriotism': Globalism and Back

Does the Keynes-Polanyi model of a sovereign democratic nation-state – small, or at least small rather than large in relation to its state system – constitute a 'relapse' into an outmoded economic nationalism, or, perhaps less threateningly expressed, patriotism? Economic patriotism, in the sense of an economic policy directed towards the improvement of the economic situation of a particular territory, has existed for as long as politics itself; a 'relapse' is therefore only a problem from the perspective of an ideal neoliberal world that cannot materialise. In fact, globalisation was also driven by economic patriotism in the countries that pursued it, in the widespread belief at the time that a country could only preserve and increase its prosperity by opening its economy to the world. This applied to large as well as small states: in the US too, a globalist economic policy was always sought for reasons of economic patriotism, either through the integration of its own economy into the world economy, or the reverse.[107]

Findings on whether and how small states can orient and assert themselves in a global economy in terms of economic patriotism, and under what conditions, date to the 1980s, the early days of modern globalisation. Particularly relevant here is Peter Katzenstein's study *Small States in World Markets: Industrial Policy in Europe*.[108] In summary, Katzenstein's message is that the small states of Europe were by no means condemned to obsolescence by the coming of globalisation, notwithstanding the widespread expectation among the larger states that this would happen. The seven European countries he examined – Sweden, Norway, Denmark, the Netherlands, Belgium, Austria, and Switzerland – were able to engage with a world market whose fluctuations had to be accepted as a fact of life, without having to forego active discretionary policies in their national interests. Despite a high (and increasing) dependence on successful exports, they were able, as a result, not only to achieve social peace and political stability but also to preserve and increase the prosperity of their citizens, along with a relatively egalitarian distribution of wealth, high employment, extensive systems of social security, and reliably democratic institutions.

Why was this? *Small States in World Markets* is set in a phase of economic development when countries could obtain considerable welfare gains by opening themselves up to the world market: they could export more in order to increase imports accordingly, and thus realise their comparative advantages. For small countries more than for large ones, this meant the need for ongoing adaptation to changing market

---

107   The theme of economic patriotism is examined in *Economic Patriotism in Open Economies*, edited by Ben Clift and Cornelia Woll (London: Routledge, 2013). Both editors and their contributors emphasise the diversity of goals and the variety of participants in the movement, as well as the omnipresence of the politics of economic patriotism in the tense force field where nation-states with spatially defined jurisdictions and international markets meet. Both subnational and supranational political systems can pursue policies of economic patriotism, say Clift and Woll; but the most important bearers of economic patriotism continue to be nation-states, which, even in an open international economy, attempt in manifold ways to help the societies they rule and represent succeed through a wide range of active interventions.

108   Peter J. Katzenstein, *Small States in World Markets: Industrial Policy in Europe*, Ithaca, NY: Cornell University Press, 1985.

conditions, often extending to their societies as a whole – a compulsion to be permanently prepared for profound changes to their economic and social structure. Where a large country may have been tempted to shape the world market in such a way that suited it (the example of the US is always in the background for Katzenstein), smaller countries had, in a sense, to follow the market as *price takers*. They were also exposed to greater foreign-trade risks than big countries: the smaller the country, the more goods it had to obtain from abroad and export abroad, and the more dependent it was, as a result, on the comparative advantages enjoyed by its export economy. Small countries, as a condition of remaining substantial enough in their segments of the market to remain globally competitive, were thus compelled to specialise ever more intensively according to increases in the international division of labour. But this approach, in turn, left entire countries vulnerable to market fluctuations in their chosen sectors.

According to Katzenstein, who was writing in the mid-1980s, the industrial policy of small countries in the early stages of globalisation consisted of using the equipment of the sovereign nation-state to organise an ongoing adaptation of the national economy to unforeseeable changes in international market conditions. If a country was extremely ambitious, it could develop a national-international niche strategy aimed at conquering a leading position in the world market for selected historically or geographically privileged sectors of the domestic economy, defending and extending its position by employing all the institutional resources of the nation-state – from education and research to monetary and foreign policy. Examples of 'sectoral specialisation' in this sense include Switzerland with financial services, top-end tourism and luxury goods, Denmark with maritime logistics, management consultancy and mid-level tourism (occasionally the sale of mink skins as well), and the Netherlands with youth tourism, the port of Rotterdam with its associated transport and business services, and Amsterdam as a global base for corporate headquarters. As long as such a strategy works, a nation's economy can organise itself around designated leading sectors and raise the funds required to maintain social cohesion, as well as to produce necessary public goods by siphoning off part of the quasi-monopoly rents from its leading sectors. Problems arise when international competitive conditions worsen for the nation's export industries, for instance through a shift from quality to price competition.

A frequently cited example of the typical risks of sectoral specialisation is Finland, which converted itself after the fall of the Soviet
Union from an exporter of timber products and paper-making
machines into an information technology specialist, but then fell into
a severe national economic crisis due to the temporary failure of
Nokia's corporate strategy and the complementary industrial policy. A
country in such a position is faced with the difficult challenge of
quickly refocusing its specialisation so as to prevent the collapse of its
international export market from leading to the collapse of its national
economy as a whole.

It was not Katzenstein's intention to produce a book of recipes for
industrial policy; what interested him was the political system which
had enabled the small states he was investigating to master the challenge
presented by the opening of their national economies to the world
market so well that their populations were able to benefit from the onset
of globalisation and wanted to participate in it. What all seven countries
had in common, he says, was that in response to the danger of ending up
as the losing side in the sharpening competition on the world markets,
they fell back on historically developed national institutions that enabled them to manage the structural changes demanded by the world
market together in the national interest, transcending class boundaries.
Katzenstein locates the origin of these institutions – he speaks of
'democratic corporatism' – in national class compromises, like the Swiss
labour 'peace agreement' or the Swedish Saltsjöbaden Agreement, that,
notwithstanding their differences in form, were negotiated between the
state, capital, and labour in the 1930s, when national existence was
threatened.[109] There is no need to compare the various national versions
of these institutions here; the details can be found in Katzenstein. It is
enough to note that later on, during the Trente Glorieuses after the
Second World War, the democratic corporatism of the inter-war period
became an important element in what I have described above as the
standard model of capitalist democracy, including in particular the
institutionalised involvement of the trade unions in the nation-state's
administration of political economy.

Katzenstein's thesis of 1985 held that the source of the great political
stability of the small states, despite the pressures of the world market, lay

---

109   Ibid., 80–135.

in their corporatist institutions, and that the remarkable ability of their economies to act and adapt to the world market, the cause of their continued prosperity, was both the result and the condition of this political stability.[110] The institutional inheritance of a national peace agreement was a political resource enabling them to cope patriotically with new, perhaps less existential but still threatening, crisis situations. Katzenstein reports that there was consensus in the countries he studied that a politically capable democratic nation-state – at the time, this meant including its organised working class – as the steering body for structural change was an indispensable prerequisite for the successful participation of a small country in an internationalising world economy. Of course, there were no guarantees, and in the mid-1980s, the first clouds were already gathering in the sky for the small states adapting themselves to the world market with flexibility and solidarity, in the form of supposedly unstoppable technological progress in the US or a catching-up of 'developing' countries in traditional industrial sectors.[111] Labour conflicts began to appear on the horizon, even in a country like Sweden, and the nation's consensus-building institutions were increasingly used to defend national competitiveness by enforcing reductions in wages and social benefits ('tighten your belts') instead of through consensual industrial policy. But the predominant feeling was still one of optimism: 'More severe international constraints', writes Katzenstein, 'will make the domestic politics of the small European states more cohesive, at least in the medium term.'[112]

But not *in the long term*, as we now know. If Katzenstein's world is compared with today's, the difference could hardly be greater. It is true, as we have seen, that small countries are still more than able to hold their own, economically and socially, with big countries. But the democratic corporatism which held small nation-states together almost forty years ago, allowing them to organise a politically consensual adaptation of their economies to international competition, has almost disappeared. The trade unions have long been in decline, and their voices count for less and less. In the labour market, wages are no longer set by collective agreement, while trade associations have yielded to the big corporations

---

110 Ibid., 191.
111 Ibid., 193.
112 Ibid., 198.

and limit their activities to lobbying.[113] Meanwhile, the parties of the political centre, which had supported the corporatist 'second tier of government' and had been supported by it, are shrinking under the pressure of new protest movements fuelled by increasing discontent over social insecurity, economic and social decline, growing inequality, social fragmentation, and the aggravated stress of competition combined with falling levels of compensation.[114] All these developments are related to the same inexorably advancing internationalisation of economy and society against which democratic corporatism had originally afforded some protection on the basis of national opposition.

Why has the magic formula of the 1980s lost its effectiveness? This is not the place to expand Katzenstein's portraits of seven small European countries in detail. But, when rereading his well-informed and comprehensive book, in its time an epoch-making theoretical work, it is hard to avoid thinking of the great change still to come at the beginning of the 1990s, a turning point that was actually an acceleration of existing trends: the transition from globalisation to hyperglobalisation. For the small states, hyperglobalisation as a form of transnational liberalisation meant a renunciation of exactly those political capabilities they had used for so long to shore up the compromise between labour and capital over the opening of their national economies. This renunciation was also motivated, strictly speaking, by economic patriotism because it too was intended to promote the competitiveness of the economy by releasing it from the grip of the nation-state's democratic politics. After all, the policy of the 'Third Way', as it began to unfold fully a good decade after Katzenstein was writing, meant that the state not only *declared* itself incapable of acting as a source of national protection against the international market but *made* itself incapable of this by abandoning its sovereignty over economic policy. Instead of negotiating the 'flexible adaptation' demanded by the neoliberal utopia in an economically patriotic and politically consensual fashion, governments of the 'Third Way' intended to enforce it by deactivating the protective authority of the

---

113   Wolfgang Streeck and Jelle Visser, 'Conclusions: Organized Business Facing Internationalization', in Wolfgang Streeck et al., eds, *Governing Interests: Business Associations Facing Internationalization*, London: Routledge, 2006, 242–72.

114   Stein Rokkan, 'Norway: Numerical Democracy and Corporate Pluralism', in Robert A. Dahl, ed., *Political Opposition in Western Democracies*, New Haven, CT: Yale University Press, 1966, 70–115.

state, thereby leaving their populations defenceless against the storms of change.

The free trade agreements of the time exemplified this. They were instrumental in ending the national control exerted until then over the economy by dismantling external barriers; the most glaring case of this was the internal market of the European Union, which entered into force in 1992 and denied member states virtually any possibility of an independent policy in trade, industry, and the regions worthy of the name. The Economic and Monetary Union following it transferred member states' monetary policies to a colossal technocratic authority without a political mandate and beyond any democratic accountability. The intended result was a de facto gold standard to neutralise national democracy, to discredit it by making it powerless, and to place the burden of potentially endless economic and social adjustment to the unforeseeable dictates of the European and global market solely on national societies – and, above all, their territorially bound work-forces – without any possibility of guarding their political flanks by altering their currencies' exchange rates.[115] Three of the seven countries in Katzenstein's study joined the EMU, while in Denmark and Sweden, the pro-European elites were forced by their fellow citizens to preserve remnants of their ability to act and take responsibility for the nation's policies. Switzerland and Norway even stayed out of the EU, also under pressure from their citizens and against the wishes of the political class's intention at the time to detach them completely from national democracy.

The capstone of the whole process was a contractual obligation by the participating countries to unlimited global capital mobility, whether generated within their borders or not, both within the EU itself and beyond it – a ban on capital controls that opened almost infinite opportunities for businesses and investors to use extortion for tax cuts and

---

115 Mark Blyth, *Austerity: The History of a Dangerous Idea*, Oxford: Oxford University Press, 2013. The impact of this was felt in Finland, among other places, where the reorientation of the country's sectoral specialisation in reaction to the Nokia crisis was hampered by the fact that by then it had entered the EMU, and so no longer had recourse to the monetary measures necessary to safeguard an economy in the throes of yet another wave of structural change. In a situation like this, effective adaptation to changes in the external economic environment can only be achieved through internal devaluation, if at all, and even then, only cautiously and against intense political resistance.

legal, semi-legal, and illegal means of tax avoidance. This marked the transition from globalisation to hyperglobalisation and thus amounted to the very economic sterilisation of the nation-state that had been at the heart of neoliberalism since the 1980s. Then, the negotiated change carried out by the small states had taken too long for impatient capital, and the compensation it had had to pay to national societies for the fulfilment of its dream of boundless social flexibility in the service of the smooth progress of capital accumulation had turned out to be too expensive; where profit-making is involved, such costs always have to be checked thoroughly. In this way, capital was able to shatter, or at least dismantle, the institutional structures that had up to that point under-pinned globalisation, but which had also slowed its pace and made it liable to compensation. Yet this was a bridge too far, and the attempt to enshrine an all-embracing, undemocratic mega-state, or a virtual single state, as a global empire of capital mobility provoked the countermovement of a new nationalism unwilling to accept the elimination of national politics as means of protecting living standards and ways of life.

Today, it is obvious why the transition from economic patriotism to economic globalism could never ultimately succeed. With the demo-cratic corporatist negotiation of globalisation, the corresponding state, in its role as peacemaker, found itself increasingly overwhelmed by capital's growing impatience, fuelled by enthusiasm first over Japanese and then Chinese methods of production. The risks of sectoral special-isation also became increasingly evident, among them the fact that sectorally specialised states could all too easily become, and would in fact have to become, the servants of giant internationalised firms with roots in their own countries. The borderless world market produced not convergence but crises, such as the one in 2008, and it gave rise to an increasing dependence on fragile and overextended value chains, while the half-completed European superstate was in no position to ensure anything like equalisation among its member countries, now down-graded to regions of an integrated political economy. For this reason, too, and in the wake of a rapidly spreading awareness of the acuteness of the risks, the political stability still admired by Katzenstein also dis-appeared along with the active nation-state, sacrificed as it was to an acceleration of globalisation in favour of a worldwide balance of marginal utility as the highest value of political economy. This prevailed until the old patriotism returned from below in a new, more resistant form as a sovereigntist, national counter-movement to the denational-ised globalism of the 1990s and demanded the resuscitation of the surviving elements of the nation-state to reactivate national economic policy.

Big Crisis, Small States

One result of this retrospective of the last wave of globalisation is that the Keynes-Polanyi model of a sovereign democratic state of moderate size suddenly seems much less exotic. In some respects, a downward exit from the post-neoliberal stalemate would amount to nothing other than the restoration of a capacity for political action which, a few decades ago, was not only a self-evident element of a state's character but had also, for a time, proved itself impressively when faced with the challenge of the expansion of economic horizons. It was only abolished when democratic-national statehood as such entered the crosshairs of neoliberalism, in the misguided expectation that its selective decommis-sioning would speed up the revitalisation of capitalism. We now know that the transition from globalisation to hyperglobalisation has led to a destructive interplay of systemic and social integration crises. Is it not obvious that the proper course is to return to the institutional form of the democratic, and therefore small, non-imperial but sovereign nation-state, whose intended sacrifice to capitalist progress resulted not in capitalist progress but in the stagnation of both capitalism and society?

There is no 'solution' to the great civilisational crises of modern cap-italism, either technocratic or market based, waiting in some scholar's study to be put into effect – even if the operators of the old global gov-ernance gigantism assert that there is 'no alternative' to their miracle cures. A worldwide counterforce with an alternative global vision does not currently exist; the last one was Soviet Communism. This does not mean that the possibility of an alternative can be excluded. Nor can it be excluded that something new might emerge in the prolonged process of globalism's decay, in connection with the development of global poly-centrism, the dissolution of the capitalist empire of the US, the resulting reduction and regionalisation of international economic interdepend-ence, the ever more urgent search for national protection against global risk, the increasing desire for collective control over economic and social development, the broadening insistence on the specificity of the economic conditions and needs of each society, and the wish of a settled community to escape dependence on the volatile benevolence of international investors and central bankers.

Here, I would like to illustrate the possibilities offered by these endeavours. Their objective and purpose is to regain a capacity for collective action by a reduction in the scale of political communities, in a retreat from an ungovernable global or continental context to a governable national one. The guiding principle is a loss of confidence in the ability of overly large jurisdictions to bring order and a sense of identity, and in the intentions of the political class that has taken root in them. Under fortunate circumstances, this could lead to a revitalisation, this time not of capitalism but of democracy: in small, but not too small, political units; in states charged with protecting their populations instead of re-educating them according to 'flexible adaptation'; and in democratic sovereignty as the alternative to the technocratic gigantism of a global governance far removed from democracy and incapable of governing.

But what about 'solving' the 'problems' – overcoming the cumulative crises of global capitalism? Could there be a crisis policy, especially in the economic field, that a democratic and sovereign Keynes-Polanyi state might pursue with some prospect of success? There is now an astonishingly broad stream of ideas on the subject that points beyond the old globalist horizon, and that could be useful to a revitalised nation-state for a *policy of overcoming crises in a decentralised way from below.* The tasks it would have to accomplish today are more complex than those mastered so impressively by Katzenstein's small states in their time. Today, the task would be to unwind hyperglobalisation and in its place to establish, or, more realistically, to allow the growth of, a less destructive system offering a chance of greater security and more equality, as well as – in the longer term – an escape from the dictatorship of endless private-profit maximisation for the self-perpetuating purpose of the endless maximisation of the same. Here, I would like to identify five areas where an emerging Keynes-Polanyi state has to prove itself and, I believe, would also be able to do so. These are fields in which favourable developments are already, to some extent, underway, and could be pursued.

(1) Firstly, it would be necessary to take up and strengthen the aforementioned worldwide tendency towards a *shortening of supply chains*

and a territorial reshoring of systems of production that have recently expanded globally. In the emerging polycentric world, states must endeavour, in the interests of their populations, to bring back the production of indispensable goods to a reliable proximity, so as not to be dependent on one or another of the great powers, and to avoid being cut off from vital supplies in a possible conflict between other states. A greater degree of autarchy should be sought, not only for 'national security' as defined militarily, and the avoidance of political blackmail, as over energy supply, for example, but also in order to be able to forgo imports from countries to which a state wishes to signal disapproval on account of gross human rights violations.[116] So-called social media also need to be deglobalised and nationalised, insofar as at present they effectively constitute a part of the public infrastructure held in private foreign hands; here, nation-states would be obliged, and able, to demand an operational subdivision of the relevant corporations into national units, analogous to banks, making it possible to regulate and tax the respective subsidiaries according to local laws.

(2) A restored democratic nation-state on the Keynes-Polanyi model could, and should, commit itself openly to economic patriotism, and even *protectionism*. There is no more important function for a democratic state under capitalism than the protection of its citizens from capitalism's risks and adverse side effects. A country in retreat from hyperglobalisation needs to change its internal structure so as to compensate for the dismantling of its global interconnectedness by broadening the range of the national economy – or, if you like, by despecialising, and putting an end to the blind glorification of economies of scale.[117] A transition of this kind to production 'in the region' – to *make more, buy less* – can only be brought about step by step and must be shielded against undercutting by foreign competitors, at least temporarily; this demands a national industrial and regional policy which can separate the domestic economy from the outside world. Both sectoral change and the fight against regional disparities may require governmental assistance ('state aid', in EU jargon); this is not permitted under market-unifying free trade treaties like those underpinning the EU internal market regime.

---

116   On the concept of autarchy in the sense applied here, see p. 318.
117   On this see Keynes, 'National Self-Sufficiency', discussed on pp. 295–301.

Protectionism has many facets, from the practice increasingly pre-
valent today, though mainly sub rosa, of government intervention to
prevent the sale of key national businesses to foreigners who do not (any
longer) belong to the empire, such as China, to the shielding of cultural
producers from international commercialisation (see, for example, the
defence of the French film industry by the Jospin government during
the struggle over the Multilateral Agreement on Investment), and the
creation of jobs by the conversion of local and regional economies to
environmentally friendly production. Protectionism, in the sense of a
move away from risk-laden integration into unreliable and asymmetric
global production systems, has a better chance of succeeding in cooperation with like-minded and similarly structured neighbouring states – in
other words, by using 'regional planning', as is right and proper for
Keynes-Polanyi states. Agreements of this kind, involving a jointly operated selective industrial policy in pursuit of national economic
self-sufficiency, would be voluntary in character and would only be
renewed if both parties wanted them to continue – unlike the free trade
treaties of the 1990s or, indeed, the EU Treaties.

(3) A retreat from hyperglobalisation means a shift of economic
policy towards *internal growth*: domestic production for domestic consumers. Here, too, it is possible to build on trends now long underway,
such as the growth of the service sector – particularly the rise of personal services, but public services as well – and an increasing inclination
on the part of consumers to prefer regional products, and not just
regarding food.[118] The fight against climate change, too, if it is to amount
to more than mere conference rhetoric, takes place locally above all, and
it requires largely local investment, for example in the insulation of
houses, conversion to renewable energy, the creation of a national infrastructure of charging points for electric vehicles, and the development
of new, more sustainable methods of building houses and planning
urban development. There also needs to be an increase in expenditure –
as triggered by the COVID crisis – on public health and the care of the
elderly, as well as on investment in research and education, with the
latter conducted in the local language, so as to avoid dependence on
foreign digital suppliers and provide job opportunities for the country's

---

118   Jim Tomlinson, 'De-globalization and Its Significance: From the Particular to
the General', *Contemporary British History* 26, no. 2 (2012), 213–30.

teachers. Domestic growth occurs mainly in labour-intensive sectors, whose future depends to a high degree on national policy, perhaps involving precautions against future pandemics. Although this can take place jointly with other countries, it is chiefly a national matter if it costs money, and, as is absolutely necessary, if local circumstances have to be considered. Reorientation from export-driven to domestically generated growth can generally be promoted by an appropriate monetary policy, provided that a state still retains its monetary sovereignty. Thus, revaluation can reduce the proportion of workers employed in export-oriented sectors, and labour market policies can accelerate the structural change towards the service sector, while cheapening imports in sectors where they do not compete with domestic production, such as tourism, thereby helping to increase the prosperity and real purchasing power of the majority of the population.[119]

(4) A democratic nation-state adjusted to domestic growth can and will devote itself to what has been called the infrastructure of everyday life – the *foundational economy*.[120] These are the *collective goods* enabling people to live normal lives in a modern society: public transportation, health care, public safety, schools, and universities close at hand. In short, they are the physical and social networks that determine whether and how a society 'functions'. Collective goods benefit all citizens equally, or they can be designed to do so in practice: they are in essence egalitarian, belonging to the public (or, where privately operated, communally regulated), and they are, or can be, subject to local democratic decision-making and self-determination. In this context, I have written of a 'communism of the everyday' underpinning modern capitalism, indeed making its existence possible, but which is constantly threatened with misappropriation by capital, in the latter's search for new opportunities for profit-making,

---

119   In the 1969 Bundestag elections, the SPD, following its then economics minister, Karl Schiller, won enough votes by calling for a revaluation of the Deutschmark to oust the CDU/CSU from the federal government for the first time, making Willy Brandt chancellor. Schiller had campaigned for revaluation as a means of reducing the endemic German export surplus and switching to domestically driven economic growth – or, to put it another way, he sought to counter the increasingly asymmetrical early 'globalisation' of the German economy.

120   See Julie Froud et al., *Foundational Economy: The Infrastructure of Everyday Life*, Manchester: Manchester University Press, 2018.

above all through privatisation and commercialisation.[121] First-class collective goods can be expensive; but we know from the Scandinavian countries, for instance, that citizens can be ready to pay high taxes for them and to remain in the country partly on their account, but also because they can be a source of patriotic pride in the excellence of their own society. In the present age of a fading neoliberalism, people in many places are considering, or actually undertaking, the reversal of the privatisation of waterworks, swimming pools, piping systems, and the like. After COVID, the question of equal and rapid access to high-quality health care is at the forefront of political debate. The same can be said of transportation, where one can well expect a new kind of demand for emissions-free individual travel. The further expansion of collective infrastructure as a growing enclave of non-profit public economic activity within a shrinking private market economy will require considerable resources, mainly from the state, only a very small proportion of which in Europe can be drawn from the overrated COVID Recovery and Resilience Facility. Such efforts will test the ability of the democratic nation-state to tax citizens fairly and effectively, and in general to raise funds for investment despite high and continuing indebtedness – and thus to deal with the 'financial crisis of the state'. States with their own currencies will be able to pass this test more easily than others.[122]

---

121   Wolfgang Streeck, foreword to Foundational Economy Collective, *Die Ökonomie des Alltagslebens*, Berlin: Suhrkamp, 2019, 7–30.

122   On the 'fiscal crisis of the state', see pp. 93ff. on the connection between small states, democracy and the share of public expenditure in the national economy, see Karen L. Remmer, 'Why Do Small States Have Big Governments?', *European Political Science Review* 2, no. 1, 2010, 49–71. Remmer shows that the more public character of the economies of small states is not just a result of economies of scale but is also independently determined by democratic politics, where it exists. In smaller, and therefore more homogeneous populations, it is easier for the advocates of an active government policy, involving greater expenditure, to assert their will as that of the majority: 'The impact of size is conditioned by regime type and the related strength of citizen pressures on politicians.' According to Remmer, 'Size . . . influences spending via political channels, shaping the relative capacity of citizens to organise, monitor, contact or otherwise influence elected politicians.' The results of Remmer's study are all the more impressive in that the author appears to lean more towards the 'public choice' school than social democracy, as can be deduced from the slight undertone of regret in her assessment that 'decentralisation may well achieve greater political accountability but at the expense of raising the overall costs of government' (68–9).

(5) Finally, and following from this last point, a sovereign and democratic 'small, but not too small' state emerging from below, at the ground level of the state system, must attempt to create its own non-capitalist, or less capitalist, *capital*, bypassing global capitalism or acting beneath its radar. Many instruments and types of organisations can (and must) be considered for this purpose, and there is by no means a lack of available building blocks, or at least their remnants. But these must rest on solid ground; no one will seriously believe that collective or communal property can be newly created and promoted at a global level. This is what is required: a national banking system, along with a regional savings banks and sectoral credit cooperatives, each with limited powers, with regulatory protection against both the grip of the world market and the temptation to gamble in the New York casino, detached from the big financial institutions, shielded from the intervention of Brussels-based European international competition lawyers, favoured by 'competition-distorting' state guarantees, and operating alongside mutual credit unions and similar organisations.[123] All these measures are in line with Keynes's dictum that finance, above all, should remain national. There needs to be a crackdown on tax evasion, not just in countries of destination but at the source, in countries of origin. Capital controls must also apply to foreign direct investment, and, not least, 'patriotic' capital in the shape of new forms of communal or responsible ownership (for example, in the UK, community interest companies) should be encouraged and cultivated. Further desiderata are: state-owned blocking stakes in strategically important enterprises, new forms of home ownership (both individual and collective), a return to municipal control of the housing stocks privatised in the orgy of neoliberalism, the promotion of cooperatives and foundations, and, finally, subsidised infrastructure linking town and country by, for example, obliging investors to contribute to local collective assets in the areas where they are investing. Wherever the issue is what one might call the constitution of capital, the

---

123   Such organisations would be similar to the German savings bank system, for decades the target of the European Union's competition watchdogs, going back to the Monti era (1995–2004). The reason was (and remains) that savings banks are able to grant certain credits to local enterprises at lower interest rates than the business banks owing to guarantor liability. On Germany's savings bank system, see, most recently, Mark K. Cassell, *Banking on the State: The Political Economy of Public Savings Banks*, Newcastle upon Tyne: Agenda Publishing, 2021.

conflicts will be particularly fierce, but the gains may also be exceptionally high.[124] Conflicts of this kind can only be won through broad
democratic mobilisation, in the course of which the need to regain
national sovereignty, including monetary sovereignty, as a prerequisite
for an independent economic policy will become clearer with each step
forward.[125]

Wherever a downward exit from the crisis of neoliberalism may lead,
seeking it out and pursuing it means nothing less than a project of radical
democratisation: the attempt to adapt the capitalist economy to an
egalitarian collective will. Its horizon could be termed a participatory
economy – an economic democracy far exceeding what the mainstream
of academic theory on the subject conceives of as democracy, namely
discussions among educated strata with media access and no obligation
to work on subjects related to the material reproduction of society. A
popular democracy that forces its way into areas where the market and
technocracy are sovereign and shapes society's material reproduction
could (and would) no longer be restricted to making use of opportunities
granted from above to share in the 'input' of the political system – in the
formulation of claims to an 'output' to be distributed across society. It
would instead be part of what, in the language of systems theory, is called
'throughput': the process of creating collective goods through social
labour. Democracy in a Keynes-Polanyi state would amount to citizens
taking effective responsibility for their collective fate. It would be both
self-defence and self-government, the pursuit of both solidarity and their
own interests, lively activity instead of passive-regressive expectation of
salvation or politically correct declarations of faith. It would be a

---

124   On new or restored forms of public or semi-public property, see the remarkable studies of Thomas M. Hanna at the Washington-based Democracy Collaborative,
among them *Our Common Wealth: The Return of Public Ownership in the United States*,
Manchester: Manchester University Press, 2018. For Germany and its cooperative
system, see Rolf G. Heinze, 'Gestaltungspotentiale genossenschaftlicher Steuerung',
paper presented at the 'Great Transformation: Die Zukunft Moderner Gesellschaften'
conference, Friedrich-Schiller-Universität Jena, 23–27 September 2019.

125   Likewise, in the Europe of the EU it became clear that the whole structure of
the Union, not to mention the EMU, can and must be read as a collection of draconian
precautions against any experiment with socialist (as opposed to capitalist) capital
formation. Here, if anywhere, the self-proclaimed pro-Europeans are quite serious. For
example, the COVID Recovery and Resilience Facility can also be understood as an
attempt to control the modernisation of member states' infrastructure from above, so
as to exclude the use of COVID-related resources in support of new forms of property
as vehicles for the day-to-day operation of local economies.

self-reliant communitarian practice instead of an institution of moral improvement, where individual initiatives are taken with the knowledge that ultimately nothing can succeed in a democracy that is not willed, done, and answered for by its citizens themselves – as a determined awareness of their own power and duty.[126]

From the perspective of hyperglobalisation and its proponents, downscaling politics with the aim of restoring democracy and containing the risk posed by the economy to society runs against the grain of capitalist development. The politics of the Keynes-Polanyi state curbs the profit-promoting expansion of markets and subjects the resources invested in capital accumulation to political evaluation and social regulation; it rejects the unlimited flexibility demanded by the unrestricted world market; it favours Indigenous over mobile capital; it enlarges rather than reduces the public sector; and it makes society's foreign trade dependent on its general acceptability as well as, using the 'polluter pays' principle, its actual costs. Resilience to crisis is the goal, and security takes precedence over risk – especially for those who have to bear the risk but have nothing to gain from it. Stability and governability are the trump cards; 'resilience' is the highest priority, with the aim of making the economy adapt to society, not the reverse. One could argue at length over whether this would end in anything other than a new version of capitalism, the last in a long series; perhaps it would merely be a recurrence of what has so often come to pass: democratic politics saving capitalism from itself by imposing limits on it, in a new, more contemporary form.[127] This time, however, and perhaps especially on this occasion, capitalism would have a price to pay. In the end, the capitalism to emerge would differ from the present version, regardless of whether it undergoes revolution or reform, or whether this development 'breaks the system' or not.[128]

---

126   Here, as so often it, is worth rereading the final chapter of Karl Polanyi's *The Great Transformation: The Political and Economic Origins of Our Time* (Boston: Beacon Press, 1957 [1944]), titled 'Freedom in a Complex Society'. The Foundational Economy Collective's paper 'What Comes after the Pandemic? A Ten-Point Platform for Foundational Renewal' (Foundational Economy Collective, March 2020) is written in much the same spirit.

127   No one has described this dialectic better in recent years than Francesco Boldizzoni, *Foretelling the End of Capitalism: Intellectual Adventures since Karl Marx*, Cambridge, MA: Harvard University Press, 2020.

128   On this, André Gorz, *Zur Strategie der Arbeiterbewegung im Neokapitalismus*, Frankfurt am Main: Europäische Verlagsanstalt, 1967, is still key. See also Mitchell and Fazi, *Reclaiming the State*; and William Mitchell and Thomas Fazi, 'Make the Left Great

The Question of Money

Can Europe as a world region be organised in any other way than as an empire? The answer is: it *must*, because in the long run it *cannot* be organised imperially, any more than it can be organised as a superstate. The semi-imperial Europe of the present is not sustainable; it is in a state of incurable structural imbalance, vulnerable to crises, with institutions which inspire little confidence and which are constantly being redefined in crisis mode. Any attempt to change this, and to make Europe a regional planned community, inevitably raises the question of the monetary system, if not in the short then in the medium term, and most certainly in the long run.[129] This might, at first glance, seem to be setting the bar too high; but, on closer inspection, one finds that a reorganisation of the monetary system is due not only in Europe but throughout the world. It must, at the very least, adapt the role of the US dollar as the world's reserve currency to the rise of the Chinese renminbi (also known as the yuan), but presumably it must also provide space for independent regional monetary systems in areas like Latin America (Mercosur), thereby turning away from the hegemony of the US dollar. To be able to address this task, we need to be clear that money has always been an institution in flux, in development, and therefore capable

---

Again', *American Affairs* 1, no. 3 (2017), 75–91, on what is perhaps the most advanced recent investigation into the anti-capitalist possibilities of a renationalised political economy.

129   This perception seems to be slowly penetrating even the minds of the European establishment. In 2020 the economist Bert de Vries, formerly a leading Dutch politician and a minister under Ruud Lubbers when the Maastricht Treaty was being negotiated, announced a proposal to move the EU towards a 'milder form of coordination' and to restore political responsibility to the nation-states, because a European federal state was not desired by Europe's citizens. Bert de Vries, *Ontspoord kapitalisme: hoe het kapitalisme ontspoorde en na de coronacrisis kan worden hervormd*, Amsterdam: Prometheus, 2020. De Vries described the introduction of the euro as a 'frivolous' action, adding that in his view the euro had 'failed': there was no additional growth, no convergence, high political instability, and animosity among the European countries. The Dutch government, of which he himself was a member at the time, had not given much thought to the consequences of joining the common currency. After inspecting the minutes of the Dutch cabinet for the years 1989 to 1994, he found they confirmed his recollection that it had not once had a serious discussion about the subject. See also his interview with the *NRC Handelsblad*, 26 May 2020, nrc.nl.

of political modification – but it is also, without question, the most important institution in contemporary capitalism, ruling not only people's daily lives but also the relations among states, and between national societies and world society. Here, too, one can draw on the insights of Keynes and Polanyi.

The decisive task of an anti-capitalist policy – or, less ambitiously, but with the same objective, a policy to make capitalism more socially embedded and politically governable – would then consist in adapting an out-of-control monetary system to the social order, and not the reverse, as neoliberalism so programmatically but futilely attempts to do. This is the task of the moment, and, in principle, it is feasible because money as an institution is, on the one hand, anything but trivial, and on the other, internally contradictory and therefore dynamic – more precisely, it has its own dynamism – hence it moves independently.[130] The notion of the *triviality* of money goes back to the monetarist school in macroeconomics, for which money was nothing more than a neutral medium of exchange, a veil in front of the real economy consisting of commodities, not money – a system of signs that does not change anything in what it signifies. Structural functionalist sociologists, namely Talcott Parsons and the normative systems theorists Luhmann and Habermas, adopted the theory of money from the classical economists, thereby losing sight of Max Weber's observation that money is a weapon in the 'market struggle', favouring different social groups according to the particular institutional shape it assumes.[131]

The notion that all money's forms of appearance are ultimately commensurable and can be viewed and treated together as a single unitary currency is just as unrealistic as the veil theory. Money has, in fact, always been pluralist. It has regularly existed in various manifestations, originating from different sources and linked with different interests and modes of economic activity. These have often been in competition and, at times of crisis, have tended to undermine each other, while the state has repeatedly been obliged to intervene to establish a more or less lasting peace. Things are no different today, with the

---

130   See, among many others, Michel Aglietta, *Money: 5,000 Years of Debt and Power*, London: Verso, 2018.

131   Wolfgang Streeck, 'Warum der Euro Europa spaltet statt es zu einigen', *Leviathan* 43, no. 3 (2015), 365–87.

coexistence of credit money, central bank money, monetarised state debt, and reserve and non-reserve currencies, as well as the rise of cryptocurrencies. The rapid growth of the latter, among which Bitcoin is only one variety, will sooner or later necessitate a reordering of the world monetary system. At present, the worldwide production of Bitcoin by means of supercomputers consumes as much electricity daily as the whole of Germany, a quantity that is rising progressively. Some recent intrusions by hackers into various supercomputers were suspected of being attributable to the need of Bitcoin producers (also called 'miners') for ever more exorbitant processing power.

That monetary reform is desirable and probably necessary, especially for the emergence of a cooperative and associational Europe, does not mean that the path to such a Europe is closed. The euro itself was a political compromise between very different national goals, most of which were not realised. The side effects of this compromise are now dividing the European state system, and there is no reason why, if the crisis it detonated becomes severe enough, such a compromise should not be revised and replaced by a new one. There is every indication that in the not-too-distant future, against the backdrop of the multipolar world order currently taking shape, a monetary and currency reform will fall due in Europe, and that it will need to be sufficiently radical to bear comparison with the Bretton Woods agreement of 1944. Whatever its details, this reform could, if desired, begin with a partial restoration of the monetary-policy autonomy of at least the Mediterranean countries. This could be realised relatively easily by resuscitating Europe's so-called 'exchange rate mechanism II', in which presently only Denmark remains, on account of its eventual decision not to join the euro – for good 'populist' reasons, as we now know. Any such resuscitation would have to be accompanied by a decentralising redefinition of the tasks of the European Central Bank and of the national central banks belonging to the ECB system. Everything else would – and could – follow in due course.

Democratic Particularism and Global Collective Goods

But is it not true that global problems can only be solved through global inter-state cooperation, and that this can only occur through global governance – through the intervention of top-down authority, invested, formally or informally, in empires which must be able to discipline their members so as to make them pursue long-term (instead of short-term) interests, forget their own special interests, and contribute obediently to the production of common goods for the whole of humanity? Is more hierarchy and less sovereignty, more unity and uniformity with less autonomy, a prerequisite for a collective response to crises affecting the whole of humanity? On the contrary, I should like to argue that, here too, there is little to be said in favour of solving problems by scaling up through a system of large states, by global governance and global empires in their various forms, but surprisingly much in favour of the assumption that a state system divided into a multiplicity of small, independent, democratic and sovereign countries of the Keynes-Polanyi type might prove just as capable as blocs of countries conjoined hierarchically – and could even be superior.

I would like to illustrate this suggestion with the example of climate policy. In this area, all the hopes of recent decades have been placed in global governance, within the framework of the multilateral and rules-based 'liberal' international order, the so-called LIO. But a nearly endless series of international conferences and summit resolutions have achieved virtually nothing; climate change continues unabated. If experience is to be taken into account, it will be necessary at some point to consider the possibility that the problem may have been incorrectly defined. In fact, I would propose as a hypothesis that the established theory and practice of combating climate change both suffer from a commitment to a rational choice model of international state action, whereas a sociological model would be more effective. The latter relies on the mobilisation of collective moral energy at the level of the society to make policies more climate friendly, rather than utility-maximising action at the state level. The main difference between the two approaches is that under the sociological model, the communal production of collective goods takes place without resorting to large, hierarchically ruled state structures. It would function instead in an environment of small, democratic and sovereign national units.[132]

Why has the global-governance approach been unable to point the way to an effective solution to the problem of climate change? I suspect that this is due to its close association with a premise that has since the 1960s become a matter of course in Western social theory: cooperative action to secure a collective good requires solving a problem similar to the so-called 'prisoner's dilemma'; specific means are needed, but regrettably they are not yet available, or insufficiently available, for inter-state cooperation.[133] The problem consists in this: that every member of a collective who takes part in the collectively rational production of a collective good must reckon with a loss of individual rationality, while members who act in a collectively irrational manner by abstaining from the process gain more as individuals – either as 'free-riders' if the collective good is still produced through others' contributions, or, if that is not the case, because they have at least not sacrificed anything for a lost cause. Since this calculation applies to everyone in the collective, as long as they act independently of each other as rationally calculating individuals – and as individuals they are all too 'small' to be able to produce the good privately for themselves and thus as a secondary benefit for others – the collective good cannot materialise. This problem can only be overcome in practice through the establishment of a higher authority that either curtails the autonomy of the participants in their own long-term interest, ordering them to act in a collectively rational manner, or rewards them for their cooperation by offering special benefits to individuals ('outside inducements').

Nothing of the kind has happened in the fight against climate change, and there is no indication that the 'rational irrationality' predicted by the theory could be corrected either by imperial or superstate global governance, hegemonic self-interest or outside inducements. Even if one does not adhere to rational choice theory, there is something to be said for the idea that states and other formally organised large corporate

---

132   A similar argument has been advanced by Anatol Lieven in *Climate Change and the Nation State: The Case for Nationalism in a Warming World*, New York: Oxford University Press, 2020.

133   On the 'logic of collective action' from this perspective, see Mancur Olson, *The Logic of Collective Action: Public Goods and the Theory of Groups*, Cambridge, MA: Harvard University Press, 1965.

actors, such as large firms, are 'rational fools'.[134] But perhaps things might look different with a change of paradigm. In a theory of international relations characterised by the rational choice paradigm, the dominant assumption is that humanity's global problems, such as climate change, must be solved with the help of rational incentives, positive or negative, by somehow redirecting the individual calculations of participating states towards the collective good. But, as already mentioned, this has so far achieved very little, and one might consider whether the problem lies with the calculations of utility themselves instead of with the incentives, and whether the former are fundamentally unsuitable for solving humanity's problems. Even the best institutional design cannot create a sufficient quantity of private incentives for individuals. When one then goes on to ask if it is possible to find functional equivalents to such calculations, using a different paradigm from that of rational choice, it makes sense to focus on moral actions and the feelings of duty motivating them. The hypothesis here is that cooperation in the pursuit of collective, universal human interests could only be mobilised to a sufficient extent if one could ensure that it would be carried out in accordance with a moral imperative allowing for no actual choice. That is, it would not really be voluntary in a rational sense; it would, rather, be the result of a collective reassessment, a reversal, which led people to act in a way that was collectively desirable, not because it conferred any direct or indirect individual advantage but for the sake of the cause itself, and because individual identity had been reformed.

In this situation, what Weber would call 'value-rationality' in action, one could not help but cooperate, regardless of what others did – the same others whose actions, under the rational choice paradigm, determine one's own – and irrespective of what real consequences this has for the aggregated end result of these actions and those of others. A reassessment of this kind can only proceed from real human beings and a specifically human need, awakened (or reawakened) at critical moments, to be morally at peace with oneself and with humanity; it cannot be produced by large bureaucratic state apparatuses dependent on rational

---

134 Amartya Sen, 'Rational Fools: A Critique of the Behavioral Foundations of Economic Theory', in Jane J. Mansbridge, ed., *Beyond Self-Interest*, Chicago: University of Chicago Press, 1990, 25–43.

calculation.[135] A cultural and moral turn towards the general interest of humanity need not preclude influence over the calculus of a corporate homunculus; but the latter would remain a rational calculus, albeit one that, given the appropriate institutional incentives, might take into account the emergence of a population 'out in the country' with the potential to grow restive if states were to ignore the prevailing normative principles and carry on as before.

Cultural revolutions of this kind have been known to take place; they are sparked by social movements that, in moments of collective efferves- cence – an exuberant feeling of community[136] – spread or revive moral attitudes that, once internalised and identified with, can be betrayed only on pain of self-contempt, for reasons of rational self-interest.[137] Social movements provide societies with ideas about themselves and identities; they run their course at the level of society, not the state, but if they become strong enough, they set objectives for and limits to state action; they produce an emotional normativity, a contagious passion transferable to others, one that is better than anything else at fomenting and stimulating the engagement of the many for a common goal.

By contrast, in the rational choice world as projected onto inter- national relations, there are no real people; we see instead artificial, hence emotionless, and therefore amoral, corporative actors, capable at most of moral judgements towards the individuals who are managing them, but all too often incorporated by the apparatus and made com- patible with it. The moral action of human beings overrides the paradoxes of rational irrationalism produced by the emotionless world

---

135   These are moments when Weber's principle of value-rationality, according to which 'man does not live by bread alone', is acutely felt, and charismatic prophets – Greta Thunberg or John the Baptist – come forward to cry out to people caught up in their daily routine with the New Testament word *metanoeite!* (μετανοείτε), translated by Luther as '*tut Buße!*' (repent), or, more precisely, 'turn around', literally meaning 'change your mind!'

136   Émile Durkheim, *The Elementary Forms of the Religious Life*, London: Allen & Unwin, 1915 [1912].

137   See in this context the recent discussion by Simone Schiller-Merkens, 'Scaling Up Alternatives to Capitalism: A Social Movement Approach to Alternative Organizing (in) the Economy', MPIfG Discussion Paper 20/11, Max Planck Institute for the Study of Societies, Cologne, 2020. A prerequisite for this is that a society can (still) bring forth a sufficient number of people who are stubbornly resistant to the temptation of material advantages – and to everyday capitalism's apparatus of discourse, which does everything it can to prepare them for the rationality trap of the prisoner's dilemma.

of the apparatus because it is, to a large extent, its own reward and therefore needs no sophisticated incentives. One does not do what one feels to be immoral, *irrespective of whether others do it or not* – such as eating dead factory-farmed animals, buying and selling slaves, flying by air to a holiday destination, and soon, perhaps, driving a car powered by internal combustion. One does not do this, because 'it just isn't done', at least not by human beings who want to be together with other human beings, after seeing Greta Thunberg on television or listening to a new partner.

One example from the field of climate change is the increasing number of cities committed to becoming climate neutral or carbon-free by a certain date. They are aware that their efforts, taken individually, have no impact on a global scale. The impact of their own conscientious actions on global temperatures cannot be demonstrated, but that does not matter to them. Municipal authorities which commit themselves to environmentally virtuous policies are reacting to a growing desire on the part of their residents to live in an environmentally virtuous city. What others do is irrelevant; it is enough to have done the right thing and set an example. Moral renewal through social movements spreads horizontally, not vertically; one can hope that this will happen, but one cannot be certain, as would be necessary in the world of rational choice. *But certainty is not a necessity.* Local authorities, finding they are obliged to join in, will justify their efforts in the language of rational common sense by referring to the advantages that accrue to the private individual: fewer traffic accidents, cleaner air, less noise, improved public health, more families with children moving in – strictly speaking, however, these are rationalisations of a policy which is desired by its supporters *for its own sake*: an emotional, sentimental project whose benefits are imagined as extending beyond one's own lifespan.

Here, the architecture of the state and the politics of scale come into play. There is some evidence that the spread of movements of moral renewal is favoured by a system of dispersed small states. Social movements arise in centres of moral infection, from which they grow laterally. They have more opportunity to gain possession of state power in a system subdivided into small states than when they have to assert themselves immediately throughout the system as a whole. It is appropriate to recall Gibbon here, but also certainly Hayek: in a fragmented state system, the new does not need to prevail immediately everywhere; it is enough if initially it prevails only in one state, even a small one.[138] If it proves to be successful, others who were at first indifferent will adopt it (according to Gibbon, 'The progress of knowledge and industry is accelerated by the emulation of so many active rivals'); if it turns out to be a failure, the damage remains limited to only one part of the system, and all the other parts will have learned how not to do it.[139]

A reduction in scale has other effects too. In small states, the population is more homogeneous than in large states, ceteris paribus; new ideas, if they catch on at all, can therefore more easily become the ideas of the majority, with which the whole society identifies, and for the sake of which it hopes to be respected or admired by others.[140] In state systems consisting of small states, rivalries between neighbouring

---

138   See also the recent research of political scientists into the veto points in political systems, of which there are all the more in a state the larger and more heterogeneous its society.

139   See also what was once described as the 'California effect', in which a mixture of moral and material forces drives the horizontal diffusion of progress. The US state of California, which for a long time did not produce any automobiles locally, was politically in a position to prescribe stringent safety and environmental standards for any vehicle that was allowed to enter its territory. Automobile producers who wanted to sell their vehicles in California – and no one could afford to miss out on the Californian market – had to observe California's rules. After they had succeeded in doing this by making costly investments, it was cheaper for them to sell their vehicles, now built to Californian standards, all over the US, especially as many customers outside California were no longer prepared to accept vehicles which were less safe or more polluting ('trading up'). The significance of the 'California effect' has been questioned in more recent research. But, in any case, it was the Californian authorities who were first to discover the fraud committed by Volkswagen and other German car manufacturers.

140   A similar point, but with an opposite intention, is made by the 'federalist' Madison, as quoted by Jörke (*Die Größe der Demokratie*, 69): 'The smaller a community, the fewer the parties and special interests that exist within it, the more often can a majority be formed from the same party. The fewer persons needed to form a majority, and the closer together they live, the easier they will find it to coordinate and to put into effect their plans for the oppression of others' – by this he means majority rule. 'If the territory is larger, it will include a greater diversity of parties and interests, and this will make it less likely that a majority of the people will have a common intention and harm the rights of the other citizens' – this chiefly refers to their property rights. The argument is in principle the same as the one used by Hayek in his 1933 essay on the contribution of 'interstate federalism' to world peace, only in Hayek it is explicitly related to economic policy. Friedrich A. Hayek, 'The Economic Conditions of Interstate Federalism', in Friedrich A. Hayek, ed., *Individualism and Economic Order*, Chicago: University of Chicago Press, 1980 [1948], 255–72. To use the language of contemporary political science, the political systems of small states have fewer veto points.

countries can be conducted over moral virtue and cultural prestige, particularly if they belong to a common cultural sphere (as in the successor states of the Western Roman Empire) and can therefore observe each other empathetically. If an associated state is prepared to contribute to the fight against climate change based on ethical convictions or value-rationality, it could be difficult for its neighbours to lag behind. In Gibbon's words, 'some sense of honour and justice is introduced into the most defective constitutions by the general manners of the times'. What is today sometimes called virtue signalling can contribute more effectively to raising the overall level of civilisation than ultimately unenforceable decrees issued by a central authority – through a moral race to the top, in contrast to market-driven behaviour, where there is reason to fear a race to the bottom.

This mechanism can be expected to work most effectively when the states involved are sovereign democracies of the Keynes-Polanyi model. Social movements thrive best in democracies; they flourish in the free spaces a democratic constitution guarantees to its citizens. Freedom of association, assembly, and opinion facilitate cultural rethinking and political innovation. Democracy also underpins citizens' identification with state and society, and supports their patriotism, which in small states must be based more than anything else on moral excellence – for example when a country (or a city) has voluntarily done something for the good of humanity in adherence to a moral imperative. Patriotism of this kind can do good far beyond the society itself, by setting an example for others. This is comparable, on a larger political scale, with the establishment of carbon-free towns, as mentioned earlier. But without sovereignty, the value of democracy is drastically reduced. A country which, for moral reasons, has restricted the number of pigs permitted per square metre in a pigsty must be free to limit the import of foreign pork only to items produced according to domestic standards – unlike in the European Union and its single-state internal market, where everyone must be brought on board first, including those who have not yet come under the influence of moral motives, and where opponents of moral progress can let the price tag to speak for itself, or invoke the 'competitiveness' of the domestic industry and the jobs associated with it.

There are many reasons why global problems would be better solved by horizontal diffusion of bottom-up, morally grounded collective and cooperative modes of action in small state structures, than by exerting authority from the top down in a framework of global governance or through an imperial system of superstates. The transmission of moral principles in a system of dispersed states takes place step by step, from the original hotspot and the state in which the new idea is first established, outwards. Dispersed statehood makes it possible to adapt the spread of a moral orientation to different local situations, so that the rationality trap of rational action can be neutralised in a more differentiated, and therefore more effective, manner. The greater readiness of the citizens of small states to feel themselves responsible for their country and its policies is also likely to be helpful. The path from decision to policy enactment will tend to be shorter and clearer in small states, and this should foster a willingness to participate in politics and to assume political responsibility. If smallness is accompanied by relative homogeneity, as is usually the case, civic engagement and a sense of responsibility can also be expected to increase. The miserable results of the system of large states prevailing in human politics should, in any case, be reason enough to try a state system that offers a chance at a grounded, and ultimately, in a generic sense, religiously motivated overcoming of the paradox of rationality.

Cooperative, Not Imperial: A Prospect of a New International Order

To conclude: What sort of international order does a Keynes-Polanyi state require? Democracy depends on sovereignty, and the restoration of democracy depends on the restoration of sovereignty: of dispersed sovereignty in a decentralised state system, organised as a cooperative confederation instead of as an empire or a superstate. There can be no democracy, and no reconstruction of democracy, under the crisis conditions of the present without an international sociotope that nourishes (rather than destroys) small-statism – that promotes loose, self-chosen, horizontal, and even reversible ties among states, and renounces fixed, irreversible, hierarchical-vertical linkages. What in the theory and practice of international relations is called the liberal international order, or LIO, is not suitable for this. I referred earlier to the change in the meaning of the word 'liberal', which originally had social democratic connotations, in line with American usage, in the sense of the 'embedded liberalism' of the post-war era.[141] With the rise of neoliberalism, however, a downgraded meaning took hold in the American-dominated discipline of 'international relations', so that it now referred to a legitimate order based not on power but on rule-setting and rule-enforcing institutions, multilateral and binding even for its strongest members.[142]

From the outset, this was just as ideological as the old social democratic meaning had gradually become, until both lost their last connection with reality in the transition from state-administered to neoliberal capitalism. In relation to this phase – still ongoing, though evidently waning – it is therefore appropriate to stop referring to a *liberal international order* and speak instead – as we saw above – of a *neoliberal imperial* one (abbreviated as NIO). The question would then be whether its increasing disorganisation in the crises of the first two decades of the twenty-first century might raise the prospect of a further transition, this time to a *polycentric nation-based order* (PNO, if abbreviation is absolutely necessary), as would be required for the institutional ecology of a state system based on the Keynes-Polanyi model.

The cornerstone of a post-neoliberal international order is the nation-state; nothing else will do. As shown above, the system of nation-states became firmly established in the twentieth century; the demand for national statehood is as strong as it ever was; attempts to rationalise the system of nation-states by mergers and acquisitions have failed; instead, the number of nation-states claiming sovereignty has continuously increased. By no means are all nation-states democracies – not even the small ones. But the nation-state is the only social formation capable of being democratised. In any case, according to Hedley Bull, the nation-state system is irreplaceable; international order can only exist on this basis, and never within a world state, any more than it can in substate regions lacking state sovereignty.[143] Accordingly, Amitai Etzioni has proposed, in view of the crisis of hyperglobalisation, taking leave of the LIO and instead thinking in terms of a 'nation-centred system' (perhaps abbreviated NCS) – an international regime without imperial control and allowing its states the freedom to take care of their

---

141   See chapter 5, p. 82.

142   For an example, see Robert O. Keohane and Joseph S. Nye, *Power and Interdependence: World Politics in Transition*, Boston: Little, Brown, 1977.

143   Hedley Bull, *The Anarchical Society: A Study of Order in World Politics*, 4th ed., New York: Columbia University Press, 2002 [1977].

own affairs.[144] In a concluding discussion, I will return to this and two other currently circulating proposals for a more strongly nation-centred organisation of the international system.

Could there really be a window of historical opportunity today for the introduction of a polycentric and nation-based international order that meets the needs of democratic, small-state, sovereign autonomy in an interconnected world? The most important relevant development – the major world-political event of our time – is likely to be the end of the US claim to global rule, combined with the rise of China, which consequently amounts to the emergence of a new global bi- or multi-polarity. We may, therefore, currently find ourselves in a situation where, for the first time since 1945, the central condition for 'regional planning' as Polanyi described would be met: a *Polanyi moment*, as it were. If one puts present-day China in the place of the Soviet Union of the immediate post-war period – two world powers with no missionary need to universalise their social orders – it would no longer be necessary to worry about the peace-endangering, capitalist market-economic expansionism of the United States, as Polanyi did in 1945. This problem has most likely been solved, whether in the coming years and decades the US is governed by Democrats or Republicans. Whereas the Chinese social order cannot even be exported within Asia – any such attempt would meet with fierce cultural, ethnic, and nationalist resistance – the US may be busy in the years ahead with the restoration, as far as possible, of its broken society; this will force it to curtail its imperial ambitions and the global presence they demand.

Multipolarity and polycentrism allow for diversity – an absence of uniformity – in the organisation of the world's regions. The Chinese pole of the newly divided world will probably be structured differently from the US pole, perhaps as a regional free trade zone instead of a 'backyard' along Monroe Doctrine lines, and both China and the US will have to deal with their own internal conflicts. This may open up room for alternative architectures of statehood elsewhere in the world. From the perspective of the emerging world system, there is no reason why its European pole could not be organised according to the principles of small and multi-statehood, in keeping with European traditions, and cooperative and confederal

---

144   Etzioni, *Reclaiming Patriotism.*

instead of imperial or superstate-federalist – without the need for permission from Beijing or Washington. As explained earlier, the future structure of the European state system depends in no small part on the outcome of the conflict between France and Germany over a European army;[145] at stake is whether Europe should react to the decline of the United States by organising and functioning as an imperial power, according to the French conception, or follow the German tendency to remain, for as long as possible, a regional subdivision of the incomplete American world empire, whose dissolution would compel Europe to decide between the French path and an alternative route.

The establishment of polycentric pluralism at the level of the global state system, with a PNO in Europe, would be anything but a step backwards from the LIO. To make such a comparison is to forget that the LIO has almost always existed only as a promise and never as a reality, especially in the last three decades. Before comparing it with any alternative, it is therefore necessary to understand the reasons for its failure to materialise. I have written extensively above about the technical and political failure of global governance as a substitute for world government and a world state.[146] Ultimately, this was due to the fact that the *internationalism* of the LIO was never anything other than the *nationalism* of the imperial nation holding it together – just as its *liberalism*, with its supposedly equally binding rules for all participants, was largely a result of the global extension of the legal system of the governing state at the imperial centre. At its core the LIO, too, was and remains a nation-centred order, albeit one centred on a single nation: asymmetrical and monocentric, rather than polycentric.

So long as the interests of the states and the political classes on the periphery of the empire coincided, or could be made to coincide, with the interests of the US as the hegemonic power, this need not have been noticed. But once this identity of interests dissolved, partly because the United States' client states gradually developed into its economic competitors, the chasm between the reality of empire and the promises and expectations legitimating its existence grew increasingly visible. For example, if liberalism in international relations meant the same laws and obligations for everyone, 'the West' was actually never liberal, because

---

145 See chapter 8, pp. 206ff.
146 See especially chapter 9.

its leading power was from the outset unprepared to be bound by the rules it required its clients to obey.[147] The US has in fact always reserved the right to alternate between multilateral, bilateral, and unilateral pursuit of its goals, as in, for example, negotiating the so-called Plaza Accord (1985) or its Structural Impediments Initiative (SII) in relation to Japan.[148] This applies even more to its military interventions, from Vietnam to Iraq (with a 'coalition of the willing'), and particularly to its dealings with the nations in its Central and South American domain, from Mexico to Nicaragua, and from Cuba to Chile.

It would therefore be inappropriate to equate a change from the LIO to a PNO with a nationalist abandonment of internationalism; in truth, it would be a shift from an asymmetrical, monocentric nationalism to a symmetrical and polycentric one. It is therefore far from clear that a withdrawal of the US into itself and a transition to a polycentric nation-based order would increase what internationalist rhetoric describes as a 'danger of nationalism'. There are different forms of nationalism, as there are of internationalism. A democratic nationalism directed against impe-rialist domination is not the same as a nationalism which seeks its fulfilment in dominating other nations. To name two examples, the nationalist separatism of the Scots and the Catalans, which I examined in detail in an earlier chapter, is not even remotely comparable to the nation-alist internationalism of the US in terms of the danger it poses to life.[149]

---

147   The laws of war are one example. As mentioned already, the US has never signed up to the statute of the International Criminal Court (ICC) in The Hague, so as to ensure that its soldiers have worldwide immunity. While the US makes no objection when Serbian or African war criminals are brought before the court, it applies personal sanctions to ICC officials when they attempt, by indirect means, to investigate American war crimes. This happened to the chief prosecutor of the ICC, Fatou Bensouda, in autumn 2020, on the instruction of the Trump administration, as a result of her investi-gations into war crimes in Afghanistan. It is the logic of the use of state power to exempt those who are charged with exercising it as far as possible from criminal prosecution for the overzealous exercise of authority; this even applies domestically to police forces, especially in the United States.

148   On this, see Mitsuo Matsushita, 'The Structural Impediments Initiative: An Example of Bilateral Trade Negotiation', *Michigan Journal of International Law* 12, no. 2 (1991), 436–49; and Frank K. Upham, 'Retail Convergence: The Structural Impediments Initiative and the Regulation of the Japanese Retail Industry', in Suzanne D. Berger and Ronald Dore, eds, *National Diversity and Global Capitalism*, Ithaca, NY: Cornell Univer-sity Press, 1996, 263–97.

149   See chapter 2, passim.

But what about international solidarity, the good side of internationalism? A PNO recognises no superpower that would be willing or able to act as the self-appointed representative of all others, acting as the world's moral guardian and police officer, simultaneously its prosecutor, judge, and executioner, constantly in danger of confusing morality and interest – its own interest. In a system of dispersed democratic sovereignty, international solidarity is first and foremost anchored in the domestic politics of the member states, where it must prevail democratically and by which it must be supported, as Marcel Mauss convincingly demonstrated in his work on the nation.[150] This may, at first, appear a challenging requirement; but it prevents international solidarity from being kidnapped by states and associations of states which then employ it as a means of asserting their dominance and projecting their power.[151] This was the case with the bombardment of Belgrade in connection with the repurposing of NATO for American-led 'out-of-area' operations (Operation Allied Force, May 1999) after the fall of the Soviet Union.[152]

---

150   Mainly published posthumously, and collected together in a volume which appeared in 2013 (republished in 2018) under the title *La nation, ou le sens du social* (and in German in a somewhat peculiar translation: Marcel Mauss, *Die Nation, oder Der Sinn fürs Soziale*, Frankfurt am Main: Institut für Sozialforschung, 2017). See also Hobson's *Imperialism: A Study*, published in 1902, and quoted by Michael Lind ('The New Class War', *American Affairs* 1, no. 2 [2017], 44): 'The hope of a coming internationalism enjoins above all else the maintenance and natural growth of independent nationalities, for without such there could be no gradual evolution of internationalism, but only a series of unsuccessful attempts at a chaotic and unstable cosmopolitanism.'

151   Cunliffe, *Cosmopolitan Dystopia*.

152   According to the impressive book by Danilo Zolo, *Cosmopolis: Prospects for World Government*, Cambridge, UK: Polity, 1997, the peak phase of the US takeover of the LIO began almost a decade earlier, at the time of the First Gulf War (1990–91), just after the end of the Soviet Union, when the 'New World Order' was being proclaimed by Bush I, coinciding (appropriately) with the beginning of the decade of hyperglobalisation. The entry of the US into the war was approved by the UN Security Council. The mandate to implement the Council's resolutions was given to the US, the only remaining great power, which happened to have for decades been deeply entangled in the part of the world in question. The US had the lion's share of the war expenditure reimbursed by the countries of the region and, above all, by Germany and Japan, countries prohibited by their constitutions from taking part in military campaigns of this kind; the conduct of operations was reserved to the chief of staff of the US Army. The forces of the 'coalition' registered 177 dead in battle, 111 of them US service personnel. Total Iraqi losses were estimated at between 20,000 and 65,000 soldiers and between 142,000 and 206,000 civilians, during the war itself and the subsequent

Moreover, as in climate policy, foreign policy concessions made by a state and rejected by its civil society usually have no effect anyway. Thus, US approval, under Obama, of the resolutions of the Paris climate conference had no impact within the country because it had neither a popular nor an electoral basis. This was, in turn, linked to the failure of the government at the time to make any political investment in its nation's climate-political collective consciousness. A political class that cannot or will not convince its society that anthropogenic climate change exists – but can convince it of the existence of weapons of mass destruction in Saddam Hussein's Iraq, or of the need to finance further Israeli settlements in the occupied West Bank – cannot present any convincing arguments in favour of global governance and its own leading role in it, or against an international order based on solidarity and organised democratically from below around the nation-state.

There are by now an astonishing number of suggestions in circulation as to how a nation-centred international order might function, in place of the pseudo-universalism of the LIO.[153] Notably, it seems that

---

uprisings in 1991 (see 'Casualties and Losses' in 'Gulf War', wikipedia.org). In accordance with the Security Council's mandate, the president of the US, acting as supreme warlord, refrained from pushing on to Baghdad to bring about a regime change, for which he was blamed at home as a demonstration of weakness. (The so-called militias, terrorist groups which developed in the American Mid-West during the 1990s, based their fear of a UN takeover of the US government on this episode.) Then, in 2002, Bush II accomplished the regime change in Iraq his father had avoided ('Mission accomplished'), and which was already regarded in the US under Clinton as overdue (Clinton had been in the habit of occasionally firing off a cruise missile at Iraq when he was facing domestic difficulties). This operation had no UN mandate, owing to Putin's opposition. The US paid for it, and it was conducted with the aid of an international posse assembled by the Americans.

153   These considerations are all the more useful the less they are understood as detailed blueprints for a 'correct' international order, of the kind that used to be put forward by the cosmopolitan planners of a world government. On this point, see Bull, *The Anarchical Society*: 'The search for conclusions that can be presented as "solutions" or "practical advice" is a corrupting element in the contemporary study of world politics . . . Such conclusions are advanced less because there is any solid basis for them than because there is a demand for them which it is profitable to satisfy' (308). See also Zolo, *Cosmopolis*: 'I do not believe in the usefulness of institutional engineering worked out on the drawing board . . . The libraries of the West are full of treatises expounding in minute detail all the rules and regulations to be brought into action in various projected reforms of international institutions that are designed to usher in stable and universal peace . . . produced by the fervid imaginations of

these are regarded as far less sensational or eccentric in Anglo-Saxon countries than in Germany. I shall now look briefly at three of them.

(1) With regard to the global economy in particular, already in 2011, and again in 2018, Dani Rodrik proposed an international rule book with seven guiding principles, founded on the priority of nation-states and national democratic systems.[154] Rodrik stresses (a) the need for markets to be embedded in regulatory regimes and (b) notes that political communities capable of democratic regulation are organised solely in nation-states and will likely remain so for the foreseeable future. For that reason, (c) a globalisation ignoring this cannot be legitimate or efficient. Moreover, there is more than one path to economic prosperity; different countries have different forms of capitalism, and this allows for experimentation with different institutions – something that a global order should not suppress in the interest of its further evolution. Furthermore, (d) countries should be entitled to their own rules and institutions; to ensure that this right does not exist on merely on paper, they must also be able to protect their national institutions, when necessary by closing their borders, as for example 'when trade demonstrably threatens domestic practices enjoying broad popular support'.[155] The conflict between free trade and protectionism – between 'the benefits of open economies and the gains from upholding domestic regulations' – can and must be adjudicated in the domestic political debate. This, according to Rodrik, means also (e) that no country may impose its institutions on other countries: 'Nations have a right to difference, not to impose convergence.' International institutions (f) should be restricted to shaping the interfaces among national political economies so that, despite their differences, exchange is facilitated where it is mutually desired. Rodrik cites as an example the exchange rate mechanism of the Keynesian Bretton Woods regime. Finally, (g) non-democratic countries should not have the same rights and privileges in the international economic order as democracies:

---

solitary thinkers, jurists, political scientists, philosophers, moralists, theologians, visionaries' (180f).

154   Dani Rodrik, *The Globalization Paradox: Why Global Markets, States, and Democracy Can't Coexist*, Oxford: Oxford University Press, 2011, 236–47; Rodrik, *Straight Talk on Trade*, 222–7.

155   Rodrik, *Straight Talk on Trade*, 224.

What gives [these] principles their appeal and legitimacy is that they highlight democratic deliberation – where it really occurs, within nation-states. When nation-states are not democratic, this scaffolding collapses. We can no longer presume a country's institutional arrangements reflect the preferences of its citizenry.[156]

If global governance of this kind came into existence, according to Rodrik, it would serve democracy rather than globalisation, and it would do this 'through global norms and procedural requirements designed to enhance the quality of domestic policy-making – instead of rules aimed at increasing global trade and investment'.[157]

(2) Another approach, perhaps less ambitious at first sight, is found in Amitai Etzioni's book *Reclaiming Patriotism*.[158] Etzioni, with Judis, distinguishes between globalism and internationalism, equating globalism with the LIO, which he regards as having failed, and internationalism, as mentioned earlier, with a nation-centred system (NCS), which he sees as developing out of the LIO.[159] The communitarian Etzioni aims in this book to return normatively and culturally integrated human societies as social formations to their rightful place in social and political theory. The globalism of the LIO, he writes, has rushed too far ahead of the emergence of a worldwide sense of community that might perhaps exist at some point in the future; however, political systems and structures must rest on a communitarian foundation if they are to gain legitimacy, and thus stability and functionality. The transition from the LIO to an NCS would reverse the excessive progress of institutional globalisation, in line with the overwhelming preferences of the world's populations; it would preserve and promote communitarian structures on the national as well as inter-state level, because an NCS 'is less focused on the promotion of individual rights, democratisation, free movement of people and goods and the quest for democratic global governance – and more on stability and peace'.[160]

---

156   Ibid., 225–6.
157   Ibid., 226.
158   Etzioni, *Reclaiming Patriotism*.
159   John B. Judis, *The Nationalist Revival: Trade, Immigration, and the Revolt against Globalization*, New York: Columbia Global Reports, 2018.
160   Etzioni, *Reclaiming Patriotism*, 143.

In some detail, Etzioni identifies four characteristics of the emerging NCS of which he approves: (a) greater respect for national sovereignty than under the LIO; (b) renunciation of the spread of liberal democracy by force, and no more coercive regime change (the promotion of liberal democracy now taking place by 'non-lethal means' and cooperation between civil societies);[161] (c) 'managed' trade so as to protect workers from job losses and social decline;[162] and (d) limited immigration, at a level allowing for the integration of new citizens into the social and cultural life of the receiving society. Note that Etzioni's catalogue of principles has less to do with political economy than Rodrik's; it is primarily concerned with US foreign policy, particularly the Bush I–Clinton–Bush II–Obama policy of basically uninterrupted global armed interventionism.[163]

(3) Finally, one must mention Italian philosopher Danilo Zolo's brilliant critique of the idea of a world government in a world of sovereign states, following the hierarchical model of a 'holy alliance' which 'superimposes the hegemonic tactics and aspirations of a narrow elite of superpowers on the sovereignty of all other countries'.[164] Zolo, whose arguments are more fundamental than Etzioni's, considers a world order achieved by alliances of large law-enforcing states to be in essence not liberal but monocentric; it is also, in the final analysis, not an order at all, because it cannot but fail to pacify the multiplicity of local conflicts

---

161   Ibid., 153.

162   Ibid., 156–7.

163   Etzioni's argument can be read as a gently worded attempt to dissuade the liberal centre of the US ruling elite from its fixed idea that it and its military are called upon to free the world of its evils by decisive intervention, only to release it, now democratised, into a global 'West'. Thomas Pogge has shown in a remarkable essay ('Can Liberalism Envision a Widely Acceptable World Order?', in Yun-han Chu and Yongnian Zheng, eds, *The Decline of the Western-Centric World and the Emerging New Global Order: Contending Views*, London: Routledge, 2021, 129–45) that by performing the role of world police and world judge according to its own national interests, the US has utterly corrupted the LIO. According to Pogge, there is need for a supranational *impartiality requirement* for every country intending or claiming to enforce its principles in the name of the system as a whole: 'We should popularize the idea that it is as shameful to subvert the justice of our global institutional order for the benefit of your own country or (more likely) its elites as it is to subvert the justice of one country's legal system for the sake of benefiting oneself and one's family and cronies' (145).

164   Zolo, *Cosmopolis*, 164.

from above:[165] the world cannot be ruled in a centralist manner, and anyone who believes and attempts this makes its condition worse rather than better.[166] Political realism, according to Zolo, demands a retreat from the hierarchical centralism of a world order run by large states, to an anti-cosmopolitan political order of 'weak interventionism' and 'weak pacifism', geared towards regional self-organisation, horizontal coordination, and inter-state negotiation – without centralised means of control, as they inevitably become instruments of the strongest, who, even with the best intentions, cannot avoid identifying the interests of all with their own.

The goal, Zolo argues, must be a 'minimal international order', essentially to 'coordinate the political and economic strategies of individual states within a network of "juridical regimes" and to set up decentralised circuits of preventive diplomacy'.[167] Part of a strategy of 'weak interventionism', aimed at 'a level of theoretical complexity adequate to meet the growing complexity of the international environment', would be a 'realistic pacifism', analogous to proposals for a 'selective restructuring of "international aid" based on a notion of "bottom-up" economic and human growth . . . at a low technological level and in harmony with local values, traditions and resources'.[168] Zolo continues:

> Economic and human growth, like peace and democracy, is not an 'exportable' commodity. The advancement of poor and weak countries, if and when it comes, will be the result of their autonomous capacity to organise themselves politically and economically and to defend their own collective identity through effective national means . . . Likewise,

---

165   Ibid., 166.

166   Zolo's book (the Italian original of which appeared in 1995) was written before the US had, in the course of the Balkan wars, converted NATO into a worldwide instrument of intervention under American control – until none other than Trump, in view of its failure to fulfil this function, publicly recalled that with the end of the Soviet Union, NATO had already outlived its usefulness. US deep-state and military resistance to this point ensured that it remained inconsequential. See, along the same lines as Zolo, Philip Cunliffe's basic critique of international relations theory and the LIO: 'This is a book about the character of liberal international order over the last thirty years of the post-Cold War era and how it came to be characterized by repetitive military interventions that effectively collapsed into an era of permanent war' (*Cosmopolitan Dystopia*, vii).

167   Zolo, *Cosmopolis*, 181.

168   Ibid., 168.

within individual countries, protection of the basic rights of democratic citizenship will depend much more on the 'struggle for law' conducted by the citizens themselves than on the protective or repressive intervention of regional or international jurisdictional bodies. Given the relations of growing interdependence and even, it may be said, of recurrent causality between internal democracy and international order, it is difficult to conceive of a more ordered and pacific world if democracy is not above all first realized within nation states.[169]

---

169   Ibid., 168–9.

Coda

Inventory of Propositions

The state

1. Due to the particularism of human society formation (socialisation) there are only states, not 'the state'. States never walk alone; they are always embedded in state systems.
2. For this reason, there will necessarily be international in addition to domestic state relations and politics. Political economy is inherently both national and international.
3. States differ. They come in all shapes and sizes, due in part to their different positions in the different state systems of which they are members and the way these affect their member states' state capacities.

States and state systems

1. The organisation of states and state systems must allow for the particularism of human societies if national and international governance is to be based on consent rather than on force – in other words, if it is to be non-imperial.
2. States and state systems are layered on top of a landscape of resident social communities with continuous transitions between them. State architectures entail binary boundaries between state jurisdictions

imposed on the fluid border areas between neighbouring societies. Dealing with the conflicts between soft social and hard state borders is a problem for most states and state systems.

3. Larger nation-states are often multinational states as they include more than one national society. One way of dealing with internalised national diversity is by decentralisation of governance, granting social-territorial subunits political autonomy, in the extreme case close to single-state sovereignty.

4. There is no example of sovereign states merging voluntarily into a superstate, whereas there are many examples of nations breaking away from multinational states in pursuit of a nation-state of their own. Demand for state sovereignty is high; see Ukraine and Palestine. There are now 193 UN member states, covering almost the entire globe, up from 99 in 1960 and 127 in 1970, all of them subject to international law.

5. State systems may be imperial, with a hegemonic centre controlling a periphery. Or they may be egalitarian, like the Nordic Council, or something in between. Similarly, multinational states may be unitary, which requires a strong (quasi-imperial) centre, or they may be federations, allowing for semi-autonomous, indeed sometimes near-autonomous subnational governance ('devolution'), typically instituted to pre-empt subnational separatism if violent suppression is not available as an alternative.

Size

1. Small countries in state systems that allow for small-state sovereignty are not inferior, and often are superior, to large states with respect to economic prosperity and productivity, social equality and solidarity, cultural and social creativity, democratic governability and accountability, and support for international peace under international law.

2. Benefits, democratic and administrative, may be gained by subdividing large polities into small ones, or preserved by not merging small polities into large ones. Small-statism may open a space for democratic responsibility taking the place of bureaucratic or imperial hierarchy, and for competition and cooperation between

neighbouring states experimenting with alternative solutions to similar problems. Resistance to large-statism counteracts disempowerment of local communities and prevents delegation of governance to bureaucracies seeking uniform solutions to multiform local needs and problems.

3. Management of complex systems may be improved by downward delegation of sovereign powers to subunits; whereas moving sovereignty upward may diminish overall governability and invite the dysfunctions of bureaucratic and technocratic hierarchy.

4. Deglobalisation as a form of decentralisation of the global political economy began early, already before the world financial crisis of 2008, in response to the unmanageability and the resulting instability of neoliberal trade connections, supply chains and financial markets, the one-sided distribution of the benefits of globalisation, and its 'creative destruction' of established ways of life in the societies involved in it.

Democracy

1. There is no democracy outside of a state, nor can there be a democratic state in the absence of state sovereignty.

2. The possibility of national state democracy depends not just on national but also on international conditions, both structural and institutional.

3. Today the future of democracy as backed up by state sovereignty depends on the United States giving up its claim to world rule, voluntarily for internal or involuntarily for external reasons – that is, for loss of domestic political support or of international military superiority or of both.

Capitalism

1. Capitalism in its historically changing forms was always closely tied to imperial states and their state systems. Both the organisation and the capacities of the classes of capitalism and the relations of power between them were from the beginning shaped by state public

policy, including the political institutions and historical compromises needed for capital and labour to join in capitalist 'plus-making' (Karl Marx).

2. The neoliberal architecture of the contemporary state system has failed to deliver what is needed in a democracy to contain capitalism inside a social contract, or compromise, that provides for a legitimate order and sustains a sufficient level of confidence on the part of both capital and labour enabling them to cooperate from compromise to compromise in capitalist value creation.

3. Containing capitalism within social bounds by contesting it, subjecting capitalist development to social development, requires a state system that provides for both democracy and governability, the latter through the former and the former supported by the latter. Moving towards a state system of this kind requires a reversal of neoliberal centralisation in favour of decentralised rather than hierarchical interest formation and problem-solving.

4. The architecture of states and state systems affects the performance of states in dealing with collective needs, which in turn affects states' legitimacy.

5. To be able to govern and thereby to establish legitimacy for itself, the left must be able to serve collective interests by delivering public goods while also suggesting credible pathways out of capitalism as a condition for even better public goods delivery.

Neoliberalism

1. The neoliberal era was one of global centralisation, integration and unification, aimed at disempowering all states except one, the United States.

2. Neoliberalism needs a strong state while globalised neoliberalism needs a strong imperial state substituting for a world state.

3. Neoliberalism tried to replace national political democracy with global economic oligarchy-cum-technocracy sustained by a world government-in-waiting, the United States, acting as guardian of a 'liberal international order' (LIO).

4. Also referred to as a 'rule-bound international order', the LIO obliged all nation-states except the United States to abide by rules

issued by the United States, extending the domestic order of the United States to the world at large, as the late-twentieth-century version of 'globalisation'.

5. Neoliberalism failed because of the failure of universalist bureaucracy, technocracy, marketocracy, and juristocracy to do justice to the collective particularism of social life, making it unable to provide for a legitimate social order. Global governance's lack of both social responsiveness and governing capacity contributed to the dual crisis of capitalism and democracy that accompanied the decline of globalist neoliberalism.

6. Decades of forced integration by centralisation (of globalisation-turned-hyperglobalisation) have contributed to a dual crisis of both capitalism and democracy. For progressive politics this recommends exploration of the democratic political and economic potential of a more decentralised political economy in states and state systems, global as well as continental. This would imply giving up futile attempts to overcome the dysfunctions of over-centralisation and hyperglobalisation by more centralisation and globalisation. Instead it would suggest a change in direction toward decentralisation and deglobalisation, in line with the political nature of human societies and the diversity of local interests, needs and problems, the opposite direction of the neoliberal revolution.

Europe

1. The EU of the Treaty of Maastricht was conceived as a continent-sized miniature model for the global-sized neoliberal economy-cum-society of the American New World Order after 1990; ultimately it was intended to dissolve into it. The EU's critical democratic and administrative governance deficits mirrored and continue to mirror those of global governance.

2. With the post-1990 New World Order broken up by the rise of China and the resurgence of Russia, there is a need for the Western European state system to find a place for itself in an emerging New World Order Mark Two, which may be uni-, bi-, tri-, or multipolar.

3. European democratic and strategic autonomy is incompatible with NATO transatlanticism designed to serve US-American interests in global hegemony.

4. Western Europe lacks an internal unifier capable of transforming its state system, organised in the EU, into a centralised superstate equidistant from the United States and China. While France does and Germany does not want to be Europe's unifier, neither of them can, whether acting separately or together.

5. Western Europe can be turned into a centralised superstate only by the United States as external unifier. This would divide the Eurasian continent between NATO and Russia along a border from the North Cape to the Caucasus.

6. The failure of the European centralised unification project – of 'European integration' as pursued by the European Union – opens up an opportunity in principle for an egalitarian European state system of democratic and sovereign Keynes-Polanyi states.

7. For the European Union as an international organisation, a productive future could be secured by transforming it into a platform for planning and implementing voluntarily adopted cooperative projects of member states, away from an outdated hierarchical regime of top-down control over democratic nation-states by a supranational bureaucracy, towards a flexible horizontal network for problem-centred mutual cooperation.

8. The war in Ukraine threatens to foreclose the path, opened by the exhaustion of the neoliberal European integration project, towards a more decentralised and less transatlanticised European state system. There is today a clear and present danger of a resumption of centralisation under military auspices, with NATO enlisting the EU for American revisionism after the end of the end of history, in confrontation not just with Russia but also with China.

9. European participation in the American war for global supremacy against Russia and, in the near future, China, with the EU as global auxiliary and Germany as America's European lieutenant, is likely to eliminate for a long time the Keynes-Polanyi option of an autonomous egalitarian European order respecting and cultivating the historical diversity of European societies and political economies.

10. If the European state system, currently organised in the European Union, is to allow European countries democratic autonomy, it

must be reorganised as a cooperative of independent nation-states with equal sovereignty, aligned worldwide with other non-aligned countries and embedded in a regional and global international security regime. Compared to the superstate model of today's European Union with its illusory integrationist *finalité*, this would amount to seeking 'more Europe through less Europe'. Alas, the prospects of such a program being adopted, let alone successfully pursued, are miniscule short of a secular defeat of Biden-Democratic expansionism in the domestic politics of the United States.

Index